To Stanley, who will never see it,
and Shirley, to whose talent it is
irrelevant, with every good wish.

John

10 April 1957

? /
irrelevant?

[Stanley Edgar Hyman
and his wife
Shirley Jackson]

CATASTROPHE
AND IMAGINATION

CATASTROPHE AND IMAGINATION

An Interpretation of the Recent English and American Novel

BY

JOHN McCORMICK

LONGMANS, GREEN AND CO
LONDON · NEW YORK · TORONTO

LONGMANS, GREEN AND CO LTD
6 & 7 CLIFFORD STREET LONDON W 1
BOSTON HOUSE STRAND STREET CAPE TOWN
531 LITTLE COLLINS STREET MELBOURNE

LONGMANS, GREEN AND CO INC
55 FIFTH AVENUE NEW YORK 3

LONGMANS, GREEN AND CO
20 CRANFIELD ROAD TORONTO 16

ORIENT LONGMANS PRIVATE LTD
CALCUTTA BOMBAY MADRAS
DELHI VIJAYAWADA DACCA

First published 1957

PRINTED IN GREAT BRITAIN
BY WESTERN PRINTING SERVICES LTD BRISTOL

To

PERRY MILLER

ACKNOWLEDGMENTS

We are indebted to the Editor for permission to reproduce an extract from an article by Richard Ellman which first appeared in the summer 1954 issue of *The Kenyon Review*, and to Random House Inc. for material from *The American Background: Selected Essays* by William Carlos Williams.

CONTENTS

FOREWORD

A BOOK should be its own justification and should require neither the defensive nor the aggressive feints of the usual author's introduction; nevertheless I am reluctant to let this particular book go nakedly forth without a preliminary, unapologetic word concerning its history, together with a brief explanation of what I agree with Mr. R. P. Blackmur in calling the 'burden' of the critic. Arithmetic indicates that I have been reading novels for the past twenty-five years, or roughly since age twelve; I have been reading books about novels and novelists for a briefer period, but the total in each instance is high. Books about novels, particularly those written in America and England, have never satisfied me, while books about novelists do not matter to anyone except novelists anyway. American critics (this term includes scholars, for the accepted distinction is irrational and denigrating) to a man ignore the important influence of the English novel, though they may occasionally bow in an easterly direction, while too often discussions of American Literature descend into flag-waving at one extreme, or into false humility at the other. English critics invariably annoy the American reader, and, I trust, some English readers as well, either by ignoring the existence of the American novel as an entity, or by raking selected American writers over to the English stack with the greedy gesture of a man winning at roulette. Thus it has seemed important to discuss the novel from a national approach, not out of nationalistic prejudice but to distinguish national modes which have had tremendous weight in determining the balance of modern sensibility in the art-form of the novel.

Another source of dissatisfaction which brought me to this labour is the common critical habit of distinguishing between 'the traditional', meaning the dead, and the contemporary, or the living. It is indeed difficult to judge the living; we tend to dislike a living novelist, just as we may secretly and uncharitably dislike our friends who are cleverer than ourselves. We read our contemporaries with our guard up; the least critical reader lives with his consciousness of the necessity for distance from the writer and from the writer's subject. In short, our criticism of our contemporaries differs curiously from our criticism of writers of the past, even the recent past. Yet the critic who shirks judgment of his contemporaries, I believe, shirks criticism. As Mr. Blackmur has said with eloquent accuracy, 'I take it the critic is a relativist; but his relativism does not need to be either deterministic or positivistic, as in our time it usually is; he may rather be the relativist of insight, aspiration, vision. He is concerned with choice, not prescription, with equity, not law; never with the dead hand, always with the vital purpose.' And again, 'Besides analysis, elucidation, and comparison, which Eliot once listed as the functions of criticism, criticism in our time must also come to judgment.' I can devise no better rubric of my own ambitions for this book. Contrary to the criticism of poetry, elucidation, analysis and comparison of novels of excellence is rather like explaining the wit of a good joke; while bad novels, like bad jokes, do not need explanation. But this is the particular burden of the critic of the novel.

If my judgments have wounded, I would say with Marie Antoinette on the scaffold, when she trod on the foot of her executioner, 'Monsieur, je vous demande excuse. Je ne l'ai pas fait exprès.' My intention has not been to wound, but to concern myself only with the 'vital purpose'.

About technical matters. I have used the term 'English' to refer to inhabitants of the United Kingdom, rather than 'British', a term which the British never seem to use; just as I have referred to my countrymen in the United States as 'Americans', without intending to include (or to offend) Mexicans, Canadians, or Peruvians. In the notes, I have followed American practice because it is consistent and concise; a full citation is given only in the first reference to a particular work. For brevity, and because

they are commonly available, I have cited novels only when a
specific novel or edition is rare. I should like finally to acknowledge the invaluable assistance of my wife, and to thank Miss
Ursula Brumm, who read much of the book in manuscript and
contributed pertinent criticisms.

LONDON, 1954
BERLIN, 1955

Chapter One

BACKGROUND TO CATASTROPHE

EXTERNAL catastrophes to mankind in the form of wars, revolutions, social upheavals and apocalyptic horrors have plagued the world since history began. Art, in retrospect, has always been produced in competition with the enormous distractions of politics gone bad. In the light of this record, it may seem arrogant to assume that the evil winds of history have suddenly become hurricanes, and that in the last fifty years the artist has had to face, encompass and survive events unknown to his forebears. And yet this has indeed seemed to be the case. The tempo of catastrophe most certainly has accelerated, and mutations have occurred in the body politic that have demanded mutations in the forms of art. It is now possible to see that between 1900 and roughly 1925, the arts at large and the art of the novel in particular experienced fundamental changes in form and tone, in concept and essence, which we are just beginning to place in meaningful perspective.

A vague relationship between changes in art-forms and the political fact of World War I is habitually assumed, but commentators have consistently evaded most of the problems arising from their assumption. World War I dislocated the life of imagination, and World War II induced virtual paralysis. Writers were killed off young by shot and shell, while many of the survivors were less dramatically silenced by the distractions of recent history. History, in fact, is no longer a quiet backdrop to the social scene, but an enemy to overcome. The multiplication of industrial processes in modern war as in modern peace denies humaneness and impedes literature, for it places all the mighty stimuli of society in the wrong places. When it is not ignored, art is regarded at best as luxury and at worst as subversion. The potential audience diverts its attention to physics or econometrics;

B I

Business Administration is followed as a respectable intellectual discipline; the Geiger-counter becomes mightier than the pen. The argument of recent years about the 'death' of the novel would never have arisen, I suspect, in a community which had not been subtly corrupted by the glorification, however necessary, of an industrial economy. It comes as no shock to discover that a large public prefers the memoirs of Prime Ministers, Presidents, and Nazi generals to even the greatest fiction, that sociology threatens the existence of literature.

Writers have responded in an untraditional manner to the wars and revolutions, to the statistical tabulations, the advertising slogans and the Geiger-counters. The resulting changes in our literature have transformed not only manner and style; they have driven to the very core of literary expression, metamorphosing literature itself. It is tempting to compare recent changes in our literature to the shift of taste that occurred in the last quarter of the eighteenth century and the early years of the nineteenth, but that comparison will not serve. The changes we know are no mere shifting in taste, they are a revolution; they are basic, reaching deeply into our social experience, our customs, institutions, our ways of thought and our imaginative processes. To observe differences in form, tone, and attack between Thackeray and Rex Warner, or between Hawthorne and William Faulkner, is to return not to the eighteenth century, but to the seventeenth for an experience comparable to our own. The difference between medieval and renaissance forms of thought, the apocalyptic strain in Jacobean drama and poetry, the formal experimentation of Shakespeare or Herbert—these alone offer a parallel to our time in totality if not in excellence.

Recent scholarship has measured every turn and gradient in the line of the revolution in seventeenth-century sensibility, just as recent criticism has been concerned with our own revolution in sensibility, mainly in poetry and the non-literary arts. With significant, though few, exceptions, criticism of the novel has lagged behind with the perfunctory notation of literary historians and the pot-boiling comments of literary journalists. Broadly speaking, novelists have outstripped their critics. While the patterns of Boccaccio, Cervantes, Richardson, Fielding, Jane Austen, Constant, Stendhal, George Eliot, even Flaubert, are still adumbrated, the modern novel assumes forms more complex and even more arrogantly ambitious than in the past. Events have forced the novelist to deal with matters which previously belonged to the politician, the physician, the revolutionist or the historian. This is not to say that the novelists of the past did not deal with history or politics; they did. But in the work of Defoe or Fielding, Dickens or Thackeray, even in so fine an artist as George Eliot, history, politics, philosophy, sociology, all were submerged in the secondary layers of their novels.

The first concern of novelists in the English pantheon, from Defoe to Hardy, that is, has been man in society and society in its totality, an organism which has been examined with varying degrees of acuteness and emphasis as taste and fashion in the novel has ebbed and flowed. Maria Edgeworth's *Manœuvring*, of 1809, contains political history only in that one of her characters goes off to the Navy; the Napoleonic wars impinge hardly at all upon the society she was examining, and the faint historical consciousness of the novel must be mined out, for her first attention went to the stylized plot of money and marriage. In *Bleak House* we learn a good deal about judicial processes in mid-nineteenth-century England; Dickens clearly intended to preach to his readers about that judiciary, but his first intention was to present the story, the plot, in all its ramifications. The point has been made too many times that the novelists of the pantheon could emphasize their stylized plots, allowing the formal problem to concern them slightly or not at all, because they wrote out of a stable social order, for a stable social order. The aristocratic remnants of medieval Europe allied to the well-filled wallets of empire and industrialism gave the novelist his form. Novels became enormous footnotes to that social order which all, writers and readers alike, could accept.

Thus far, the conventional view is admissible with the large reservation that nineteenth-century stability was more apparent than real; controversy about its reality is off the point. The fact that members of the society recognized and accepted certain dominant social formulas is what matters for the novel. The conventional cliché goes on to develop the notion that because the twentieth century has been deprived by a cruel history of the 'stability' of foregoing centuries, the novelist no longer has a true subject, and the novel as such is no longer viable.[1] It would be foolish to deny that the eclipse of widely held values in the nineteenth century had profound effects for all art. But to maintain that those effects destroyed the climate for the production of art is to deny humanity its resilience and to exile art into the jungles of dogma where the sun of experience never penetrates. Among the many inadequacies of this view is the fact that it cannot account for the nineteenth-century novel in America: it tells us little or nothing about the achievement of Cooper or Hawthorne or Melville, about Howells or Norris or Crane. The First World War so obviously accounts for much of the change in Western society that we are in danger of seeing the revolution in the arts as following in comfortable historical progression from the war and of ignoring other potent factors which lead well back into the eighteenth century. Before examining the complexities of the relationship between the English and the American novel, it is useful to look first to certain assumptions of nineteenth-century England and America, that time when, according to the pall-bearers of the corpse of the novel, writers did their finest work in the form.

Although our generation has been taught to distinguish carefully between early, middle, and late Victorian, it is peculiarly hard for us to see the Victorians. We have lived through at least two arcs of taste's pendulum—that arc of disillusion which began with the Edwardians, increased its momentum in the early Georgian period and finished its long sweep in the 'twenties. We learned that the Victorians were proto-Fascist in politics, tribal in family relationships, narrow and miserable in theology, ruthless in business, barbarous in their colonial wars, hypocritical in sexual matters, greedy, nasty, materialistic, best interpreted as a society of Podsnaps and Veneerings. The pendulum paused, then began to reverse its course with Lytton Strachey's *Queen Victoria* (1921), begun 'with cynical doubts', but ended 'in a state

[1] Chapter III will take up this problem in detail.

of respect and praise'.[1] Since Strachey's day, we have seen the full return sweep of the pendulum. The Victorians are purged of crude utilitarianism and other embarrassments and are portrayed as reasonable, questioning people, deeply troubled by contradictions within their society, charitable, profoundly Christian, diffident exploiters of the Africans and Asians—bearers of the white man's burden, victims with all humanity of man's darker side. Tennyson the doubter dominates Tennyson the singer, and the characteristic novel is not *Our Mutual Friend* but *Jude the Obscure*. Victoriana becomes chic and one's friends' houses are littered with horsehair love-seats and porcelain sitting-hens.

As ever the undramatic truth probably lies somewhere in between, and most recent work on the period avoids the extremes of the pendulum.[2] No one can read Victorian literature or intellectual history without being made keenly aware of Victorian doubt and even despair. Tennyson in his black visions, Arnold, Hardy and Hopkins were no apologists in verse for Victorian complacency, nor were Thackeray, Dickens, Disraeli, George Eliot, Newman, or Hardy in prose. But we have lived too briefly with moderation, and most contemporary readers of any enlightenment seem to come away from their reading with the anti-debunking, pro-Victorian view uppermost. One must emphasize that some of the insights of the Edwardian and Georgian reaction were indeed accurate.

Matthew Arnold's poetry of doubt, like Melville's in *Clarel*, spoke for a significant minority, but still a minority. Arnold must be contrasted with that very characteristic writer, Carlyle, who could say of Byron, 'Here was a man of great genius who had never reached maturity, an artist who had never achieved the Everlasting Yea and who, therefore, had little to offer a generation in search of assent.'[3] In broad outline, I would conclude that the Victorian generations found assent, for all the dissent of many of

[1] *Letters of Queen Victoria from the Archives of the House of Brandenburg-Prussia*, ed. Hector Bolitho, New Haven, Yale University Press, 1938, Preface, p. vii.
[2] For example, Jerome H. Buckley, *The Victorian Temper: A Study in Literary Culture*, London, Allen & Unwin, 1952; also Joseph E. Baker, ed., *The Reinterpretation of Victorian Literature*, London, Princeton University Press: Cumberlege, 1950.   [3] Cited in *The Victorian Temper*, p. 19.

their better artists. In the novel, Victorian assent took the form
of the society's feelings about itself and its assumptions that for
lack of a better term I shall call a 'sense of society'. A sense of
society is important to all art, but to the novel as we have known
it, it has been indispensable. It is possible, I think, to discover
whether the modern novelist can possess a sense of society—
whether that sense is capable of adaptation and mutation—by
observing the sense of society as it existed in the Victorians, both
English and American.

To define further, a sense of society is equivalent to, though not
identical with, our awareness of man's associations with man,
whether in politics, religion, education, philosophy, economics,
science, or any other branch of activity in which communal tradition, value, and judgment play their parts. By observing a few
of the social assumptions of the Victorians, both as writers and
readers, we can gain a necessary perspective for an examination
of the differences between the Victorian and the modern novel.

The lesser Gibbon and Victorian Toynbee, Thomas Henry
Buckle, whose *History of Civilization in England* was widely read
in England and in America, illustrates a striking facet of the
Victorian sense of society in science, education, religion, and
historiography. Buckle was an agnostic, devoted to 'scientific'
method rather than to God, critical of his society yet a pure product of it. His diatribes against superstition in the Scottish Church
or the machinations of the Papacy in Spain are amusing, but their
final meaning only bears out the conviction that he was a product
rather than a shaper. In Buckle's system, the terms 'laws of
nature', 'advancement', and 'improvement' take on transcendent
overtones; they are the formulas for the good life. In its social
and moral outlines, his world has the simplicity of Ptolemaic
astronomy; Buckle exemplifies social Darwinism and progressivism in combination with the simple-minded determinism of
Herbert Spencer.[1] 'The more we know of the laws of nature',
Buckle wrote,

[1] For a useful résumé of the Victorian idea of progress, see: John Bowle and
Basil Willey, 'Origins and Development of the Idea of Progress', in *Ideas and
Beliefs of the Victorians*, London, Sylvan Press, 1949, pp. 33–39.

the more clearly do we understand that every thing which happens in the material world, pestilence, earthquake, famine, or whatever it may be, is the necessary result of something which had previously happened. Cause produces effect, and the effect becomes, in its turn, a cause of other effects. In that operation we see no gap, and we admit of no pause.[1]

This test-tube notion of history dominates Buckle's view and supplies the infirm basis for his social meliorism, which he best expresses in the whooping mixture of metaphors that concludes his book:

> This age, haply, may not witness the emancipation [from ignorance]; but, so surely as the human mind advances, so surely will that emancipation come. It may come quicker than any one expects. For, we are stepping on far and fast. The signs of the time are all around, and they who list may read. The handwriting is on the wall; the fiat has gone forth; the ancient empire shall be subverted; the dominion of superstition, already decaying, shall break away, and crumble into dust; and new life being breathed into the confused and chaotic mass, it shall be clearly seen, that, from the beginning there has been no discrepancy, no incongruity, no disorder, no interruption, no interference; but that all the events which surround us, even to the furthest limits of the material creation, are but different parts of a single scheme, which is permeated by one glorious principle of universal and undeviating regularity.[2]

In his philistine rationalism, Buckle looks to education as the magical elixir which will cure all ills. His view of education is Hobbesian, anti-humane. It suspects the arts of falseness and values literature only as a device for discovering 'physical and mental laws'. Buckle was in fact writing one more chapter in the history of European anti-intellectualism, a large and pernicious component of English and American society in the nineteenth century and a component which helps to account for the cleavage between writers and their audiences today.

[1] Thomas Henry Buckle, *History of Civilization in England*, 2 vols., New York, 1885, II, 469. Guizot's *History of the Origin of Representative Government in Europe* might also be mentioned in this connection as a representative and widely read work.

[2] *History of Civilization in England*, II, 472.

Buckle's *History* closely paralleled the social and economic philosophy of the Utilitarians, a group who from the best of motives supplied their century with a complex process in which government, greed, self-interest, and what M. Halévy calls 'the natural identity of interests' could combine,[1] a philosophy geared precisely to the open, expanding society of nineteenth-century England and America. It is unfortunate, in retrospect, that early nineteenth-century England recognized no stronger system than Jeremy Bentham's, whose second-rate mind fashioned a philosophy from second-hand ideas. The very catch-phrase of the Utilitarians, 'the greatest happiness of the greatest number', tawdry and inadequate as it was, Bentham borrowed from Joseph Priestley's *Essay on Government* (1768).[2] Utilitarianism, the only coherent philosophy in Britain in the nineteenth century, was not a product of that century but of the great figures of the eighteenth: of Hume above all, but also of Bernard Mandeville, Priestley, Helvetius, Beccaria, and Paley. Bentham, James Mill and their circle collated the ideas of their masters, popularized them and remoulded them into the needs of their society, but in no sense were the early Utilitarians original. So it was that the Utilitarians passed on to Victorian society another kind of stability, the stability that results from a scarcely realized but none the less real consciousness that its principles belong to tradition. The Victorian sense of society was buttressed by the circumstance that its philosophers did not venture into the uncharted regions of Blake, Godwin, or Paine among native thinkers, nor into the foreign deserts of Kant, Hegel, or Marx. Bentham and his followers saw themselves as radicals, and indeed they were radical in their assertion to an inimical aristocracy of democratic principles, yet those radical principles were very easily pre-empted by the increasingly powerful middle class and cited in rationalization of social abuses. Politically, the influence of Utilitarian philosophy was ultimately conservative.

[1] Elie Halévy, *The Growth of Philosophic Radicalism*, London, Faber & Faber, 1949, p. xvi.

[2] Priestley had taken the phrase from Francis Hutcheson. John Plamenatz, *The English Utilitarians*, London, Oxford University Press, 1949, p. 47; and Halévy, p. 433.

British and American economics of the nineteenth century were similarly based firmly in eighteenth-century theories. Adam Smith's adherence to Hume was demonstrated in 1759 in the 'Theory of the Moral Sentiments', while *An Enquiry into the Nature and Causes of the Wealth of Nations* appeared in 1776. Malthus published his famous *Essay on the Principle of Population* in 1798. Although Ricardo's *Principles of Political Economy and Taxation* was not printed until 1817, he is best understood as an eighteenth- rather than a nineteenth-century figure; he was born in 1772 and died in 1823. With a few exceptions in the way of utopian experiments, the English-speaking community went unscathed by continental nineteenth-century economic theory. Liberal Party economics as expressed by free trade were hardly more than variations upon utilitarian thought; we must look to the Fabians and finally to Keynes to discover any considerable figure in economics after Ricardo.

The peculiar fascination of Utilitarianism for the nineteenth century lay not in its apparent radicalism nor in its more genuine conservatism, but in its pretensions to 'scientific' authority. Just as the latter-day Utilitarian historian, Buckle, sought so earnestly for 'physical and mental laws', so his masters, Bentham and James Mill, pursued the 'laws' of politics and economics. The Victorian sense of society was accordingly grounded in eighteenth-century tradition, but unlike many another traditional society, it was not impeded by tradition, for its scientism gave it a necessary dynamic impulse. It is this dynamism, immensely fortified by Darwin and Huxley, that accounts for Herbert Spencer's vast system; Carlyle (no slight authority on asininity), who judged Spencer 'the most immeasurable ass in Christendom', doubtless received a certain negative impetus from the same source. Froude and Seeley, the jingoists of Empire, were similarly indebted to the political dynamism of Utilitarianism.

Queen Victoria herself is a superb witness to the nineteenth-century sense of society. Her achievement was incredible—to revive from disgrace the idea of royalty, to embody that idea in herself as figurehead, and to wield great political power as well. One doubts that Victoria ever heard the term 'utilitarian', or that she would have cared to. Comparatively innocent of education beyond politics, profoundly non-intellectual, she possessed political instinct and a certain cunning. She apparently was able to lead her society not through superior powers, but because she was so completely attuned to it, able to give the British people a centre of reverence that was comfortable and familiar, royal and *insouciante*. But Victoria speaks for herself, as in this note of 1893 to Gladstone, whom she despised:

> The Queen would wish Mr. Gladstone to consult his colleagues on the present state of affairs abroad, and to ask them if they are satisfied with the condition of our army and navy in the event of the outbreak of war with any of the Great Powers. The dislike of the French to us cannot be concealed, and their alliance with the Russians may lead to a combination which might prove disastrous to our small forces. The Queen firmly believes that the supremacy of our navy would always be supported by the country. . . .
>
> The Queen thinks that no time should be lost in increasing our navy with men and material, and in strengthening our army, already too weak for the duties they have to perform.
>
> The Queen is no alarmist; but she thinks the state of affairs very serious, and there is great alarm abroad about the Mediterranean. The Queen wishes Mr. Gladstone to read this letter to the Cabinet.[1]

With a strength based upon the solidity of the society, the Queen can patronize her Prime Minister, confident that she knows what the country needs better than he. Victoria's epistolary assaults upon Gladstone were not limited to matters of high policy. She approves of Canon Basil Wilberforce's appointment, but objects to his 'very strong total abstinence language' in his preaching at Westminster. 'Total abstinence is an impossibility,' she continues, 'and, though it may be necessary in individual cases, it will not do to insist on it as a general practice; and the Queen relies on Mr. Gladstone's speaking strongly to him in this sense.'[2] In her journal, Victoria describes a dinner party which the American ambassador attended: 'Mr. Bayard is very American,

---

[1] Victoria to Gladstone, 7 December 1893, *The Letters of Queen Victoria*, Third Series, ed. G. E. Buckle, 3 vols., London, Murray, 1931, II, 328.

[2] Victoria to Gladstone, 10 February 1894, *Letters*, Third Series, III, 359.

but he was very civil and kind, and said how devoted the Americans were to me.'[1] Her 'but' is Jamesian in implication; it implies much about the relationship between society in England and America. The Empress rather than the Queen wrote,

> I had a long conversation with Mr. Rhodes (such a remarkable man). He said he had had great difficulties, but that since I had seen him last he had added 12,000 miles of territory to my Dominions, and that he believed in time the whole would come under my rule. He also believes that the Transvaal, which we ought never to have given up, would ultimately come back to England. The Germans were causing us much difficulty, and would never succeed as Colonists.[2]

Victoria's innocent cunning, her home-brewed politics, her maternalism towards that anonymous abstraction, 'the poor', her utter certainty of her own rectitude, were impossible even in the reign of Edward VII, while the dullness of the papers of subsequent monarchs demonstrates once and for all the cohesiveness of Victorian society, that last point in modern history when insularity, imperiousness and insouciance could rule the social day.

The tradition in American historiography of emphasizing uniquely national experience, of concentrating on the frontier and, more recently, upon the various waves of immigration can easily cause us to overlook the fact that the sense of society in England in the nineteenth century was similar to that in America. The complaints of travelling Englishmen about American manners from Mrs. Trollope to Evelyn Waugh combine to demonstrate that English manners and English social assumptions were and remain similar in America. Most adverse English comment arises from those very similarities, for we criticize not the foreign and exotic but the variations from our own standards, which they appear to reject. Political historians have emphasized that the American nineteenth century was a period in which the revolution against England was consolidated; the period in which the United States found its national feet and assumed a national stance; the period, above all, when Americans consciously parted

[1] 2 March 1894, *Letters*, Third Series, III, 367.
[2] Journal, 4 December 1894, *Letters*, Third Series, III, 454–455.

company with the remnants of their Englishness. Yet to emphasize political history at the expense of intellectual history[1] is to
distort to the point of falsification.

In the nineteenth century two currents ran side by side over
the loam of the American intellectual landscape, creating a delta
that was the sole product of neither, but which forms a source of
thought that only recently can be called American. One current
obviously is English; the other is continental, specifically German
and French. At a time when Englishmen were consolidating an
empire in Asia and adding to that empire in Africa, Americans
were expanding into the south and west of what they regarded
as their continent, appropriating the phrase 'manifest destiny' to
justify the near extinction of the natives and appropriating, very
like their English counterparts, utilitarian ideas to justify an unprecedented industrial expansion in the years after the Civil War.
Nineteenth-century America and England alike received their
economic philosophies from the same sources: Alexander Hamilton, Washington's First Secretary of the Treasury, had given the
country its economic philosophy, and Hamilton's ideas, like
Bentham's, smacked of Hume, Adam Smith and Ricardo. The
European sources of American thought were of course modified
in form, particularly by the agrarian prejudice of Thomas Jefferson, but in outline they were hardly to be distinguished from
English thought. The principal American deviations were deviations in emphasis; where Free Trade was the slogan of the English
Liberals, *laissez-faire* and from 1861 a policy of protective tariffs
were virtually the only expression of American economic thought
until Theodore Roosevelt and Wilson.

English historians commonly regard the American Revolution
as an historical accident, an unfortunate result of the circumstance
that the empire was heavily engaged elsewhere. American historians, on the other hand, are likely to see the American Revolution as a total rejection of all things English, an absolute departure
from a decadent if not moribund civilization. This view has
attained the quality of myth, a myth which has sometimes

---

[1] As most writers of history for primary and secondary schools do. It is from
these sources that Americans at large form their ideas of themselves.

strengthened and other times weakened American literature. But to accept the myth is to ignore the probability that American political institutions were not revolutionary, even though the separation of the American colonies from England was revolutionary. The unwritten English constitution was in effect written down by the Americans, with modifications deriving from the Enlightenment, and particularly from John Locke; but once we subtract the principle of monarchy, differences between English and American custom are comparatively insignificant. American political practice, as opposed to political theory, was to differ considerably from English practice as it evolved in the nineteenth century. It was to influence English political practice powerfully, a process which is not confined to politics, and one which has continued in so many areas of social experience that Englishmen today can deplore the 'Americanization' of their country. The American party system was a direct outgrowth of the English; ideas of representative government, of the conduct of elections and countless other practices were taken over with their virtues and vices from the English. Above all, the idea of government responsible to the electorate as we know it today is a joint product of English and American theory and practice. English common law rather than Roman law was the source of the American legal system. All the concepts, in short, of a modern liberal democracy were made possible by English experience and through American modifications of that experience.

In spite of the American rejection of official religion under the constitution, and in spite of the American taste for nonconformist sects, religious thought and, more important, popular attitudes towards religion did not differ materially as late as the nineteenth century. Throughout the seventeenth and eighteenth centuries the same Divines were read on both sides of the Atlantic; Calvinism was nowhere so strong as in New England. Edinburgh could tell Boston nothing about doctrine, and long after doctrinal struggles had been settled in Edinburgh and rural Ayrshire, they continued to agitate Boston and rural Connecticut. Throughout the eighteenth and nineteenth centuries, Americans shared with Englishmen a sharp appetite for sermons and popular theology.

This common taste stresses in turn the fact that English and American literature were virtually identical until the Revolution.

The question of when American literature became American is ultimately unanswerable, for the very question must be so hedged with reservations and defined assumptions that the answer can only be multiple, complex and unsatisfying. It may be sufficient to note that printing was not fully established in the colonies until 1763, though the first press operated at Cambridge, Massachusetts, so early as 1637. The colonists read English books throughout the seventeenth and eighteenth centuries, a habit their posterity has not lost. They read the King James Bible, Foxe's *Actes and Monuments*, Raleigh's *History of the World*, and Bishop Burnett's *History of the Reformation in England*. In poetry they knew Herbert, Quarles and Cowley; some read even *The Faerie Queene* and *Paradise Lost*. Pope, Addison and Steele were the most popular writers of the American eighteenth century. Classical learning was far from unknown; Harvard, founded in 1636, William and Mary, founded in 1693, and Yale, founded in 1701, were sources of classical study; Thomas Jefferson believed Tacitus to be the wisest of all writers.

This is not to say that English and American intellectual history was identical. Over two centuries, geography itself, events and men accounted for considerable differences. In the earliest writing on the American continent—William Bradford's *History of Plymouth Plantation* (completed 1651), in the work of Samuel Sewell, of William Byrd, of William Bartram—in a multitude of sources, a distinctly American prose style developed, displaying among the New Englanders a Puritan prejudice for plainness and uniquely adapted to the necessities of the times[1]—to survey, to report, to explain, and in the eighteenth century to complain, to protest, and to justify. In the novel, American and English literary experience diverged after 1820 with the American hospitality to continental romanticism. It is no accident that German transcendentalism impressed only isolated English figures—Coleridge and Carlyle—while it swept over New England and was so

[1] Howard M. Jones, *Ideas in America*, Cambridge, Massachusetts, 1944, pp. 70–106.

earnestly cultivated that it was virtually transformed from its European aspect into a central source of American literary achievement in the generation between 1830 and 1860. To a society in danger of growing away from the principles of the Enlightenment, the transcendentalism of Channing, Emerson, and Thoreau served at once as a moral check upon the rough-and-ready politics of pre-Civil War America, and as a source of energy to a literature in danger of provincialism and sallow imitativeness. Transcendentalism not only served as a link between Europe and America, but its fierce idealism prepared the way for post-Civil War progressivism, for the meliorism which was a defining characteristic of the society until 1920. Ironically, transcendentalism itself was lost and all but forgotten under the impact of the Civil War. In its effect upon prose style in particular, American transcendentalism differed materially from its European sources. The American transcendentalists' doctrine of nature, which insisted upon the necessity of registering the specific, the closely observed, the minutely realized facts of external nature within the framework of a generalized abstractly apprehended philosophy of Nature, maintained continuity with the older Puritan tradition of simplicity in prose style and prepared for the wide American acceptance of naturalism.

By 1870, roughly, American writers had departed very considerably from the English in prose style, hence in their basic conception of society, even though both American and English writers were subject to approximately similar social forces. Henry Adams wrote of the America of 1868,

> Society in America was always trying, almost as blindly as an earthworm, to realize and understand itself; to catch up with its own head, and to twist about in search of its tail. Society offered the profile of a long, straggling caravan, stretching loosely towards the prairies, its few score of leaders far in advance and its millions of immigrants, negroes, and Indians far in the rear, somewhere in archaic time. It enjoyed the vast advantage over Europe that all seemed, for the moment, to move in one direction, while Europe wasted most of its energy in trying several contradictory movements at once; but whenever Europe or Asia should be polarized or oriented towards

the same point, America might easily lose her head. Meanwhile each newcomer needed to slip into a place as near the head of the caravan as possible, and needed most to know where the leaders could be found.[1]

In spite of Adams's lucid statement of differences, his own *Education* is eloquent proof of the fact that the two societies, English and American, shared a common political philosophy; social piety mingled with agnostic doubt was present in roughly equal portions; scientism, the urge towards synthesis, progressivism and social meliorism dominated the intellectual climate; Bentham's utilitarianism reinforced society's walls wherever a breach threatened.

The 'sense of society' can perhaps be more readily perceived and its place in the novel more easily evaluated against this background in which the similarities rather than the differences in nineteenth-century English and American society are given their due. Without such stress, I would insist, discussion of the modern novel in English can be superficial and misleading. For convenience, the novel from Maria Edgeworth's time to the present can be considered in three successive phases, the first two of which occasionally overlap.

In the first phase, character and society are equivalent. The fictional character may very often question the rightness of the ways of society, but he never challenges their inner reality, their existence. Betrothals, marriages, connivance to gain or enlarge property, to impress one's superiors or inferiors, to make one's way—these are the conventional and stylized moulds for the nineteenth-century plot, made possible by the acceptance of convention and stylization within the society. This first phase obviously includes the novel of manners, but it also includes a nineteenth-century version of the eighteenth century's sprawling, rowdy, comic novel—that form in which Dickens, Trollope, Thackeray, George Eliot and Meredith often wrote, using certain devices of the novel of manners, omitting eighteenth-century bawdiness but sharing its energy, constructing a world for which

[1] Henry Adams, *The Education of Henry Adams*, New York, Modern Library, 1931, pp. 237–238.

the usual term 'social novel' is pale and inadequate. The few American critics who have bothered with the question have assumed that because American nineteenth-century society was not identical with European and specifically English society, that society is lacking in the American novel as a whole, from its inception to the present. Although nineteenth-century America produced no Jane Austen, it produced both the novel of manners and novels exhibiting a strong sense of society. Confining attention for the moment only to parallels to the first phase in England, we must note James Fenimore Cooper's too often ignored *Home As Found* (1838) as the first example in America of the novel of manners, even though Cooper's point was that Americans lacked European manners.[1] Cooper's trilogy of 1845–46, the *Littlepage Manuscripts*, is a further example. The novel of manners had its full day much later in America than in Europe in the work of Henry Adams, William Dean Howells, Henry James, and Edith Wharton. Whether in the brief novel of manners of Jane Austen, the loose unconfined narrative of Trollope in *Orley Farm*, or in the nostalgic re-creation of the society of Colonial New York State by Cooper in *Satanstoe*, this first phase in nineteenth-century novel-writing presents a common acceptance of order and hierarchy, together with a series of assumptions about social experience intimately related to nineteenth-century intellectual history, assumptions which remain assumptions and need not take the form of proofs.

Maria Edgeworth's *Manœuvring* (1809), a novella of domestic intrigue in which money, inheritance and social identity supply the theme, could be considered the prototype of the novel in its first phase as the novel of manners. Here are incidents which in the second or third phases could only be treated with irony. When young Beaumont, for example, comes of age, the village bells are rung, an ox is roasted whole, and the tenants are invited to dine and dance in the manor house. The social structure of the village is presented without being dissected, as it would be in the

---

[1] Cooper's first novel, *Precaution* (1820), a direct imitation of Jane Austen's *Persuasion*, was English in setting and might well have been written by an Englishman.

C

later novel; primogeniture is celebrated in roast ox, the tenants are willing tenants and they will eat and dance in the manor house with free, uncomplicated hearts. The line of plot is strong, arising out of social custom, and a contemporary could accept the theatrical machinations of Mrs. Beaumont over Amelia's marriage because he believed in the usages which the author was manipulating. Jane Austen's *Emma* (1814–16) was and remains credible because of her subtlety in placing us in her fictional situation, even though she shared Maria Edgeworth's stylization and borrowed her themes—money and marriage. Emma Woodhouse, of impeccable social standing in the village of Highbury, would defy social decorum by marrying her less well-born protégée, Harriet Smith, to the young vicar, Elton. When Emma discovers that Elton prefers to marry her rather than Harriet, her scorn conveys a world. She feels that Elton dissimulates love in order to better himself and is 'insulted by his hopes. . . . She need not trouble herself to pity him. He only wanted to aggrandize and enrich himself; and if Miss Woodhouse of Hartfield, the heiress of thirty thousand pounds, were not quite so easily obtained as he had fancied, he would soon try for Miss Somebody else with twenty, or with ten.' 'He only wanted to aggrandize and enrich himself.' The firm, sure world of Highbury rejects the thruster, the social climber; earth and possessions are not to be jeopardized in the name of love. Love has its place, but rash love is intolerable. Manners to this society are more than a code, more than certain assumptions about human conduct: they are the iron-hard framework whose bounds neither Harriet nor Elton nor Emma herself —and here lies the irony—can transgress except at their peril. Manners to Maria Edgeworth and to Jane Austen alike were identical with the sense of society. At first glance, it might appear that a sense of society and the conventions of the novel of manners are one and the same. This is hardly the case. While the novel of manners of course embodies the sense of society, the sense of society is discovered in novels light-years away in impulse from the novel of manners.

James Fenimore Cooper's reputation as 'the American Scott' has completely obscured his position as a novelist of manners, yet a significant amount of his work apart from the Leather-Stocking series and the novels based in European history takes its force and meaning from manners. Himself a political conservative torn between the democratic and the aristocratic ideal, at once a defender and an accuser of the American way, Cooper used his own inner struggle to rich advantage, particularly in his late work. The second novel of the *Littlepage Manuscripts, The Chain-Bearer* (1845) begins thus:

> My father was Cornelius Littlepage, of Satanstoe, in the county of Westchester, and State of New York; and my mother was Anneke Mordaunt, of Lilacsbush, a place long known by that name, which still stands near King's Bridge, but on the Island of Manhattan. . . .
> Of my progenitors further back, I do not conceive it necessary to say much. They were partly of English, and partly of Low Dutch extraction; as is apt to be the case with those who come of New York families of any standing in the colony.

Cooper's world in *The Chain-Bearer* is not, admittedly, the world of Maria Edgeworth or Jane Austen; it lacks the assurance and depth of those worlds. But neither is it vastly remote; social status and theories of property make up its movement, and if there is less stylization, there is more freshness. Cooper's curious achievement is to bring about a junction between the classic mode of the novel of manners and the romantic mode of the depiction of natural man. Conflict in the entire trilogy arises between legality—written laws of property and natural law—the right of squatters, men in nature, to the property they feel they have made their own by having occupied and worked it. The most interesting difference between Cooper and the early English novelists of manners is one of tone. Cooper sounds a note of nostalgia for a way of life that has passed; the present and the future, in his novels, represent a threat to the good life, a falling away from an ideal of the good society which is never developed nor made thematic. It is a tone heard many times in American fiction and in some English fiction, and it is closely related to a sense of society.

It is a tone that we may hear, if we are attuned to it, in Dickens's work. It is muted, impossible to isolate in quotation, and probably not to be defended in Dickens's own logic. His reformer's zeal marks him as a devotee of progress, even though he never bothers to indicate the direction that the idea of progress implicit in his criticism is to take. Dickens's method of satire through burlesque and caricature is the intellectual failing which roots him firmly on the near side of greatness; that method was inadequate to the problem which Dickens the artist set for Dickens the entertainer. Yet Dickens could carry his inadequate method to remarkable successes; in spite of it he is an unusual novelist of society. *Great Expectations* (1860–61) demonstrates how Dickens was able to present the social theme memorably. As Lionel Trilling has remarked, the very title conveys the social theme; it is a specifically nineteenth-century title, containing the confidence, the energy, the sense of growth and progress that Dickens's readers so well understood. Before the point in the novel where young Pip is to come into a mysterious fortune, Pip himself, the Pumblechooks, his foster-parents, and the multitude of minor characters are hardly more than Dickensian stock-types until the appearance of Jaggers, the lawyer who is to administer the mysterious trust fund for Pip. When Jaggers explains that 'It is the desire of the present possessor of that property, that [Pip] be immediately removed from his present sphere of life and from this place, and be brought up as a gentleman—in a word, as a young fellow of great expectations', we know where we are: deep in the folk-lore of nineteenth-century society, whose theme is ambition and the latent urge of industrial society toward progress; whose effect is to force individuals to thrust upward through the hostile levels of a society paying lip-service to gentility, honesty, and honour, while rewarding only material success, however achieved. The invention of Pip is brilliant. He is the honest and innocent man, forced by circumstance into the equivocal position of the social thruster. His situation, which allows for degrees of irony and a depth of social meaning uncommon in Dickens, is all the more effective in that Pip himself is aware of it. Just before Pip leaves his village for London and the fulfilment of his 'expectations', he pays a call on Miss Havisham. He has been wearing his new clothes, and when he is about to return to his foster-parents' home, he writes, 'I . . . took off my new clothes, made them into a bundle, and went back home in my older dress, carrying it,—to speak the truth—much more at my ease too, though I had the bundle to carry.' Through such muted symbolism Dickens moves away from surfaces and deep into social reality. Jaggers, the lawyer who represents the fantastic convict, Magwitch, is one of the long line of figures in Dickens who express utilitarian principles. 'Take nothing on its looks', he says to Pip; 'take everything on evidence. There's no better rule.'

Like Dickens's many other commercial villains, Jaggers is not so much a caricature of materialism as a figure out of allegory. It is always a temptation to dismiss these characters as caricatures, together with remarks about Dickens's 'vitality'. Dickens's animus against society transcends the satirical energy and the ironies of the novelist of manners. His successes and his failures relate directly to the technique of allegory. Behind the social protest, behind the sense of outrage at a commercial society, it is not hard to see the figure of the author himself who shares in the very excesses he allegorizes, a willing victim of the system which provides his material. It is tempting to compare Dickens with a modern American social allegorist, Sinclair Lewis. Lewis's sense of society, like Dickens's, is marked by his revulsion from vices which he perceives with his mind, and in which he himself shares. But Lewis's satire dates as Dickens's does not, for Lewis was incapable of Dickens's saving ability to project symbol and myth. Both Dickens's and Lewis's 'vitality' is the desperate vitality of an eloquent criminal defending himself at the bar. Both writers' sense of society is founded upon passionate conviction which may be two parts reformist in constitution, but which is surely one part self-confession and self-exoneration. While Dickens belongs fully to the first phase of the novel, Lewis, in his sociological (as against social) emphasis, his political awareness, his neglect of plot, belongs to the third phase, of which more later.

It is difficult to remember that Dickens and Trollope were almost exact contemporaries. Where Dickens derived from the renaissance tradition of humours and from the novel of Fielding and Smollett, Trollope belonged more closely to the tradition of the novel of manners. Dickens's reality is mythic and in truth unreal; in Jane Austen's or Trollope's sense, he was not interested in reality, though he was intensely interested in society. Dickens's plots are mad, fantastic, fairy-tale creations; Trollope's are closer to 'life' as it is lived. With Trollope, we are back in the world of betrothals, marriages, wills and codicils. Trollope knows so much; his actual social experience prepares him to deal with society far more expertly than Dickens. His political scenes in *Phineas Finn* have life, blood, and a conviction of knowledge in them that is lacking in Dickens's stray jabs at Parliament; Trollope's characters have none of the woodenness of Disraeli's. In *Orley Farm* (1862) Trollope explored the dimensions of English society with breadth, though without the intensity of virtually any other English novelist. The gradations of the nobility, of the law, of the merchant classes down to clerks and book-keepers are all here, as are the serving maids, the social climber, and the social outcast.[1] The utilitarian spirit in business is coolly regarded and precisely conveyed early in the novel by the unscrupulous Dockwrath, who when challenged in his right to use the commercial room of an inn at Leeds, remarks, 'In this enterprising country, all men are more or less commercial.' The loose plot involves one of those endless nineteenth-century legal trials, but never boringly. And yet, despite the range and expertness, however brilliant the characterization, regardless of the importance of his problems, this novel, together with the rest of Trollope's work, is best described by the critic who calls it 'calisthenic'; a series of moral exercises that prove to be nothing but vagaries. Because we know the lasting significance of his moral problems, 'it is not Trollope's failure to "solve" them that we resent, so much as his pretence that they can be solved with a catchword and a betrothal'.[2] In an earlier novel, *The Warden* (1855), Trollope's wilful subordination of moral effect to the trivialities of plot is even more obvious. Here the scene is confined to the provinces,

---

[1] For an excellent analysis of the novel, see Robert Martin Adams, '"Orley Farm" and Real Fiction', *Nineteenth-Century Fiction*, VIII, No. 1, June 1953, 27–42.

[2] '"Orley Farm" and Real Fiction', p. 38.

and because manners survive longer there than in the capital, we see at once Trollope's able handling of the genre together with his variations upon it. His most interesting variation is his satirical presentation of the nineteenth-century reformer, the surgeon John Bold, an example of the interesting bungler. He intends to correct the 'abuse' of an annual payment of £800 to the Warden of Hiram's Hospital; Bold considers the amount excessive and hopes to divert it to broader social welfare. When his sister Mary asks about his intentions, he replies:

> 'You might ask the same question of anybody else,' said he: 'and according to that, the duty of righting these poor men would belong to nobody. If we are to act on that principle, the weak are never to be protected, injustice is never to be opposed, and no one is to struggle for the poor!' And Bold began to comfort himself in the warmth of his own virtue.

Such priggishness is Trollope's weapon against reformers, against the Victorian meliorist. Meliorism is further satirized when Bold's cause is taken up by *The Jupiter*, Trollope's scornful version of the reforming newspaper. The issues one perceives are basic and interesting, but they lapse into triviality as Bold woos and wins Eleanor Harding, the Warden's daughter, and is persuaded to drop his case, though not before he has done damage to the good Harding by his reforming zeal.

Trollope was not an intellectual, but he was uniquely attuned to the society he described. In Bold's controversy with the local Bishop, we sense overtones of the coming conflict between science and religion; on the evidence of *The Autobiography* it is clear that Trollope was not particularly moved by that conflict. His unfailing sense of society led him to it, as it led him to his depiction of the utilitarian spirit, the political conniver, or the foolhardy reformer. If we go to Dickens for partial explanation of Sinclair Lewis, we go to Trollope for enlightenment upon the methods of William Dean Howells. Holding to a closely reasoned theory of realism, Howells admired and undoubtedly imitated the English masters. In his best novels, *A Modern Instance* (1881), *The Rise of Silas Lapham* (1885), Howells took up the great nineteenth-century theme of 'the rise' through the social and economic scale, in the first instance of the unscrupulous Bartley Hubbard, and in the second of the scrupulous Lapham. An intelligent craftsman, fully able to portray American manners, highly aware of all the implications of the problems he considered, Howells like Trollope consistently evaded the full meanings of his own insight and solved his dilemmas by theatrical removals, absurd romances, and all the outworn paraphernalia of stylized plot inherited from the beginnings of the novel. In the end we return to Trollope and to Howells to appreciate the vividness of their apprehension of society, their very virtuosity in the creation of character, their admirable grasp upon their material. But we return to Dickens even more readily, in spite of the tasteless sentimentality, the embarrassing mock heroics, for his intuitive flashes when the manner transcends itself, caricature becomes mythic, and the resulting reality causes Trollope, Howells and a dozen others to appear as quaint and superficial creators of period studies.

It is increasingly difficult for the present generation, at least in America, to read Thackeray. But if we can still read him, it is because, like Queen Victoria herself, he rises to the mind as a lost landmark; he is uniquely *the* Victorian novelist. Our nostalgia results in biographical rather than critical studies; we wisely do not want to look too closely at the work and we concentrate on the life. But when we do return to the work, we find that Thackeray's woodenness and sentimentality is at once disguised and relieved by his satirical awareness of social gradation and by his portrayal of the movement and restlessness of Victorian society. His technique is to describe the social mean, then to place in the foreground a character who does not apparently 'belong' but who in reality delimits the society for us—a Becky Sharp or a Barnes Newcome. Society is his theme; not the underside, not Dickens's underworld of Thames dockside and slum, but the world of the pushing new bourgeoisie, the would-be elbow-rubbers with the lesser aristocracy. Since the First World War the satirist has stood outside society flicking a bull-whip, like Evelyn Waugh and Nathaniel West; Thackeray belongs to the first phase of the novel because he remained within society, for all his sharpness and point. So Trollope, so George Eliot, so even

Dickens. Our slight addiction to Thackeray and our contemporary revival of Trollope are probably due to our nostalgia for the time when the serious, if minor, novelist could write critically from within society.

Thackeray's sense of society frequently falters, and he presents neither Dickens's myth-laden caricatures nor Trollope's carefully observed, fully dimensioned people, but wash-drawings of people which are too slight to convince. Thackeray's successes are few but striking. When in *The Newcomes* (1853-55) the innocent Colonel Newcome returns from long residence in India to be introduced to London 'society' by his upstart nephew, Barnes, we are aware of still another context in which the Victorian novelist's sense of society could function. Of 'the Rummun', a wealthy Indian present, Barnes explains,

> 'By Gad, a fellow who's rich in London may have the pick of any gal—not here—not in this sort of thing; I mean in society you know,' says Barnes confidentially. 'I've seen the old dowagers crowdin' round that fellow, and the girls snugglin' up to his India-rubber face. . . . Gad, for a settlement, I believe some of 'em here would marry—I mean of the girls in Society.'
>
> 'But isn't this society?' asked the Colonel.
>
> 'Oh, of course. It's very good society and that sort of thing—but it's not, you know—you understand. I give you my honour there are not three people in the room one meets anywhere, except the Rummun. . . .'

Now this is all invented without being inventive, and is therefore the essence of vulgarity. Yet we do not mind, just as we do not particularly mind the confused narrative thread, or the author's preaching interruptions, for the security of money in the bank, the power of the British Empire, the dangerous glitter of London where merchants and baronets and predatory women mingle and jostle are all implied, while the Colonel's pathetic question, 'But isn't this society?' inevitably places the entire complex in our minds. Barnes Newcome believes that he *knows* what society is, and so does Thackeray. Society to Thackeray and novelists of the first phase consists in the presence of certain elements: birth or lack of birth, money, a particular manner of speech, the maintenance of a standard in dress, loyalty to family, to class, to social decorum.

One quality lacking in Thackeray and the rest of the Victorians before Hardy was sustained intensity, that sense of emotional and mental urgency which infuses human affairs, no matter how trivial, and gives them an added measure of meaning. George Eliot possessed intensity. It allowed her to construct into a splendid entity the advantages of the convention of manners, the range of Trollope, the satire of Thackeray, and the sureness of touch of a novelist rooted in society; she brought to the novel, in addition, an intellectual awareness of social experience that was rare in the nineteenth century and which remains fresh and valuable in the twentieth. *Middlemarch* (1872) (with *Moby Dick* one of the finest novels of the nineteenth century) is indebted to Jane Austen as an examination of manners; to Dickens for the minor character Raffles; it is, superficially, a novel of the tradition. But essentially *Middlemarch* remains original. The controlling voice and mind is George Eliot's own. She proves by example that any convincing treatment of manners depends upon style, that style ultimately is manners. Mrs. Cadwallader is not a new figure in English fiction, but George Eliot's presentation of her is:

> Her life was rurally simple, quite free from secrets either foul, dangerous, or otherwise important, and not consciously affected by the great affairs of the world. All the more did the affairs of the great world interest her, when communicated in the letters of high-born relations: the way in which fascinating younger sons had gone to the dogs by marrying their mistresses; the fine old-blooded idiocy of young Lord Tapir, and the furious gouty humours of old Lord Megatherium; the exact crossing of genealogies which had brought a coronet into a new branch and widened the relations of scandal,— these were topics of which she retained details with the utmost accuracy, and reproduced them in an excellent pickle of epigrams, which she herself enjoyed the more because she believed as unquestioningly in birth and no-birth as she did in game and vermin.

George Eliot is prodigal, for Mrs. Cadwallader is a very minor character indeed; manners are manipulated at second remove through her in order to give intensity and reality to the social

subject. 'Great affairs' exist in George Eliot's world as they do
not in Jane Austen's, and the resulting sense of society impresses.
Plot is less important in *Middlemarch* than in most nineteenth-
century novels; character and idea are at least equally balanced
with plot. The various themes—the incompatibility of Dorothea
and Casaubon, of Lydgate and Rosamond; the commercial and
social ambition of Bulstrode; and the romantic ambition of the
unconvincing Ladislaw, are devices to create the necessary tension
against which George Eliot's ideas can be presented. Lydgate,
one of the finest portraits in nineteenth-century fiction, dramatizes
scientific meliorism, the struggle of research against ignorance
and superstition. At the same time he is the full expression of the
snobbery of a beautiful wife, solid silver, and a house too great
for his income. As a man of intellectual distinction, he is finely
aware of his predicament; thus in stature he approaches the tragic.
'Science', he reflects, 'is properly more scrupulous than dogma.
Dogma gives a charter to mistake, but the very breath of science
is a contest with mistake, and must keep conscience alive.'

Jane Austen ignored the Napoleonic wars; George Eliot plunges
us into politics. We go to the hustings with Brooke and learn
through the action of the novel the problem of the lack of representation in the large towns of 1829–32. Will Ladislaw fails as a
character because the method for once is too mechanical; he is the
'Romantic' (like Dorothea), as well as a figure of the uprooted
individual in the new society. He is in a sense George Eliot's Pip, a
man of great expectations: '. . . Why should he not one day be
lifted above the shoulders of the crowd, and feel that he had won
that eminence well?' Dorothea and Casaubon between them
represent two seminal ideas in Victorian society: Casaubon the
need to synthesize, which is satirized in his 'Key to all Mytholo-
gies', and Dorothea in her moral meliorism, her belief 'that by
desiring what is perfectly good, even when we don't quite know
what it is and cannot do what we would, we are part of the divine
power against evil—widening the skirts of light and making the
struggle with darkness narrower'. In the wide cast of her intellectual net, George Eliot apprehended the breaking up of Victorian
society—we think of the countrymen near Middlemarch meeting

the surveyors for the railroad with pitchforks—thus anticipating the novelists of the second phase. In her breadth lay her weakness; as Henry James said, *Middlemarch* is 'an indifferent whole'. James also complained that the novel 'is too often an echo of Messrs. Darwin and Huxley';[1] a complaint which emphasizes George Eliot's sense of society and suggests James's own deficiencies as a novelist. George Eliot brought intelligence, passion, and intensity to the comedy of manners, lifting it, in *Middlemarch* and in *Daniel Deronda* very near to the level of tragedy. In these novels she did not pretend to write tragedy; she placed side by side manners and history, money and politics, ambition and idealism. With other novelists of the first phase, she was still given to the convention of the 'catchword and betrothal'. Plot still distorts life; the human dilemma is seen in the round but still not allowed its full sum of meaning. The Mary Garths, Fred Vincys and Will Ladislaws are allowed to shoulder the Lydgates out of the way.

If the first phase of the nineteenth-century novel was so directly connected with the presence of the social edifice, the second phase was that in which the writer moved away from society to encamp on its outer boundaries. Instead of accepting a basic social framework he questioned it; instead of social comedy he began to write social and personal tragedy. He attempted a greater depth of psychological truth, sacrificing plot as he went; stylization gave way to paradox, and the modern, third phase of struggle and total alienation was anticipated.

While the novel of the first phase remains the 'characteristic' novel of England in the nineteenth century, the novel of the second phase was characteristic of America. The American masters after Cooper—Hawthorne, Melville, Mark Twain, Stephen Crane—have much more in common with English writers of the second phase—Hardy and Conrad—or with the lesser writers like Gissing and William Hale White (Mark Rutherford), than with the writers of the first phase. The reasons for this circumstance are

[1] Henry James, 'George Eliot's *Middlemarch*', *Nineteenth-Century Fiction*, VIII, No. 3, December 1953, 169–170. James's review first appeared anonymously in *Galaxy* in 1873.

as fascinating as they are complex; I would limit the present discussion to what I see as the central cause: the American attitude
toward history. The United States has been interpreted as a
country without a pre-history, a country which came into being
at a given moment in recorded history.[1] American society,
according to this theory, did not develop like traditional communities, but is closer to a human artifact, manufactured to
satisfy conscious, reasoned needs. Lacking the nourishment of
pre-historical traditions, it paradoxically lacks a history: 'a society
born in a certain moment of history comes to find itself outside
history; . . . it lacks any deep-rooted consciousness of history'.
One function of pre-history is to provide a necessary body of
myth, necessary in that myths are 'projections which answer a
certain number of questions about life and therefore satisfy a
number of spiritual needs'.[2] With reference to the novel, such
myths make for a common body of accepted ideas and help to
build the social edifice. The American novelist, living in a con-
tractual society without a body of myth, has had to become his
own myth-maker; forgoing elegance and stylization, the imagination of the nineteenth-century American novelist was split in
two directions in an effort to reconstruct the colonial past and to
cope with the historically difficult present. The novelist had to
be both the glass and the mercury coating without which the
glass cannot be a mirror. English glass alone could not suffice.
Whether vociferously like Cooper, or quietly like Hawthorne,
American novelists recognized and coped with the problem of
imitation in their individual ways. Henry James's explicit 'international' theme, the theme of the impact of Europe on Americans,
was hardly original with him.

Little wonder, then, that Hawthorne groped compulsively for
symbols which would unite and interpret the deeply varying
elements of his art. Hester Prynne's scarlet letter 'A' is a product
of Hawthorne's conscious historical research into New England
seventeenth-century history, of his function as a myth-maker, and

---

[1] F. G. Friedmann, 'America: A Country without Pre-History', *Partisan Review*,
XIX, No. 2, March–April 1952, 141–153.

[2] Friedmann, p. 142.

of his not so conscious sense of alienation from the nineteenth-
century present. For Hawthorne's sense of alienation was not
total; in *The Marble Faun* the problem of history takes another
form, and one meets the first convincing treatment, in the
relationship between Kenyon and Hilda on one side, Miriam and
Donatello on the other, of the 'good' American faced with the
wicked European. A similar pattern of rejection and acceptance,
of alienation from and apology for American society exists in
Melville's work. More completely than Hawthorne's, Melville's
imagination turned to myth, allegory and symbol. Born to
Calvinism, like Hawthorne, Melville took his departure from
theology into philosophy by way of the art-form of the novel.
Keenly aware of contemporary history, cut off from society by
reason of temperament and the very fluidity of society, Melville
was to set a pattern for future American novelists. The line from
Melville to Faulkner is a clear one. For all his myth-making,
Melville did not neglect society; his work often suffered when he
took pains to explain the workings of his mythic apparatus and
to make clear the social application of his symbols. One resents
being told that the *Pequod* is a world in microcosm. *Mardi* (1849)
is virtually unreadable in its vast litter of myth and symbol, but
even there Melville went directly to the social theme by way of
satire. Combining the fairy-tale motif of the quest with echoes
from Swift, Melville caused his characters to cruise among undis-
covered islands of the Pacific, one of which, 'Vivenza', represents
the United States:

  The throng that greeted us upon landing were exceedingly
boisterous.
  'Whence came ye?' they cried. 'Whither bound? Saw ye ever
such a land as this? Is it not a great and extensive republic? Pray,
observe how tall we are; just feel of our thighs; are we not a glorious
people? Here, feel of our beards. Look round; look round; be not
afraid; behold those palms; swear now, that this land surpasses all
others. Old Bello's [England's] mountains are mole-hills to ours;
his rivers, rills; his empires, villages; his palm-trees, shrubs. . . .'
  'Where is your king?' asked Media . . .
  'Ha, ha, my fine fellow! We are all kings here; royalty breathes
in the common air. . . .'

It is all too possible to concentrate on Melville's myth and symbol to the exclusion of his subject, which after all is man and his actions, whether in pursuit of the white whale, whether working out methods for duping his fellows, as in *The Confidence Man*, or expiating the imagined sin of a father, as in *Pierre*. Neither men in reality nor men in Melville's fiction exist apart from society; Melville's insights are social, and his themes are comprehensible only in terms of our social understanding. That they include alienation and estrangement only serves to identify and to delimit the themes, not to remove them from society.

It is tempting to place Mark Twain among writers of the first phase, and on the evidence of his first novel (with Charles Dudley Warner), *The Gilded Age* (1873), that is where he belongs. Colonel Beriah Sellers is frankly modelled on Micawber, while the entire novel is a Dickensian excoriation of American society in the decade after the Civil War. But in his major work, *Huckleberry Finn* (1884), and in his late, bitter, minor tales, *The Man that Corrupted Hadleyburg* (1899), *What Is Man?* (1906) and *The Mysterious Stranger* (1916) Twain made clear that he belonged with writers of the second phase. He did not abandon the social theme, but he approached the mythic in his treatment of that theme. *Huckleberry Finn* in particular interprets the recent American past, establishes an ethical vision, and emphasizes the distance between primitive virtue and social corruption. This theme is of course a traditional one, a hoary romantic cliché, yet Twain saw it freshly and incorporated it into an American myth which persists with vigour in much subsequent work. As in Melville and Cooper, the social theme in Twain appears through the devices of satire; satire in America, in fact, becomes not merely a device, but an integral method for the novelist grappling with his large and difficult task.

Stephen Crane's work between *Maggie*, his first book of 1893, and his death in 1900 marked the farthest point to which the novel of the second phase could be taken. Crane's best work is a landmark both in technique and in the nature of the problem he set for the novel; the third and modern phase in America was made possible by his example. Crane was not the first American novelist to go to school to the continental masters; James and Howells before him had taken what they could use from the Russians and the French, and what they could use proved to be refinements upon the novel of the first phase. In spite of his express denial, Crane either read Zola or was familiar with his theory of the *roman expérimental*, and he was responsible, with Frank Norris, for importing the enormously influential theory of naturalism into American writing. It is clear that Crane perceived society in *Maggie* (1893) and in *George's Mother* (1896) much as Zola did in the *Rougon-Macquart* series, that is, as the doomed environment into which the novelist inserted his characters to observe more or less objectively their disintegration. In these two embarrassingly deficient novels, Crane shared a habit of many American novelists of the second phase, the literal rendering of local dialect in an attempt to reach a high degree of realism. Crane was far from crippled, though, by his momentary kinship with second-rate writing either of Zola or of the 'local colour' school of Edward Eggleston and Bret Harte. His vindication was *The Red Badge of Courage* (1895), a study of a young soldier's conduct in Civil War battle, in which Crane reached a quality of psychological truth unknown in the earlier American novel, and rare in the novel in any time or place. Here the break with conventional plotting is complete; emphasis upon psychological motivation determines the total movement of the novel, and while society in the dissolution of Civil War is his subject, that subject may seem to be submerged in the consciousness of Henry Fleming, the central character. But Crane's originality in technique, his arresting emphasis upon psychological exploration, his ability to project depth as well as width should not continue to obscure the fact that society, a society at war with itself, is still his controlling subject. Crane's lesser work, like *The Third Violet* (1897) or *Whilomville Stories* (1900), placed him more conventionally with his contemporaries in the second phase of the novel. *The Third Violet* in particular shows how conventional and merely 'calisthenic' Crane could be; it shows him, too, displaying a full awareness of society in the more traditional sense.

In England the break between the first and the second phase of the novel was more orderly than in America. We have seen how, despite their differences in theme, tactic, and emphasis, novelists from Maria Edgeworth to Trollope wrote in a consciousness of the social edifice. Their sense of involvement in society resulted in the luxury of the long, loose plot; the novel was conceived as an artifice rather than as a solemn commentary. The distance between the frankly stylized plots and the reality of English life remained as large as the difference between Verdi's libretti and the realities of Italian life. In the second phase, stylization was driven underground, and the novel took on a new and ponderous seriousness. Life and art, seemingly, began to merge; the old conventions no longer existed, and society became subjected to a process in which we are still involved, a process of erecting new conventions, new manners and mores. While society still loomed large, the hero now opposed it. One result was a distinct kinship between writers of the second phase in England and in America. Hawthorne, Melville and Hardy have far more in common than have, say, Melville and his contemporary, Trollope.

The second phase in England belongs to novelists like George Gissing and William Hale White, to George Moore, but above all to Thomas Hardy. Writing out of bitter personal experience with the underside of Victorian life, seizing by instinct or acquaintance with continental writing upon some of the devices of naturalism, these writers anticipated many later modes in the novel. Because the great edifice of Victorian society still remained, they would not or could not dispense with the conventionally plotted novel. Containing such contradictions and sustained by only minor talents, it is no wonder that Gissing's and White's books were not widely read. Nor is it any wonder that Hardy despaired of the novel after the public savaging of *Jude the Obscure* in 1895. This novel is similar in theme to Melville's *Pierre*, the theme of characters in sexual conflict with society, and similar in that the reception of *Pierre* turned Melville away from the novel form for many years, just as *Jude* turned Hardy away for good. *Jude* marks the exact point in English fiction at which society as a subject withdraws in favour of the individual. Society is still present, but Hardy's characters live in defiance of society,

D

not as the villains they would have been in Dickens, but as forlorn heroes. Jude and Sue live in religious and particularly in sexual conflict with Victorian society, while the power of their story is created by the totality of social disapproval, which they feel like physical weight upon their bodies. It is not to flatter our own time to say that it is this conception of his material that makes Hardy a 'modern', and which allows him the ironies of the scene at the conclusion when Arabella traps Jude once again into marriage; Arabella whose monstrous vulgarity speaks for the society Jude has tried vainly to defy. Arabella gets Jude drunk, then leads him to the altar:

> 'Mrs. Fawley, I presume?' said Tinker Taylor, with mock courtesy.
> 'Certainly. Mrs. Fawley again,' replied Arabella, blandly pulling off her glove and holding out her left hand. 'There's the padlock, see. . . . Well, he was a very nice, gentlemanly man indeed—I mean the clergyman. He said to me, as gentle as a babe, when all was done, "Mrs. Fawley, I congratulate you heartily," he says. "For having heard your history, and that of your husband, I think you have both done the right and proper thing. And for your past errors as a wife, and his as a husband, I think you ought now to be forgiven by the world, as you have forgiven each other," says he. Yes; he was a very nice, gentlemanly man. "The church don't recognize divorce in her dogma, strictly speaking," he says, "and bear in mind the words of the Service in your goings out and your comings in: What God hath joined together, let no man put asunder." . . . But Jude, my dear, you were enough to make a cat laugh! You walked that straight and held yourself that steady, . . . though I knew you were seeing double all the time, from the way you fumbled with my finger.'
> 'I said I'd do anything to—save a woman's honour,' muttered Jude, 'and I've done it!'

This prepares for the final, wonderful irony of Arabella's going off to the boat-race celebration though she knows that Jude lies dead. Greater novelists had created greater characters than Hardy's Jude, but Hardy was the first to sense and to reproduce the break between the fictional character and the society of which he is a member; Jude is the most eloquent fictional protest we have against Victorian notions of progress and education. The distance between character and society was widened in Conrad's novels, and culminated in a totally new conception of what the novel was and could do, in the years after 1918.

It was John Galsworthy's wry honour to compose the *Götter-dämmerung* for both the first and the second phases of the English novel. His failure was proof, if proof is required, of the division of sensibility in the English novel in the years under scrutiny. Prepared technically in the 'classical' Victorian school, Galsworthy produced his Forsyte novels in such a way that they read like the work of a lesser Thackeray or a minor Trollope. Yet they can be read at all because Galsworthy perceived the very cleavage in sensibility of his time, and took it for his theme. An inadequate technique which was the result of an inadequate imagination accounted for the slightness of his early work, and for the down-right shoddiness of his later work. He wanted desperately to describe society; he was intellectually aware of the social theme, but a sense of society is precisely what was missing. His characters are social types *manqués*, unliving attempts to demonstrate a thesis. The opening passage of *Swan Song* (1920) indicates that to stand outside character without the social audience of an earlier century results in a cheap slickness:

> In modern Society, one thing after another, this spice on that, ensures a kind of memoristic vacuum, and Fleur Mont's passage of arms with Marjorie Ferrar was, by the spring of 1926, well-nigh forgotten. Moreover, she gave Society's memory no encouragement, for after her tour round the world, she was interested in the Empire—a bent so out of fashion as to have all the flavour and excitement of novelty with a sort of impersonality guaranteed.
>
> Colonials, Americans, and Indian students, people whom nobody could suspect of being lions, now encountered each other in the 'bimetallic parlour,' and were found by Fleur 'very interesting,' especially the Indian students, so supple and enigmatic, that she could never tell whether she were 'using' them or they were 'using' her.

And with this we are off down the road of social decay presented through the general strike of 1926. But when Galsworthy's writing is not cheapened by obvious devices it is simply dull.

Because of the inadequacy in technique, we cannot believe either Galsworthy's people or the problems set for them.

The transition from the second phase in England was almost entirely one of material; writers like Arnold Bennett and Galsworthy realized with their minds that politics and wars were changing the nature of reality for the novelist, but they modified Victorian techniques only in the direction of a watery naturalism. In America, the transition affected technique rather than material, since the overt social theme had never been so dominant as in England. Crane's hospitality to continental influence was symptomatic of the technical differences which were strongly to mark American and English fiction well into the twentieth century. But Galsworthy and his generation looked to the past; by 1914, the revolution in the novel had struck the provinces, and those who were capable of seeing knew that the Capitol would fall. There was no one to share Flaubert's aesthetic meliorism as he expressed it in a letter of 1858 to Louise Colet:

> The more Art develops, the more scientific it will be, just as science will become artistic. Separated in their early stages, the two will become one again when both reach their culmination. It is beyond the power of human thought today to foresee in what a dazzling intellectual light the works of the future will flower.[1]

[1] Francis Steegmuller, trans. and ed., *The Selected Letters of Gustave Flaubert*, London, Hamish Hamilton, 1954, p. 135.

Chapter Two

AN EXPERIMENT IN DEFINITION

THE late Theodore Spencer once defined the novel as

> . . . a narrative in prose which describes the progress of one or more
> imaginary characters through a series of events so arranged as to
> produce the illusion that those events have a necessary relation to one
> another and to the characters experiencing them; which describes
> those characters and the subsidiary characters involved in the narra-
> tive, against an environment creating the illusion of factual reality,
> and which implies a set of moral and emotional standards by which
> the behavior of the main characters is to be judged.[1]

Spencer himself was aware of the tortured nature of his definition,
and he presented it as evidence of the difficulty one encounters in
attempting even to describe the modern novel. Spencer's problem
is of recent vintage. No one in nineteenth-century England or
America had any particular difficulty in recognizing what the
novel was: a dramatic narrative with a beginning, a middle, and
an end, whose purpose was to entertain and to instruct. And as
long as the novelist wrote his narrative with a certain skill and did
not violate social taboos, he was reasonably assured of a public
large enough to support him in comfort, if not in luxury.

Broadly speaking, the nineteenth-century novelist's task was
one of social synthesis. As society became more complex, the
novel became longer in the writer's effort to encompass the many
discordant elements. The length of the Victorian novel has usually
been explained by the convention of serial publication for the
consumption of a population that lacked radio, films, or television.
But once the break had been made with the feudal conception of
society which persisted until Jane Austen's time and the Victorian
industrial free-for-all had begun, the novelist was forced to fill

[1] In an unpublished lecture at Harvard University, 1947.

much space in constructing the rules of behaviour to which his characters might or might not conform. An avowed novelist of manners, like Trollope, exceeded Jane Austen's novels in length many times over. Americans still write long novels, for they are still surveying the social ground. Until the emergence of the third phase of the novel, between 1910 and 1920, discordant social elements were dealt with by embellishment to beginning, middle, and end; synthesis, closely allied to meliorism and progressivism, was still a powerful motive, and the novelist remained, if not at peace, at least in a state of truce with society.

The First World War was an unusual historical event, for every literate European realized as it occurred that the war marked the end of an age which had begun with the French Revolution. The wars and revolutions of 1914–25 disintegrated the social and moral codes of the Victorians and Edwardians, and where order had once existed, confusion, if not chaos, ruled. In those years, Americans reached the same general conclusions as Europeans through a national experience which differed from the European in political outline, but which held the same meanings for the writer. In the novel, fragmentation took the place of synthesis. The generation of the First World War was prompt to recognize that the social, political, and psychological fundament of reality had been transformed, and that the tradition which they as writers had inherited was inadequate for coping with their new and appalling problem. The uneasy truce was broken and the long rebellion began, the conclusion of which we may be seeing only now, a generation in time and a Second World War in politics later.

One result of that rebellion has been a modification, in the minds of writer, critic, and reader alike, of what the novel is and of what it might be. Traditional techniques have been turned to untraditional uses, and new techniques have been invented; like the other arts, the novel has rapidly become cosmopolitan and familiar national themes and patterns are no longer comfortably recognizable. The term 'modern' became first either a rallying cry or an insult, associated in some minds with freakishness— Gérard de Nerval's lobster paraded in the boulevard on a pink

ribbon—with a false *avant-gardisme*, with beggary and buggery.
Then to other minds the modern movement meant the effort to
reach new levels of meaning, a break with the past and an openness before the present and the future.[1] In our time, 'The Modern
Novel' has developed into a loose, omnibus idea which can mean
virtually anything in the way of technique, though it is usually
allied in a vague manner with that other omnibus idea, 'experimental'. Without attempting to legislate what the novel should
or should not be, I would define the modern novel as it has
existed in actual practice, and to suggest at the same time a few
things that the novel is not.

In the face of much insensitive and obscurantist legislation by
critics of limited vision, the effect of which has been theoretically
to rule out the writing of novels, Northrop Frye has made a contribution that deserves wider circulation than it has received.
Observing the novel historically, Frye would eliminate any archetypal idea of The Novel, and would classify prose fiction according
to the limits set by writers themselves. Something is wrong with
the term 'novel', he suggests, when it makes Defoe, Fielding,
Jane Austen, and Henry James central to its tradition and Borrow,
Peacock, Melville, and Emily Brontë 'somehow peripheral'.
The term 'novel' suffices for the traditional well-made fiction of
Jane Austen and her stylistic descendants. But Frye would use
'romance' to describe prose fiction such as *Wuthering Heights*; the
difference from the novel is one of characterization. In Emily
Brontë's work, we do not find 'real' people; we find instead
Jungian libido, anima, and shadow; a gloss of subjectivity and the
'glow' of allegory.[2] The third category is the confession, in
which 'autobiography [has] merge[d] with the novel by a series
of insensible gradations'. In itself, autobiography is not a form of
prose fiction, but in the writing of St. Augustine, in the *Religio*

[1] I do not mean to imply the notion of progress in the art of the novel by the
historical division of the novel into three phases. I believe firmly, however, that
the novel is still maturing as an art-form, and that the third, modern phase has
extended the possibilities of the form. The distinction between progress and
maturation is obviously important.

[2] Northrop Frye, 'The Four Forms of Prose Fiction', *Hudson Review*, II,
1950, 582.

Medici or Newman's *Apologia*, a pattern larger than the self becomes apparent. In Rousseau, 'the confession flows into the novel, and the mixture produces the fictional autobiography, the *Künstler-Roman*, and kindred types'. Idea is prominent in the confession, whereas in Jane Austen idea is subordinate to personal relationship. 'The confession is . . . introverted, but intellectualized in content.'[1] Frye names his fourth and last category the 'Menippean satire', or the 'Anatomy', after Burton, its foremost exemplar, and traces its venerable ancestry from Menippus through Lucian, Varro, Petronius and Apuleius to its modern form in Voltaire's *Candide*, Swift's *Gulliver*, the fiction of Peacock, and *Brave New World* of Aldous Huxley. In the Anatomy men are classified according to their humours and are generally satirized.[2]

Although Frye's categories create many problems in their turn, they carry forward the necessary work of providing a vocabulary with which to discuss prose fiction. The categories are meaningful here in that they supplement the previous discussion of the three phases of the novel, and they set apart as the 'confession' one kind of prose fiction that we meet so frequently in modern literature. Frye shows considerable insight in his emphasis on the confession that is 'intellectualized in content'. This is another way of insisting upon the rightful place of ideas in the modern novel. The continental novel in the nineteenth century was more hospitable to ideas than either the English or the American; the work of Rousseau and Constant, Goethe, Stendhal, Dostoievski and Flaubert was most frequently dominated by ideas, by a discernible intellectual purpose that was quite literally foreign to Anglo-American practice. An occasional writer like George Eliot could cope with ideas, though even she failed more often than she succeeded. The success of *Middlemarch* must be countered by the historical morass of *Romola*, an instance in which idea floundered in a historical bog; again, the woodenness of *Felix Holt* vitiates the intellectual purpose of the writer of genius struggling with an alien idiom. In America, Melville's finest work, *Moby Dick*, went unread, as did *Pierre* and *The Confidence Man*; all novels of ideas

[1] Frye, p. 584.　　　　　　　　[2] Frye, pp. 587–588.

served up to a public that wanted entertainment in the form of realistic narrative.

The catastrophe of the First World War not only altered society, it affected men's sensibilities as they had not previously been affected in modern times. The catastrophe brought into modern society a sense of urgency and a new tempo; it made for a new consciousness of self and of the place of the self in society; it created an atmosphere in which the loss of old certainties, the presence of new anxieties, and the thrusting forward of public issues combined to isolate man from man and group from group. The novelist promptly discovered that new techniques were required to express the new fragmentation of society. The novel of ideas, particularly for the English and American novelist, to whom ideas were traditionally distinct from literature, took on particular importance, for they learned belatedly what the continental writers had learned from Stendhal—that the novel was the unique instrument of the imagination for dealing with catastrophe. One important result for the Anglo-American novel in the third phase was a growing awareness of the novel as an art-form, as a particular instrument beautifully fitted for certain kinds of communication, but totally unfitted for other purposes.

The period of experimentation which began with Joyce (and which is still in progress) perfected some techniques and displayed the limitations of others. Experiments in stream-of-consciousness techniques, in the shaping of narrative in accordance with a new consciousness of time, expressionism, surrealism, new manipulations of symbol, myth, and allegory aided both writer and reader in discovering the limits of prose narrative. All involved a heightened consciousness, particularly for the Anglo-American writer, of the nature of prose, hence we might first examine certain theories of prose diction which lie embedded in the best, and the worst, novels of the third phase.

It may seem simple-minded to say that the medium of the novel *is* prose, and that prose by definition, derivation, and the best practice of the best writers, implies the communication of a more or less logical, more or less apprehensible version of human experience; but one must say this because of a confusion, traditional and contemporary, about the nature of prose in the novel. One would not rule out the exalted, the esoteric, or any manner of imaginative flight, nor banish from the novel the least seemingly-logical of literary approaches to experience, whether surrealist, Dadaist, Vorticist—*any* usable mode; the beribboned lobster may always parade the boulevards of the novel—but it is to insist upon the uniqueness of the novel as an art-form, and prose as its medium. The novel is not poetry nor painting, any more than it is ballet or opera. Prose, all kinds of prose, the novelist's unique instrument, has its own movement and its own specific gravity. A bastard confusion of prose with poetry has existed in the Anglo-American novel at least since Dickens in England and William Gilmore Simms in America, but experiments in the third phase of the novel have led to an alarming acceleration of the confusion among both writers and critics.

The importance to the novel of psychoanalytical research was acknowledged from the time that Freud began his public lectures, about 1909. The various experiments in depth psychology in the modern novel of sensibility have been fully traced, and the techniques which make that novel possible competently analysed. But no one has given more than passing attention to the technique of poetic prose, a technique which has implications for the novel of sensibility second only to psychoanalytical theories in importance; no one seems to have recognized the negative place of poetic prose in modern experiment.[1] English prose style as we practise it is of course a recent development. Our distinction between prose and poetry owes its existence, significantly, to the rise of the novel as an art-form in the eighteenth century. The distinction had been observed in Middle English, but it became clouded in the sixteenth century by the vogue of Euphuism in the prose of Lyly, Lodge, and Greene, while the confusion was perpetuated in the seventeenth-century baroque, meditative prose

[1] Joel Springarn touched on the distinction between prose and poetry in *Creative Criticism*, New York, Henry Holt, 1917, p. 102; Edmund Wilson's essay, 'Is Verse a Dying Technique?', *The Triple Thinkers*, New York, Oxford University Press, 1948, mentions the problem, as does Lionel Trilling in *The Liberal Imagination*, New York, Viking, 1951, pp. 271-273. But none of these critics bothered with the major implications of his statement.

of Donne, Jeremy Taylor, Browne, and Burton. This is not to say that baroque prose was poetic prose, but that it contributed to the 'poetic' character of prose narrative before the neo-classic reform in the late seventeenth century. By the nineteenth century the pure baroque of the seventeenth century had deteriorated into the sterile confusion in style in the work of Landor and De Quincey.

In the novel proper, both Fielding and Dr. Johnson may have contributed to the confusion in their theoretical writing, though in their practice they observed a strict distinction. Fielding wrote hard, clear, logical prose in *Tom Jones* (1749), but in the famous interpolated essays he presented his theory of the novel as 'comic epic'. Johnson's *Rasselas*, again, was written in the prose of the time, unconfounded by lyric flights, rhythm, rhyme, or any other device of versification, while in an earlier *Rambler* essay Johnson had said that '. . . works of fiction . . . are such as exhibit life in its true state, diversified only by accidents that daily happen in the world, and influenced by passions and qualities which are really to be found in conversing with mankind. This kind of writing may be termed not improperly the comedy of romance, and is to be conducted nearly by the rules of comic poetry.'[1] These writers' mere use of the terms 'epic' and 'poetry' is unimportant against their expert practice in the medium of prose, but the harm was felt a century later, on the side of theory, in the writing of William Gilmore Simms in America, and in practice in the purple passages of nineteenth-century English novelists like Dickens.

I have no doubt that Simms was influenced by Fielding's theory when he wrote in his preface to *The Yemassee* (1835) that the 'Romance', by which he meant the unhistorical historical novel,

is of loftier origin than the Novel. It approximates the poem. It may be described as an amalgam of the two. It is only with those who are apt to insist upon poetry as verse, and to confound rhyme with poetry, that the resemblance is unapparent. The standards of the Romance—take such a story, for example, as the Ivanhoe of Scott, or the Salathiel of Croly,—are very much those of the epic. It invests individuals with an absorbing interest—it hurries them

[1] Samuel Johnson, *Rambler*, 31 March 1750.

rapidly through crowding and exacting events, in a narrow space of time—it requires the same unities of plan, of purpose, and harmony of parts, and it seeks for its adventures among the wild and wonderful. It does not confine itself to what is known, or even what is probable.

Simms, a lesser Fenimore Cooper who wrote historical novels about the South and the southern Indian tribes, indulged his theory rather less than Cooper, confining his use of the 'poetic' elevated style to moments of highest tension. Dickens did not theorize about style, but his actual procedure is important for its effect upon his wide audience and for his influence upon other writers. Capable of fleeting genius as a stylist, Dickens was also capable of a gaudy lyricism and declamatory rhythms that are embarrassing when they are not revolting. It is false modesty to explain away these excrescences as Dickens's concessions to Victorian taste, when in fact they are downright bad writing. The lingering deaths and the candied portaits of suffering age can be effective as long as Dickens remained faithful to his own conception; he failed by any standard when he indulged in poetic embellishment, as in the climactic moment in *Our Mutual Friend* when John Rokesmith-Harmon determines to clear away the mystery of his identity:

> And John Rokesmith, what did he? He went down to his room, and buried John Harmon many additional fathoms deep. He took his hat, and walked out, and, as he went to Holloway or anywhere else —not at all minding where—heaped mounds upon mounds of earth over John Harmon's grave. His walking did not bring him home until the dawn of day. And so busy had he been all night, piling and piling weights upon weights of earth above John Harmon's grave, that by that time John Harmon lay buried under a whole Alpine range; and still the Sexton Rokesmith accumulated mountains over him, lightening his labour with the dirge, 'Cover him, crush him, keep him down!'

In his effort to construct high drama, Dickens borrowed from poetry the devices of inversion, thematic repetition, and metaphor, but his metaphor, absurdly mixed from nautical diction, geology, and burial-rites, produces bathos. An insensitivity to language caused Dickens to use the devices of poetry without achieving the effects of poetry; with him the baroque tradition degenerated into fretwork and gingerbread. Hardy was able to use many poetic devices in his novels, but he used them legitimately, that is to say, *as prose*; thus he avoided Dickens's inflation and false emotion. Flaubert supported this view when he wrote, '. . . I detest so-called poetic language. When there are no words, a glance is enough. Soulful effusions, lyricism, descriptions—I want all these embodied in Style. To put them elsewhere is to prostitute art and feeling itself.'[1]

Dickens's stylistic successes and failures call attention to the habit of one of his critics of falling back on the term 'poetic' whenever he wishes to praise without qualification, a vicious habit which is not confined to critics of Dickens and which displays as basic a confusion about the differences between the novel and the poem on the part of the critic as on the part of delinquent authors. The irascible Dr. Leavis (I almost wrote Johnson) says that for its texture, imaginative mode, display of symbol, and resulting concentration, *Hard Times* is a 'poetic' work. 'The final stress may fall on Dickens's command of word, phrase, rhythm and image: in ease and range there is surely no greater master of English except Shakespeare. . . . Dickens is a great poet.'[2] For Dr. Leavis, Hawthorne and Henry James are also poets, though they were not up to Shakespeare in standard.[3]

One powerful influence upon American poetic prose came not from a novelist, but from Walt Whitman, poet, journalist and essayist. Whitman's undoubted stature as a poet and the excellence of some of his essays must be set against the fact that his influence upon the novel has ranged from deplorable to disastrous. Whitman's effect upon poets was apparent shortly after his death in 1891, but the tones of his prose are not heard in the novel until

[1] To Louise Colet, 6 July 1852. *Selected Letters*, p. 140.
[2] F. R. Leavis, *The Great Tradition*, Chatto & Windus, London, 1948, p. 234; p. 245.
[3] Leavis, pp. 128–129. Marius Bewley follows Leavis in congratulating James upon the 'poetically organized' *Golden Bowl: The Complex Fate*, London, Chatto & Windus, 1952, p. 93.

later, mainly in the work of D. H. Lawrence,[1] Thomas Wolfe, John Steinbeck, and their imitators, evidence that while the experiments of the 1920s released new energies, they also gave licence to infatuation with lists, catalogues, a neo-transcendental mystique of nature, and to Wolfe's defiance of the existence of form. Whitman's verse, by turns fine and true and crashingly bad, could all too easily be confused with the prose of, say, *Democratic Vistas*. One kind of experimenter could read Whitman's thoughts about 'the democratic literature of the future' and find authority in the content, and more particularly in the style, for further confusion of the two disciplines:

> For us, along the great highways of time, those monuments stand —those forms of majesty and beauty. For us those beacons burn through all the nights. Unknown Egyptians, graving hieroglyphs; Hindus, with hymn and apothegm and endless epic; Hebrew prophet, with spirituality, as in flashes of lightning, conscience like red-hot iron, plaintive songs and screams of vengeance for tyrannies and enslavement; Christ, with bent head, brooding love and peace, like a dove; Greek, creating eternal shapes of physical and esthetic proportion; Roman, lord of satire, the sword, and the codex;

and on in the same sentence Whitman strides through the centuries to 'Dante, stalking with lean form, ... rich Shakespeare, luxuriant as the sun . . . and so to such as German Kant and Hegel, where they, though near us, leaping over the ages, sit again, impassive, imperturbable, like the Egyptian gods.'[2] If Christ

---

[1] 'Whitman, the great poet, has meant so much to me.' Lawrence in *Studies in Classic American Literature*, New York, 1923, p. 253.

[2] Walt Whitman, *Democratic Vistas*, London, Routledge, n.d., p. 61. The following incantation from the editorial page of the *New York Times* shows that Whitman's influence is even more potent among reporters than novelists: 'We are the city of the skyscraper and the one-family home; city of subways and the private automobile; city of tunnels and bridges, of the narrow, winding street downtown and of the great boulevard on "the island". We are the city of the Negro and the white man, the Catholic, the Protestant, the Jew and uncounted other religions and shades of belief and disbelief; of Irish, Italian and plain American—as all eventually became; of East and West, of North and South. We take pride in our tolerance, yet know our unfortunate moments of prejudice. We are America, we are the world and democracy in a ferment of striving, introspection and extrovertism such as must know no parallel.

'In this mixing bowl we call New York we know wealth and poverty, the

precedes the Greeks, no matter so long as the rhythms roll and the list rings impressively. In Thomas Wolfe's prose, Whitman's unmistakable hand lies heavy in the infatuation with rhythm, the catalogues which enlarge without clarifying, the forced *brio* which reflects the writer's mood at the moment of writing rather than the demands of the material.

Wolfe's poetic prose, like that of his imitators, is the result not so much of conscious experiment as of the climate of experiment combined with a failure of sensibility. When we look for the cyclones and anti-cyclones of the experimental climate, though, we must go back to the beginnings of modern experiment, to the work of the imagists in England and America, and particularly to Amy Lowell.[1] Her highly conscious experiments in 'polyphonic prose', like those of the American poet, John Gould Fletcher, have had more effect upon the novel than has been generally recognized. Amy Lowell wrote that polyphonic prose is not really a prose form, but a free and elastic form that 'follows at will any, and all, of the rules which guide other forms'. It can go from the 'laws' of both metrical and cadenced verse in one and the same piece of verse without incongruity. She traced her theory to the variations upon the alexandrine of the French poet, Paul Fort, explaining how she compared the rhythm of the alexandrine to the iambic pentameter of English and discarded both in favour of 'the long flowing cadence of oratorical prose'. She then noted her use of rhyme, assonance, alliteration, and return; return 'is usually achieved by recurrence of a dominant thought or image, coming in irregularly and in varying words, but still giving the spherical effect . . . imperative in all poetry'.[2] A brief sample from 'Hedge Island: A Retrospect and a Prophecy' demonstrates Amy Lowell's theory in her actual practice:

expression of man's noblest sentiments, and of his degradation. It is the city of opportunity, beckoning to all, to rise with high acclaim or to fall unnoticed, unwept.'

'New York 1653–1953', *The New York Times*, International Edition, 2 February 1953, p. 4.

[1] For a good discussion of Imagism, see Stanley K. Coffman, *Imagism: A Chapter for the History of Modern Poetry*, University of Oklahoma Press, Norman, 1951.

[2] Amy Lowell, *Can Grande's Castle*, Boston and New York, 1921, Preface, pp. x–xv.

Hedges of England, peppered with sloes; hedges of England, rows and rows of thorn and brier raying out from the fire where London burns with its steaming lights, throwing a glare on the sky o'nights. Hedges of England, road after road, lane after lane, and on again to the sea at the North, to the sea at the East, blackberry hedges, and man and beast plod and trot and gallop between hedges of England, clipped and clean; beech, and laurel, and hornbeam, and yew, wheels whirl under, and circle through, tunnels of green to the sea at the South; wind-blown hedges to mark the mouth of Thames or Humber, the Western rim. Star-point hedges, smooth and trim.

Starpoint indeed, with all His Majesty's mails agog every night for the provinces. Twenty-seven fine crimson coaches drawn up in double file in Lombard Street. Great gold-starred coaches, blazing with royal insignia, waiting in line at the Post Office. Eight of a Summer's evening, and the sun only just gone down.[1]

With all deference to the author's insistence that this is a form of poetry, I can only insist that poetry's demands are not so easily slighted. At best *Can Grande's Castle* is a ludicrous compromise between verse and prose which performs a disservice to both. Amy Lowell's acknowledgment of the 'oratorical' in polyphonic prose gives her hand away; it can be demonstrated that very often when the novelist, particularly the American novelist, moves from the metropolis of prose into the suburbs of verse, he tends to fall back on oratory. Again, witness Thomas Wolfe, or Faulkner at his worst in *Pylon* or portions of *A Fable*.

If Virginia Woolf ever read Amy Lowell she made no record of it. Yet her efforts to escape from the confines of the 'plain prose' she hated led her to experiments in the novel that are curiously parallel to Amy Lowell's efforts to leave behind the 'laws' of verse. As a highly conscious and wonderfully dedicated artist, Virginia Woolf was aware of the novel as a formal entity, but she was willing to wander into the province of verse out of impatience with what she saw as her failure to achieve her ambitions for the communication of her vision of human experience. She half distrusted and half approved her 'lyric vein'; *Orlando*, she wrote, was to be a satire on 'My own lyric vein. . . . For the

[1] *Can Grande's Castle*, pp. 101–102.

truth is I feel the need of an escapade after these serious poetic experimental books whose form is always so closely considered.' This was March 1927; a month earlier she had asked herself, 'Why not invent a new kind of play. . . . Away from facts; free; yet concentrated; prose yet poetry; a novel and a play.'[1] After an illness in 1926, she noted that returning health 'is shown by the power to make images; the suggestive power of every sight and word is enormously increased. Shakespeare must have had this to an extent which makes my normal state the state of a person blind, deaf, dumb, stone-stockish and fish-blooded.'[2] This statement in particular reminds us that she was contemporary with the Imagists and partially explains her conception of the novel— as a series of images, 'poetically' conceived and placed in meaningful relationship one to another. She did not go to novelists, writers of prose, when she found her mind returning to normal after illness, but to Shakespeare. Her purposeful confusion of prose and poetry resulted among other works in *The Waves* (1931), large stretches of which are uncomfortably like Amy Lowell's polyphonic prose in style though their ultimate effect is different. *The Waves* begins,

> The sun had not yet risen. The sea was indistinguishable from the sky, except that the sea was slightly creased as if a cloth had wrinkles in it. Gradually as the sky whitened a dark line lay on the horizon dividing the sea from the sky and the grey cloth became barred with thick strokes moving, one after another, beneath the surface, following each other, pursuing each other, perpetually.
>
> As they neared the shore each bar rose, heaped itself, broke and swept a thin veil of white water across the sand. The wave paused, and then drew out again, sighing like a sleeper whose breath comes and goes unconsciously. Gradually the dark bar on the horizon became clear as if the sediment in an old wine-bottle had sunk and left the glass green. Behind it, too, the sky cleared as if the white sediment there had sunk, or as if the arm of a woman couched beneath the horizon had raised a lamp and flat bars of white, green and yellow spread across the sky like the blades of a fan. Then she

[1] Virginia Woolf, *A Writer's Diary*, ed. Leonard Woolf, London, Hogarth Press, 1953, pp. 104–105.
[2] *A Writer's Diary*, p. 97.

E

raised her lamp higher and the air seemed to become fibrous and to tear away from the green surface flickering and flaming in red and yellow fibres like the smoky fire that roars from a bonfire. Gradually the fibres of the burning bonfire were fused into one haze, one incandescence which lifted the weight of the woollen grey sky on top of it and turned it to a million atoms of soft blue.

And the characters are introduced on the second page of the novel like this:

> 'I see a ring,' said Bernard, 'hanging above me. It quivers and hangs in a loop of light.'
> 'I see a slab of pale yellow,' said Susan, 'spreading away until it meets a purple stripe.'
> 'I hear a sound,' said Rhoda, 'cheep, chirp; cheep, chirp; going up and down.'
> 'I see a glove,' said Neville, 'hanging down in a drop against the enormous flanks of some hill.'
> 'I see a crimson tassel,' said Jinny, 'twisted with gold threads.'
> 'I hear something stamping,' said Louis. 'A great beast's foot is chained. It stamps, and stamps, and stamps.'

The alliteration of 's', 'i' and 'f' sounds, the wealth of rhythms, the extended (and awkward) simile comparing the sun to a woman raising a lamp, added to the uncomfortably obvious symbolism of the characters' monologues creates a fare too rich for the novel form, marmalade on beefsteak. It is the inevitable product of the author's neglect of the real nature of poetry. Both in the *Common Reader* series and in the *Writer's Diary*, Virginia Woolf displayed her essential lack of interest in poetry as poetry.

The line of experiment in poetic prose that begins with Amy Lowell is continued in contemporary England by William Sansom[1] and Philip Toynbee. Sansom's indulgence is brief and tongue-in-cheek at least half the time, but Toynbee's, in *The Garden to the Sea* (1953), is sustained and ambitious. Although this novel is no more successful than *The Waves*, its avoidance of the lyricism of extreme sensibility gives it a harder core than *The Waves* possesses. When we read the first chapter heading, 'Noel

[1] William Sansom, 'Corrida at the Marble Arch', *Punch*, CCXXVI, 24 March 1954, pp. 372–373.

Insists that He is Still in the Garden', we say, 'Oh Lord, please not of Eden', but Eden it is. Like Steinbeck's *East of Eden* (written in still another vein of poetic confusion deriving from Whitman), Toynbee borrows the symbolic mechanism of the Fall from *Genesis*, adds to it concepts from Freud and later Christian theology, and places the narrative within the frame of dramatic monologue spoken in loose rhyme and pronounced iambic rhythm. The dialogue is carried on in the mind of Adam, who we learn has lost his Eve (Daisy) to a rival, who has Fallen through taking part in the war as a fighter pilot, and whose guilt is incurred by having shot down an enemy. Adam awakens in hospital, and in Toynbee's stage directions is answered by his own voices from the past: . . . 'Noel, the Voice of his Innocence. Tom, the Voice of his Fall. Charley, the Voice of his Punishment.' In theme, Toynbee appears as a latter-day, low-powered Hawthorne, who substitutes Freudianism for Calvinism up to the point where the novel ends with the promise of Adam's regeneration through his consciousness of divine power. In style the book reads as though Christopher Fry had written closet drama; neither the heavy symbolism of Eden and the Fall nor the prosaic 'poetry' of the style that is neither prose nor competent verse saves the experiment from failure, and the novel lies on the mind heavily, incapable of stimulating the imagination in the manner of poetry, or of communicating anything but its own confusions to the intelligence.

It was precisely in his attitude toward the intelligence that D. H. Lawrence often lost control of his prose and lapsed into a pseudo-poetic trance. Not even Lawrence's most undiscriminating champions will say that his work was uniformly successful, and when his prose fails to convince, it is most often because Lawrence allowed his pose as exile, martyr, and public prosecutor to get in the way of his artistry. Lawrence's temperament, at once feminine and bisexual, his arrogant reliance on intuition, his mystique of the flesh and the 'dark strength' of the blood, all these were combined with his self-made-man's suspicion of disciplined reason to obscure the boundary between verse and prose and to encourage his indulgence in poetic inflation. 'My great religion',

Lawrence wrote in 1912, 'is a belief in the blood, the flesh, as being wiser than the intellect. We can go wrong in our minds. But what the blood feels, and believes, and says, is always true.'[1] That Lawrence was capable of writing superb prose is obvious from most of his short stories, occasional moments in *Sons and Lovers*, *The Rainbow*, *St. Mawr*, and some of the other novels; his excellence was most often sustained, significantly, in his travel-writing. But too often, particularly in his late novels, he relied on the devices of repetition, rhythm and the catalogue to create incantation, and on symbolic paraphernalia often extraneous to the novel, boring, or embarrassing. *The Plumed Serpent*, with its Aztec trappings and its unconscious comedy of phallic absurdity, is a good example of Lawrence's enormous defects, while in brief passages of landscape description, in some of the portraits of the Mexican people, it is as good as anything he ever wrote. Lawrence blundered when he entered the minds of his female characters. In Kate Leslie's mind but with his own voice and beard, Lawrence wrote essays on the familiar old themes—race, blood, male, female—tempted constantly to poetic prose in order to disguise the essay as prose fiction, to substitute mystique and italics for characterization:

> Kate was of a proud old family. She had been brought up with the English-Germanic idea of the *intrinsic* superiority of the hereditary aristocrat. Her blood was different from the common blood, another, finer fluid.
>
> But in Mexico, none of this. Her criada Juana, the aguador who carried the water, the boatman who rowed her on the lake, all looked at her with one look in their eyes. *The blood is one blood. In the blood, you and I are undifferentiated.* She saw it in their eyes, she heard it in their words, it tinged their deference and their mockery. And sometimes it made her physically sick: this overbearing blood-familiarity.
>
> And sometimes, when she tried to hold herself up, in the proud old assertion: *My blood is my own. Noli me tangere*, she would see the terrible ancient hatred in their eyes, the hatred which leads them to atrocities and fearful maimings.

[1] Quoted by Aldous Huxley, *The Olive Tree*, 1936.

They would defer to her spirit, her knowledge, her understanding.
. . . But back again they demanded her acquiescence to the primeval
assertion: *The blood is one blood. We are one blood. . . .*
To this she must submit. Or they would persist in the slow
revenge.
And she could not submit, off-hand. It had to be a slow, organic
process. Anything sudden or violent would destroy her.
Now she understood Ramón's assertion: Man is a column of
blood: Woman is a valley of blood. It was the primeval oneness of
mankind, the opposite of the oneness of the spirit.

Sometimes there is a mad, Carlylean strength in such essays, but
the insistent, declarative sentences do not argue an essayist's
point, they assert an angry man's obsession, as though Lawrence
had been a Hearst or Beaverbrook, pounding the public on the
front page of a controlled newspaper.

Thomas Wolfe, the most shameless writer of poetic prose in all
fiction, continuously resembles D. H. Lawrence. Like Lawrence,
Wolfe did not merely write, he was driven and compelled to
communication by a personal mystique which he assumed to free
him from the minimum demands of prose, and to allow him to
float his vision in mellifluous 'fine' writing, speeches, essays,
incantations and sibylline utterances. Like Lawrence, Wolfe was
capable of writing impressive fiction in 'pure' prose, the short
stories, 'Chickamauga' and 'Only the Dead Know Brooklyn',
or the episode of old Gant's death in *Of Time and the River*. But
the failure of his sensibility to register adequately what prose, as
opposed to verse, really is, was more serious than Lawrence's
failure. Wolfe wrote two kinds of poetic prose. One was trance-
like, flowing from the narrative compulsively; the second was
written in his notebooks as verse, then transferred to the novel and
printed as prose. An example of the first kind occurs at the conclusion of *You Can't Go Home Again*, in the form of a letter from
the writer-hero to his editor:

Something has spoken to me in the night, burning the tapers of the
waning year; something has spoken in the night, and told me I shall
die, I know not where. Saying:
'To lose the earth you know, for greater knowing; to lose the life

you have, for greater life; to leave the friends you loved, for greater loving; to find a land more kind than home, more large than earth—

'—Whereon the pillars of this earth are founded, toward which the conscience of the world is tending—a wind is rising, and the rivers flow.'[1]

And the second kind, from *Look Homeward, Angel*. Eugene Gant is mourning the death of his brother, Ben; he stands with Ben's mistress over the grave, and Wolfe writes, 'A light swings over the hill. (We shall not come again.) And over the town a star. (Over us all, over us all that shall not come again.) And over the day the dark. But over the darkness—what?' This is followed in a few lines by the 'poetic' motif which pervades the novel: 'O lost, and by the wind grieved, ghost, come back again!' Thus Wolfe destroys the legitimate, muted emotion which he has built up in the chapter, and urges the conclusion that Eugene Gant's graveyard 'ghost' is not that of Ben, but of Lydia Huntley Sigourney, one of the lady graveyard poets of the American 1840s, or that of Young in *Night Thoughts*. With depressing logic, an admirer of Wolfe has extracted numerous passages of this sort of writing from Wolfe's texts and printed them separately as 'verse'.[2]

I have noted previously the way in which critical confusion over Dickens's writing has come about and has perhaps added authority to still further confusion among writers and critics. Further instances come all too easily to hand. It is not surprising to find among Lord David Cecil's many easy generalizations an easy generalization about Hardy's 'poetic' quality in the novels,[3] even though Hardy was admirably aware of the distinction between verse and prose. It is surprising that so good a critic as Francis Fergusson should mix examples from D. H. Lawrence's prose and verse to explain the Laurentian style,[4] or that Irving

[1] Thomas Wolfe, *You Can't Go Home Again*, New York, 1942, p. 743. In fairness to Wolfe, it should be noted that this novel was put together from various manuscripts by Wolfe's publisher after his death.

[2] In *The Face of a Nation*, ed. John Hall Wheelock, New York, 1939.

[3] David Cecil, *Hardy the Novelist*, London, 1943, pp. 138–140.

[4] Francis Fergusson, 'D. H. Lawrence's Sensibility', in John W. Aldridge, ed., *Critiques and Essays on Modern Fiction: 1920–1951*, New York, 1952, pp. 328–339.

Howe in an otherwise admirable book on William Faulkner should fall back on the meaningless term 'poetic' to summarize Faulkner's achievement.[1] Faulkner has had more than his share of 'poetic' criticism; still two other critics examine his use of imagery, particularly in *The Hamlet*, and call his ironic lyricism there examples of 'poetry',[2] though in truth they are very carefully constructed passages written by one of the most successful modern experimenters in the resources of prose. Faulkner does indeed fall into the trap of poetic rhetoric, in *Pylon* and in some of his other remarkably bad novels, among which *The Hamlet* cannot be included. A more interesting form of critical confusion over Faulkner results when one critic returns to Coleridge's famous distinction between prose and poetry in Chapter XVIII of *Biographia Literaria*, but then goes on to demonstrate that in Coleridge's sense the Faulkner of *The Sound and the Fury*, the Lawrence of *The Rainbow*, and much of Hardy is actually 'poetry'. By identifying the effects of poetry with those of prose, as Coleridge seems to do but doesn't actually, this critic confounds confusion.[3]

There is no real mystery about the differences between poetry and prose; some of our best critics have discussed the matter with final authority, but always with their central attention upon the writing and interpretation of verse. Various statements of Ezra Pound,[4] William Empson's work on the subject in *Seven Types of Ambiguity*, I. A. Richards's in *Science and Poetry*, and Robert Graves's in *The Common Asphodel* provide a foundation for Herbert Read's most interesting conclusions. In 'Poetic Diction', Read says that poetry is a more primitive form of expression than prose, and that the language of primitive peoples is more 'poetic'

[1] '. . . if the price of his rebellion has come high in rhetoric, so has the gain in poetry.' Irving Howe, *William Faulkner*, New York, Random House, 1952, p. 202.

[2] H. M. Campbell and R. E. Foster, *William Faulkner: A Critical Appraisal*, University of Oklahoma Press, Norman, 1951, pp. 20–21.

[3] Robert M. Adams, 'Poetry in the Novel: or, Faulkner Esemplastic', *Virginia Quarterly Review*, XXIX, No. 3, Summer 1953, 419–434.

[4] Particularly 'The Serious Artist', *Literary Essays of Ezra Pound*, ed. T. S. Eliot, London, Faber, 1954, pp. 48–57.

than ours. He then develops his central theory, with the support
of modern Italian aesthetic theory, the Platonic language of
which varies considerably from Empson's or Richards's, but
resembling Richards in conclusions that belong, like his, as
properly to epistemology as to aesthetics. Read quotes Leone
Vivante, 'Notes on the Originality of Thought':

> 'In the poetic period not only the attribute, but every word, every
> moment of thought, gathers up, renews the whole. The subject is
> recalled in its concept in every word of the proposition, . . . progres-
> sively takes fresh value, fills up of itself and governs every new
> moment. Thus reality at every point is drawn up from the unknown.
> The new expressive moment in its particular significance forms itself
> in the meaning of the whole, which in the new moment is not
> inferred but renewed: and myriads of *nexus*—resemblances, accords,
> unities, *ex principio*—form themselves. On the other hand, con-
> structive thought loses the *nexus* or necessities of principle proper
> to thought in its integral originality: if we except the *nexus* belonging
> to formal logic, to a conception schematically material and spatial
> —a position of mere existences and of spatial and quantitative rela-
> tions and ideal abstract identities. In other words, in constructive
> thought *nexus of inherence* are comparatively prevalent, in poetic
> thought *nexus of essence*.'

Vivante develops the familiar idea that the diction of prose and
the diction of poetry are qualitatively different; words in poetry
have 'boldness', as he rather quaintly puts it. Read then sum-
marizes:

> All art originates in an act of intuition, or vision. But such *intuition*
> or vision must be identified with *knowledge*, being fully present only
> when consciously objectified. This act of vision or intuition is,
> physically, a state of concentration or tension in the mind. The
> *process* of poetry consists firstly in maintaining this vision in its
> integrity, and secondly in expressing this vision in words. Words
> are generally (. . . in prose) the *analysis* of a mental state. But in the
> process of poetic composition words rise into the conscious mind as
> isolated objective 'things' with a definite equivalence in the poet's
> state of mental intensity. They are arranged or composed in a
> sequence or rhythm which is sustained until the mental state of

tension in the poet is exhausted or released by this objective equiva-
lence.[1]

I linger over the problem of poetic prose not to carry forward
a semantic quibble, but to discover its bearing upon a larger area
of meaning in the recent novel. With relation to the modern
novelists' sense of society, it is clear that prose is closer to society
than poetry; a regrettable but real product of social fragmentation
in our day. The main objection to poetic prose in the novel, then,
apart from questions of taste and sensibility, is that it impoverishes
the novelist's sense of society by encouraging him to evade, in
Vivante's terms, the 'nexus of inherence', while it entices him
into the 'nexus of essence', a locality in which he cannot from the
nature of his medium be accepted. One is tempted to say that the
presence or absence of poetic prose in recent experiment is a
measure of success or failure. The mixed success of Virginia
Woolf or Faulkner—conscious, controlled writers—can be set
against the abdication of control in Thomas Wolfe or Philip
Toynbee, to establish an angle of critical vision.

The bastard form of novel-as-film-script is a second kind of
negative experiment which aids in the definition of what the novel
is not. Here the Americans are the chief offenders, for the elemen-
tal reason that Hollywood and its dollars is located in California
and not in London or Paris or Palermo. A Frenchwoman has
written a book called *L'Age du roman Américain* to prove that the
work of leading American novelists, Hemingway, Faulkner, and
Dos Passos, is structurally related not to the novel of English or
even of American tradition, but to the structure and devices of
the film.[2] For all its brilliance, this book strikes an American as
the familiar French lack of understanding of English tradition in
the novel, although it is fruitful for emphasizing the undoubted
influence of the film upon certain lesser novelists. John Steinbeck and James M. Cain exemplify the procedure of an all-too-
large number of novelists who seem to write with one eye on

[1] Herbert Read, *Collected Essays in Literary Criticism*, London, Faber, 1951,
pp. 42–45.
[2] Claude-Edmonde Magny, *L'Age du roman Américain*, Paris, Editions du Seuil,
1948.

Hollywood; their novels tend to be written principally in dialogue, while exposition and point of view no longer are integral devices of an imaginative projection of character and situation, but serve as notes to the director and other film technicians. The following passage from *Of Mice and Men* speaks for itself: Lennie, a power-fully built but gentle moron, has killed a woman quite by accident, and George, his only friend, has been forced to shoot him to save him from lynching.

> Slim came directly to George and sat down beside him, sat very close to him. 'Never you mind,' said Slim. 'A guy got to sometimes.'
> But Carlson was standing over George. 'How'd you do it?' he asked.
> 'I just done it,' George said tiredly.
> 'Did he have my gun?'
> 'Yeah. He had your gun.'
> 'An' you got it away from him and you took it an' you killed him?'
> 'Yeah. Tha's how.' George's voice was almost a whisper. He looked steadily at his right hand that held the gun.
> Slim twitched George's elbow. 'Come on, George. Me an' you'll go in an' get a drink.'
> George let himself be helped to his feet. 'Yeah, a drink.'

This is not the dimension of fiction, but of film: essentially flat, cheaply 'dramatic', and totally unreal as reality is understood in the novel.

One regrets Steinbeck's willingness to merchandise his ability in this fashion, for he might once have developed into an enduring minor novelist. In the case of James M. Cain and his commercial brothers in fiction, the writers of blood-and-breasts 'historical' novels, art has suffered no loss; I only resent the cliché that Cain and the rest are descendants of Hemingway. Essentially Cain has no more in common with Hemingway than he has with Maria Edgeworth, but he has borrowed and cheapened certain of Hemingway's devices and adapted them to the requirements of the scenario-novel.

In England, the influence of the scenario has been happier, perhaps, for the added influence of the legitimate theatre. It has undoubtedly influenced the work of Henry Green, who composes highly effective experiments in the novel entirely in dialogue, and though this is speculative, I think that film may have had its influence upon Ivy Compton-Burnett, whose novels are written almost entirely in dialogue.

The writing of Miss Compton-Burnett and Henry Green returns us to the question of what we mean, precisely, by 'experiment' in the third phase of the novel, and of whether experimentation has contributed either to the development of the novel or to the metamorphosis of its form. The novel-reading community is far from agreement regarding experiment. In one sense, it is clear that all writers experiment; the nature of the novel induces a constantly shifting approach to the raw material of the art. As 'experimental' is used of the modern novel, however, the term means something more radical—the conscious search for new techniques, dedicated intensity, rebellion, ambition. C. P. Snow speaks for a large number when he rejects the very idea of experiment in literature. He remarks that the phrase, 'experimental novel', was borrowed from science, that it never was a very good idea in the first instance, and that efforts to change the form of the novel have only resulted in the novelist's imitation of the specialization of science. Only Proust and Stendhal may have 'experimented', but for the rest, the form of the novel has not changed for thirty-five years.[1] This sort of obscurantist criticism ignores the development of the techniques of stream-of-consciousness; important perceptions of the relationship between narrative, meaning, and the placing of events in time and space; the appearance of the contemporary sensibility; more seriously, it ignores the organic relationship between art and events even while it pretends to acknowledge the notion of society.

The two developments basic to modern experiment, the rise of psychiatry and the emergence of the stream-of-consciousness techniques that psychiatry made possible, are well known and need not be reviewed here. It might be useful, though, to emphasize stream-of-consciousness techniques for their connection with

[1] C. P. Snow, 'Storytellers for the Atomic Age', *New York Times Book Review*, LX, No. 5, 30 January 1955, 1 ff.

those apparently extra-literary considerations—historical and social fragmentation. In an authoritative discussion, Robert Humphrey notes that there is no single 'stream-of-consciousness' technique and that the term itself is ambiguous, since 'consciousness' in psychology defines 'the entire area of mental attention, from preconsciousness on through the levels of the mind up to and including the highest one of rational, communicable awareness'. Proust's work, then, is not stream-of-consciousness, for it treats only the remembered aspect of consciousness. But in stream-of-consciousness proper, the novelist places first emphasis on the exploration of 'pre-speech levels of consciousness for the purpose, primarily, of revealing the psychic being of his characters'.[1] The novelist is concerned not with formulated thought, but with the margins of thought. Interior monologue, direct or indirect, is most frequently confused with stream-of-consciousness, and again Humphrey's distinction is valuable: interior monologue, indirect when the author guides us through the character's mind, direct when the author effaces himself, is 'the technique . . . for representing the psychic content and processes of character, partly or entirely unuttered, just as these processes exist at various levels of conscious control before they are formulated for deliberate speech'. To the technique of direct and indirect monologue, Humphrey would add two more traditional devices for a comprehensive definition of stream-of-consciousness: omniscient description, and finally the soliloquy.[2]

Stream-of-consciousness techniques can be viewed as the devices by which historical and social fragmentation are at once recorded, shaped, and transformed through the writer's necessary task of selection and emphasis. At the same time, they prove beyond possibility of doubt the compulsion of the writer to move as close to actuality by effacing himself as his art will allow. This demand for immediacy which stream-of-consciousness techniques make possible is as much a political and historical fact as it is literary. Prodded by events that cannot be ignored, hounded by

[1] Robert Humphrey, *Stream of Consciousness in the Modern Novel*, University of California Press, Berkeley, 1954, pp. 2–4.

[2] Humphrey, pp. 23–24.

a history that insists on writing its bloody page before our eyes, writer and reader alike seize upon the technique which will best enable the beginnings of understanding, an understanding that begins with the unit, the individual mind, the individual consciousness. One result is a kind of paradox. The stream-of-consciousness writer, like the naturalist, searches for the fullest accuracy, the closest possible approach to actuality. Total objectivity is the ideal; the writer, his prejudices and his comments are ruled out, for the writer is merely the agent by which the reader is placed in touch with the flow of reality. Viewed traditionally, these demands are not strictly 'literary', and one of the curious developments of our time has been an apparently non-literary literature which is, nevertheless, very much the product of a sophisticated literary technique. Stream-of-consciousness apparently rules out mind and seems to slight or ignore the place of free will; Dos Passos's *USA* is made to seem more narrowly and traditionally naturalistic than it really is, while Joyce, who admired the naturalists and at least took his departure from them, does not seem more than incidentally a naturalist in *Ulysses*, because he had mastered his techniques. Stream-of-consciousness, then, is not a wilful evasion of society, but as its relations to naturalism help to demonstrate, it offers the writer one more means for getting to society, for seeing society in all its complexity rather than merely accepting society's own myths, official or folk, about itself.

Stream-of-consciousness techniques in their turn have opened the way for still other forms of experiment which have had little direct but considerable indirect effect upon the Anglo-American novel. The very names of these experiments, 'expressionism' and 'surrealism', are borrowed from the theatre and the fine arts, and the dejected air of the borrowed clings to most of the work done in their name. Definitions of expressionism and surrealism in the novel tend to fade into each other, though defining differences exist to separate them. Expressionism can be most coherently defined with reference to Germany, where the term arose and where it was truly a movement rather than a vague adjective. German expressionism was not only a movement in the arts, but it was a rejection of the political, social, and moral precepts of the *Wilhelminische Bürgertum*—Germany's Edwardian period—an attempt to break up the old patterns, in art as in society, and to achieve social justice, to regain civic honesty, and to substitute either a mystical, vaguely oriental religious concept, or a political concept of the brotherhood of man, for what seemed to be the exhausted notions of Christianity. Expressionism was opposed to positivism in science, it was irrational, anti-intellectual, and pacifistic. The expressionist novelist opposed the dominant realism and naturalism in favour of abstraction of subject; stereotyped characters became symbols of a reality out of focus; the very syntax of prose was broken up in order to present the writer's organized disorganization. Allegory was approached but not completely adopted; physical settings were shifted about mechanically, and while time was tampered with, it remained time-linear, the time of the clock-face.[1] The expressionist's imagination is aware of fragmentation but reaches towards synthesis, in the manner of the nineteenth-century tradition. Hermann Hesse's *Der Steppenwolf* (1925), one of the few unqualified expressionist successes in the novel, is the story of Harry Haller, the post-World War I German so cut off from society that he thinks of himself as a wolf of the Steppes. Haller's experiences are an allegorical treatment of post-war Germany, and the typical expressionist

---

[1] I must emphasize that no satisfactory definition of expressionism exists. German critics, who have treated the subject more thoroughly than the Americans or the English, are agreed only in asserting the vagueness of the term. Max Krell emphasizes the ambiguity of a movement that is at once of 'classical purity' and of 'anarchic turbulence, at times completely annulling . . . meaning'. 'Expressionismus der Prosa', *Weltliteratur der Gegenwart*, Bd. *Deutschland*, II, Teil, Leipzig, 1924, p. 3. See also Fritz Martini, 'Der Expressionismus', *Deutsche Literatur im zwanzigsten Jahrhundert*, Heidelberg, 1954, p. 107; Wolfgang Stammler, *Deutsche Literatur vom Naturalismus bis zur Gegenwart*, Breslau, 1927, p. 100; and Heinrich Neumayer, *Der Expressionismus*, Vienna, 1956, p. 8. I am also indebted to Jürgen Born, Free University, Berlin, for his unpublished essay, 'Toward a Definition of Expressionism'. I would add that in many ways German expressionism was an attempt to catch up with the rest of the world; in poetry, the expressionists did nothing that the English metaphysicals had not done. Expressionism was, typically, romantic and anti-romantic, posing objectivity against the characteristic (and untranslatable) '*Schrei*', the cry of pain at the impossibility of communication.

manipulation of setting occurs in a section called the 'Magic-Theater', where Haller's imagined experiences are presented in the form of magic-lantern scenes. Rex Warner's political allegory, *The Wild Goose Chase* (1937), with its wild goose as the symbol of man's political and spiritual hope, is almost a masterpiece. It fails at the point in the final fifth of the novel where Warner introduces a fantastic landscape of mysterious rock caverns, sliding walls, secret passages—the trappings of Gothic romance. The parallel with the theatre is instructive here; expressionism has its fullest success in the plays of Bert Brecht, which depend so heavily upon the revolving stage and the tricks of production that require the collaboration of designers, carpenters and electricians —all foreign to the novel.

Surrealism accepts total dissociation. The surrealist shares with the expressionist a fondness for symbol and allegory, but the surrealist's symbol is dream-like, illogical, juxtaposed shockingly in space rather than in linear time; the surrealist does not hesitate to abolish 'natural' time and to substitute the chronology of dreams. Surrealism is more adapted to the novel, for it does not require the exterior and intrusive apparatus of expressionism. Kafka's novels are usually described as surrealist, but they are closer to expressionism. Some of his stories, though, are pure examples of surrealism. A more typically surrealist writer is the American, John Hawkes, whose *The Cannibal* (1949) is again an allegory of Germany after World War II. At one point Hawkes describes a starving, ragged 'Habsburg' Duke who leaves his room in the middle of the night to run down a fox, kill it and hack it up for food with a sword-cane. The incident is brutal, shocking, and apparently unrelated to the novel proper. This novel, like the writer's *The Beetle Leg* (1951), demonstrates the essential triviality of surrealism as a structural, controlling device; *The Cannibal* is made up of a series of shocking, brutal and nauseating scenes that never really cohere. Hawkes flogs his sewer-like imagination, and one can read him only for his competent prose style.

The important contribution of surrealism to fiction has been its effect upon the modern novelists' conception of time, and the realization of the possibilities of that other dimension of time, space. In the first two phases of the novel, writers apprehended only dimly the dimensions of time and space. Time for the most part gave the framework to the dramatic novel; events took place in the sequence of the clock-face and the calendar, and when the writer tampered with that rational sequence, he carefully explained to his readers where, in time, they were. Edwin Muir suggests the term 'spatial novel' to describe the novel of a society, that novel in which dramatic sequence is subordinated to the social milieu;[1] the concept of space is still mechanical, however, and its symbol would be the picture frame rather than the clock or the calendar.

Marcel Proust, whose theme *is* time in his great novel, *À la recherche du temps perdu*, conceived his material, with minor variations, in the manner of the traditional novelist: in temporal sequence, but a sequence given aesthetic shape and the beginnings of spatial form by the sensibility of his narrator. In the final volume, *Le temps retrouvé*, Proust describes a discovery—'pure' time, a point in a mystical experience at which he was enabled to escape the domination of time, to rise above the passage of time.

> Each such experience . . . is marked by a feeling that 'the permanent essence of things, usually concealed, is set free and the true self, which had long seemed dead but was not dead in other ways, awakes, takes on fresh life as it receives the celestial nourishment brought to it.' This celestial nourishment consists of some sound, or odor, or other sensory stimulus, 'sensed anew, simultaneously in the present and the past.' . . . Only in these moments did he attain his most cherished ambition—'to seize, isolate, immobilize for the duration of a lightning flash' what otherwise he could not apprehend, 'namely, a fragment of time in its pure state.' . . . but 'pure time' . . . is not time at all—it is perception in a moment of time, that is, space.

Characters are juxtaposed not in temporal but in spatial units.[2] In *The Magic Mountain*, Mann experimented in temporal and

[1] Edwin Muir, *The Structure of the Novel*, London, Hogarth Press, 1946, pp. 62–87.

[2] Joseph Frank, 'Spatial Form in Modern Literature', in *Critiques and Essays in Criticism: 1920–1948*, ed. R. W. Stallman, New York, Ronald Press, 1949, pp. 315–328.

spatial relationships much as Proust had done, though neither writer's work should be called surrealist. Surrealism contributed to Proust's basic spatial concept the material of dreams and the apparently illogical, temporally detached symbolic object. *Ulysses* remains the most convincing employment of surrealism in the modern novel, and *Finnegans Wake* is perhaps the only interesting work in which surrealism is a fundamental structural device. At the same time, the impenetrability of *Finnegans Wake* provides the most cogent criticism of the techniques of surrealism.

The technical experiments which created the third phase of the novel allowed the craftsman to shape and to project his response to catastrophe. The actual devices were few in number but rich in possibility. The devices of stream-of-consciousness liberated the individual sensibility from the schematic patterns of tradition; the devices of expressionism and surrealism made possible, in alliance with stream-of-consciousness, structural changes in the novel—Faulkner's hesitant unveiling of motive and plot—and in turn made possible the merging of two seemingly disparate forms, the novel of sensibility and the novel of ideas.

In themselves, the purely 'experimental' novels, with the great exceptions of the work of Proust and Joyce, contributed little, and they were responsible, in the hands of writers rather less than masters, Gertrude Stein or Henry Miller, for the branding of the entire modern movement as chi-chi and false. But if we list modern novels which might still be read a century from now, we realize at once the debt of the modern writer to tradition and realize anew the importance of the less-than-great work of the experimenters in refreshing tradition and making it accessible to the modern consciousness. List-making is at best a self-indulgent game that merely enrages the other players, but it can be useful; my own would include, from America, Fitzgerald's *The Great Gatsby*, Hemingway's *A Farewell to Arms*, Faulkner's *The Sound and the Fury* and *Light in August*, and Ralph Ellison's *Invisible Man*. From England, Forster's *A Passage to India*, Rex Warner's *The Aerodrome*, Malcolm Lowry's comparatively unknown *Under the Volcano* and Anthony West's similarly unknown *One Dark Night*, Rosamund Lehmann's *The Echoing Grove*, and P. H.

F

Newby's *The Retreat*. For all their obvious differences, these writers have in common the ambitiousness essential to greatness, a mastery of structure, an absolute command of prose diction, an awareness of both the lineal and spatial possibilities of fiction, a consciousness of history and politics, while in varying degrees each novel is a novel of ideas. Without the example of traditional achievement in the novel in English, notably the stylistic mastery of Jane Austen or George Eliot, or the structural contributions of Henry James and Conrad, all of these writers would be the poorer. But without the experiment of Joyce and Kafka, neither *The Sound and the Fury*, *The Aerodrome*, nor *Under the Volcano* would be the works they are; without Proust, without the work of Virginia Woolf, both Miss Lehmann and Anthony West would be impoverished. This is not to say, of course, that the novelist writes with the work of his masters open before him; literary influence does not necessarily work that way. The writer may be no more aware of the influences upon him than the general public is aware of the atomic radiation which the scientists say is all about us. Literary influence is a climate, an ambience to which the writer at once responds and, if he has elements of greatness, contributes. Our best writers have responded each in his way to that climate; to define modernism is to approach a definition of the novel as we know it. Confusion regarding the place of experiment in Anglo-American writing since World War I has led to the strange cult of 'the death of the novel', a cult whose ritual we must next examine.

Chapter Three

DEATH, MANNERS, AND IDEAS

In William Dean Howells's novel, *The Rise of Silas Lapham* (1885), an exchange takes place at a dinner party:

> 'There was talk some years ago,' said James Bellingham, 'about novels going out.'
> 'They're just coming in!' cried Miss Kingsbury.
> 'Yes,' said Mr. Sewall, the minister. 'And I don't think there was ever a time when they formed the whole intellectual experience of more people. They do greater mischief than ever.'

The James Bellinghams of criticism have outnumbered the Miss Kingsburys for the past century and a half, and the Mr. Sewalls have been heard from hardly at all. Valéry set the problem for the modern writer by saying that he could not accept the novel as a serious literary form when it obliged the author to write, 'La marquise sortit à cinq heures . . .'; his demand, in short, was for experimentation, for enlarging the possibilities of the form. But when the novelists obliged, a comic situation developed. In any other art, new techniques are normally regarded as a sign of high health, and as those techniques emerge, artists and critics congratulate themselves with a certain justifiable fervour. But when novelists experimented with new techniques after World War I, they were damned for ignoring tradition, for not being sufficiently reactionary, and accused of inducing the 'death' of the novel in their very efforts to give it life. Since 1925 the attack on experimentation in the novel has increased in range and scope, until now hardly a month passes when some critic or reviewer fails to administer the oils of extreme unction to the expiring corpse.

The year 1925 is not arbitrary, for that was when Ortega y Gasset's influential essays, 'The Dehumanization of Art' and

'Notes on the Novel' appeared. According to Ortega, it is implicit in the 'historical process' of our time that the minor gap which existed between artist and public in the nineteenth century should become immeasurable in the twentieth. The evidence is most obvious in music and painting but it applies as well to the novel. With Nietzschean overtones, Ortega wrote that whatever its form, art is produced for an élite: 'A time must come in which society, from politics to art, reorganizes itself into two orders or ranks; the illustrious and the vulgar.'[1] When the writer ceased to concentrate upon the narrative element of his art, the novel parted company with the vulgar and became the property of the illustrious. They, in turn, very rapidly set about exhausting the possibilities of the genre: 'I believe that the genre of the novel,' Ortega continued, 'if it is not yet irretrievably exhausted, has certainly entered its last phase, the scarcity of possible subjects being such that writers must make up for it by the exquisite quality of the other elements that compose the body of the novel.'[2] Psychology, the 'scientific' analysis of a character's motives, indicates the moribund state; a Proustian contemplation takes the place of action.[3] The true novelist must learn to forget much of his actual experience and create an 'extramural world'—the world of Cervantes and Dickens, of Dostoievski and Stendhal. 'Hence every novel is still-born that is laden with transcendental intentions, be they political, ideological, symbolical, or satirical.' When such intentions appear, the reader loses the illusion of art and returns to the world of immediate experience.[4]

For all their surface gloss and their small kernel of validity, Ortega's pronouncements strike me as fallacies, developed in blindness to literary tradition and flatly wrong in their conclusions. They sound a loud warning to the legislative critic. It goes without saying that the regimes of Hitler, Mussolini, and Franco have buried deep Ortega's political remarks about 'the illustrious and the vulgar'. The parallel in the arts is not axiomatic, but it is

[1] José Ortega y Gasset, *The Dehumanization of Art and Notes on the Novel*, trans. Helene Weyl, Princeton, N.J., 1948, pp. 1–7.
[2] Ortega, p. 60.
[3] Ortega, pp. 80–87.
[4] Ortega, pp. 92–93.

worth remarking that an outstanding cultural fact of our society since Ortega wrote in 1925 has been the increasing opacity of the distinction in the arts between the illustrious and the vulgar. Abstract art is no longer considered revolutionary by a large public, but representative art is; anthologies of experimental writing are bought by thousands in the United States for fifty cents; the best short history of Roman Britain costs half a crown; the audience for 'serious' music has increased astonishingly in the past fifteen years. Having suffered long and grievously from industrialism, the arts are finally beginning to benefit from its techniques. It is entirely possible that these developments may have unfortunate results for the arts,[1] but whatever their future, they testify to the trend away from Ortega's prophecies.

If we look at Ortega's own evidence in the novels of Cervantes, Dickens, Dostoievski and Stendhal, it is impossible to admit that these writers lack 'transcendental intention', or that their work can be read apart from their political, ideological, symbolical or satirical meanings. Is not *Don Quixote* a satire, and among other things, an ideological parable? Dickens creates an 'extramural' world, to be sure, but it is firmly based in his own experience, in his satirical view of contemporary society, and embellished with symbol and prosaic idea. Which novelists are more 'psychological' than Dostoievski or Stendhal? Separate from their novels their transcendental intention and little remains; the very process is unthinkable. To accept Ortega's premises, then, would be to rule out the achievements of modern fiction, and also to rule out those writers whom he presents as archetypal and legitimate.

Moving from Spain in the 1920s to contemporary England, we find a leading academic speaking for many of his colleagues when he says bluntly that he dislikes the novel and considers it inferior to poetry and drama as an art-form;[2] while Sir Harold Nicolson represents the small but vocal philistine element in literary journalism when he writes that the novel's history has

---

[1] Malcolm Cowley notes that one result of the paper-backed book publishing industry in America may be only to insure the wider circulation of fewer titles, an ominous prospect. *The Literary Situation,* New York, Viking, 1954, pp. 104–107.

[2] F. W. Bateson, in an address on the B.B.C. Third Programme, 1953.

been brief, bright but finished, and that the future of imaginative prose belongs to history and biography.[1] Miss Dorothy Sayers, a latter-day Romola who combines detection with salvation, agrees with Nicolson's argument, but gives the future to the film rather than to history and biography.[2] When Nicolson accuses the novelist of ignoring character and of confining his technique to an interior monologue made up of 'agreeable or painful reminiscences or conceits', it is hard to know whose work he is describing, for that is not the way the contemporary English novel is written. It is fairly easy to see, lingering in the wings, the hoary accusation that the contemporary novelist is remote from society, withdrawn, uninterested in ordinary people, in science, politics, or the real ways of the real world.

No one since Ortega has written so authoritatively or so well about the death of the novel as Lionel Trilling, whose essays have circulated widely on both sides of the Atlantic. His arguments appear to have influenced Harold Nicolson in England and a larger number of his American compatriots,[3] and his authority seems to have silenced all opposition. Trilling concentrates his argument on the American novel, but he ranges to other literatures and includes them in his attack. 'Attack' does not do justice to Trilling, for his essays on the novel are more like clinical dissections, deductive rather than inductive in procedure, and more devastating than any mere attack. He always proceeds from a rigid definition of what the novel ought to be, though he is too urbane a writer ever to use so bald a term as 'ought'. The American novel, he says, 'diverges from its classic intention, which . . . is the investigation of the problem of reality beginning in the social field. The fact is that American writers of genius have not turned their minds to society.' What Poe and Melville sought to do 'was only tangential to society'. Hawthorne wrote

---

[1] Harold Nicolson, 'Is the Novel Dead?', *The Observer*, London, 29 August 1954. Sir Harold was admirably answered by Philip Toynbee: 'The Defence Brief', *The Observer*, 5 September 1954.

[2] Dorothy L. Sayers, 'Some Other Views', *The Observer*, 5 September 1954.

[3] Particularly John Aldridge, who brashly adds a heavy frosting of morality to Trilling's argument. In 'Manners and Values', *Partisan Review*, XIX, May 1952, 347.

what he himself called 'romances', consciously evading the novelist's proper object, and was himself aware 'of the lack of social texture in his work'. William Dean Howells 'saw the social subject clearly', but would never accept its full seriousness.[1] Trilling writes, echoing Ortega, I suspect, that the main task of the novel was established in *Don Quixote*. Cervantes once and for all set the theme of appearance and reality in that seminal work, while Don Quixote's poverty established the theme of money, the importance of which lies in the circumstance that in society money makes for differences and illusion, for social snobbery, for the marvellously entangled apparatus of society: '. . . every situation in Dostoievski, no matter how spiritual, starts with a point of social pride and a certain number of rubles'.[2] These various elements, appearance versus reality, ambition, snobbery, the possession or lack of money, the awareness of rank and degree, constitute manners, and manners are the novelist's raw materials. Trilling's explicit definition of manners is so felicitous that writers have been reluctant to wrangle with him: manners are 'a culture's hum and buzz of implication . . . the whole evanescent context in which its explicit statements are made'.[3]

Trilling implies that American society lacks manners, and he quotes James's famous complaint about American society in the *Life of Hawthorne*, a familiar complaint that goes back at least to Washington Irving's remarks about the commonplace character of America in *The Sketch-Book*, and one which Fenimore Cooper developed in *Notes on the Americans* (1828):

There are no annals for the historian; no follies (beyond the most vulgar and commonplace) for the satirist; no manners for the dramatist; no obscure fictions for the writer of romance; no gross and hardy offences against decorum for the moralist; nor any of the rich, artificial auxiliaries of poetry. . . . I have never seen a nation so alike in my life, as the people of the United States, and what is more, they are not only like each other, but they are remarkably like that which common sense tells them they ought to resemble. No doubt, traits

[1] Lionel Trilling, *The Liberal Imagination*, p. 212.
[2] *Liberal Imagination*, pp. 207–211.
[3] *Liberal Imagination*, p. 206.

of character that are a little peculiar, without, however, being either very poetical, or very rich, are to be found in remote districts; but they are rare, and not always happy exceptions. . . . There is no costume for the peasant, (there is scarcely a peasant at all,) no wig for the judge, no baton for the general, no diadem for the chief magistrate.[1]

James's characteristic addition to Cooper's list is, 'no Epsom and no Ascot'. For Trilling, James alone in the nineteenth century perceived the social intention, but he lacked a society to write about, and fled to Europe. In the recent American novel, Trilling says, society is only a backdrop for Dreiser and Dos Passos; Faulkner's society is provincial and severely limited. American writers in fact resist a close examination of society: 'They appear to believe that to touch accurately on the matter of class, to take full note of snobbery, is somehow to demean themselves.'[2] The great character in American fiction, an Ahab or a Natty Bumpo, is set apart from class, set apart from manners, abstracted into myth because of his lack of connection with social reality.[3]

'I do not believe that the novel is dead', Trilling writes, though he proceeds to demonstrate just why the novel is all but dead. In the United States, the necessary class-structure never has existed; in England 'the middle class is in the process of liquidating itself'; in France, Proust's writing showed that the process of liquidation had already been completed, and his lifework is witness to the ruins. The net result is a 'falling off in the energy of mind that once animated fiction'.[4] This total condemnation is not casual; it is fundamental and thorough. The nineteenth-century American novel together with the entire recent novel displays a crippling failure of intelligence, of perception, of sensibility; a failure to impose meaningful organization upon reality, upon multiplicity. If this is not indeed death, Trilling is being either dishonest or too sparing of his readers' feelings. Trilling combines fineness of perception with logic; if we accept his terms, we can

[1] J. F. Cooper, *Notes on the Americans*, 2 vols., London, 1828, II, 142.
[2] *Liberal Imagination*, pp. 213–214.
[3] *Liberal Imagination*, p. 262.
[4] *Liberal Imagination*, p. 215; p. 255.

only accept his conclusions, and nothing remains but to hope for a revival of poetic drama or a sudden burgeoning of genius among television script-writers.

The burden of Trilling's argument is that the novel of manners is the only proper novel in the first phase; the novel of manners depends upon a kind of social organization that passed into eternity with the death of Edward VII; since the modern novelist everywhere and the American novelist of the nineteenth century lack that particular social organization against which to pose their material, the novel is finished. Who are the vital novelists for Trilling? Henry James alone in America, and James only because he turned away from America and had the artistic taste to live out his life abroad. Trilling accepts the recognized masters of the European nineteenth century, because they fit his social formula. In England he admires that last Edwardian, E. M. Forster, and has written the best criticism we have on Forster to demonstrate his admiration. In fact Trilling himself seems to be culturally an Edwardian who rejects his own tradition because it does not fit his rigid ideological demands.

His rigidity is apparent just beneath the surface of his own argument. He appears to accept Cooper's and Hawthorne's and James's catalogues of the defects in American society as a subject for the writer, but he slights the fact that all three writers did indeed turn their attention to American society, not wholly in the manner of their English contemporaries, in the case of Cooper and Hawthorne, but according to their perception of how they *could* organize and give meaning to their admittedly difficult material. Trilling is too subtle and sophisticated a critic to accept the simple-minded view that James 'fled' America and turned himself into a stage Englishman, yet he fails to deal with James's American novels, or to take into full account the meaning of James's international theme, in those novels which explore dramatically the tensions and variations between American and European experience. The key words for Trilling are 'society' and 'reality'. By society, in the novel, he really means the novel of manners; by reality he means 'social morality', the special concern of the novelist of manners. I have already suggested the inadequacy of manners as a universal and timeless formula, and urged the conception of the sense of society in place of manners.

Trilling's fondness for abstraction together with his trick of lending abstractions an illusory concreteness is responsible for his use of the term 'reality'. Whenever the word appears, it is followed by his accusation that the recent novel everywhere, and the American novel throughout its history, has failed to deal with the theme of appearance and reality ('the investigation of reality in the social field').[1] That theme is particularly evasive, for it is fundamental to all art, not only to the novel or one kind of novel. But if the theme of appearance and reality is placed against the concept of the sense of society, that sense which allows for the moral concerns of the novelist of manners as well as for the projection of moral awareness through other modes and other techniques, Trilling's objections tend to dissolve. In *The Complex Fate*, Marius Bewley analysed with brilliance Henry James's use of the theme of appearance and reality in his later novels, particularly in *The Golden Bowl*. He sees James not as a lonely expatriate aping European masters, but as a distinctly American writer whose greatest single influence was Hawthorne; as one who stands meaningfully in the line of American novelists from Cooper and Melville. Without wishing to put out even the most discreet flag, I can only agree, and I would add that this theme is also a conscious theme for American novelists from Cooper to Saul Bellow. It pervades Hawthorne's work and much of Melville's; it is by definition the theme of the novelist who is tempted to allegory, and allegory had an almost deadly attraction for nineteenth-century American writers. Particularly in the third phase of the novel, the theme of appearance and reality appears constantly: in Fitzgerald's *The Great Gatsby*; in Hemingway's *The Sun Also Rises*; certainly in the so-called naturalistic *USA* of Dos Passos; certainly in the best work of Faulkner.

Instead of discouraging the novelist's conception of the discrepancies between the apparent and the 'real', American nine-

---

[1] Trilling does not mean, of course, the reality of the naturalist or the neorealist; that kind of reality, he feels, has dogged and bedevilled the American novel to the exclusion of a larger social morality.

teenth-century history forced those discrepancies upon his attention. The differences between the announced ideals of post-Civil
War society and the realities of the Gilded Age, to use Mark
Twain's title, provided rich fare not only for Twain himself, but
for Howells, Henry Adams, Edith Wharton, Stephen Crane, and
even Frank Norris. The very 'self-liquidation' of the middle
class in England and on the Continent since Edwardian times
which Trilling deplores, has made for an intensification of the
writer's awareness of the differences between the apparent and
the real. Social fragmentation has opened a mine of material for
English satire, and Ronald Firbank, Aldous Huxley, Evelyn
Waugh, V. S. Pritchett, William Sansom, and Kingsley Amis,
among others, have been working the seam to good effect. The
work of Forster, Rex Warner, Rosamund Lehmann, Anthony
West, or P. H. Newby, again, depends in large part for its success
upon the author's treatment of appearance and reality. The
development of American satire since 1945 in the work of Mary
McCarthy, Randall Jarrell, Flannery O'Connor, Elizabeth Hardwick, Saul Bellow, and Ralph Ellison,[1] together with the increasing intellectualization of recent American fiction, demonstrates
the degree to which American and English writers have come to
share similar, if not identical, impulses, just as these events measure
the area into which Trilling and his followers are unwilling to
penetrate.

But something is surely wrong, something lacking, in arguments which demonstrate that nothing of merit has appeared in
English since Henry James and E. M. Forster. Further, a principle
is at stake. Perhaps every war generation is arrogant and sentimental in believing that it has particular insight into the literature
it produces, a loyalty to itself out of shared experience, but the
conviction will not down. Trilling in America, Nicolson in
England, and the rest seem to me to be the White Russians of
literature, bemoaning their lost estates, fondling in memory the
lustre of their bartered jewels, recalling with fond melancholy the

[1] Neither Miss Hardwick, Ellison nor Bellow is a pure satirist, but they use
satire as a technique to establish idea in narrative, as opposed to the clowning of
Sinclair Lewis or Thomas Wolfe.

moujiks in the fields, happy even under the knout. These retrospective critics would cut off the novel in its second phase. Because
they are ill at ease in modern society, they insist that modern
society does not exist. Jane Austen had it better. To quarrel with
Trilling is an act of ingratitude, for his perceptions have taught
much to a generation of writers; I feel rather like a contemporary
of Dante praising the *Divine Comedy* but complaining because it
is written in Tuscan. Yet the flaw cannot be polished out. Trilling
appears to share the broad social concern of Matthew Arnold (on
whom he has also written a book) and of T. S. Eliot, to which he
brings the perceptions of the intellectual steeped in extra-literary
matter: politics, psychoanalysis, and just a hint of the jargon of
'social relations'. The result is a blunting of his reading of the
literary text; a heavily schematic set of requirements that are too
rigid to follow the novel in its bendings and turnings. The
requirements, in short, are admirably adapted to the novel in its
first two phases, but they reject, by implication, the revolution in
sensibility of the third phase.

Paradoxically, Trilling's own novel, *The Middle of the Journey*
(1947), raises still another question which neither his theory nor
other theories of the death of the novel take into account: the
place of the novel of ideas. Here again one feels cloddish and
ungrateful to Trilling. His essay, 'The Meaning of a Literary
Idea', is satisfying, right, and wise; no one but Richard Blackmur
has written so well of the peculiar relationship between literary
form and the substance of literature which we call idea. Trilling
says that 'whenever we put two emotions into juxtaposition we
have what we can properly call an idea'; and again, 'The very
form of a literary work, considered apart from its content, so far
as that is possible, is in itself an idea.'[1] As long as the discussion is
confined to literature in general, one can only applaud. It is when
Trilling turns his attention to contemporary American literature,
measuring it against the greatest European literature of the nineteenth and twentieth centuries, that one begins to have reservations. For one thing, the burden of his attack is upon the novel;
he specifically exempts American poetry, and he deals only with

[1] *Liberal Imagination*, p. 283.

Eugene O'Neill among dramatists. But surely the novelist's problem is very different from the poet's or the dramatist's. When Trilling says that Wolfe and Dos Passos are finally unsatisfying for their lack of 'intellectual capital', he is right, but for the wrong reasons. And when he says that Hemingway and Faulkner 'are intensely at work upon the recalcitrant stuff of life',[1] that they thus create a literary idea which is intellectually satisfying, again he is right but for the wrong reasons.

Trilling's assertions force us to one of those terrible and complicated junction-points where criticism, literary, social, political history, and taste must meet and mingle. There is first the formal problem, which in turn leads to the other elements in my gaudy list. The history of the novel in English differs considerably from the history of the continental novel in that the catastrophe which was brought home to England and America in 1914 had been apprehended on the Continent from Napoleonic times. This meant that intellectual content—ideas—became prominent in the continental novel long before they did in the English novel. At the same time, English and American writers tended to utilize the meditative lyric for 'literary' ideas, at the expense of the novel, perhaps; one thinks of Melville, the novelist, and his fine Civil War lyrics. Melville wrote no novel about the literary idea of war. The novel in England through the convention of stylization remained calisthenic and, in a way, immature; thought *and* feeling in the sense I mean were more mature in poetry than in the novel, where feeling preceded idea, or thought, until very recently. Thought was comparatively unassimilated in the novel until after the naturalists, after the early period of experimentation in the third phase of the novel. The continental novel, on the other hand, became 'pure', intellectualized, fairly early in the day, but then it tended to freeze in its purity. The German novel has never become unfrozen, while the French novel required the combined genius of Proust, Gide, and Malraux to induce a degree of thaw.

Thus it is unfair of Trilling to compare Dos Passos's *USA* to *L'Education sentimentale*, for at base they are not comparable. Dos Passos was introducing a needed maturity into the form and

[1] *Liberal Imagination*, p. 297.

substance of the novel, where Flaubert was writing against a totally different background—political, historical, and intellectual, in quite another manner. Trilling does not include the English novel in his discussion, but he might have; if the American novel is lacking in idea, intellect, as Trilling defines them, the English novel is even more lacking. The problem of ideas for the novelist writing in English, then, needs fuller examination than Trilling concedes it. And this takes us back to techniques and devices.

In the traditional English novel, in all its impurity, writers followed one of two procedures when they wanted to deal with ideas. The most common practice was to turn aside from the narrative proper and to say, in effect, 'I shall now allow my characters to go along by themselves while I describe An Idea, reader.' A modification of this technique was to disguise the Idea faintly by speaking through the character, who lectures the other characters (in the author's voice) for a time, to their annoyance as well as the reader's. This was Dickens's practice, Thackeray's, even George Eliot's, though she was slightly more subtle than most. The second method was to write a novel around an Idea, Chartist politics, for example, and to subordinate characterization to idea: this is Disraeli's practice in *Sybil*, and Mrs. Humphry Ward's in *Robert Elsmere*. This method might be called the novel as geometrical theorem, in which characterization, point of view, and the other devices are only axioms, lines, and angles. Without wishing to revive the ancient and pointless quarrel between truth and beauty, Horace's *utile* against *dulce*, form against content, one can only say that recent formal changes in the novel have made for a happy meeting between the novel of sensibility and the novel of ideas; in the jargon of the day, modern novelists have achieved the principle of organic form.

Mme Magny returns us to the discussion of time in modern experiment, establishing more clearly the relationship between ideas, form, and experiment, and affirming at the same time the vitality of the modern novel;

> 'Time,' Schelling says somewhere, 'is the bad conscience of every empty metaphysic.' It would not be arbitrary to begin an aesthetic of the novel by saying that Time is the central character of the novel;

that the novel is the literary genre whose task is to explore and reveal
all the aspects and all the dimensions of Time; and that in the novel's
vogue and very real triumph it is doubtless not irrelevant that the
modern conscience is an uneasy one: a conscience which has allowed
the rapport . . . with eternity which it had succeeded in preserving
almost to the Renaissance to decline, and which from then on was
seriously wounded by a trauma of Time, whose presence is so
apparent in most great contemporary novelists, from Faulkner to
Virginia Woolf. One of the functions of criticism, then, is to uncover the trauma of Time and to analyse it, thus probing the wound,
however impossible so radical a cure may have proved.[1]

This is valuable for its description of the way in which one kind
of novel of idea comes into being; time in Faulkner is more than
a form of organization, a frame for the narrative. It is itself an
idea, relating in part to political history, in part to manners, in
part to that trauma which Mme Magny mentions, and from which
Faulkner's imagination takes flight. Form and idea in a novel like
Light in August are inseparable. They are indeed 'organic'.

   The Middle of the Journey, however, offers a better starting-point
for analysis of the novel of ideas, for it is less complex than *Light
in August*, and Trilling's conception is closer than Faulkner's to
that of many Anglo-American novelists. Trilling has written
much and well about his theory of the absence of social reality
in the American novel, and one is tempted to say that *The Middle
of the Journey* is an exercise in compensation for the asserted defi-
ciency. His theme is social reality, or rather conflicting views of
social reality in America in the mid-thirties. The modern, urban,
committed mind is contrasted with the rural New England community in which the novel is set; the force of ideology upon the
intellectual of the period, in the character of Maxim, the Communist apostate,[2] who feels in his apostasy that he 'no longer

---

[1] Claude-Edmonde Magny, *L'Age du roman Américain*, pp. 142–143. My translation. Jean Paulhan's *Temps et roman*, Paris, Gallimard, 1946, is pertinent in this
connection, as is A. A. Mendilow's *Time and the Novel*, London, Peter Nevill,
1952. Mendilow's discussion is both more comprehensive and more academic
than Paulhan's.

[2] Trilling was writing three years before the theme of the Communist apostate
became fashionable, and his treatment of that unrewarding subject remains by
far the best.

exists', contrasts with the similar withdrawal from 'life' of John
Laskell, the central character, an intellectual architect who is
recovering from a near-fatal siege of scarlet fever, and who represents the debilitated 'liberal' mind. Laskell's liberalism differs
from that of his country hosts, Arthur and Nancy Croom, who
are 'committed to life', committed to New Deal progressivism,
to the future. With their child, their rural summer house where
they live in Arthur's vacations from University lecturing, their
rather smug self-satisfaction, they cannot see, much less accept,
Laskell's partial rejection of life, nor the meaning of Maxim's
apostasy, which they sentimentalize.

This complex of American reality is posed against the life of
the small New England community: the good, solid Folgers, who
have lived in the area for generations, and who in spite of Trilling's
best efforts emerge as clichés, and the more interesting Duck and
Emily Caldwell. Duck is the neighbourhood handy-man, described at one point as a Mellors-the-gamekeeper type, indepen-
dent, drunken, scornful of the summer people, a jack-of-all-trades
cum natural man and villain of the piece. His wife, Emily, is at
first glance a half-educated, arty-crafty intellectually pretentious
woman, who proves more 'real' than the intellectuals who are
embarrassed by her enthusiasm for Spengler, and who brings
Laskell back to 'life', to reality, in a Laurentian sexual relationship.
Reality, then, reality as it appears in manners and mores with
particular reference to political ideology in a given time and place
is the subject of this highly competent novel.

In technique the novel does not differ essentially from the novel
of 1847 or 1880, but it belongs to the third phase rather than to the
first because of the manner in which ideas are treated. Without
its ideas, the novel would be a slight piece of melodrama, building
up to the final episode in which Duck Caldwell is responsible,
unwittingly, for his daughter's death. Trilling, having gone to
school to E. M. Forster, presents the episode ironically, so that we
read it in the context of the idea he is developing—the relationship
between the standard American conception of the good fellow,
Duck, and the man of reflection, Laskell. The central idea of the
novel investigates how the various characters relate the present

to the future. Trilling presents the idea in terms of his plot, the Crooms' reactions to Maxim's Party activity. At one point Laskell becomes convinced that Nancy Croom has acted as a courier for Maxim. Laskell's thoughts further the plot, and they give Trilling the opportunity to develop his theme of manners:

> . . . he did not know whether he was frightened for Nancy or by her.
>
> He lay a long time in the dark that night, listening to the very faint movement of the tree outside his window. Once more he turned over in his mind just what it meant to feel that the future was no longer real, or that, if it was real at all, it was coexistent with the present. And once more he thought of the future as a characteristic concept of the well-loved young man of the middle class, brought up on promises.
>
> And what has changed? he asked himself. Was it that he was not well loved? Or not of the middle class?
>
> Oh, surely of the middle class. Perhaps not so well loved as he once had been. And surely no longer young.
>
>   .   .   .   .
>
> Arthur was a political man, but even for him the Party was not really political, and a break with it was not an action in politics—in practical politics, as people said, wishing to make a distinction between that unfortunate kind of politics and some other, better kind—but rather an action in morals.
>
>   .   .   .   .
>
> But Nancy was involved. Of that Laskell was sure. Why had she said yes? [to Maxim] Was it because she, like him, had been reared as a well-loved child of the middle class, brought up on promises which had to be fulfilled? If at first Laskell had been ambiguously frightened by his knowledge of what she had done, now, as he thought of her in the light of their common past, thought of her as the spirited girl in the genteel suburb to whom so much was promised and so much given, he had a kind of tenderness for her action. It had a directness and innocence about it, a fresh, young immediacy.

There is a qualitative difference between this way of dealing with ideas and the Victorian novelist's, 'And now, reader . . .'.

A less successful meeting between manners and idea occurs when Laskell attends a church supper and bazaar at which Emily Caldwell is selling the wooden bowls she has decorated for the

G

occasion. Loyal to Emily, Laskell tells her that he wants to buy one:

'So modernistic,' said Mrs. Parks, secure in the established tradition of her tatting patterns.

'Yes, isn't it?' said Laskell, as if that were a recommendation.

What aspiration was contained in the unprincipled designs of these bowls he did not know. He could see the forms of Cubism as it had been picked up from the brushes of Parisians who had dropped it two decades before, picked up by men of small intellect and less passion. He could see in the angles the embodied talk about the machine age and the beauty of the functional which had always implied angles. There was arts-and-crafts and a touch of the folk and even of the peasant, the saving myth of *hand* work. There was the deep sullen modern mysticism of the abstract and non-representational, here scarcely understood. Oh, it was so thoroughly not good, it was so bad and silly and derivative and yet somehow it contained so much that, though badly transmitted and ill understood, had been tried and fought for in confusion and pain and pride that it went to his heart through all the firm barriers of judgment and taste. Each of the designs was in bad taste and each, with its red and blue and its unorganized swoops of angle and curve, was deeply depressing, precisely because it denied the sunny fleshy quality of the meeting by the river. Was she at all what these darkened unhappy designs implied—as well as the woman who at first sight had suggested an ancient goddess to him, as well as the woman who had been foolish and social and pretentious at the Crooms', and as well as the woman on the river bank?

Ideas, here, are not merely calisthenic; they are proposed with subtlety and faced with courage. But the place of the wooden bowl in Laskell's and Emily's relationship suggests another literary bowl, the golden bowl that stands between Maggie Verver and Prince Amerigo in Henry James's novel. It suggests the bookishness of much of Trilling's writing. We hear frequent echoes, of Forster, Lawrence, James, and in the first quoted passage, of the wonderful ending of *The Great Gatsby*, where the narrator thinks of the Dutch sailors seeing Long Island for the first time, 'a fresh, green breast of the new world . . . for a transitory enchanted moment man must have held his breath in the presence of this continent, compelled into an aesthetic contemplation he neither

understood nor desired, face to face for the last time in history
with something commensurate to his capacity for wonder.' And
then the organizing phrase that lives on in the memory, 'Gatsby
believed in . . . the orgastic future that year by year recedes
before us.' The difference between the two writers' use of the same
idea is that Trilling gives the impression that idea preceded narrative; idea determined narrative pattern. Fitzgerald, a less 'intellectual' writer, reached idea through a theme which preceded
idea; his idea has an inevitability which Trilling's lacks. This is
borne out by the structure of the two novels. *The Middle of the
Journey* splits down the centre and becomes two novels, one about
Laskell and one about Maxim; it is, in fact, a skilled amateur's
work, where *Gatsby* is a writer's book, having the centrifugal
force of the novel in which emotion and mind are in the proper
balance—and no one but the writer can say what 'proper' is for
his particular novel.[1]

It is unjust to compare *The Middle of the Journey* with *The Great
Gatsby*, for they represent two different strains in the novel of
ideas; they represent, in fact, two of the three discernible strains
that need to be sorted out. The most obvious strain might be
called the 'pure' novel of ideas, or the novel in which the author's
political or philosophical hypothesis dominates the conception,
the structure, the characterization. This is the novel of Orwell in
1984, of Arthur Koestler in *Darkness at Noon*, of Rex Warner in
The Aerodrome, or of Norman Mailer in *Barbary Shore*. A year
after reading *1984*, for example, we are more likely to remember
Orwell's description of Newspeak than the central character,
Smith; more likely to recall with our minds Orwell's conception
of the totalitarian State than to remember with our emotions the
effect of totalitarianism upon the puppet-characters. The same
applies to *Darkness at Noon*. Although *The Aerodrome* is a better
novel than *1984*, its basic reality is the reality of idea rather than
of fictional narrative. Its validity is as great and no greater than

[1] Jean Genet's definition of talent helps to clarify my meaning here. Genet
said, 'Talent is courteousness in regard to matter; it consists in giving song to that
which was dumb.' *The Thief's Journal*, trans. Bernard Frechtman, Paris, Olympia
Press, 1954, p. 121. In Genet's sense, Fitzgerald has talent, and Trilling has not.
Trilling gives clarity to that which was vocally in existence.

the validity of the idea of Fascism from which it springs; again the same applies to *Barbary Shore*. In spite of Trilling's best efforts to make it otherwise, *The Middle of the Journey* belongs with this strain of the novel of pure Idea; its validity is finally an intellectualized validity rather than an emotional one.

The second strain in the novel of ideas is that of the *roman-fleuve*, as adapted by modern novelists. The basic assumption of the *roman-fleuve* in the nineteenth century to which it belongs was that objective social reality could best be presented through the life-stories of many single characters or families, existing contemporaneously in the same or in varying milieus. Trollope wrote the *roman-fleuve*, as did Galsworthy; the last novel in the strict genre was probably Roger Martin du Gard's *Les Thibault*, published between 1922 and 1940 but belonging to the nineteenth century in conception and execution. These novelists wanted to show the flow of life, rather than to compel life into narrative and plot. Their conception was useful to the naturalists in the second phase of the novel, while the modern adapter of the *roman-fleuve* has changed the traditional technique by giving the flow a direction, his apprehension of social fragmentation and his political and ideological ideas acting as the alidade for determining direction. Consistent with the fact that naturalism has been stronger in America than in England, American writers, far more than the English, have used the *roman-fleuve*. John Dos Passos in *USA*, James T. Farrell in his *Studs Lonigan* trilogy, Norman Mailer in *The Naked and the Dead* are just a few examples, while in England one must go back to the avowed naturalists like Bennett, to Galsworthy, or to the Tietjens novels of Ford Madox Ford. Apart from technique, the *roman-fleuve* differs from the pure novel of ideas in that the idea, or the direction, tends to be diffuse, more closely allied to a sociological, economic, or historical view in the round than to a distinct, personal interpretation of one place *in* history, politics, or sociology. John Dos Passos has said that he regards his first allegiance as a novelist to social history,[1] and his career bears out his theory.

[1] John Dos Passos, 'Credo', *Bookman*, LXVIII, September 1928, 26. Reaffirmed in a letter to the writer, 27 October 1947.

While I do not want to extend the jargon of criticism, I am forced by the meagreness of our critical vocabulary to borrow from psychology a term to describe the third and most important strain in the novel of ideas. I would call that novel in which sensibility and ideas mingle inextricably the novel of cognition, or the cognitive novel. Cognition in psychology combines knowledge, or what one has learned in the past; perception, or what one is learning in the present, together with the mechanical means by which knowledge is apprehended; and sensibility, the organization of past knowledge and present perception within the individual's unique mental and emotional make-up. The cognitive novel, then, is the most characteristic strain of the novel of ideas in the modern period. The cognitive novelist, generally speaking, is the writer who has encompassed with his mind the order-defying history of our time, and he has in addition comprehended and accepted that history with his emotions to the degree that he is able to project his dual comprehension meaningfully in the novel. He is neither a disguised sociologist nor a masked political scientist, but a writer who directs his first attention, as writers have always done, to story, to the realization of three-dimensional characters who live on in our minds as characters, not as disguised ideas or disembodied editorials. In the novel of the first phase, the reader can remove the thin layer of idea, and the movement of the whole is more often improved than impeded. In the second phase, in James, Conrad, or Meredith, idea was expressed as motif or theme; James and Conrad in particular were moving towards the cognitive novel, but there remained, even in their finest work, an aesthetic impatience with idea. But in the cognitive novel, ideas, character, and situation become meaningless if we attempt the operation of removing from their total dimension the objective framework of idea in which the characters live and have being. Malcolm Lowry's extraordinary *Under the Volcano* (1947) and Rosamund Lehmann's *The Echoing Grove* offer concrete illustrations of my meaning.

The central character in each of these novels is a rare, fine and needed personality displayed in a state of disintegration before the demands made upon him for love and stability. Geoffrey Firmin of *Under the Volcano* is a dipsomaniac, and Rickie Masters of *The Echoing Grove* suffers from a duodenal ulcer which causes his death. The controlling situation in each novel apparently hinges upon the realization of individual, private sensibility, and at the level of sensibility, each novel succeeds totally; each novel is a study of the failure of marriage and of the nature of love in a fragmented society. But we have had many such studies, and if Lowry and Miss Lehmann stopped there we would not give them a second thought. We return to them for their ability to transcend sensibility, to reach into our society and to tell us something about ourselves. In this effort, too, they succeed with distinction. Geoffrey Firmin is the British consul in a small Mexican city whose American wife, Yvonne, has left him a year previously through a misunderstanding. As the novel opens, Yvonne has returned to Mexico to attempt reconciliation. The time is about 1937, and the action of the novel takes place in the last week-end of Firmin's life. At the level of sensibility the novel succeeds through Lowry's ability to present Firmin as a commanding figure. Firmin is not merely a theatrical drunkard flinging himself at destruction; he rises from the page as a tragic, real, rounded man of mind and emotion, beautifully realized from the inside. His drinking creates a chain of ungrasped opportunities, of leapable barriers never cleared for the communication of his deep love for Yvonne, a chain which she on her side is equally unable to break. Drunkenness causes Firmin's loss of Yvonne, of Hugh, his half-brother, of his friends, of his grasp upon reality, and finally of his own life, when he is thrown over a cliff, literally under the volcano, by a gang of Mexican Fascists.

While the narrative is confined to one week-end in time, it ranges back to Firmin's boyhood before the World War and into the twenties and thirties. The black facts of the World War and of the Spanish Civil War in progress exist both as elements in the narrative and as ideas which give the novel the depth and resonance we demand of the greatest writing. The exotic Mexican setting is not an evasion of society, but a background of which the geography, history, religion, customs, and day-to-day facts provide the discrete symbolism that Lowry needs for the projection of his secondary background, the English and American society to which his characters belong. Mexico allows this writer's sense of society to function.

To state Lowry's ideas in this novel baldly is to impoverish them by removing them from their rich context, but it is also to see that they belong with the greatest writing of our time. His first idea, implicit in every page, is the necessity of love and the virtual impossibility of realizing it. Secondly, he is concerned with the relationship between action and contemplation, between life and death; action means death, contemplation life. Existentialism is turned about, and yet Lowry would not deny the existentialist's emphasis upon action. 'We all live in a time when we must act and live too much, thus we miss life', he seems to say. Finally, war and Fascism as ideas counterbalance the personal and individual themes. We are not taken to the wars, nor does Lowry take sides and preach; yet he is on the side of the angels, and both the idea of war and of Fascism are condemned. Firmin had commanded a ship in the World War, and he carries a burden of guilt for having killed a German submarine-crew he had taken prisoner. Hugh, too young for the war, is the modern romantic who roams the world as a newspaperman looking for the war he missed as a boy. Hugh, Geoffrey, and Yvonne attend a bull-riding exhibition; they are bored, the performers are drunk, and at one point Hugh himself enters the arena and rides a bull: not to show off, Yvonne tells Geoffrey, '. . . No, he was simply submitting to that absurd necessity he felt for action, so wildly exacerbated by the dawdling inhuman day.' This moment of action brings Geoffrey and Yvonne closer together than they have been and almost leads to the reconciliation and the escape from Mexico they both so badly want.

Lowry uses the traditional method of an argument between Geoffrey and Hugh to present the idea of war, but by making the intellectual positions belong firmly to the sensibility, the turn and bend of the characters, he leaves behind the staleness of the device. In the last conversation with Hugh before Yvonne's and Geoffrey's separate deaths, Geoffrey is quite drunk, but lucid as ever:

'. . . Why should anybody interfere with anybody? . . .

'Or more specifically perhaps, Hugh, I was talking of nothing at all. . . . Since supposing we settled anything—ah, *ignoratio elenchi*, Hugh, that's what. Or the fallacy of supposing a point proved or disproved by argument which proves or disproves something not at issue. Like these wars. For it seems to me that almost everywhere in the world these days there has long since ceased to be anything fundamental to man at issue at all. . . . Ah, you people with ideas!

'Ah, *ignoratio elenchi*! . . . All this, for instance, about going to fight for Spain . . . and poor little defenceless China! Can't you see there's a sort of determinism about the fate of nations? They all seem to get what they deserve in the long run.'

'Well . . .'

A gust of wind moaned round the house with an eerie sound like a northerner prowling among the tennis nets in England, jingling the rings.

'Not exactly original.'

'Not long ago it was poor little defenceless Ethiopia. Before that, poor little defenceless Flanders. To say nothing of course of the poor little defenceless Belgian Congo. And to-morrow it will be poor little defenceless Latvia. Or Finland. Or Piddle-deedee. Or even Russia. Read history. Go back a thousand years. What is the use of interfering with its worthless stupid course? Like a barranca, a ravine choked up with refuse, that winds through the ages, and peters out in a—— What in God's name has all the heroic resistance put up by poor little defenceless peoples all rendered defenceless in the first place for some well-calculated and criminal reason . . .'

'Hell, *I* told you that——'

'—to do with the survival of the human spirit? Nothing whatsoever. Less than nothing. Countries, civilizations, empires, great hordes perish for no reason at all, and their soul and meaning with them, that one old man perhaps you never heard of, and who never heard of them, sitting boiling in Timbuctoo, proving the existence of the mathematical correlative of *ignoratio elenchi* with obsolete instruments, may survive.'

Firmin continues, arguing brilliantly from *War and Peace*, confusing that book with *Anna Karenina*, as Hugh points out, and finally turns his argument into a cruel reproach to Yvonne for interfering with his drinking. Thus it is that the idea, the logical argument, the man, the character emerge full and rounded—a major achievement. Lowry's themes are those of the greatest novelist of ideas, André Malraux, but *Under the Volcano* has a compassion and above all a sad and wild humour that is foreign to Malraux, as it is to most of modern literature.

The Echoing Grove (1953) is a novel of sensibility in greater degree than *Under the Volcano*; both Miss Lehmann and Lowry may be said to have begun where Katherine Mansfield and Virginia Woolf left off. Sensibility for these later writers is not an end but a means; in this area experiment continues to take place, not dramatic experiments in technique, but experiments in the possibilities of human communication which utilize earlier techniques. *The Echoing Grove* is firmly rooted in English society of the last thirty years; it is an explicit novel of manners, as well as a novel of sensibility and a novel of ideas. The scene is London and rural England. Masters, the central character, has been dead some years as the novel opens, but we see him through the minds of his wife, Madeleine; his mistress, Dinah, who is Madeleine's sister; and in part we know his own view of the impossible triangle. Again, the wars and uprisings of recent history are finely examined, not as syllogisms or hypotheses, but for their effects upon the characters. As in Miss Lehmann's earlier novel, *The Ballad and the Source*, the unifying theme is the fragmentation of Victorian and Edwardian social patterns from 1914 to the present. Mrs. Burkett, the mother of Madeleine and Dinah, is a representative of that earlier stability, living on into our silver age, judging not at all, but approving even less. Masters is born well into a county family, a civil servant of some distinction, who realizes that his birth and his acceptance of fragmentation are tearing him in two. Madeleine accepts her mother's principles in the main, while Dinah is a total rebel who leaves the safety of her own upbringing for a promiscuous and sordid existence in the pale London Bohemia. This basic conflict between generations, ways of life, is everywhere implicit in the novel, and once explicit, a good example of how Miss Lehmann copes with ideas. The Second World War is in progress, and Dinah and her mother are talking about the past, about Dinah's rebellion, and about Masters:

'I suppose,' mused Dinah, 'if ever a generation knew its own strength it was yours: or rather *didn't* know it, as the saying goes, meaning it's so tremendous it hasn't got to be consciously considered, for good or ill. We inherited your Juggernaut momentum; but of course not your sphere of operations.'

'Indeed!'

'That started to be blocked. And we seized up. Rickie must have known it in his bones long before we did. We weren't conditioned like him, not deeply, by ruling class mentality. You needn't get on your snobby-horse'—for her mother had snorted—'I couldn't be more thankful for the good sound upper-middle stock I come of. It's meant a sort of solid ground floor of family security and class confidence that's been a great stand-by. But Rickie hadn't got it. He was a romantic orphan boy, irrevocably out of the top drawer. He was never at home in his situation, was he?—I mean the contemporary one, the crack-up—not just the general human situation of wondering why you're born.'

Despite the awkward inversion 'mused Dinah', and despite the uncharacteristic tastelessness of 'snobby-horse', in its context this passage, like Lowry's, effects the union between sensibility and idea, between narrative and statement. *The Echoing Grove* also shows how the cognitive novelist can fail; Miss Lehmann wants to present the tendency among American women to 'psychologize', to analyse every situation in terms of half-baked psychiatric lore. Georgie, the American woman who is intended sympathetically, is made to say of Dinah, 'She could have been bust right open, she wouldn't have resisted it; after a while she'd have integrated into something pretty fine. Rickie is a honey, but he was the wrong guy for her to settle for.' The underlying idea is valid, but the failure is one of diction, for Georgie's speech is not American any more than it is English. It is like no speech known to man. This is a minor flaw in an otherwise excellent novel, but it typifies a tendency among English novelists to bungle their American characters and to weaken the effect of the idea behind the portraiture. Isherwood's *The World in the Evening*, an example of how bad the cognitive novel can be, fails totally for the author's curious neglect of American diction and rhythms of speech.

The existence of manners in *The Echoing Grove* returns us to the counter-attack upon Trilling's idea that in England 'the middle class is in the process of liquidating itself' and that manners therefore no longer exist as material for the novelist. When Masters goes to his final interview with Dinah, he goes in response to her request, for he has tried to break off their relationship and has avoided her for months. He discovers that she is leaving the flat he has rented for her, and that she wants to return some of his belongings. He resents her having made further demands upon him, and he hurries their cold business proceedings so that he can return to his home in time to take Madeleine, his wife, out to dinner. Masters and Dinah take a taxi to Masters's home; he leaves her in the taxi, having given the driver a pound note to deliver her wherever she wishes. As he leaves, Masters senses that she has no address to go to, as is the case, and he senses the girl's agony in the knowledge that her final, unspoken appeal has gone unanswered.

Masters's giving the note to the driver is a pure and very typical example of manners as they exist in the modern English novel. His act is a moral act which concentrates his past, his character, his training, his divided loyalty, his insoluble problem. The situation itself would not be possible in the novel of the first phase; it is a clear result of social fragmentation and of the disappearance of traditional guides to conduct. Religion does not enter into Masters's decision, nor does traditional sexual hypocrisy: he does his best to be honest with both women, and the only hypocrisies Masters indulges in are to spare his children—one instance of traditional values that do persist. Masters's conduct to be sure does not represent a social standard; it is the unique result of his particular sensibility and his particular system of ethics. Yet Masters's standards are recognizable and in their context admirable. The assumption that when traditional religion and traditional codes fail men lapse into brutality is a partial truth at best. It is anti-humane and reactionary, and it implies that traditional codes were effectual in restraining men from brutality, an implication which history denies. Wherever men live together they formulate codes of behaviour, they act according to manners.

We need not apologize for our manners; if our recent history has shown us our depths, it has often displayed our heights. The modern novelist at his best has been priest and prophet in Shelley's sense, rather than a sorcerer attached to a dying cult.

It is not necessary to multiply examples of manners from other English novelists; as I have interpreted them, manners are the basis of the novels of Elizabeth Bowen, of L. P. Hartley, of C. H. B. Kitchin, of Anthony Powell, Evelyn Waugh, William Sansom—the list is long. No one who had lived in contemporary England for any length of time could ignore the existence of manners in every reach of English society. The Welfare State has assuredly changed many traditional and fundamental facts in English political and social life, but it has also created new situations in which manners are prominent. If anything, the Welfare State has enriched the novelist's materials by setting up one more source of tension between new and traditional patterns of existence. Far more people than before the war, for example, attend a university, but the differences between the graduate of an 'old' university and a 'red-brick' university have been exacerbated. Levelling has occurred, but the ways of the levellers have been unpredictable: the militant *New Statesman and Nation*, as distinguished for its unwinning nationalism as for its socialism, is capable of printing an esoteric supplement on wine-tasting. Whether a man covers up his native provincial accent with B.B.C. English or with the tones of Oxford is important; he can be placed by whether he owns a poodle or a greyhound, by whether he wears a homburg or a cap, and by whether the cap has a button on top or is sewn to the visor. Accent, dress, social conduct and its moral bases are still present and are still being drawn upon by novelists. Faced with the necessity, one finds it easier to list the contemporary English novelists who do not write of manners than those who do. One is confined mainly to the novelists of pure idea—Orwell or Warner—and then only in certain novels; and to sub-literary writers of adventure, detection, and science fiction. Serious English novelists remain novelists of manners. To ignore the fact is to be beguiled by doctrinaire political theory and blind to recent literary history.

The attack upon the English novel of manners might better have been completely reversed; a case could be made for a falling off in English literary energy not because it has ignored manners, but because it has relied too heavily upon them. Novelists like L. P. Hartley, Anthony Powell, or Elizabeth Taylor have consigned themselves to the limbo of the minor by their preoccupation with manners, their nostalgic theme of the bright past against the grey present. One is tempted to say that without idea the novel of manners tends to a feminine preoccupation with technique, the proliferation of detail that is fascinating in itself but ultimately distracting, as in the later novels of Elizabeth Bowen, or Hartley's *The Boat*. Henry James has often served the English novelist badly.

In America the novel of manners has had a complex evolution. I have remarked how mid-nineteenth-century American novelists departed from their English contemporaries by treating society at one remove. Instead of writing novels of manners, they wrote allegories or elaborate metaphors of society out of their need to create the myths by which society functions. A second reason for the relative neglect of the novel of manners until recent times was the American writer's compulsion to sort out in his work the relationship between his own country and Europe. The idea of Europe floats through the American novel like a corked bottle containing a coded message. Cooper thought that he knew the code, though he was never at ease with his knowledge; Hawthorne toyed with the mysterious bottle as a boy with a wooden raft, pushing it here and there with the sapling of his Calvinist conscience, until in *The Marble Faun* he tried to crack open the bottle and failed. In *Redburn* Melville sent his hero to Liverpool, provided with a guide which had belonged to Redburn's father and which no longer corresponded to the twists and turnings of the actual city. Howells became the propagandist for Europe in America; as editor of the *Atlantic Monthly* he introduced contemporary French and Scandinavian writers in particular to the American audience, attempting through translations and exploratory essays to make clear the meaning of Europe to his countrymen. Stephen Crane fled from America to gasp out his brief life in England and to leave his body in Germany. Generations of writers spent long years in Europe; Hawthorne as Consul in Liverpool; Howells as Consul in Venice; Melville more briefly as a merchant seaman; Henry Adams spent eight years in the American Embassy in London; again the list is long, reaching to our own day. After each of our World Wars, young writers have settled abroad to make their peace with their idea of Europe.

Henry James's expatriation, for the history of the American novel, is archetypal. Coming to maturity in a period of unparalleled economic and social swinishness, James left America with one part of his mind, but with another part he remained there. His divided allegiance made him into the first American novelist consciously to exploit the European theme. In his European novels as in his American ones, the bottle is opened with ease and the message accurately decoded. The result was a new kind of novel of manners; James was not rooted in English society as George Eliot had been or, in French, as Stendhal had been. His novels of manners have nothing of the strongly regional aspect of the earlier European novelists. He observed European manners with detachment and with an un-European, morally critical eye. At the same time, he was Europeanized enough to observe American society with the same detachment and the same quality of criticism in his American novels. But his great achievement was the novel in which both societies, to use one of his words, reverberate. In *Portrait of a Lady*, *The Ambassadors*, and *The Golden Bowl*, a solution to the century-long American search was found, for the idea of Europe had been squarely confronted. In his international novels, James was not so much compromising with the traditional novel of manners as he was seeing with a fresh eye what had long been an American dilemma, and constructing from what he perceived an American substitute for the traditional novel of manners. He was the first major American writer to dispense with the metaphysic and the metaphor of the American romantic movement.

In his view of society, James belongs to the second phase of the novel, while in his technical experimentation he belongs to the third. Like Virginia Woolf, he ruled out idea and substituted technique; in this decision lies the strength and the weakness of both.[1] If James's influence on contemporary English writing has often been unfortunate in its tendency to create monstrosities of artificiality, his influence has been entirely for the good in contemporary American writing. The doctrinaire naturalism of Norris and Dreiser which flatly denied the discipline of form in fiction needed the corrective influence of James and his disciples. James's influence has been widespread in America, appearing in strange places; none more strange, possibly, than the work of Ernest Hemingway. Until recently Hemingway has been conceived by most Europeans and too many Americans as a kind of gangster of literature, a Neanderthal *Ur-Mensch* of the novel, violent, illiterate, an unfortunate accident of literary history, rather than as the very conscious artist he is. Hemingway's novelty has obscured his literary debts, while an unhealthy and wilful confusion between his life and his work has prevented many readers from seeing the work. James's influence is apparent throughout Hemingway's work as a quality of concern, a single-minded insistence upon moral behaviour. This sort of influence cannot be proved, it can only be pointed to. But the second kind of influence, which is technical, can be isolated: it appears in points and flecks of detail, as when in *The Sun Also Rises*, Jake Barnes, in love with Lady Brett Ashley, fails to turn over to Robert Cohn, a rival of sorts, a telegram from her, preferring to paraphrase the contents.[2] Hemingway does not seem to belong to James's tradition because he adds to the Jamesian framework of moral impulse the concerns of the cognitive novelist—he is a

[1] Virginia Woolf's comment on *The Wings of the Dove* might apply to much of her own work: 'His manipulation becomes so elaborate towards the end that instead of feeling the artist you merely feel the man who is posing the subject. And then I think he loses the power to feel the crisis. He becomes merely excessively ingenious. This, you seem to hear him saying, is the way to do it. Now just when you expect a crisis, the true artist evades it. . . . The mental grasp and stretch are magnificent. Not a flabby or slack sentence, but much emasculated by this timidity or consciousness or whatever it is. Very highly American, I conjecture, in the determination to be highly bred, and the light obtuseness as to what high breeding is.' *A Writer's Diary*, p. 40.

[2] I have discussed James's influence on Hemingway in greater detail in 'Hemingway and History', *Western Review*, XVII, 1953, 87–98.

novelist of ideas. Each of his novels and many of his short stories present an organized view of society, a view which would be meaningless to James, but in a style which James would recognize and welcome. Certainly James would recognize Hemingway's treatment of the international theme, that theme which he made possible for later writers and which has been in an important sense *the* American novel of manners.

Still another reason for the comparative neglect of manners as such in the American nineteenth century was the vogue of what literary historians rather unsatisfactorily call local colour. American local-colour writing was only superficially related to the regionalism of English novelists like Maria Edgeworth, Jane Austen, or George Eliot. Local-colour writing, or regionalism, was the price America had to pay for being new. The regionalist answered to the familiar exhortation for a native, American literature, and consciously turned his back on Europe. Thus from the beginning, regionalism was immersed in the sentimental mystique of 'the folk'; it produced in the work of Augustus Longstreet, George Washington Cable, and Joel Chandler Harris in the South; of Sarah Orne Jewett and Mary Wilkins Freeman in New England; of Edward Eggleston, Bret Harte and the frontier humorists of the Mid-West and West, a sub-literature which is often unreadable for its dialect, teeming with humorous, pathetic, or crooked 'characters', slight in narrative, filled with local detail (often badly observed); it remained essentially an oral rather than a written record of the new life in a new land. Regionalism in the nineteenth century produced no writer of merit but Mark Twain; a necessary clearing of the ground, a preliminary exploration, it made possible the work of Faulkner and other contemporary southern writers, but it left an anti-intellectual imprint and the willingness to be satisfied with second-rate work which still blights some American writing.

Since the Second World War regionalism has outgrown its provincialism, its home-made, hacked-out appearance and has blended with the novel of manners to produce novels of some distinction. The work of Jean Stafford, Elizabeth Hardwick, Saul Bellow, and Peter Taylor is often regional, an examination of

Boston or Iowa City or Chicago or St. Louis—but in no sense is it provincial, any more than Stendhal is provincial when he writes of Dijon, or Italo Svevo when he writes of Trieste.

The American regionalists and 'realists' of the seventies and eighties were unknowingly responsible for clearing the way for naturalism, that movement which virtually by-passed England, but which has had so profound an effect upon subsequent American writing. Naturalism has been attacked, with some justice, as an unfortunate influence in the American novel; for the moment it is sufficient to note that doctrinaire naturalism also served to turn the American writer away from manners; for a full generation, society was conceived as a specimen in biology, as a geological force, as a chemical, but not as a collection of people leading diversified lives in diversified ways. To a man, writers of strictures on the death of the novel have observed that the naturalist and the novelist of manners have little in common; naturalism has therefore been presented as something evil and second-rate, a view which must be discussed at length in another chapter.

Elizabeth Bowen once made an inspired comment on the argument about the connection between literature and society: 'My books', she wrote, '*are* my relation to society.'[1] I have tried to say something like this at vastly greater length—that even in their own terms, the mourners at the death of the novel have by turns ignored, twisted, and denied the facts of contemporary literature. The falling-off in literary energy of which they complain is their own, not that of living, breathing writers. Every week-end they demand a masterpiece, and when it is not forthcoming, they conclude that it is all up with us, and they mourn for the social certainties of 1814. The ultimate absurdity of their view is stated by one of the lesser followers of Lionel Trilling who has written,

> There are only two cultural pockets left in America; and they are the Deep South and that area of the north-eastern United States whose moral capital is Boston, Massachusetts. This is to say that these are the only places where there are any manners. In all other

[1] Elizabeth Bowen and others, *Why Do I Write?*, London, 1948, p. 23.

H

parts of the country people live in a kind of vastly standardized cultural prairie, a sort of infinite Middle West, and that means that they
don't really live and they don't really do anything.[1]

I conclude from this that the falling-off in energy affects editors,
too, when they allow such egregious silliness to be printed. In
the quaint words of Howells's Mr. Sewall, novels still form, if
not the whole, then a large part of the intellectual experience of
many people. May they long continue to do great 'mischief'.

[1] John Aldridge, 'Manners and Values'.

Chapter Four

THE TWO NATURALISMS

As an art-form, the novel is diffuse, difficult to grasp, now as wide-ranging as pollen on the wind, now as deeply encrusted as a geological deposit. It is probably this refusal of the novel to fit into categories that has caused so many critics to categorize, to place novels in genres and to legislate about the art as a whole, even though the categories and genres of their invention might apply only to certain historical periods or to certain clusters of novels. The fallacy of genre criticism with regard to the novel of manners has been examined; I next propose to look at the strange and wonderful dogma that has developed around the idea of naturalism in Anglo-American writing. Since the beginning of the modern period, naturalism has appeared as a monster in the Faerie Queene world of the novel to be slain by the Red Cross Knight whose weapon is variously form, manners, morals, pure technique, metaphor, symbol, or myth. Naturalism has been vilified as a means of evading the novelist's proper task, as a substitution of 'the endless bookkeeping of experience' for the re-creation of experience in all its richness and meaning.[1] Writers who are actually or apparently committed to naturalism have been relegated to the sub-basement of literature, when they have not simply been ignored as beneath critical contempt. The denunciation of naturalism has been so widespread and so effective that when James T. Farrell, one of the few admitted naturalists in existence, discusses the subject, he takes the defensive: 'I have been called a naturalist', he says, 'and I have never denied it.'[2] Coming from Mr. Farrell, an aggressive man, this is craven; it

[1] Philip Rahv, 'Notes on the Decline of Naturalism', *Image and Idea*, Norfolk, Conn., New Directions, 1949, pp. 128–139.
[2] James T. Farrell, *Reflections at Fifty*, New York, Vanguard, 1954, p. 150.

lacks even the defiance of Jean Genet defending thieving and sodomy. The American Nobel Prize winners, Hemingway and Faulkner, safely enshrined at last in the Pantheon, are subjected to a de-naturalizing process not unlike the delousing of prisoners of war. Faulkner, for instance, has been saved from naturalism by the sudden discovery that he is a 'religious' writer.[1] The fact that the quarrel over naturalism has raged in America, not in England, is of high significance to an examination of the Anglo-American novel; it also hints at a confusion and a complexity that cry out for fuller treatment.

Few people who use the term 'naturalism' bother to define it. The assumption that naturalism is a dirtied kind of realism and responsible for much formlessness in the novel (*tranche de vie*), for encouraging moral obtuseness in young writers, for the development of a naïve trust in documentation, for Kathleen Winsor's variety of 'historical' novel, and ultimately for the insults to language in the journalism of that evil Trinity, *Time*, *Life*, and *Fortune*, is general, and in a limited sense all true. Yet it ignores the considerable service that naturalism has done to the novel and abbreviates literary history, particularly in America, unpardonably.

Naturalism in literature is associated with the doctrinaire programme for constructing the novel as announced by Zola in his essay, 'Le roman expérimental' of 1880, and by his practice in the twenty-volume cycle of the *Rougon-Macquart* (1871–93). Zola's theory is well known and does not need to be reviewed in detail. What should be noted is that Zola's theory was a simple-minded adaptation of nineteenth-century scientific thought, of the impulse we have noted in Buckle to discover fixed laws, and to apply those 'laws' to literature. Zola saw environment as a laboratory in which human beings could act only in accordance with 'laws' of behaviour. The fact that Zola was a second-rate novelist did not prevent his theory from spreading widely, for it answered a need of the day; it was superficially consistent with Darwinian thought, and even more consistent with Herbert Spencer's system. In purely literary terms, Zola's vogue was probably as

---

[1] William Van O'Connor, *The Tangled Fire of William Faulkner*, Minneapolis, University of Minnesota Press, 1954.

great as it was because it carried forward Balzac's practice and
seemed to support writers like Stendhal, Flaubert, and Maupassant. One must emphasize that Zola's programme *was* doctrinaire
and narrow, based upon a grave confusion between science and
art. It is this aspect of naturalism that Mark Schorer seems to have
in mind when he describes the 'structural machinations of Dos
Passos and the lyrical interruptions of Steinbeck as the desperate
manœuvres of men committed to a method of whose limitations
they despair. They are our symbolists *manqué*, who end as
allegorists.'[1]

If naturalism were only the doctrinaire programme of Zola,
we should need to pay no more attention to it than to Wyndham
Lewis's Vorticism, but in point of fact naturalism was and
remains many different things to many different people. According to the *Oxford English Dictionary*, 'naturalist' came into the
language about 1587 as a theological term; this ancestry emphasizes
that naturalism is not only a literary movement, but a way of
seeing experience as ancient as man. A naturalistic philosopher
defends his position by saying that naturalism is commonly and
erroneously identified with extreme Materialism or Mechanism;
it is, rather, 'an earnest and courageous desire to find out and
face the truth'. It is not propaganda, not self-deception, not the
will to believe. The naturalist believes that 'Nature, the world
of reality, has a character, a structure of its own, and our opinions
are true only in so far as they conform to this actual situation.'
Theologians and Idealistic philosophers too often speak of
naturalism 'as a kind of evil conspiracy against all that is spiritual
and ideal, a devil's invention with only malevolent aims. Such a
picture is sheer caricature.'[2] If we substitute critics and literary
historians for theologians and Idealistic philosophers, we approxi-
mate the situation in literature. As a philosophy and as a literary
movement, naturalism comes under attack for its real or supposed
adherence to determinism. But again, while determinism is a

[1] Mark Schorer, 'Technique as Discovery', *Forms of Modern Fiction*, ed. Wm.
Van O'Connor, Minneapolis, University of Minnesota Press, 1948, p. 26.
[2] James Bissett Pratt, *Naturalism*, New Haven, Yale University Press, 1939,
pp. 2–4.

large factor in Zola's doctrine, few 'Naturalists' have been deter-
minists. Naturalism has contributed to literature not a doctrinaire
programme, but an obsession with actuality which amounts to
an ontological view, and a technique for communicating that
ontology. To clarify this assertion, one must first trace the confused history of the transformation of Zola's doctrine outside
France into a useful mode for the modern novel.

That history in England is brief. French naturalism in the work
of Zola, Maupassant, the Goncourts, Flaubert, even the mild
Daudet, was offensive and repellent to the Victorian sensibility.
The literary reviews of the seventies and eighties presented a solid
front against the Gallic invasion, and Vizetelly, Zola's English
publisher, was tried, fined a hundred pounds, tried again, and
imprisoned for propagating the 'foul animalism', in the words of
the *Scottish Review*, of the French masters. It is characteristic of
Victorian literary society that while the sixty-nine-year-old
Vizetelly was released because of a petition circulated in literary
circles, the naturalists' work aroused no excitement, created no
English school, was at worst reviled and at best snubbed by writers
as well as by the more philistine reviewers, churchmen, and
guardians of public morality. A grudging public accepted the
naturalists in the nineties and the first decade of the new century,
but the list of Anglo-Irish writers who actually answered to
naturalism is brief and unimportant.[1] Claims, for the most part
doubtful, have been made for the influence of French naturalism
upon George Moore, Thomas Hardy, Arnold Bennett, Henry
James, George Gissing, Hubert Crackanthorpe, H. D. Lowry,
Henry Harland, G. S. Street, Arthur Morrison, Somerset
Maugham, Rudyard Kipling, and Richard Whiteing.[2] Ignoring
the excessively minor here, one can say that George Moore alone
was an out-and-out naturalist, and then only in *A Mummer's*

[1] In spite of some carelessness, Clarence R. Decker's *The Victorian Conscience*,
New York, Twayne, 1952, particularly the chapter 'The Naturalists in England',
is valuable; I have used Mr. Decker's account of Vizetelly above.
[2] The claims appear in two studies: Margery Oliver, *The Influence of French
Naturalism on English Fiction*, University of Chicago Library, 1913; and W. C.
Frierson, *L'Influence du naturalisme français sur les romanciers anglais de 1885 à 1900*,
Paris, Girard, 1925.

Wife and *Esther Waters*. *A Modern Lover* and *A Drama in Muslin* have elements of doctrinaire naturalism, but already Moore's later style, personal and impressionistic, is apparent. Arnold Bennett was eager, in his journals, to assert kinship with the French and Russian nineteenth-century masters, but his naturalism is a pallid affair and no more than incidental. Henry James's appearance on the list confounds and amuses; in any case, for literary purposes, he must be discussed as an American. The brief for Hardy, Gissing, and Kipling must be so hedged with reservations as to explain it away. They belonged to the second phase of the novel, without doubt, but they derived from the English tradition of social realism rather than from contemporary continental models; in their work the ethical, moral strain which survived through the Edwardian period was strong. In one sense this strain was opposed to Victorian social experience, producing a *Jude the Obscure*. But in another sense it supported the dominant Victorian view at a point where doctrinaire naturalism would deny or negate it. Naturalism in France, as in the United States, presented the literary side of the struggle between science and religion, idealism and materialism. In England naturalism failed to attract support because the issues were apprehended and decided on a terrain apart from that of the novel: in poetry; in Buckle's variety of historiography; in theology and philosophy. It is likely that the decadence of the nineties was England's naturalism; the decadence and its invitation to stylization absorbed the energy which in other countries went to naturalism. Naturalism remains imperfectly understood in England,[1] though it is making an impact of sorts upon the modern novel; not in doctrinaire form, but through the work of Joyce and other experimenters, and through the broad though elusive influence of American writers upon their English contemporaries.

[1] For example, Mr. Owen Holloway said in a B.B.C. Third Programme broadcast: '... I think it was futile for narrative to court the limitations of the naturalistic drama. We cannot afford to require what one of Jane Austen's early reviewers welcomed in her, namely "the perfect appearance of reality". That could only be a picture, and a novel is not a picture—or even what Hugo called it, a variety of pictures . . .', 'The Novel and Private Life', *The Listener*, LI, 4 February 1954, 227 ff.

Even though the majority of Americans in the seventies and eighties would have found no quarrel with the English reception of French naturalism, American society did not present the solid phalanx of the English against the movement. By 1893, when Zola had completed *Les Rougon-Macquart*, most of the twenty volumes had been translated by Americans. The novels received their share of abuse as filthy, corrupting and obscene, but publishers were not imprisoned, and more important, Zola found American champions in Howells, Frank Norris, and Hamlin Garland. Perhaps the bitterness of the English attack served to blunt the sharp edge of American genteelness, but the reasons for the success of formal, doctrinaire naturalism in America are grounded deep in American literary tradition. A country founded in protest and formed in two centuries of intimacy with violence, committed by its very geography to a close and unceasing examination of the 'reality' of life on a series of frontiers, was not so likely to be startled by a literary programme which set out to deal with the unsavoury, the underside of daily experience, the supposedly unmentionable. A country long and intimately familiar with theological determinism in the systems of Calvin and Luther was not to be startled by determinism as a literary creed, nor was the leap from 'Manifest Destiny', the slogan of the Mexican war, to the determined lives of Zola's *Nana* or Norris's *McTeague* a large one. Americans, that is to say, had long known determinism in its theological and political contexts, even while they shaped a contrary philosophy, individual, pragmatic, idealistic and democratic.

These considerations are of course only peripheral to literature; in the foreground is the literary fact of the development of an American sensibility and its expression in a prose style which was quite different from anything in England, and which can be interpreted within the philosophical meaning of naturalism: the belief that 'Nature, the world of reality, has a character, a structure of its own, and [that] our opinions are true only in so far as they conform to this actual situation.' From the earliest writing on the American continent (by Englishmen), Nature, external nature, had a rich significance; first as a subject, later as a transcendent idea which helped to explain America to itself and to the world. Colonial American prose from 1598 to the Revolution, whether devoted to accounts of voyages and discoveries, theology, economics, agronomy, history, Indian relations and the general literature of geopolitics, autobiography, natural history, or the polemics of justification and complaint, had in common a lively concern for brute facts, precise detail, the rendering of actual experience. It was a practical, pragmatic literature in the main, containing a maximum of content and, with the obvious exception of theology, a minimum of speculation. In no sense was it a 'closet' literature; the writer with notebook in hand in the midst of an active life—of reality, if you will—was familiar in America long before the notebook became a sacred, ritual object to the doctrinaire naturalist. The prose style of the earliest writing in America was of course the prose of the Elizabethans and the Jacobeans: inventive, lively, rhythmical, admirably suited to the task of exploration and description; logical and ordered when it needed to be. The colonists of Massachusetts Bay were more ardent to purge their prose of embellishment than were their relatives, friends, and enemies in England. The puritan plain style became the dominant American style, for New England was more literary than the Cavalier Virginia Colony and the later southern colonies. The Elizabethan and Jacobean florid style survived, I would suggest, in the southern oratorical tradition, a style which became the dominant oratorical style of the American nineteenth century and one which is far from dead in Congress and State legislatures to this day. But the most meaningful development for American fiction was the blending over a period of many generations of the florid style, the Puritan and neo-Classic plain style, with the native strain—a realistic, proto-naturalistic style. Not illogically, the result of the blending process is most obvious in contemporary southern writing, in the elegance of Katherine Anne Porter, the rhetorical prose of Robert Penn Warren, and particularly in the prose of William Faulkner. One of the scenes in the saw-mill in *Light in August* is representative of Faulkner's middle style, the style which carries the burden of narrative in his best novels:

And on Monday he did return to work, in the overalls; they saw them, Brown and Christmas, down at the sawdust pile. They had been watching the two of them down there from the day when Brown went to work: Christmas jabbing his shovel into the sawdust slowly and steadily and hard, as though he were chopping up a buried snake ('or a man,' Mooney said) and Brown leaning on his shovel while he apparently told Christmas a story, an anecdote. Because presently he would laugh, shout with laughter, his head backflung, while beside him the other man worked with silent and unflagging savageness. Then Brown would fall to again, working for a time once again as fast as Christmas, but picking up less and less in the scoop until at last the shovel would not even touch the sawdust in its flagging arc. Then he would lean upon it again and apparently finish whatever it was that he was telling Christmas, telling to the man who did not even seem to hear his voice. As if the other were a mile away, or spoke a different language from the one he knew, Byron thought.

In addition to its kinetic effectiveness, the simile of the buried snake has the observed precision of the best of naturalism. The movement of the passage as a whole, however, is at once literary and flamboyant (the 'flagging arc' of the shovel), oral and easy; a result of Faulkner's device of writing in the third person, but adapting the cadence and diction to that of the poor-white characters.

Faulkner's relation to doctrinaire naturalism can be more clearly apprehended if we can first sort out the components which make up the blend of American naturalistic prose. Captain John Smith was not only the first professional Indian-fighter in the Virginia and Massachusetts Bay settlements, he was also a kind of land agent. Wanting to attract settlers from England to the colonies, he wrote *A Description of New England* (1616), setting forth the advantages of the New World for gentlemen and artisans, for fishermen and for labourers, in a prose whose characteristics became common in American writing:

Heer nature and liberty affords us that freely, which in *England* we want, or it costeth us deerely. What pleasure can bee more, then (being tired with any occasion a-shore, in planting Vines, Fruits, or Hearbs, in contriving their owne grounds to the pleasure of their owne minds, their Fields, Gardens, Orchards, Buildings, Ships, and other workes, &c.) to recreate themselves before their owne doores in their owne boates upon the Sea; where man, woman and childe, with a small hooke and line, by angling, may take divers sorts of excellent fish, at their pleasures? . . . He is a very bad Fisher [that] cannot kill in one day with his hooke and line, one, two, or three hundred Cods: which dressed and dried, if they bee sold there for ten shillings a hundred, though in England they will give more then twentie, may not both the servant, the master and marchant, be well content with this gaine? If a man worke but three daies in seaven, he may get more then hee can spend unlesse he will be excessive. Now that Carpenter, Mason, Gardiner, Taylor, Smith, Sailer, Forgers, or what other, may they not make this a pretty recreation though they fish but an houre in a day, to take more then they can eat in a weeke?[1]

Apart from its rough-and-ready grammar, this prose is notable for its abundance of nouns, concrete rather than abstract, standing for objects in nature, and arranged as a catalogue. Verbs are next in importance. One is reminded that in Smith's prose, in William Bradford's *History of Plymouth Plantation* (written between 1620 and 1647), in Samuel Sewall's journals for the period 1673–1729, in William Byrd's journals and histories of the Virginia region of the early eighteenth century, nouns, verbs and catalogues continue to predominate. It was not by accident that Gertrude Stein was to construct a mystique of the noun and to beatify the rhetorical device of the catalogue.

That Captain Smith was sadly in error about nature's abundance in New England, that the bitter experience of the early seventeenth century belied his catalogue of facts, is also very much to the point. From the beginning, the American continent invited dreams of what Scott Fitzgerald called the 'orgastic future', dreams which it often fulfilled, but in a manner disillusioning to the sleeping or waking dreamer, and establishing from the beginning a curious tension between the vision of reality and its literary expression; between the reality as it was conceived and as it was

[1] Reprinted from Captain John Smith, *Works, 1608–1631*, ed. Edw. Arber, English Scholar's Library, No. 16, Birmingham, 1884, in Blair, Hornberger, Stewart, *The Literature of the United States*, Chicago, Scott, Foresman, 1949, p. 24.

lived. William Carlos Williams, the great contemporary poet
who has insisted upon the uniqueness of the American language
and wrought a quiet revolution in American verse out of his
theory and practice,[1] has stated this with classic finesse:

> They saw birds with rusty breasts and called them robins. Thus
> from the start, an America of which they could have had no inkling
> drove the first settlers upon their past. They retreated for warmth
> and reassurance to something previously familiar. But at a cost.
> For what they saw were not robins. They were thrushes only
> vaguely resembling the rosy, daintier English bird. Larger, stronger,
> and in the evening of a wilder, lovelier song, actually here was some-
> thing the newcomers had never in their lives before encountered.
> Blur. Confusion. A bird that beats with his wings and slows himself
> with his tail in landing.
>
> The example is slight but enough properly to incline the under-
> standing. Strange and difficult, the new continent induced a torsion
> in the spirits of the first settlers, tearing them between the old and
> the new. And at once a split occurred in that impetus which should
> have carried them forward as one into the dangerous realities of the
> future.
>
> They found that they had not only left England but that they had
> arrived somewhere else: at a place whose pressing reality demanded
> not only a tremendous bodily devotion but as well, and more
> importunately, great powers of adaptability, a complete reconstruc-
> tion of their most intimate cultural make-up, to accord with the new
> conditions. The most hesitated and turned back in their hearts at
> the first glance.
>
> Meanwhile, nostalgically, erroneously, a robin.[2]

The puritan plain style was adopted in America as in England
on theological grounds, but one feels certain that even if puritan
plainness had not extended to prose style, the New England
plainness of expression would have evolved anyway. A form of
insurance was needed against mistaking the American thrush for
the English robin. When Samuel Sewall, a pious man of business

---

[1] I have developed this idea at length elsewhere: 'Poet and Anti-Poet', *Western
Review*, XIX, Autumn 1954, 65–72.

[2] William Carlos Williams, 'The American Background', *Selected Essays*, New
York, Random House, 1954, p. 134.

and public official of Massachusetts, wrote in his diary for January 1686, 'This day so cold that the Sacramental Bread is frozen pretty hard, and rattles sadly as broken into the Plates',[1] he was preparing the way for American naturalism; his plainness was more than a literary affectation, it belonged to a way of life, a manner of seeing. Similarly, English neo-classic literary theory was read and accepted wholeheartedly in eighteenth-century America; Addison and Pope continued to be read widely until at least 1850. Their popularity, however, was not due to a theoretical conviction on the part of the Americans, but it arose from the fact that rationalism and plainness answered to the felt and observed needs of their readers. For the same reason, John Locke was read on Virginia farms and in New England villages as a guide to action first, and as an epistemologist and philosopher of government second.

Benjamin Franklin belongs to the American eighteenth century as Voltaire belongs to the French and Joseph Addison to the English, which is to say that his career has a representative quality that cannot be explained by the sum of his activities. His service to American prose is fully as memorable as his service to science and to the American government at its difficult birth. In his *Autobiography*, Franklin wrote that he first read the *Spectator* about 1721, when he was fifteen, and that he tried to model his own style upon Addison's. He was later to perfect a style which was still Addisonian, but with a difference. Franklin reduced the Latinate elements in the Addisonian style without eliminating them; he achieved clarity without sacrificing grace and fluency. His can be described as the first native American style, for the very qualities that make Franklin the main representative of a native as opposed to an English strain. Subject-matter determined his style: as a journalist, he gained an eye for fact; as a scientist, he needed a style which would explain and report without ambiguity; as a man of business, he combined legal shrewdness with humour and grace; and as a diplomat concerned as a matter of principle to deviate from European court-practice, he perfected a style that was logical and direct, blunt without clumsiness. Franklin's imagination was utilitarian and scientific; in no sense was he an

[1] Samuel Sewall's *Diary*, ed. Mark Van Doren, New York, 1927, p. 29.

artist. His importance to art is that his style became a fundament in later American writing. The contemporary European notion that American writers are only incidentally artists, if artists at all, owes much to Benjamin Franklin.

The rationalistic, deistic aspect of the American eighteenth century, not omitting the American version of the eighteenth-century theory of 'natural' man, is summed up in the writing of Thomas Paine. Paine did not set foot on American soil until the age of thirty-seven, nor did he put pen to paper for publication until 1775, when he was thirty-eight. Yet Paine's angry career as the polemicist of the American Revolution is even more important for literature than Franklin's. His prose is American, and his contribution to the pattern of Franklin's prose was anger and drive, qualities appropriate to the existing situation, and needed to take the curse of slightly inspired commonplaceness away from writing such as Franklin's. Paine set the plain style on fire, often doing less than justice to the complexity of the ideas he was treating, but driving his points home with absolute clarity. The peroration of *Common Sense* reads in part:

> Ye that tell us of harmony and reconciliation, can ye restore to us the time that is past? Can ye give to prostitution its former innocence? neither can ye reconcile Britain and America. The last cord now is broken, the people of England are presenting addresses against us. There are injuries which nature cannot forgive; she would cease to be nature if she did. As well can the lover forgive the ravisher of his mistress, as the continent forgive the murders of Britain. The Almighty hath implanted in us these unextinguishable feelings for good and wise purposes. They are the guardians of his image in our hearts. They distinguish us from the herd of common animals. The social compact would dissolve, and justice be extirpated from the earth, or have only a casual existence were we callous to the touches of affection. The robber and the murderer would often escape unpunished, did not the injuries which our tempers sustain, provoke us into justice.[1]

Published a few months before the outbreak of hostilities in 1776, *Common Sense* might look like the text for a rabble-rousing speech;

[1] *The Life and Works of Thomas Paine*, ed. W. M. Van der Weyde, New York, 1925, II, pp. 149–150.

there lies the relevance of Paine's style, however. *Common Sense* was a pamphlet, written to be read, but Paine used the turns and cadences of spoken, or at least orated, language; a development which American writers fostered and made into a native contribution to English prose, particularly the prose of naturalism. Paine's strong anti-intellectual bent was again a quality of American naturalism.

To this point I have tried to indicate the remoter sources of a native American style, and to demonstrate how even in its beginnings that style anticipated significantly the special concerns of naturalism. Next I should like to try to account for the curious relationship between romanticism and naturalism in America, a relationship that did not exist in either continental or English naturalism. Unless this relationship is satisfactorily explained, much recent American writing cannot be properly understood.

Frank Norris, the noisiest American theorist of doctrinaire naturalism, emphasized at length what he saw to be the 'romantic' element of Zola's work and insisted dogmatically upon the necessity for the American naturalist to be a romantic, to devote himself to grand themes and extraordinary events. He noted that the difference between Howells's realism and Zola's romanticism is that Howells's characters are ordinary, bourgeois; they are the people across the street from us. But in *Les Rougon-Macquart* the characters are extraordinary:

> The naturalist takes no note of common people, common in so far as their interests, their lives, and the things that occur in them are common, are ordinary. Terrible things must happen to the characters of the naturalistic tale. They must be twisted from the quiet, uneventful round of every-day life, and flung into the throes of a vast and terrible drama that works itself out in unleashed passions, in blood, and in sudden death. The world of M. Zola is a world of big things; the enormous, the formidable, the terrible, is what counts; no teacup tragedies here.

Norris lists at lurid length the unhappy fate of Zola's heroes, then continues:

> Everything is extraordinary, imaginative, grotesque even, with a vague note of terror quivering throughout like the vibration of an

ominous and low-pitched diapason. It is all romantic, at times unmistakably so, ... closely resembling the work of all modern roman-
ticists, Hugo [*sic*]. We have the same huge dramas, the same,
enormous scenic effects, the same love of the extraordinary, the vast,
the monstrous, and the tragic.

Naturalism is a form of romanticism. . . .[1]

It is just to remark of this that Norris was mistaking for
'romanticism' Zola's inveterate moralizing. Zola was far from
being his own best exemplar. At the same time, Norris was
justifying his own practice in the novel; his theory of the romantic
aspect of naturalism is an accurate description of *McTeague*, of his
incomplete epic of wheat, as well as his more minor efforts.
Above all, Norris's theory is the logical culmination of one trend
in the American romantic movement, a movement whose connections with European romanticism have only been surveyed,
and whose meanings we are only beginning to understand.

As with its European counterpart, the motifs of American
romanticism extend deep into the eighteenth century and even
into the seventeenth, appearing in opposition to the predominant
neo-classic theory. Daniel Gookin's seventeenth-century historical studies of the Indians, John Lawson's early eighteenth-century
historical accounts of Carolina—more folk-lore than history—but
more particularly the mid-eighteenth-century work of the Quaker
John Woolman and of Crèvecœur established the romantic view
of the 'noble' savage and helped to propagate a Rousseau-like
vision of virtuous man living close to the bosom of nature in the
New World.[2] William Bartram's *Travels through North and South*

---

[1] Quoted in Lars Åhnebrink, *The Beginnings of Naturalism in American Fiction*,
Upsala, American Institute, 1950, p. 158. Norris's intuition of the conjunction
between romanticism and naturalism is accurate with reference to many writers;
one thinks of Flaubert's *La Tentation de Saint Antoine* and *Salammbô*; of Heming-
way's early romantic verse; of Faulkner's Keatsian, pastoral poems in *The Marble
Faun* (1924); and of Norris's own early writing. His first published essay was
'Ancient Armour', 1889, and he wrote three cantos of a romantic narrative poem,
'Yvernelle', in 1891.

[2] The most authoritative short account is Kenneth B. Murdock's 'Woolman,
Crèvecœur, and the Romantic Vision of America', in A. H. Quinn, ed., *The
Literature of the American People*, New York, Appleton-Century-Crofts, 1951,
pp. 124–136.

Carolina, Georgia, East and West Florida (1791), based on his experiences prior to 1778, is a good example of the exploratory nature of this strain in American eighteenth-century prose. A painter and the son of a noted botanist, William Bartram had the naturalist's eye for precise detail together with the romantic (and naturalistic) fondness for the exotic, the vast, and the sublime, qualities which recommended his work to so varied a group as Coleridge, Wordsworth, Chateaubriand, Southey, Campbell, Mrs. Hemans, Shelley, and Tennyson.[1] Although Bartram did not confuse the robin with the thrush, he did confuse crocodiles with alligators, using both terms to describe the beasts during his travels in Florida. He was at once a prototype of the naturalistic writer who moves with notebook in hand, and the kind of pantheist who later would be called transcendentalist; the two elements combined were distinctly in the tradition which produced Frank Norris and Jack London. Even though Bartram's Seminole savages are noble and his alligators crocodiles, when he describes their habits his prose is sharp and clear, the product of exact observation:

> . . . On turning a point or projection of the river bank, at once I beheld a great number of hillocks or small pyramids, resembling hay cocks, ranged like an encampment along the banks, they stood fifteen or twenty yards distant from the water, on a high marsh, about four feet perpendicular above the water; I knew them to be the nests of the crocodile, having had a description of them before, and now expected a furious and general attack, as I saw several large crocodiles swimming abreast of these buildings. These nests being so great a curiosity to me, I was determined at all events immediately to land and examine them. . . .
> The nests or hillocks are of the form of an obtuse cone, four feet high and four or five feet in diameter at their bases; they are constructed with mud, grass and herbage: at first they lay a floor of this kind of tempered mortar upon the ground, upon which they deposit a layer of eggs, and upon this a stratum of mortar seven or eight inches in thickness, and then another layer of eggs, and in this manner one stratum upon another, nearly to the top: I believe they commonly lay from one to two hundred eggs in a nest: these are

[1] Murdock, p. 135.

I

hatched I suppose by the heat of the sun, and perhaps the vegetable substances mixed with the earth, ...[1]

Sixty years later, Emerson was to rationalize both precise observation of detail in nature, and pantheism into a theory of language. In *Nature* (1836), one of the basic documents of American transcendentalism, Emerson wrote in the sub-section, 'Language':

1. Words are signs of natural facts.
2. Particular natural facts are symbols of particular spiritual facts.
3. Nature is the symbol of spirit.

'The use of natural history', he continued,

> is to give us aid in supernatural history; the use of the outer creation, to give us language for the beings and changes of the inward creation. Every word which is used to express a moral or intellectual fact, if traced to its root, is found to be borrowed from some material appearance. . . . It is not words only that are emblematic; it is things which are emblematic. Every natural fact is a symbol of some spiritual fact. Every appearance in nature corresponds to some state of the mind, and that state of the mind can only be described by presenting that natural appearance as its picture.[2]

Nature, then, is of overwhelming importance in the history of American prose, both in retrospect and in prospect. It derives from the cowshed and kitchen-hearth realism of the early period, while both Emerson's theory and practice, theology apart, provided a model for American writers from Thoreau to Hemingway.

Emerson practised what he preached. His prose is epigrammatic, concise, rich in images taken from everyday life, at once literary and close to New England speech. His journals are fascinating for their style and as a record of a full nineteenth-century life. When he thinks of power, an abstraction, he must find 'a material appearance': 'Don't trust children with edge tools. Don't trust man, great God, with more power than he has, until he has learned to use that little better. . . . Put a button on

---

[1] Reprinted from *The Travels of William Bartram*, New York, 1940, in *Literature of the United States*, p. 59.

[2] *The Complete Essays and other Writings of Ralph Waldo Emerson*, ed. Brooks Atkinson, New York, Modern Library, 1940, pp. 14–15.

the foil till the young fencers have learned not to put each other's eyes out.' Or again, 'What is there of the divine in a load of bricks? What is there of the divine in a barber's shop? . . . Much. All.' Instead of measuring natural objects, like Bartram, he records them in a striking phrase. He takes an April walk near Cambridge: 'After much wandering and seeing many things, four snakes gliding up and down a hollow for no purpose that I could see—not to eat, not for love, but only gliding'; then follows a catalogue of other natural objects which he has seen in the woods. His imagination always goes from the abstract to the specific: 'The Southerner asks concerning man, "How does he fight?" the Northerner asks, "What can he do?" '[1] By indirection, Emerson himself is the best witness to his friend Thoreau's total sympathy with his theory of language. When Thoreau died of tuberculosis in 1862, Emerson made the funeral address, which he concluded by quoting from Thoreau's unpublished manuscripts sentences to illustrate Thoreau's 'power of description and literary excellence'. They illustrate as well Thoreau's care to cultivate his powers of perception, his wit, his closeness to objects in nature, his concern for innate reality behind exterior form. While he was in an important sense a follower of Emerson, he was his own man, an original whose entire life was given over to the creation of a style. The ascending scale of intensity in the following results from the order Emerson gave them:

Some circumstantial evidence is very strong, as when you find a trout in the milk.

The chub is a soft fish, and tastes like boiled brown paper salted.

If I wish for a horse-hair for my compass-sight, I must go to the stable; but the hair-bird, with her sharp eyes, goes to the road.

We are strictly confined to our men to whom we give liberty.

Nothing is so much to be feared as fear. Atheism may comparatively be popular with God himself.

I ask to be melted. You can only ask of the metals that they be tender to the fire that melts them. To nought else can they be tender.[2]

[1] *The Heart of Emerson's Journals*, ed. Bliss Perry, Boston, 1939, pp. 55; 82; 85; 113.

[2] Emerson, 'Thoreau', *Complete Essays*, pp. 912–913.

The scale of intensity moves from mere wit allied with observation, to parable, in the hair-bird sentence, on to cool idea—fear and liberty, and finally to personal revelation. But the entire scale still depends for fullest effect upon accuracy of observation.

I would suggest that these fugitive sayings of Thoreau in their ascending scale of intensity can be interpreted as a metaphor of the connection between American naturalism and ideas in the novel. Thoreau's study of nature was not really scientific, but literary and aesthetic; he seems to have been aware of the fact, and from the evidence of his journals was attempting to become more scientific at the time of his death. He was obsessed, that is, with actuality, exterior fact, which concealed the hidden essence, reality. The two naturalisms appear side by side: the American literary tradition or habit of recording nature pragmatically, and the accompanying compulsion to order nature into a science—what I have called 'doctrinaire' naturalism. This is to deny Philip Rahv's acute, but I think erroneous, distinction between naturalism and realism, when he writes:

> I know of no hard and fast rules that can be used to distinguish the naturalist method from the methods of realism generally. It is certainly incorrect to say that the difference is marked by the relative density of detail. . . . A more conclusive test . . . is [the] treatment of the relation of character to background. I would classify as naturalistic that type of realism in which the individual is portrayed not merely as subordinate to his background but as wholly determined by it—that type of realism, in other words, in which the environment displaces its inhabitants in the role of the hero.[1]

This is accurate for European doctrinaire naturalism, but it fails to recognize the distinctions which the American tradition interposed. The American naturalist goes to actuality to uncover the hidden essence of reality, in part out of a conviction that ideas can only be presented in such a context—never as a philosophy, in the manner of the continental novelist.

It has been observed that neither Emerson nor Thoreau thought of himself as an artist,[2] but their importance to literary art in

[1] *Image and Idea*, pp. 132–133.
[2] Perry Miller, ed., *The Transcendentalists*, Cambridge, Mass., Harvard University Press, 1950, Introduction, p. 9.

America is enormous. Their style is the quintessence of two centuries of development; they stand between the remote American
past and the American present, making viable the romanticism
which continues to characterize American writing. Contemporary with Emerson's and Thoreau's high seriousness was an anti-
romantic, illiterate, low clownishness that developed slowly into
literature and prepared still another soil for American naturalism.
I mean, of course, the vernacular literature of the backwoods
settlements in which folk-lore and history mingled with the boring
tall-tales and the newspaper anecdote, the 'humorous' political
commentary and the satirical sketch. Daniel Boone and Kit
Carson, actual historical figures, became legends, American versions of knights errant wearing coonskin and deerhide instead of
armour; the backwoods scene supplied the origins of the short
story in Augustus B. Longstreet's *Georgia Scenes* (1835), and the
minor local-colour fiction of Bret Harte and Joaquin Miller
belonged to the same movement. Platform entertainers and
journalists, from Jack Downing in the Jacksonian period, through
Artemus Ward, Orpheus C. Kerr, and Petroleum V. Nasby in
the Civil War, to Mr. Dooley at the end of the century, established a convention of crude burlesque passing for political satire,
written in close, all-too-close, imitation of dialect and oral speech,
which later naturalists took over. The realism of Longstreet's
stories, or the brutish nastiness of G. W. Harris's 'Sut Lovingood'
yarns went far beyond the nineteenth-century English convention
of realism, and can only be seen as a form of naturalism.

The main service of backwoods writing was to folk-lore rather
than to literature, except for the figure of Mark Twain, who com-
pounded the various elements of humour, oral speech, dialect, the
tall-tale, and the backwoods setting into high literary art. *Huckleberry Finn* forgives many backwoods literary sins, while the
pessimistic determinism of Mark Twain's final period is a distinct
counterpart to that aspect of doctrinaire naturalism. American
vernacular literature, written either by educated men who disguised their education in the uneducated speech of their characters, or by men like G. W. Harris who were virtually without
education, accustomed a wide American audience to the literary

treatment of themes which more genteel writers avoided as indecent, crude, and sub-literary; its element of folk-lore reflected the American tendency to create mythic, generalized types, and anticipated the habit of naturalism to combine specific detail with the generalized, the banal-typical, and ultimately the mythic. And throughout the vernacular literature, apparently anti-romantic and often discouragingly down-to-earth, runs the mystique of nature and the superiority of natural man—the Daniel Boones and the Davy Crocketts—to the urban, educated, sophisticated man; a doctrine of nature that is not remote from the Emersonian, transcendental formulation.

The conventional mental image, both American and European, of nineteenth-century American society emphasizes the opportunistic, the pragmatic and the optimistic, the American willingness to reach out towards the 'orgastic future'. This image is hardly inaccurate, for it is the construction of impeccable authority, from Tocqueville, Dickens, Trollope, Thackeray, Arnold, and Mark Twain, to Henry Adams; one thinks of Mark Twain's young man in *The Gilded Age*, who brags, 'A year ago I hadn't a nickel to my name, and today I owe a million dollars.' Yet this image ignores one entire side of the American nineteenth-century mind, that side whose political meaning was contained in the Civil War, that bloodiest of wars which seemed to deny the very axioms of American society, and whose imprint pressed heavily upon the American consciousness. The most superficial reader is aware of the shattering effect of the Franco-Prussian war upon the French consciousness, yet the Civil War was more than an American 1870; it reached even deeper into the social fundament. One result for fiction was an impressive novel of the Civil War by John William DeForest, *Miss Ravenel's Conversion from Secession to Loyalty* (1867), which can only be described as a naturalistic treatment of the war by an un-doctrinaire naturalist. In conception, in documentary quality, in precise description of battlefield carnage and lifelike portraiture of character, the novel might well have come from a talented follower of Zola. DeForest's presentation of the idea of war anticipated more recent work. His earlier fiction showed him to be a follower of the current sentimental-romantic formula; that his later work reverted to that formula is probably explained by the failure of *Miss Ravenel's Conversion* to find a public. The public is notably fickle regarding war novels published too soon after the shooting has stopped. Stephen Crane, another writer who came to naturalism out of instinct rather than doctrine, had better luck with *The Red Badge of Courage* in 1895; that finest of Civil War novels was widely read upon publication and has since taken its merited place as a classic American novel.[1] Whether Crane did or did not know Zola and European naturalism, he wrote in a style that is Emersonian in clarity and sharpness of detail, and he presented war not in a romantic glow, but in an anti-romantic vision of horror. His conception of the experience of war, and of the rest of human experience as well, had a distinct affinity with naturalistic determinism. He resembles Hardy in his presentation of nature indifferent to man's struggle, but he is closer to textbook naturalism than Hardy in his selection of theme and treatment of detail. One can only agree with an English commentator on Crane's first 'naturalistic' novel, *Maggie*, that Crane put to use the materials he found about him; his picture of a girl of the streets is very like that to be found in the newspaper and magazine writers of his day.[2]

The trauma of the Civil War helps to account for the cordial American reception of English and continental *fin de siècle* writing, for the appearance of a native version of that writing, and, of course, for the pessimistic and deterministic vogue of doctrinaire naturalism. The popular image of the optimistic American must be countered by the fact that the nihilistic, doom-crying, half-baked, pseudo-scientific *Degeneration* of Max Nordau was one of the most popular books of non-fiction in America between 1895 and 1900. Nordau's thesis—that the western European was increasingly the victim of neurosis and disease, and that civilization, particularly in the arts, was characterized by

[1] A fierce struggle rages among critics as to whether Crane was or was not a doctrinaire naturalist; my only concern here is to present Crane in the line of 'native' naturalism, as a writer who treated the materials at hand in a characteristic manner.

[2] Marcus Cunliffe, 'Stephen Crane and the American Background of *Maggie*', *American Quarterly*, VII, Spring 1955, 31–45.

vanity and conceit, by Wagnerian mysticism and eroticism, by the 'idiocy' of Maeterlinck, the 'crazy' verse of Whitman, the egomania of the French Parnassians, the decadence of Huysmans and Wilde—was widely accepted in America, even though Nordau exempted the Americans, in the main, from the European afflictions.[1] Zola's ideas by contrast to *Degeneration* were Peter Pan-like. American doctrinaire naturalism, at any rate, found a certain nourishment in the foetid wind blown from Nordau's bellows.

One might object that the account to this point of the appearance of one American variety of prose could with equal ease be applied to 'realism'. The intention is not to obscure the traditional, textbook distinction between naturalism and realism, but to suggest that the distinction, borrowed from England, is not a useful one when it is applied to American literary history. The realism of Defoe, Fielding, and Smollett never really made a full appearance in the American novel. Their realism had an element of stylization, a satirical intent, for which American society was not ready. The nineteenth-century realism of Jane Austen and the novelists of manners had its American counterpart in Cooper's social novels, in Henry Adams, Henry James, and in William Dean Howells. But the social realism of the novel of manners is markedly different from the realism of the backwoods vernacular school, and it possesses nothing of the romantic-naturalistic strain I have been tracing.

What, then, was American doctrinaire naturalism like? And did it differ so materially from European naturalism? For all the fuss raised over the literary sin of doctrinaire naturalism, American doctrinaire naturalists were few in number and negligible in accomplishment: Frank Norris, Hamlin Garland, Jack London, Theodore Dreiser, James T. Farrell: a brief roster. As to accomplishment, Garland has already found the literary oblivion he so richly deserves; his work is sentimental and jejune. Norris's *McTeague* and the first two volumes of the trilogy his early death

[1] Max Nordau, *Degeneration*, New York, 1895, pp. 101; 181; 232; 238; 290. Grant C. Knight, *The Critical Period in American Literature*, Chapel Hill, University of North Carolina Press, pp. 70–75, discusses Nordau's American reception.

cut short, *The Octopus* and *The Pit*, are splendid in isolated sections, but hardly sustained, never equal to Norris's ambitions. With the possible exception of *The Call of the Wild* and one or two short stories, Jack London is interesting as a literary object rather than as a subject. His journalistic versions of Darwinian clichés— 'the survival of the fittest', 'the beast in man'—are read seriously only in the Soviet Union and its satellites as studies in the decline of capitalism. Dreiser, the Caliban of the American novel, proudly untutored and defiantly untutorable, wrote a long shelf of novels and autobiography, of which *An American Tragedy* (1925) is an undoubted masterpiece. Farrell, who has taken Dreiser as his master, has not improved on the master's sullen indifference to literary craft. The result has been another long shelf of novels, short stories, autobiography, literary polemics and cries of Marxian agony, among which only *Judgment Day*, the third volume of his *Studs Lonigan* trilogy, seems likely to find a permanent place. Mr. Farrell is still a young man, but he is so committed to a private dogma which has already betrayed him into sterile repetition that one would not predict from him a second *American Tragedy*, the best that could be hoped for.

The small success and the large failure of doctrinaire naturalism can be charged to the adjective 'doctrinaire'. Norris and the rest were prisoners of their own theories, particularly of the theory that the novel writes itself. Norris wrote to a reviewer in 1899,

> What pleased me most in your review of 'McTeague' was the 'disdaining all pretensions to style.' It is precisely what I try most to avoid. I detest 'fine writing,' 'rhetoric,' 'elegant English,'— tommy-rot. Who cares for fine style! Tell your yarn and let your style go to the devil. We don't want literature, we want life.[1]

None of the other naturalists would have quarrelled with Norris's curious anti-intellectual explosion. It disguises the ancient Platonic notion of inspiration, which, combined with the naturalists' preoccupation with documentation and their dedication to the

[1] Quoted in Åhnebrink, *The Beginnings of Naturalism in American Fiction*, p. 117. I am indebted to Mr. Åhnebrink, as anyone must be who writes of American naturalism, for his sifting of the facts and for his wise interpretations in an area which had been opaque and neglected.

vast, encompassing theme, made for lack of control, grandiosity, and fatal prolixity. Disdaining elegance, Norris, Garland, and Dreiser often fell into an embarrassing pseudo-elegance, the diction of the self-made writer who wants to prove that he too can write.

The basic European element in American naturalism was the dubious adaptation of the laws of science to the 'laws' of society, which determined men's actions. Norris insisted on the Romantic aspect of naturalism, and with Garland added still another notion, that the naturalistic novel should be American in character. Norris hated what he called the 'New England School' of Irving, Holmes, Lowell, Hawthorne, Howells, and particularly the local colourists, as imitative and superficial.[1] The novel of the future was to concern itself with American themes and scenes; a new literature was to arise not from the ashes of the old, but from new ground. In a sense, Norris joined the Emerson of 'The American Scholar', for Emerson too in 1837 had called for an American literature that would reject European models. They differed in that Emerson was not for a moment asking for a narrowly provincial literature, while Norris and Garland were. The work of American doctrinaire naturalism is ultimately provincial, in theory as in practice. In protest against England, against genteel social realism, and the fairy-tale historical romance of the 1890s, they adopted a European model and made it paradoxically into a vehicle for nationalistic provincialism. In their average work, length took the place of intensity and documentation the place of insight. Consciously rejecting the 'literary' and honestly indignant at social abuse, they cultivated a proletarian prejudice which made them the darlings of Marxist criticism with its reverence for the proletarian subject. Manner and technique were sacrificed to matter, although the naturalists made much of the necessity for objectivity. Terror, Norris said, ought to be dramatically implicit; it is not necessary for the novelist to explain or to put in the mouth of his character that a scene is terrible.[2]

The doctrine of objectivity, like the idea of determinism,

---

[1] Frank Norris, *Works*, New York, Doubleday, Doran, 1928, 7 vols., VII, 107.
[2] Norris, *Works*, VII, 188.

amounted ultimately to moral obtuseness; it accounts for the curious blunting of effect in parts of *The Octopus* and for long, dry wastes in Dreiser's work. In their best novels, the naturalists were not objective, and their moral indignation, implicit but unmistakably present, added to their stature. In spite of their credo, the naturalists performed the important function of turning the novel into an instrument of protest while maintaining, almost in spite of themselves, the novel as an art-form. They extended the traditional American belief that truth resides not in intellectual dialectic but in things—objects in the natural, tangible world. At the same time they performed a disservice to themselves and to literature with their anti-intellectualism, their suspicion of the imagination, and their elevation of action high above contemplation.

The importance of naturalism in America obviously cannot be accounted for by the accomplishment of the doctrinaire naturalists. The bitterness of formalist critics against naturalism is due to the fact that doctrinaire naturalism left a legacy to the later American novel which detracts from purity of form. If the only achievements of naturalism were the factual lists and the heavy clowning of Sinclair Lewis, the sub-literary parodies of Erskine Caldwell, the sentimental film-scripts of Steinbeck, the double-breasted bogus historical novel of Frank Yerby, the disasters to journalism of the Luce publications, or the *raffinement* of *New Yorker*-naturalism, one could only share the animus. This chapter could have been eliminated if the only contribution of naturalism to the American literary atmosphere had been H. L. Mencken's ranting espousal of the underside of American diction, his failure to distinguish between vitality and corruption in American language.[1]

I think that the virulence of the attack on naturalism is due in part to the White Russian reactionary attitude of many formalist critics; it is easier to look back and to assess the good old days than

[1] Mencken's high reputation both in America and abroad is puzzling. Only Marius Bewley has seen the meaning of the threat to American culture in Mencken's obscurantist theory of language: 'Mencken and the American Language', *The Complex Fate*, pp. 193–211.

to face the bad new days, and the critic need not risk his good name by quixotic judgments. Doctrinaire naturalism furthered the marriage of catastrophe to imagination, a ceremony whose sanctity many readers suspect, by codifying, in its emphasis upon protest, the long-standing, uneasy relationship between the American writer and society, while by its doctrine of objectivity it made possible some of the more successful experiments of the modern period.

It would be pleasant to write about the novel without any reference to the writer's place in modern society; the subject has become banal and suspect, yet it demands still further treatment. It is a fact that from Poe and Hawthorne to Whitman and James, American writers became increasingly aware that their best work went unread and that they were begrudged any position whatsoever in society. This is summed up in Melville's phrase, 'I feel myself an exile here.' The naturalists were not content merely to withdraw and passively to observe. Their solution was to turn upon society, to rebel and to reject, to discover their subject in the social underworld and to cram it, in effect, down society's throat. They set out to enrage; *épater le bourgeois* was more than their unspoken slogan, it was their aesthetic. When Norris wrote, 'We don't want literature, we want life', he was setting a course for American writing of the next forty years that was more erratic than he knew. For in separating 'life' from literature, the naturalist at once denied his own source of strength, and formed a cult of the artist, the defiant Byronic figure who lived apart from society to burn and scourge it with his wrath. As Byron maintained the fiction that he merely dabbled in poetry and did not write for money, so the American writer came to pretend that he was neither artist, intellectual, nor man of contemplation, but rather a man of action.[1] At the same time, the secret pride in being a writer led to a fondness for the Bohemian, whether in Greenwich Village, Harlem, Chicago, Paris, or San Francisco. Until very recently, the intellectual appeared in American fiction

[1] Malcolm Cowley remarks that in the entire metropolitan New York telephone directory, only one person lists himself as a writer. *The Literary Situation*, p. 212.

only as an object of satire—as a blockheaded Ph.D. in Sinclair Lewis, or as a craven villain busy selling out the working man in Dos Passos. Writers, however, abound as characters, thinly disguising the autobiography.

Thomas Wolfe, who owed a great deal to doctrinaire naturalism, wrote a collective portrait in all his novels of the dedicated writer, yet he hated intellectuals, depicting them as frauds, homosexuals and dilettantes, satirizing them as cultists, esoteric snobs, and devotees of intellectual fashion. Wolfe resembled Sherwood Anderson in his conception of writing as obsession. At the age of forty, Anderson literally walked out of a prospering business, a house and family, not so much to write—he had already begun writing—but to *be a writer*. In all of Wolfe's attitudinizing about himself and his troubles, the same distinction was always present: the distinction between writing and being a writer. For both men, the bohemian fallacy led finally to desiccation and inflation. They found social alienation a source of strength, but their self-imposed alienation from intellectuals, their obscurantism that is, was finally crippling. Hemingway, on the other hand, has often assumed a kind of obscurantism out of mockery. He deliberately created the legend of himself as soldier, newspaperman, *aficionado* of the bullfight, skeet-shooter, revolutionist, boxer, lover, big-game hunter, fisherman—anything but the careful artist which in fact he is.

Again we must pause for definition. Since Marx, the word 'intellectual' has had one meaning on the Continent and quite another in England and America. In continental usage, 'intellectual' defines anyone who uses his mind and pays allegiance to rationalism, virtually anyone, in fact, who can read and write. This meaning is extended to define a rough class division; somewhere in the European's mind is an archetypal separation between the brutish mass, the unlettered peasantry and proletariat, and the lettered, educated class, the 'intellectuals'. In English and American usage, the term 'intellectual' more often than not is an insult. It is associated with pose, pretension, and fraud. In England it implies gravy-spots on the waistcoat, indifference to games, physical and intellectual slovenliness. In America it implies politics

of the extreme Left, subversion of the constitution, hostility to
religion and the family, and a failure to share the American
reverence for actuality and observed fact. The only equivalents
in the American language for 'intellectual' are terms of denigration: 'highbrow', 'egg-head', 'long-hair'. Bertrand Russell once
wrote, 'I have never called myself an intellectual, and nobody has
ever dared to call me one in my presence.

'I think an intellectual may be defined as a person who pretends
to have more intellect than he has, and I hope that this definition
does not fit me.'[1] Russell poses the difficulty; we have no word in
English to define the concept. 'Intelligentsia' is even worse in
association, and one turns back to 'intellectual', meaning the
person of some education who pays a certain attention to rational
processes, and including by definition the novelist, as well as
most poets. Anti-intellectualism implies a schizoid condition in
the person of the writer who pretends to despise his own mental
processes and to demean the function of criticism. Thomas
Wolfe was schizoid in this sense, if not paranoid; so were Anderson and Sinclair Lewis. American literary journalists are commonly downright philistine in their schizophrenia, while their
English counterparts, in the main, are intellectual in their approach
to literature, though they would at once resent the description and
be flattered by it. This ambivalence is a direct result of modern
catastrophe, and it became explicit in the naturalistic movement.

Anti-intellectualism has accounted for many of the contradictions, excesses, and absurdities of naturalism, but the efforts of
the anti-intellectual to apprehend truth have been exerted with
the intelligence of the intellectual. The hypothesis that doctrinaire
naturalism has declined because 'What was once a means of
treating material truthfully has been turned . . . into a mere
convention of truthfulness'[2] is probably valid, but it does not take
into account the rather recent necessity for literary truthfulness.

---

[1] Quoted by H. O. Alexander, 'Communications', *Encounter*, IV, No. 6,
June 1955, 71. 'Professor' is also a term of denigration in the U.S., though not in
England. W. H. Auden's 'Note on Intellectuals' is to the point: 'To the man-in-
the-street, who, I'm sorry to say/Is a keen observer of life,/The word Intellectual
suggests straight away/A man who's untrue to his wife.'

[2] Rahv, *Image and Idea*, p. 137.

It is not long ago that Hardy gave up the novel because he felt that he could not deal honestly with themes that were important to him. It is easy to forget, in our plethora of sexual sewage, that simply in terms of subject-matter the naturalists made possible a necessary maturity in social attitudes towards sex, and sex apart, they introduced the notion that any and all human experience is material for the novel. Subject-matter in itself is of minor importance; the novel profited from a widening in the range of sensibility which the perceptions of the doctrinaire naturalists, however limited, made possible. The naturalists' idea of objectivity, falsely based and unworkable as it proved, had desirable results for modern prose style. The ideal of objectivity, the felt need in writers so diverse as James, Joyce and Gide to eliminate themselves as omnipotent authors from their material, led to the development of stream-of-consciousness techniques and to the widening of the possibilities of interior monologue. Joyce was a vocal admirer of naturalism, particularly of Ibsen. He out-naturalized the naturalists in his scrupulous accuracy of detail.[1] The very fact that Joyce so far transcended the effects of the early naturalists is proof of the importance of their work; they made possible the enlarging of the art of the novel by Joyce and others, writers who might seem to owe little to the naturalists' naïve theories and frequent inferior performances. The methods of

[1] Richard Ellmann notes: 'His imitation of reality extends painstakingly to insuring the accuracy of his details. Some curious letters to his aunt Josephine Murray have survived; in one he asks whether there are trees, and if so what kind, behind the Star of the Sea Church. In another he asks her to go to 7 Eccles Street to measure the distance from the sidewalk to the area to make sure that Bloom in his novel could have managed that descent. Joyce had seen his friend Byrne, whose exact height and weight are those which he attributes to Bloom, negotiate the drop successfully; but since Byrne was more athletic than Bloom, he needed to be sure that the distance was not too great. An even more striking anecdote of Joyce's Naturalism is that of Samuel Beckett. Beckett was taking dictation from Joyce for *Finnegans Wake*; there was a knock on the door and Joyce said, "Come in." Beckett, who hadn't heard the knock, by mistake wrote down "Come in" as part of the dictated text. Afterwards he read it back to Joyce who said, "What's that 'Come in'?" "That's what you dictated," Beckett replied. Joyce thought for a moment, realizing that Beckett hadn't heard the knock; then he said, "Let it stand." The very fact that the misunderstanding had occurred in actuality gave it prestige for Joyce.' 'The Background of Ulysses', *Kenyon Review*, XVI, No. 3, Summer 1954, 359–360.

naturalism, clumsy and obtuse, were nevertheless of first importance to the later novel. It was their peculiar virtue that those
methods were moving in the direction of a new sensibility in
fiction, at once towards exterior catastrophe and the interior
revolution: naturalism, to say it another way, anticipated the work
of both Virginia Woolf and Ernest Hemingway. I think of the
first paragraph of *The Old Man and the Sea*:

> He was an old man who fished alone in a skiff in the Gulf Stream and
> he had gone eighty-four days now without taking a fish. In the first
> forty days a boy had been with him. But after forty days without a
> fish the boy's parents had told him that the old man was now
> definitely and finally *salao*, which is the worst form of unlucky, and
> the boy had gone at their orders in another boat which caught three
> good fish the first week. It made the boy sad to see the old man come
> in each day with his skiff empty and he always went down to help
> him carry either the coiled lines or the gaff and harpoon and the sail
> that was furled around the mast. The sail was patched with flour
> sacks and, furled, it looked like the flag of permanent defeat.

The predominance of concrete nouns here, the attention to lines,
gaff, harpoon, and sail patched with flour sacks indicates the way
in which the modern writer is related to doctrinaire naturalism.
He wishes to establish the truth of things in nature; this is not
merely the convention of truth, but a passionate concern for
actuality. Hemingway is thus related to naturalism in the same
degree that Emerson was. Emerson's gliding snakes, not to eat,
not for love, belong to the real world because of the style in which
they are expressed. So Hemingway's patched sail. The degree of
stylization he brings to the naturalist's world at once removes
him from their world and places him firmly in that world.
Hemingway has frequently been explained, or explained away,
as a brutal celebrator of violence, an immature boy-man, gifted
but finally trivial. Such a reading fails to recognize that the electric
quality of Hemingway's violence derives not from brutality but
from the disparateness of the natural, actual world, and man's
failure to live up to his own ideal of himself; it is the highest
literary art rather than an attitude or a journalistic habit. The
difference between the English and the American reception of

Hemingway—the difference between veiled hostility and reluctant surrender—is the measure of the difference in degree of penetration by naturalism. Englishmen are made uncomfortable by Hemingway's apparent excess of actuality, while to the American the literary registering of the real world is where all writing begins.

Naturalism performed still another service to the modern novel by its insistence upon the place of ideas. Departing from pseudo-science to arrive at environment as fundamental to the movement of character, the naturalist tried to see entire societies. In technique he resorted to the *roman-fleuve*, but that device did not solve his problem. Thus he was forced to experiment with idea, and he attempted to work out meaningful ways of presenting a literary idea. This led for the most part only to preaching, or to a repetition of the clumsy devices of the traditional novelist. But the naturalist's failures made possible later successes. Their failures resulted from their reliance upon ideology as opposed to idea, and upon their self-induced blindness to the aesthetic content of ideas in the novel. At the same time they should be given credit for their understanding, however primitive, of the need for the extension of the literary idea to the novel. Their impatience with conventional realism and with woolly romanticism was caused by their awareness that life offered more than the novelist was taking; that ideas needed somehow to be expressed not in syllogisms but as forces that suffuse society, all human activity. The task for the modern novel was to carry forward that primitive apprehension of the naturalists to the point where ideas were not only seen in their naked social context, but valued for their utility in giving shape and structure to the novel itself.

John Dos Passos's career, in this connection, is fascinating but ultimately disappointing, for it supplies more interest to literary history than to criticism. His first novel, *Streets of the Night*,[1] begun while he was a student at Harvard, and even his second novel, *One Man's Initiation*, dealing with the First World War, are carefully weary duplications of *fin de siècle* writing in England;

---

[1] First in composition but not published until 1923, after *One Man's Initiation* of 1920 (reissued in 1945 as *First Encounter*) and *Three Soldiers*, 1921.

they owe more to *Marius the Epicurean* than to any contemporary work, celebrating impressionistically the sensitive individual in foredoomed conflict with gross reality. Dos Passos's real career began with *Three Soldiers* (1921), it became exciting in *Manhattan Transfer* (1925), and it reached its apogee in the trilogy *USA: The 42nd Parallel* (1930), *1919* (1932), and *The Big Money* (1936). Imperfect as it is, *Three Soldiers* was the first American novel to present World War I as an idea rather than as reportage or auto-biography. The ambitious theme, or idea, of the novel, to demonstrate the meaninglessness of the war through its impact on three different kinds of American soldier, was schematic and insufficiently realized. In Andrews, the educated soldier, a student of music who deserts the Army only to be captured and probably shot, Dos Passos looks back to the worn impulses of his first novels; Chrisfield and Fuselli, a farm boy and a shipping-clerk from San Francisco, anticipate the near-anonymous figures of *USA* who are the social victims, ignorant, acquiescent, dangerous when aroused, but aroused only through fraud or the corrosive and corrupting idealism of trade union and Communist Party activities. The broad theme and the objective style belong to naturalism, but the execution of idea carries the novel beyond naturalism almost into the modern mode. *Manhattan Transfer*, a far more satisfying work, has for its central character not any one of the human beings it describes, but the city itself, New York City. By this device Dos Passos advances from the crude naturalistic drive to reach society in the guise of environment to a produc-tive technical experiment in point of view. The various characters meet and react only incidentally; their meaning as people reaches us only through their reactions to the vast city. Dos Passos's accomplishment in this novel is related to E. E. Cummings's accomplishment in verse: each in his very different way evokes a brilliant intellectual image of his subject by working upon our sense perceptions in such a manner that the image comes to us not through logic or the usual syntax of prose or verse, but as images reach us in nature—in a flash of white, a whirr of wings, a glimpse of sky—and only then the 'logical' conclusion of the mind— 'a dove'. The city thus evoked lives on in the mind as it could not do through logical, traditional description. The city's meaning, too, is evoked through a similar process. The difficulty is that Dos Passos's experiment sacrifices the human being. He seems to hold his characters at arm's length, refusing to allow us to engage ourselves with them. The novel then becomes the vehicle of literary idea, but not the fullest and richest idea possible, nor indeed the idea we demand: the idea of human character in all its emotional, moral, and decision-making or decision-blundering roundness.

The comparative success of *Manhattan Transfer* encouraged Dos Passos to further experiments in *USA*; experiments which had to be made, but which benefited later writers more than Dos Passos himself. *USA* is nothing less than an attempt to write in novel form the public and private history of the United States from 1898 to 1929. Dos Passos used four devices to carry out his plan. The first, basic device is the record of the activities of the three central characters and of the multitudes of secondary characters, written in a combination of third person omniscient author and modified internal monologue. The second device is the brief 'biography' of public figures of the period, politicians, labour leaders, scientists, and business men, selected for their representative character, and interspersed among the narrative of the fictional characters. Third is the device of the 'Newsreel': fragments of headlines, popular songs, slogans, catchwords, and news stories, similarly interspersed throughout the trilogy. These three devices are obviously intended to orchestrate the public history of the period. The fourth device, fragments of the biography of a single individual written as that individual's stream-of-consciousness, presents a private history, corresponding to Dos Passos's own private history, as opposed to the public histories; it is the counterpoint in the orchestration.

These devices are hardly 'the desperate manœuvres' of a man 'committed to a method [naturalism] of which he despairs', for they are controlled throughout, and serve admirably the purpose for which they are invented. Our quarrel is only with that purpose. Ambitious to write history, Dos Passos committed himself too far in advance to one kind of historical interpretation, that of

Thorstein Veblen, an economist, with the result that we know in advance too many phases of Dos Passos's tendentious interpretations. The only remotely disinterested human beings in *USA* are the trade union men whose cause is doomed; the rest are either scoundrels from birth, like J. Ward Moorehouse, the public relations magnate, or their quality is corrupted by capitalism, like Charley Anderson, the honest mechanic turned Wall Street tycoon. Dos Passos leaves himself no space for emotional manœuvre. He is so concerned to convey his literary idea, an idea whose inadequacy his own later career as an apostate liberal so fully underlines, that he ceased to be a novelist.

For all its failure, *USA* remains important. Its techniques have directly influenced contemporary writers so diverse as Norman Mailer and J.-P. Sartre; indirectly its seriousness and its massiveness have given a tone and a direction to novelists like Saul Bellow and Ralph Ellison. There is an authority in honourable failure that is far more meaningful than the arrogance of the slight success. Dos Passos was more aware than most members of his generation of the meaning of the catastrophe, and of the necessity to grasp the catastrophe imaginatively. He took the materials at hand, which happened to be the materials of naturalism, and re-worked them to the point where a new generation could prove the validity of his first insights. His work is marred by the proletarian prejudice and the anti-intellectualism of naturalism, but his work was inevitable to the American novel. Because his idea was a literary one, it is not enough to say that history has denied the validity of his political oversimplifications; a defect of imagination was also involved, regrettable for Dos Passos the writer, but hardly crippling, and finally even a productive defect.

Dos Passos's relation to naturalism is representative for the best American writing of the past thirty years. American writers of the period have not been doctrinaire naturalists, but they have fulfilled through doctrinaire naturalism an important strain in the American tradition by carrying on the investigation of actuality to the point where it has become truly literary; they have provided a means for dealing with social fragmentation and for absorbing into the art-form of the novel the recalcitrant materials of our time—war, politics, the history that insists upon unrolling itself before our eyes.

It is a wry accident of literary history that naturalism became the mode by which the modern writer everywhere could realize the great themes of modern literature: violence, as we know it in politics and war; isolation, as we know it in the motifs of love and death; time, the special dimension in which the great themes unfold.

Naturalism had a technical meaning for the American which it lacked for the English writer. The English writer has reacted to naturalism only in so far as he addresses himself to those great themes of the modern novel. But for the most part the contemporary English novelist has been a victim of his great tradition, as well as a victim of the comfortable homogeneity of English society. England never had a Bohemia, and Englishmen to this day lack the *nostalgie de boue* of either the American or the continental writer. For all the fragmentation of society everywhere in the West, the English writer still accepts the ideals of his society in a remarkable degree. Eccentricity takes the place of rebellion and willing apprenticeship the place of defiant experiment. Naturalism has crept into the modern English novel through a side door; it appears as subject-matter in a novel like Angus Wilson's *Hemlock and After*, a vacuous, *chic* treatment of life among the London homosexuals, or in the lazy, mannered imitation of bad American novels, such as this from Elizabeth Taylor's *The Sleeping Beauty*: 'He ordered a sweet, sallow wine she liked and which made him pause in the middle of sentences while he smothered little belches. She ate *mille feuilles*, then regretted them. Waiters constantly interrupted to ask if the meal was all they desired.' To generalize dangerously, I would say that the English sense of reality differs considerably from the American, and it differs in the same direction and degree that the American literary tradition differs from the English. The implications of this loose statement must be reserved for the next chapter.

The critical confusion regarding naturalism is deeply symptomatic of our distrust of ourselves and of our wretched world. For considerable reasons, we have come to distrust nature and to

distrust things. Actuality has too often betrayed us. W. H. Auden
has said, following St. Augustine, 'Natural man hates Nature and
wants above all to be free—free of ties to inanimate nature, as
well as to his own human nature and to God.'[1] This accounts in
part for the recent desperate attempts to evade nature by resorting
to surrealism and to Kierkegaard, to the symbolism of the Fall of
man and to aesthetic religion. Luther, Calvin, Berdyaev, Cardinal
Spellman, and Jean Cocteau meet in the literary mind retreating
from reality and nature. I do not mean to mock, but only to
suggest that to evade nature, animate or inanimate, is to evade our
own humanity and to impoverish our literary record.

[1] Quoted by George McFadden, 'The Rake's Progress: A note on the Libretto',
Hudson Review, VII, No. 1, Spring 1955, 108.

Chapter Five

TRADITION AND THE NOVEL: ENGLAND

THE word 'tradition' has reached the state of depreciation where it can mean anything to anybody, with the result that one is stricken with cold vertigo whenever it appears. One of Webster's definitions, identified as '*now rare*', reads 'Delivery [or] A surrender'. This delights and enlightens, for it describes with precision and imagination one largely held modern attitude towards the past, that of the elder statesmen of literature for whom the subject stops with the death of Keats. 'Surrender' also describes the attitude of the reader for whom tradition is an absolute; when cornered, he invokes tradition with the fervour of a thirteenth-century Crusader invoking the True Cross. For contrast, there is the reader for whom the stimulus 'tradition' brings the automatic reflex, 'dead hand of'. This *garde en arrière* mind knows Proust, Joyce, Melville, Mann, Arnold Toynbee, Truman Capote, Kafka, Propertius in translation, Paul Bowles, and little else. Dr. Leavis qualifies tradition with the adjective 'great', and The Great Tradition is his Hamlet's rapier (or tennis racquet) with which he lays into the arras of modern literature, slaying his many Poloniuses. Allen Tate tells us that in the modern novel we owe all to Flaubert,[1] but for Dr. Leavis, Flaubert is one more Polonius; the great novelists, he says, lack 'anything of Flaubert's disgust or disdain or boredom, they are all distinguished by a vital capacity for experience, a kind of reverent openness before life, and a marked moral intensity'.[2] This definition is so large, and its terms of reference so personal, that they can mean whatever Dr. Leavis

---

[1] Allen Tate, *On the Limits of Poetry*, New York, Morrow, 1948, p. 136. 'Gustave Flaubert created the modern novel. Gustave Flaubert created the modern short story. He created both because he created modern fiction.'
[2] *The Great Tradition*, p. 9.

wants them to mean; only thus can he unite Jane Austen, George
Eliot, Howard Sturgis and D. H. Lawrence.

I take it as self-evident, or as self-evident as anything ever is in
literature, that the fundamental mode of the English novel from
its origins has been realism, just as the mode of the German novel
has been philosophy, and of the French novel intellectualized
morality. The English novelist has rarely been an intellectual in
the French sense, rarely a philosopher in the German sense, but he
has been concerned with what people, objects, society are really
like. Fielding mentions somewhere the necessity for the novelist
never to exceed the limits of the probable, and Smollett defined
the novel as 'a large diffused picture, comprehending the characters of life, disposed in different groupes, and exhibited in various
attitudes, for the purposes of an uniform plan'. The novel must
have a central character for unity and form, without whom it will
lack 'propriety, *probability*, or success. . . .'[1] To be useful, any
discussion of tradition, I would think, must establish what
'reality' has meant to the English novelist and how, formally and
technically, rather than philosophically, his conception of the
real world has appeared in the novel.

In discussing naturalism, I suggested that reality has been one
thing for the American and something intrinsically different for
the Englishman. Defoe has been justly credited for having a
special interest in the real and the actual, but even Defoe, standing
first in time before the long line of English realists, manipulated
the real world in a curious and characteristically English manner.
The accepted explanations for Defoe's realism—that he wanted
for political and perhaps other more obscure reasons to conceal
his identity, or that he was fond of literary hoaxes—do not account
for the technique of his remarkable narratives. Edgar Allan Poe,
too, used a kind of verisimilitude to pass off hoaxes, but he differs
from Defoe as Baudelaire differs from John Masefield. *Moll
Flanders* is Defoe at his best, and a good place to look for Defoe's
kind of realism. First, Defoe uses the familiar dodge of the discovered manuscript which he 'recommends' to the reader;

[1] Dedication to *Ferdinand, Count Fathom*, in *The Miscellaneous Works*, 6 vols.,
Edinburgh, 1800, IV, vii. My italics.

although the 'manuscript' contains a lusty account of Moll's bigamy, whoring and thievery, Defoe reassures the reader of his moral purpose. He points out in a preface that Moll atones for her wickedness, and says that the 'whole relation is carefully garbled of all levity and looseness that was in it, so it is applied, ... to virtuous and religious uses'. No one can reproach him for publishing the account:

> ... there is not a wicked action in any part of it, but is first or last rendered unhappy and unfortunate; there is not a superlative villain brought upon the stage, but either he is brought to an unhappy end, or brought to be a penitent; there is not an ill thing mentioned but it is condemned, even in the relation, nor a virtuous, just thing but it carries its praise along with it.[1]

Whether Defoe wrote this with tongue in cheek or not, it reminds us of his nearness in time to John Bunyan, and of his use of the prose style which Bunyan helped to introduce into English; the plain, unadorned style of the Puritan which worked against wilful flights of imagination and which in America contributed to the development of native naturalism.

Moll Flanders is a deeply sensual woman whose frequent, perfunctory penitence neither she nor we believe in; nor did her creator, Defoe. Moll's moralizing is at once Defoe's gesture to the hypocrisy of the emerging middle class and a source of comic effect. The large total of Moll's transgressions, equating with a precisely equal number of repentances, make for humour. V. S. Pritchett has said that Fielding and Smollett are 'the grand progenitors of the masculine school in the English comic novel'.[2] I would give Defoe that honour, for *Moll Flanders* is, among other things, a richly comic affair. And yet, Defoe was too limited a writer to make the most of Moll's comic possibilities. He lacked Fielding's and Smollett's cunning in construction of comic incident, but he understood better than many of his critics that sex and comedy are intrinsically related. Joyce knew this, and Molly

---

[1] Author's Preface, *Moll Flanders*, Boston, 1903, I, xix–xx.
[2] 'The Tough School', *The Listener*, LI, 20 May 1954, 861. This was the first of five talks on the Third Programme on the comic novel, a distinguished series which is the only adequate treatment of the subject we have.

Bloom has more in common with Defoe's Moll than her Christian name. To come to the point, hardly an original one—what Mr. Pritchett calls 'masculine' comedy in the novel is very close to realism. The plain style and the comic combine in *Moll Flanders* to create one kind of realism in the English novel. Exactly what kind of realism is it? We need to look at an example of Defoe's 'verisimilitude'. At a low point in her career, Moll takes to thieving from a child; she steals a gold necklace, and even thinks of killing the child, but resists:

> . . . I turned the child about and bade it go back again, for that was not its way home; the child said, so she would; and I went through into Bartholomew Close, and then turned round to another passage that goes into Long Lane, so away into Charterhouse Yard, and out into St. John's Street; then crossing into Smithfield, went down Chick Lane, and into Field Lane, to Holborn Bridge, when, mixing with the crowd of people usually passing there, it was not possible to have been found out; and thus I made my second sally into the world.
>
> The thoughts of this booty put out all the thoughts of the first, and the reflections I had made wore quickly off; poverty hardened my heart, and my own necessities made me regardless of anything. The last affair left no great concern upon me, for as I did the poor child no harm, I only thought I had given the parents a just reproof for their negligence. . . .
>
> This string of beads was worth about £12 or £14. I suppose it might have been formerly the mother's, for it was too big for the child's wear, but that, perhaps, the vanity of the mother to have her child look fine at the dancing-school, had made her let the child wear it; and no doubt the child had a maid sent to take care of it; but she, like a careless jade, was taken up perhaps with some fellow that had met her, and so the poor baby wandered till it fell into my hands.
>
> However, I did the child no harm; I did not so much as fright it, for I had a great many tender thoughts about me yet, and did nothing but what, as I may say, mere necessity drove me to.

The device of the first person, which Defoe maintains strictly throughout the novel, is in itself of course a source of realism. The more familiar devices are the cartographic accuracy of Moll's escape after the theft, and the notation of an exact sum for the value of her loot—£12 or £14. Yet read for its meaning in the round, the entire incident is flat and unrealistic. Moll doesn't re-create her emotions; she reports them. Reality listed is not reality realized; even the actual objects in the novel, the necklace, the sums of money that are always changing hands, are at base generalized, lacking in texture. The reason, I think, is that Defoe is using reality to a given end: to create a structure within which Moll takes on a size and grandeur larger than life, and to achieve his ironically comic effect through the juxtaposition of gross carnal behaviour with hollow repentance. Reality, in short, is stylized and turned to a given purpose.

Serviceable as it was, Defoe's style was not to be the style of the traditional novel in England. Defoe passed on to later novelists a concern for female virtue, a useful manner of dealing with the real world, and not least, a craftsman's devices for narration and pace; but not a basic style. Again we look to Mr. Pritchett for a description of the basic English style, not only in the comic novel which is his special concern here, but in the novel at large. In the eighteenth century, he writes,

> . . . a respectable, snobbish, and powerful middle-class society was being rapidly established. We can see the growing if rather trite assurance of writers who are founding the modern world in every page. The eighteenth century may be a roaring cauldron of gin, crime, and unreason, but the comic writers have invented a lid which will hold it down. They have invented a highly abstract, even imaginary thing called the World and characters whose aim is to be 'men of the world'. This man of the world was given a style in which he talked—Latinised, epigrammatic, consequential, euphemistic; and one object of this sententious manner was, by force of intellectual propaganda, to suppress the threat of anything ungovernable from without.[1]

The man of the world of the eighteenth-century comic novel talked so well in his Latinized, epigrammatic style that nineteenth-century writers until Hardy imitated him, in their own, third-person omniscient voice as well as in the voice of their characters. And while contemporary writers, perhaps under the influence of

[1] 'The Tough School', ibid.

American naturalism, have shown a tendency to return to the plainness of Defoe, the Latinized style remains fundamental.

All three of Samuel Richardson's novels, *Pamela*, *Clarissa Harlowe*, and *Sir Charles Grandison*, have a striking affinity with Defoe's, in Richardson's prurient interest in female virginity and his close attention to narrative technique. The device of the novel in letters was a brilliant solution to the problem of point of view, even though Richardson floundered desperately at times to maintain an illusion of reality through the shortcomings of the method. The epistolary device, like Defoe's use of a narrator, had two important results for the later novel: both helped to establish a satisfying depth of psychological reality, and to bring to early maturity two acceptable methods for dealing with time, methods which were indispensable until James, Conrad, and the modern period of experiment. Defoe's mechanical conception of time, in which incident follows upon incident in logical and chronological order, conformed to the human impulse to order perception and to organize experience. It is so obvious that one can forget that the novelist still must choose some sequence as a literary method. The linear conception of time (and therefore of experience) has been the choice of the great majority of English novelists, and it remains dominant in spite of modern experiment and contemporary variations upon Richardson's conception.

Richardson regarded experience not as predominantly sequential, or linear, but monolithic. *Clarissa* moves in time, to be sure, but the significant movement of the novel is psychological. The actual time sequence covers less than a year, from January 10th, to be exact, to the final letter of the eighth volume, of December 18th. But we are concerned with the chronological only by the way. Richardson wanted to present literally, in the words of his sub-title, *The History of a Young Lady: Comprehending the Most Important Concerns of Private Life. And Particularly Showing the Distresses that May Attend the Misconduct Both of Parents and Children in Relation to Marriage*. He was no tongue-in-cheek creator of comic irony; both the author and his vast eighteenth-century public saw *Clarissa* as the psychological tragedy of a paragon of virtue brought to her grave by the conflict between her pride, her obedience to her family, and the machinations of the rake-hell, Lovelace. The remarkable thing is that while we can no longer accept *Pamela* without a smile, so sternly unsentimental as we are, we can accept *Clarissa* as near-tragedy. Richardson, that is to say, succeeds in psychological realism even though his careful and constant efforts at reality of texture fail miserably. Lovelace is not an observed human being but an operatic monster who has only the symbolic reality of evil personified; I see a direct line between Lovelace and Bradley Headstone of *Our Mutual Friend*, or Dickens's numerous other villains.

Clarissa herself remains believable because of the inner reality of her struggle. Richardson avoided obvious allegory through his manipulation of fact, but finally he created allegory rather than tragedy. The reason lies, I believe, in his selection of observed fact. On her deathbed, Clarissa orders her own coffin, has it installed in the sick-room, and pays the bill for the imposing object out of her own purse,

> . . . reflecting upon herself for the expensiveness of it, saying that they might observe in *her*, that pride left not poor mortals to the last: but indeed she did not know but her father would permit it, *when furnished*, to be carried down to be deposited with her ancestors; and, in that case, she ought not to discredit those ancestors in her *appearance amongst them*.

Belford, who is writing to Lovelace, describes the coffin in detail:

> Mrs. Lovick has . . . shown me a copy of the draught by which all was ordered; and I will give thee a sketch of the symbols. The principal device, neatly etched on a plate of white metal, is a crowned serpent, with its tail in its mouth, forming a ring, the emblem of eternity: and in the circle made by it is this inscription:
>
>
>
> CLARISSA HARLOWE
> April x.
> [Then the year.]
> Ætat xix.
>
>
>
> For ornaments: at top, an hour-glass, winged. At bottom, an urn.

And so on with a precise list of the three Biblical inscriptions. The final effect of this matter-of-fact realism is to establish the reader's image of Clarissa as a Christian sacrifice to inexorable convention, a willing martyr to her own pride and the ravages of her seducer. Realism, then, as with Defoe, is used to a distinctly literary end; it is stylized and imbued with purpose over and above the demands of the observed, everyday world. Without Clarissa's psychological reality, the moral purpose would not survive, and the novel would be no more than a tract. And the style of Belford, like that of Lovelace and even Clarissa herself, differentiated though it is in each person, is the style of that 'imaginary thing called the World', and of characters who belong to the World, whether as Men of the World or as Female Virtue apart from the World. We can find in *Clarissa* and increasingly in the eighteenth- and nineteenth-century novel a discrepancy between that supple but highly literary style, and the demands of realism as society disintegrates and the writer is forced in each generation to the recreation of background and character. In subject, *Clarissa* leads straight to *Tess of the D'Urbervilles*; Tess's return to her seducer, in contrast to Clarissa's self-willed death in defiance of Lovelace, illustrates a tradition still living though moribund; it is an example of what I have described as Hardy's retrospective quality.

Despite their use of limited point of view, both Defoe and Richardson shared with the comic writers of the eighteenth century and passed on to the nineteenth century a leisurely dwelling upon incidents in all fullness. They must tell all and leave no awkward gaps in the reader's knowledge. Richardson was forced to the use of footnotes, a conclusion and a postscript in order to tie up all the loose ends of Clarissa's story and to explain his moral and Christian intent. Fielding wrote introductory essays; he too used footnotes when clarity was in doubt, and while he maintained a consistent objectivity in the narrative proper, we are always conscious of his voice and his mind framing the story. That voice, that eighteenth-century leisureliness and fullness of detail is the characteristic, traditional voice and manner of the English novel until the third phase.

In committing themselves to these techniques, English novelists committed themselves to reality; to the representation of events and details as outwardly fixed in nature, whose order in time and space is established without ambiguity. While realism in England was from the beginning recognizably English rather than American or French or German, it was of course not original with the English. Erich Auerbach proposes at the beginning of a study of reality in Western Literature that the convention of full description, the presentation of all the links in narrative goes back to Homer. He examines in detail the scene in book 19 of the *Odyssey*, in which Odysseus has come home and is recognized by the old housekeeper Euryclea through the scar on his thigh, and notes that Homer interrupts the dramatic narrative to tell us all about how Odysseus got the scar, about the characters involved in the boar-hunt of Odysseus's boyhood, their degrees of kinship, his recovery from the wound, his parents' concern—all. Auerbach demonstrates convincingly that this fullness of the Homeric style is fundamental to one broad strain in Western writing up to and through French naturalism. He contrasts the Homeric epic style with the epic style of certain Old Testament writers, analysing the story of Abraham's sacrifice of Isaac, and pointing out that the story lacks setting; we do not know whether we are indoors or out; God is merely a voice to Abraham, and we know nothing of Abraham or of Isaac as characters, nothing of their thoughts and feelings. The writer subordinates exterior reality to the creation of suspense; Homer deliberately destroys suspense in the cause of fullness. Most significantly, Auerbach remarks,

> Homer can be analysed, . . . but he cannot be interpreted. Later allegorizing trends have tried their arts of interpretation upon him, but to no avail. He resists any such treatment; the interpretations are forced and foreign, they do not crystallize into a unified doctrine. . . .
>
> It is all very different in the Biblical stories. Their aim is not to bewitch the senses, and if nevertheless they produce lively sensory effects, it is only because the moral, religious, and psychological phenomena which are their sole concern are made concrete in the sensible matter of life. The story of Abraham and Isaac is not better established than the story of Odysseus, Penelope, and Euryclea; both are legendary. But the Biblical narrator, the Elohist, had to believe in the objective truth of the story of Abraham's sacrifice—the

existence of the sacred ordinances of life rested upon the truth of this and similar stories. He had to believe in it passionately; or else . . . he had to be a conscious liar—no harmless liar like Homer, who lied to give pleasure, but a political liar with a definite end in view, lying in the interest of a claim to absolute authority.[1]

This comment by a superb historical critic is laden with meaning for the traditional novel in England. It directs our attention back to the discussion of the place of idea in fiction, and it points to the two lines of realistic writing from Defoe and Richardson to the present. It is apparent even from the foregoing brief quotations from *Moll Flanders* and *Clarissa* that two kinds of realism are at work. We can analyse *Moll Flanders* but not interpret it, and like the allegorizers of Homer, the allegorizers of Defoe and his school—and here I include Fielding, Smollett and Thackeray; Kipling, Joyce Cary and Anthony Powell—come to grief in their attempt to discover a kind of meaning that was never intended and indeed was never there.[2] *Clarissa*, however, is another matter. Richardson's novel demands to be 'interpreted' as Auerbach uses the term, for Richardson's notion of the truth of his literary idea was not far removed from that of the Biblical narrator of the story of Abraham's sacrifice. Richardson believed that virtue outraged will triumph, even in death; he presented a Christian parable charged with moral and psychological overtones. If we ignore those overtones, we cannot even read *Clarissa*, much less enjoy it. The physical atmosphere of *Clarissa* is confining, almost claustrophobic. The action seems to take place in small rooms with closed windows. This effect is partly due to the epistolary form, but more particularly to the fact that the action is inner and psychological rather than exterior. *Humphry Clinker* is also written in the epistolary convention, but Smollett takes us out of doors into the open. It is possible to forget that we are reading letters in this novel; in *Clarissa* never. So it is that when

[1] *Mimesis: The Representation of Reality in Western Literature*, trans. W. R. Trask, Princeton, Princeton University Press, 1953, pp. 3–14.

[2] For example, Dorothy Van Ghent on Defoe, *The English Novel: Form and Function*, New York, Rinehart, 1953, 33–45. Or contrast Orwell's analysis of Kipling with T. S. Eliot's and Edmund Wilson's unconvincing search for new dimensions in Kipling's work.

Richardson stops to examine a physical object, such as Clarissa's grotesque coffin, he stops for an ulterior purpose—to convey the inevitability of Clarissa's death, and to enlarge Lovelace's fury and remorse.

Richardson's conception of reality is tempered by his idea; reality is subordinated to idea and amounts to little more than a minimum of verisimilitude. His idea differs from George Eliot's and from the modern novelist's in that it is not intellectualized; it is as primitive as rape itself and depends for its validity upon the validity of the characters. Hence the success of that form which allowed Richardson to dwell upon characterization, to tell and re-tell incidents not for their effect as incidents, but for their psychological possibility. It was too intense a form, perhaps, for the wider nineteenth-century public; it found as great an eighteenth-century audience as it did because it caught a fashion in the making, the fashion for the novel of feeling, and helped at the same time to create the fashion. Maria Edgeworth and Jane Austen were to learn from Richardson and to use his subject in their own individual ways; Hardy, as I have noted, was to use it in another way. But not until James do we find Richardson's concentration in technique, his single-minded resolution of the non-intellectual idea. T. S. Eliot's famous comment about James —that he had a mind so fine no idea could violate it—might apply equally to Richardson.[1]

To move from Richardson's *escritoires* in confined rooms to the comic writers of the eighteenth century is more than to move out of doors into the English countryside, it is to move to another conception of the novel, to another technique, and to another conception of the real. Happily the great English comic writers are widely read and more fully understood than any other group. It is necessary here only to note what they contributed to tradition, how they gave a peculiar turn to the English novel, and to determine what modern writers have taken from them. Fielding

[1] Illustrations in Richardson's novels come as a shock; one feels that it is somehow wrong to try to give that kind of reality to Richardson's work, while illustrations in *Tom Jones* or *Peregrine Pickle* seem welcome and fitting. Would anyone ever try to illustrate Proust or Thomas Mann? (I have learned since writing this that Philippe Julien *has* illustrated Proust. *Tant pis*.)

L

and Sterne are to the comic novel as Defoe and Richardson are to the earlier moral tale and the tragic novel. Mr. Pritchett's useful distinction between the masculine and the feminine school of the comic novel defines the relationship between the two great progenitors. Fielding's humour is music-hall humour, lusty, tumbling, healthy and extroverted. That he learned much from the theatre we know; as he was an indifferent playwright, we cannot regret that he turned his talents to the novel. His technical contribution is so much a part of the succeeding novelist's equipment that it is easy to overlook its originality and even to undervalue its art. Fielding suffers from the massive flattery of universal imitation. A paragraph from *Joseph Andrews*, his first proper novel of 1742, can illustrate his technique and his kind of reality: the scene is the inn of the henpecked Tow-wouse, where Joseph Andrews is recovering from a tussle with a thief.

> Mrs. Tow-wouse delivered herself in the following words: 'Sure never was such a fool as my husband; would any other person living have left a man in the custody of such a drunken drowsy blockhead as Tom Suckbribe?' (which was the constable's name); 'and if he could be indicted without any harm to his wife and children, I should be glad of it.' (Then the bell rung in Joseph's room.) 'Why Betty, John, Chamberlain, where the devil are you all? Have you no ears, or no conscience, not to tend the sick better? See what the gentleman wants. Why don't you go yourself, Mr. Tow-wouse? But any one may die for you; you have no more feeling than a deal board. If a man lived a fortnight in your house without spending a penny, you would never put him in mind of it. See whether he drinks tea or coffee for breakfast.' 'Yes, my dear,' cried Tow-wouse. She then asked the doctor and Mr. Barnabas what morning's draught they chose, who answered, they had a pot of cyder—and at the fire; which we will leave them merry over, and return to Joseph.

This is scenic as a play is, and while Mrs. Tow-wouse's speech is realistic enough, it has the realism of the theatre rather than of life. It is loud, direct, and wonderfully unsubtle. We see here Fielding's trick of the descriptive surname; Tom Suckbribe and Mrs. Slip-slop are the father and mother of first a convention and later a boring habit. We see objects in the round—tea, coffee, a pot of cider—and by the fire. Fielding's world is a world of things, but things selected and used for a larger comic and moral purpose, not things in themselves having transcendental meaning *as* things. And we hear Fielding's characteristic voice, guiding, directing, lending tone and narrative pace. He never hesitates to bring down the curtain with a rush, then to fling it up again upon the next scene, rushing his characters all the while over the landscape, in and out of each other's beds, on foot, horseback or by carriage they make their hasty way through the wide eighteenth-century world, a world chaotic but uncomplex, open and uneccentric.

Smollett too peoples that world with brutalized versions of Fielding's characters. When blood flows in Fielding's stories it is stage-blood and we do not take it seriously. Smollett's blood is all too real; his clubs have weight and his swords points and cutting edges. His humour is blunter than Fielding's, and if we ponder a scene too long it may turn to horror. Smollett's most memorable comic figures are not the club-wielders but the eccentrics: Commander Trunnion arriving late at the church for his wedding because he has had to tack cross-country on horseback due to contrary winds. Smollett's comedy left reality even farther behind; he instigated an attack which Dickens was to develop to an absurd degree. The fantastic and the eccentric inhabit English fiction from Smollett to the present, intensely English and often comprehensible only to the English. Fielding and Smollett between them represent, in American terms, the frontier period in English fiction. Their kind of joke is similar to the frontier joke: ribald, loud, and physical. Their characters have in common with American frontier characters a mythic quality; they are rather larger than life, and they correspond to a basic national image of the national consciousness at a given point in time. But the comparison fails in that Fielding, and to a lesser degree Smollett, give an urbanity and a formal finish to their creations that is lacking in American frontier writing; their work is more 'literary' and less realistic.

With Laurence Sterne we retreat from the open landscape back into the Richardsonian interior, back to an intense consciousness of time, back to the restricted point of view, back to a world where the eccentric is the exception, the mad and the fantastic the rule. Behind the modern French novel stands Pascal;[1] behind the modern German novel stand both Kant and Nietzsche; behind the American novel, Emerson; behind the English novel, Sterne's great *tour de force, Tristram Shandy*. The formulation must read something like this, for later English novelists have not needed to go outside their chosen form to discover their ancestry; neither to Hobbes, Locke, nor Bentham, but to other novelists, among whom Sterne is central. Even more than the American writer, the English writer traditionally distrusted or ignored the intellectual statement of formal philosophy in favour of the felt, stylized, urbane presentation. An English *Dr. Faustus* of the order of Thomas Mann's would be inconceivable, while an Emily Brontë, a Hardy, even a Scott, often seem indeed 'peripheral' to the main line of English fiction.

Sterne's overt comedy, personal, procrastinating, smuttily sexual, is contained in a narrative in which nothing, no object, no person, no relationship lacks comedy. At the same time, Sterne can endow each incident with symbolic value, generalizing it into the sum of his reflections upon the human condition. All is stylized: the accident of Tristram's conception, Uncle Toby's wound, the widow Wadman's hot pursuit of Toby, the curse of Ernulphus, Bishop of Rochester, the Slawkenbergian treatise on noses. The effectiveness of the material depends upon a nice balance between the physical and the intellectual, the whimsical and the sexual, the fantastic and the satirical; this balance in Sterne establishes a direct line to Peacock, Dickens, Firbank, Beerbohm, and Joyce. The existence of that line in the tradition of the novel has become a truism of criticism, but as with many another truism, its meaning is more commonly assumed than explored. Sterne

---

[1] André Malraux has said, '. . . the four French writers whose work is entirely subsequent to 1916, and who are the most widely read abroad: Giono, Bernanos, Montherlant and myself, are all four bound by what can be called the French heroic tradition, the Corneillian tradition . . . (in which, to my mind, Pascal is an essential link) . . .' in contrast to the current in French writing of Montaigne, Molière, La Bruyère, Chamfort, Stendhal—'people who want to know what they are talking about, the regulators of dreams, the moralists, in fact'. 'An Interview with Malraux', *Horizon*, XII, October 1945, 241.

displays an aspect of the English mind that ultimately is defeating to the novelist. The figure of the urbane amateur, whimsical, *fée*, and quaint, is familiar in English fiction. Sterne himself was able to keep these qualities in suspension and to give them form from the very fact of suspension. But in his followers, they turn too easily into impatience with the formal problems of the novel, an eager willingness to dispense with the actual, and to create fantastic, whimsical Characters who, lacking Sterne's saving ribaldry, oppress the non-English mind. I think particularly of Dickens.

In the contemporary novel, the tradition of Sterne often combined with that of Fielding occurs in strange places. P. H. Newby allots to each of his otherwise original and impressive novels one fantastic whose effect is to weaken the novel's symmetry and to coarsen its texture. No American writer of comparable stature would dare to touch rich, ripe Characters like Hesketh Senior in *A Step to Silence*, or the baker in *The Young May Moon*; they are foreign to the American tradition, and their stylization sometimes seems like posturing. Both Joyce Cary and Anthony Powell derive very clearly from the tradition of Fielding and Sterne. Powell combines Fielding's range of incident with Sterne's deliberate lack of pace. Writing in a supple, exceedingly Latinized prose, he is concerned with the social history of the upper-middle-class, public school, Oxford or Cambridge young man of the twenties and thirties. He omits plot as such and lingers over evocative incidents whose evocations are clubbed down by outlandish, contrived, comic climaxes: a practical joke misfires, and Stripling of *A Question of Upbringing* is discovered early one morning by the guests in a country house, walking down a corridor with a chamber-pot held on high; Widmerpool, the social climber and recurrent goat, crashes his car into a stone urn filled with geraniums in *A Buyer's Market*. Such schoolboy humour is remote from the tumblings in the hay of Fielding or the witty insinuations of Sterne, and its effect is to eliminate idea and enthrone the urbane amateur. I am reminded of George Ponderevo in *Tono-Bungay*, who reflects, 'Our people never formulates; it keeps words for jests and ironies.' Powell's ironies are not thematic or structural; they are external ironies of situations that debase the currency of this writer's admirable style; it is as though Henry James and Groucho Marx had entered into ludicrous collaboration.

Although Joyce Cary is a more interesting and vigorous novelist than Anthony Powell, his concern for Character-drawing within a frame of social history identifies him, too, as a retrospective writer who derives from a once-vigorous tradition. Possessing a strong novelist's intelligence, Cary does not draw back from ideas; he does 'formulate', but his technique is inadequate to his formulations. He frequently wears the Shandyean mask, placing himself in the mind of a central character, who in turn is a Dickensian fantastic disguised as a citizen of the modern world. That character may be a half-Europeanized African like Johnson, in *Mr. Johnson*; the lusty, talkative old artist, Gully Jimson, of *The Horse's Mouth*; the cranky, obscene old man, Wilcher, whose journal in *To Be a Pilgrim* is a record of his crankiness and resistance to social change; or Sara, Gully Jimson's consort of many years, a cook turned gentlewoman who writes her story from prison in *Herself Surprised*; or again Tabitha Baskett of *A Fearful Joy*, who recites her Victorian youth, her Edwardian young womanhood, her Georgian middle age, and her old age to the point of her death about 1947. While each of these characters is quaint and fantastic, Pickwick-like, it is to Cary's enormous credit that he is able to elicit sympathy for them; in their various obsessions they share a taste for life and for experience. Although the world knocks them about, pushes and punches them, they retain their conviction that the world is a good place. Their fantasies and their old persons' evasions and half-mad way of coping with the world are a product of their determination to hang on to life, not to let their qualities escape them. This view is rare in modern fiction, one which needs statement. But ultimately cantankerous old people fail to convince, for Cary neglects to place them in a created world whose reality one can unhesitatingly accept; they are finally false and sentimental, in league with the hosts of children and madmen who crowd the pages of English fiction.

A Fearful Joy (1949) is one of Cary's best novels, and fully
representative of his strength and weaknesses. In time, the novel
covers the period from about 1885 to 1947. In events, Cary
chooses to deal with the decadence of the nineties, in considerable
detail; the Boer War; the social effect of the appearance of the
automobile and the aeroplane in the Edwardian period; feminism;
mobilization and industrialization before and during the World
War; demobilization and the slump of the twenties; the rise of
Hitler; the pacifist climate of the thirties; mobilization and the
Second World War; demobilization and the election of the
Labour government. In addition, Cary sketches in quite fully
the Victorian social background in a village near London; both
Liberal and Tory political ideology; the social and sexual mores of
the entire period; the class divisions and the conflicts among the
various generations represented. In order to cover so much
ground, Cary adapts from Fielding the device of the brief chapter
in which only one salient point is made; the novel has a furious
pace. And to achieve immediacy he writes in the historic present,
at once in the mind of Tabitha, his heroine, and apart from it—an
annoying device which is closer to Sterne, say, than to Joyce or
Virginia Woolf. One result of these devices to create pace and
immediacy is that Cary can never really penetrate his rather slick
surfaces; he is forced to frequent generalizations, like the following: the time is about 1900. Tabitha has run off at eighteen with
a preposterous dog, Dick Bonser, has been abandoned, picked up
by a pseudo-aesthete, Sturge, becomes Sturge's mistress, and has
had a son; after being left almost penniless at Sturge's death, she
has married the ancient industrialist, Gollan. She finds that
she cannot really 'run' Gollan as she had run Sturge. The
knowledge, in typical Cary paradox, comforts her, and Cary
writes:

> . . . when Gollan comes at last, full of apologies, she looks at him
> with respect as well as irritation. She thinks, 'Yes, I've been silly.
> You can see what a will he has; he's just been teaching me.'
> And in the thought she feels unexpectedly, with all her annoyance,
> a certain comfort. It is as though she has had a new reassurance. She
> feels a relaxation as into a new peace. She feels for the first time in

her life the meaning of the words 'to belong'. For the sense has not been with her since her childhood.

The voice is that of the nineteenth-century author, a Thackeray or a Trollope who has dipped into Freud, while the style is that of Michelet, who adopts the historical present at solemn moments: Robespierre murdered. But Cary does not pretend to be an interior writer. Wanting to suggest the interior through the exterior, he habitually erects a series of paradoxes to reveal character. Repeatedly in *A Fearful Joy*, as in his other novels, he presents his heroine at a moment of joy, insight, or intense unreasoning pleasure, then he deflates the situation, and joy becomes indeed 'fearful'. When Tabitha first runs off with Bonser in the illusion that they are to be married, she is unaware that Bonser is a lecher and an idle spiv. He takes her to Brighton; it is September, and the weather is sparklingly fine:

> Tabitha feels a little drunk with sensations which flow equally from sky, sea, the touch of Bonser's arm which supports her hand. She thinks, 'How nice it is here. Really, there's something in the seaside. What a good appetite I'm getting. How excited Dick was last night; how he adores me—of course he had had a good deal of whisky.'
>
> She is pleased that this piece of intuition does not trouble her, but only causes her to be aware of her new womanly wisdom. And that also exhilarates her. There is something between the air, the sea, and herself, some happy correspondence of vibrations, which turns everything into rapture.

Upon the moment, however, Tabitha learns that Bonser had run out on their London landlady and in a hundred words he has picked up an Edwardian fourteen-stone beauty and abandoned Tabitha. This technique is effective once, twice, three times, but it is too slight and obvious to carry the structure of the novel, as it is made to do. The headstrong Tabitha of eighteen turns into the hard, commercial mistress of the wealthy Sturge; into the responsible mother of her bastard son, John; into the careful and good wife of Gollan; into a religious and selfless nurse during the war; into the defender and wife of Bonser in his old age, a Bonser who has never reformed but who comes to represent a relative stability to Tabitha, in contrast to the flightiness of her grand-daughter, Nancy.

At an even more superficial level, *A Fearful Joy* depends upon Cary's competence in establishing and developing idea. As a social historian he is committed to a review of the political and social events of the period, and he is successful when he can satirize. His treatment of the aesthetic movement is convincing, even though he still plays paradoxical tricks. We first meet Sturge at the seaside, trailing admirers and framing the sea between thumb and forefinger. Sturge has financed a short-lived aesthetic review, and he takes up with Tabitha because she represents, he says, the new beauty, the Beardsley kind of woman. That Tabitha is pregnant only makes her more desirable; she has broken with the Victorian past and represents the new freedom. When Sturge is revealed as a wholesale groceryman who wants to set Tabitha up in a flat, the irony is convincing and truly comic. And when a very few years later Tabitha learns that books like *The Glories of the Decadence* are being published and that she and Sturge are heroes of a sort, the irony is nicely underlined.

But in contrast to this very English type of satire are the frequent passages in which Cary simply sketches in the social or political background. When Tabitha is keeping house for Sturge, entertaining lavishly in order to promote their new review, *The Bankside*, Cary writes:

> For several other ladies, perhaps cleverer and more beautiful, but certainly much more blown upon, have in the last ten years established the same kind of salon. There has been a change, a subterranean disturbance in the foundations of society. Some long slow process of movement, of tension, has suddenly produced large cracks, especially between the old queen's set at Windsor and the prince's set at Marlborough House. That spring of new wealth, of South African gold, whose fertilising stream has produced such a varied and fantastic growth of buccaneers in politics, idealists of Empire, adventurers in art, in science, has also split society, causing merchants to grow richer than dukes, and to give entertainments which are less tedious.

And 1913 produces a series of anonymous voices discussing the situation at Hackstraw, Gollan's country house:

'If the Austrians move——'

'If they don't, they'll be done for. Slav nationalism is out to break up the empire.'

'Nationalism; that's the trouble everywhere.'

'All the same, the Germans! What ability, what industry, what discipline, what progress. I was amazed. But one must see the danger.'

'I don't agree with you. This war scare is based on a complete misunderstanding of the German situation, indeed of the world situation. The interlocking of trade has already made wars impossible. . . .'

'Quite so; but then this naval race.'

'And the Slavs.'

'Certainly there are dangerous currents.'

This is only the slightest variation upon the Victorian presentation of idea; Cary is still turning aside from his characters and saying, in the historical present, 'now, reader, for an idea'. The first passage is dulled by the cliché of the geological metaphor. Cary, who is not given to clichés in diction, falls back on cliché because of his pace, and because of his willingness to superimpose the described idea. Technique and idea do not merge and mingle, even as they do in Graham Greene's work, or Ivy Compton-Burnett's. The technique of the anonymous voices seems a desperate one; the dialogue is stylized and unnatural on purpose, but insufficiently stylized to be convincing. Cary seems trapped between his essentially realistic motive and his traditional English carelessness regarding reality.

A Fearful Joy is an example of the *roman-fleuve*, while the Gully Jimson trilogy and the Nimmo trilogy remind us that Cary, like John Dos Passos, has been trying for many years to adapt that traditional organization of experience to the modern novel. The problem of pace is central in the *roman-fleuve*. Dos Passos solved it by foreshortening and by the Joycean method of simultaneity of events. Cary foreshortens almost not at all; his pace is the pace of the metronome set at maximum speed. Major and minor events receive virtually equal treatment, and time is linear, not spatial. The historical present or the first-person narrator achieves immediacy; the paradox of personal and social history provides a surface penetration of character, and Cary's conception of character is forced to carry the rest. Dos Passos presents carefully observed individuals as representative members of society; Cary presents Dickensian fantastics: the disparity between social history and the Dickensian Gollans, Jimsons, Wilchers, and all the rest is never accounted for. Doubtless English society does produce eccentrics that are inconceivable in American society. Dos Passos's characters have the flatness of Cary's social history, but Dos Passos's social history is not exterior and unrealized; it comes to us as a literary idea. Joyce Cary reverses the process. His characters have a life that Dos Passos's lack, but his ideas are flat and ultimately trivial. In the end the eighteenth- and nineteenth-century English conception of character does not serve twentieth-century reality. Both Anthony Powell and Joyce Cary, writers of unusual ability, seem to draw up short of their own potentialities. Like E. M. Forster, they rest content with superlative but minor performances rather than risk the possibly imperfect major performance. A great tradition cradles these writers in powerful maternal arms. Their vision remains local, astigmatic, and uncorrected to the twentieth-century vista. They reject as vulgar the ambition that a truly great writer must have. The heritage of Sterne, Fielding, Peacock, and Dickens dwindles into forced comedy, boyishness, and even coyness.

It is the fate of the masters in all literature that the harm they do to their imitators almost equals the benefits they extend by performing superlatively and inimitably. The pallor of Henry James's imitators obscures the pastels of the master in a white cloud. Kafka's vision borrowed becomes monstrous in the work of a John Hawkes. Dickens, who continues to defy neat summaries and to force his critics to inadequate adjectives, stands monolithic over the nineteenth century, tempting certain contemporary writers by his largeness, his easy solutions to problems that all novelists must face. I have already suggested that one of his conceptions of character has been an unfortunate model for Joyce Cary and Anthony Powell. Tradition, that is, can be dangerous and difficult; it can stifle where it is relied upon to release. To be specific, here is a typical speech of Micawber, one of Dickens's most successful fantastics: he is parting from David Copperfield after victimizing him as his lodger:

> 'My other piece of advice, Copperfield,' said Mr. Micawber, 'you know. Annual income twenty pounds, annual expenditure nineteen nineteen six, result happiness. Annual income twenty pounds, annual expenditure twenty pounds ought and six, result misery. The blossom is blighted, the leaf is withered, the God of day goes down upon the dreary scene, and—and in short you are for ever floored. As I am!'
>
> To make his example the more impressive, Mr. Micawber drank a glass of punch with an air of great enjoyment and satisfaction, and whistled the College Hornpipe.

V. S. Pritchett's Beluncle in *Mr. Beluncle* (1951) is a twentieth-century reincarnation of Micawber. Beluncle, a comic fraud, dreams of moving his large family from cramped quarters in a village near London to a country house, adequate to his ambitions. In physical appearance he was

> a short, deep, wide man, with grey hair kinked as if there were negro in him. His skin was kippered by a life of London smoke but it quickly flushed to an innocent country ruddiness at the taste of food: his face was bland, heavy in jowl, formless and kind, resting on a second chin like a bottom on an air cushion. It was the face of a man who was enjoying a wonderfully boyish meal, which got better with every mouthful; but in the lips and in the lines from the fleshy nose there was a refined, almost spiritual, arresting look of insult and contempt.

Early in Pritchett's burlesque upon the self-made, or the unself-unmade small businessman, street-corner religion, and popular psychologizing and sexualizing, Mr. Beluncle is discussing with his business-partner, Mrs. Truslove, his idea of a country house:

> 'You can't afford it,' said Mrs. Truslove.
> 'Afford it?' he said. 'I can afford what is right. If it is right for me to have that house or any other, nothing on earth'—and here Mr. Beluncle made a very large gesture—'can prevent me from having it. And—I'll give you a thought there,' said Mr. Beluncle, now smiling so warmly that his brown eyes seemed to buzz like

bees in his sunny creasing face, '—in case you are thinking of the price. There is only one price.' Mr. Beluncle said this solemnly, pointing a finger at her like an accusing salesman in an advertisement. 'You think too much of figures, Mrs. T., it's your training, I don't blame you, you're right to think of price; but if I believed every figure I have seen written down on paper in my lifetime'—and the word 'life' led Mr. Beluncle once more to make a large wide gesture upwards with both arms and to click the fingers of one hand very brilliantly as he did so, '—if I'd taken any notice of figures, where would I be now?'

'You'd be a rich man and not on the point of bankruptcy,' said Mrs. Truslove quietly.

'What?' said Mr. Beluncle, dropping his arms and going as green as a gorgonzola.

'I said you are on the point of bankruptcy,' said Mrs. Truslove.

'I don't want to hear you use that word,' said Mr. Beluncle. 'It's a funny word to use.'

He looked furtively as if he had heard something sexually indecent.

Micawber is a fine comic creation, and despite Dickens's eighteenth-century debts, an original one. The formula was simple, with the simplicity of a master: a figure belonging to his time and class is blown up with comic bellows to a new dimension. His dialogue is stylized and invariable. Micawber speaks usually about money, in circumlocutions, which he then translates into the vernacular. He is surrounded by a comic family off whom he lives; he trusts the future not only because it helps him to defraud his acquaintances, but because his horror of the present is real and compelling. The entire creation has the overtones of a horror more shattering than anything in Smollett. Dickens reaches reality by caricaturing it, a technique in which he is inimitable. Mr. Beluncle, who is closely patterned upon Micawber, is another matter. In describing Beluncle, Pritchett lingers over details as Dickens often does. The first part of the description quoted is evocative, realistic, and brilliant in the verb 'kippered'. The rest is Dickens adapted to 1951. Beluncle too speaks in circumlocutions and gestures with Micawber-like authority, but where Micawber would go modest and sad at the word 'bankruptcy',

Beluncle goes 'green as a gorgonzola'. Beluncle is the modern
fantastic; Pritchett has added certain elements—sexuality, smooth-
ness of pace, and a high degree of modern facility. But the basic
recipe is Dickens's, without the final ingredient of horror, and
Mr. Beluncle remains local, amusing perhaps, never more than
entertaining.

As a superb short-story writer and almost the only English
critic of the European novel, Pritchett is a surprising victim of the
Dickensian tradition. He is a craftsman in fiction, while his
awareness of the place of tradition in the novel is acute and
unassailable. *Mr. Beluncle* is doubtless an experiment, one which
helps us to measure the stature of writers who enjoy considerable
reputations for lesser accomplishments.

Between Dickens and V. S. Pritchett stands the figure of H. G.
Wells, the interesting Wells of *Tono-Bungay*, not the idea-monger-
ing Wells who wrote science-fiction and world history. Wells
is the typical novelist of the second phase; the writer who perceived the end of the Victorian order but returned to the Victorians for his technical equipment. Although he rejected the
beliefs of the society to which he belonged he was loyal, in his
scientific optimism, to the late nineteenth century. He is to the
comic novel as Hardy is to the tragic novel. The structural looseness and the whimsical characters with comic surnames are retrospective, looking back to Dickens and Fielding. His feeling for
reality is slight and inconsequential; Wells again manipulates
reality, selecting details for their place in the burlesque pattern of
events. Ponderevo in *Tono-Bungay* is a successful Micawber, but
a two-dimensional one. He looks 'energetic and knowing and
luxurious and most unexpectedly a little bounder . . .' He sits in
a chair with his little legs curled up—how false this touch—to
persuade George to come into business with him. He describes
the nostrum, Tono-Bungay:

> 'You see,' said my uncle in a slow confidential whisper, with eyes
> very wide and a creased forehead, 'it's nice because of the' (here he
> mentioned a flavouring matter and an aromatic spirit), 'it's stimula-
> ting because of' (here he mentioned two very vivid tonics, one with
> a marked action on the kidney). 'And the' (here he mentioned two

other ingredients) 'makes it pretty intoxicating. Cocks their tails. Then there's' (but I touch on the essential secret). 'And there you are. I got it out of an old book of recipes—all except the' (here he mentioned the more virulent substance, the one that assails the kidneys), 'which is my idea. Modern touch! There you are!'

Fifteen years later Sinclair Lewis was writing a similar kind of burlesque of business in *Babbitt*, but Lewis added to his burlesque the naturalist's notebook; he would have given us the chemical formulas of Tono-Bungay in the place of Wells's comic (and vague) parentheses. Lewis's burlesque bit deeper for being less stylized. Wells's burlesque, more intellectualized and more generalized, looks back to quite another tradition, and his concern is for another kind of reality.

I emphasize the comic tradition for its enormous importance in that monolithic construction, 'the nineteenth-century novel', as well as for the fact that the comic element is habitually ignored or slighted in favour of discussions of manners, morals, society, romanticism, lines of development, and all the rest of the literary historian's paraphernalia. Scott is Gothic, Hardy cosmic, George Eliot protestant *malgré lui*, and distinctions are lost or blurred in reverence for the monolithic structure itself. No nineteenth-century reputation was more monolithic than Scott's, and the monolithic aura pervades the twentieth-century atmosphere, even though the admirers of the Wizard of the North are increasingly hard put to it to rescue Scott from the nursery and the graduate seminar. His contemporary, Jane Austen, now overshadows him in the degree that he overshadowed her a century ago. Posterity (ourselves) has been just, I suspect, and it is worth relating the work of both Scott and Jane Austen to present practice in the novel.

Both writers relate slightly to the comic tradition, Scott with an occasionally heavy joke and Jane Austen with her satirical eye, but in neither case is there a comic centre, in the sense that the centre in Fielding or Peacock is comic. Jane Austen is more important to us in that she leads away from the Gothic novel of the late eighteenth century on to Trollope, George Eliot, Henry James, Elizabeth Bowen, and Rosamund Lehmann. Scott absorbs

Mrs. Radcliffe, enlarging and perfecting the Gothic mode, but he leads to Ainsworth, Lytton, Hugh Walpole, John Buchan, and saddest of all, to Margaret Mitchell and *Gone with the Wind*. He leads only casually to Emily Brontë, and I suspect that there is more of Jane Austen in *Wuthering Heights* than of Scott. Ironically enough, his continental and American influence, Margaret Mitchell apart, was another matter. His influence upon Balzac, Fenimore Cooper, Dumas, Mérimée, and Tolstoy is of the order of Poe's influence upon Baudelaire, Mallarmé, and Valéry; one always has the uncomfortable suspicion that these continental followers in each case were inventing a Scott and a Poe that never existed and admiring qualities that to the native reader remain inexplicable.

M. Merleau-Ponty has said, 'Because we are in the world, we are condemned to meaning.'[1] In terms of the novel, 'meaning' translates, I suspect, into 'reality', not photographic reality, of course, but the reality which emerges when mind and imagination combine to organize experience into a communicable entity. The difficulty with Scott is that finally his mind is uninteresting. We can accept his theory of the novel when in *The Monastery* Captain Clutterbuck quotes Villiers, 'Then, Sir, you would agree with Bayes, "What the devil does a plot signify except to bring in fine things?"' Scott, the novelist of fine things, never wrote fine novels, and he passed on to Trollope, Dickens and Thackeray a hobbling notion of narrative as a collection of fine things. As long as we consider the novel merely as entertainment, we can accept Scott's bequests, his love affairs, and his cloak-and-dagger nonsense; we can even accept his faulty diction, his 'God's bread!' 'Ods fish!' and 'Ods death!', for this diction is not intended to have anything to do with the meaning to which we are condemned. But at any other level than entertainment, it is hard to admit that Scott's vaunted morality is anything more than good Scottish piousness, that his admired Scottish peasants are anything more than local-colour writing, and that his 'realistic', 'racy' dialogue of the Scottish novels is even readable south of

---

[1] Herbert Spiegelberg, 'French Existentialism: Its Social Philosophies', *Kenyon Review*, XVI, No. 3, Summer 1954, 459.

Northumberland. Scott's version of reality invites interpretation as epic; no part of the whole stands by itself as a novel, but conceived as epic the various groupings among his novels fail to measure up, and the very effort underlines their essential triviality, their localness, and their failure in presenting either national or individual history. The failure is a failure of mind, just as in a different context Thomas Wolfe's and Somerset Maugham's and John Galsworthy's failures are failures of mind.

Historical romance and the novel of adventure: the burden of Scott's modern influence is here. When that influence appears in the serious modern novel, it is a doubtful one. Scott's present-day namesake, J. D. Scott, invites comparison with the master in *The End of an Old Song* (1954). The theme of ambition and social fluidity in the career of Alastair, a bright Edinburgh boy who leaves Scotland for the greener southern pastures of London, is an important one, often neglected in English writing. Patrick, the narrator, develops action past and action present in the first two-thirds of the novel with a social and psychological reality unusual for vividness and accuracy. But in the final third of the novel a false note sounds in the theme of Alastair's paternity, and the increasingly specious plot is resolved in a fire which burns down the ancestral manor. Sir Walter has in effect taken over from J. D. Scott to end the novel by the formula of the Waverley series. *The End of an Old Song* stands in the same relation to *The Antiquary*, with its paternity theme, as *Mr. Beluncle* to *David Copperfield*.

Where Scott's virtues have been inflated by idolatry, Emily Brontë's have been obscured. Her resemblance to Scott is slight; her Yorkshire is comparable to his Scottish settings, as is her use of dialect, with the reservation that the character Joseph, in *Wuthering Heights*, is the one of two examples in the novel of a cliché which reduces the total effect. Heathcliff is of course the other: Heathcliff is straight out of Byron, but he 'belongs' in the novel in the sense that the servant Joseph does not. The success of *Wuthering Heights* suggests where Scott most seriously fails. Both writers are at once romantic and anti-romantic, depending for their effects upon an emotional intensity set side by side with an

M

anti-romantic rationality and dryness. Scott's intensity is diffused and unconvincing through his neglect of the probable and his disregard of technique. Emily Brontë reaches and maintains a high degree of romantic, emotional intensity, and through the technique of various narrators, achieves distance and criticism; in that distance and criticism we sense the presence of a forceful and interesting mind, the quality of mind at work in *Emma* or *Mansfield Park*. Scott had attempted a Byronic Heathcliff in the figure of Ravenswood in *The Bride of Lammermoor*, but Ravenswood is little more than a sexless Giaour, a prototype for a Douglas Fairbanks film.

Heathcliff, too, is a Giaour or a Lara, but with a difference. Byron's passionate villains, like Scott's, exist quite apart from the other characters; their relations with the other characters are mechanical and determined by a preposterous plot. Heathcliff, though, is seen not only through his own actions and stilted speeches, not only through the demands of Emily Brontë's equally preposterous plot, but through his necessary relationship with Catherine, Cathy, and the Earnshaws—every fully-created character in the novel. Heathcliff has another dimension of reality, as well, which Byron only implies and Scott consciously ignores: he has a sexual reality which had been absent from English fiction after Fielding and which was not to reappear until Hardy.[1] Charlotte Brontë's universally recognized fleshliness, in *Jane Eyre* or *Shirley*, differs from Emily's understanding of sexual love as adolescent ogling differs from the passion of Antony for Cleopatra. Heathcliff's excesses are both Poesque and Byronic, but they are also the tumescent excesses of frustrated sexuality. We are more the followers of the Victorians than we know if we read the marvellously lyrical scenes between the young Heathcliff and Catherine as Platonic; their intensity serves to motivate, within the literary world of Wuthering Heights, Heathcliff's later hatreds, and his very necrophilia.

[1] Every commentator I know who discusses the subject refers to Emily Brontë's 'sexlessness'; this strikes me as insensitive and simply wrong. Muriel Spark, a moderate commentator, says that Emily Brontë was unable to understand sexual love as it might have existed between Heathcliff and Catherine. Spark and Stanford, *Emily Brontë: Her Life and Work*, Peter Owen, London, 1953, pp. 93–95.

On the night of Catherine's burial, Heathcliff relates, he went to the churchyard in the snow:

> Being alone, and conscious two yards of loose earth was the sole barrier between us, I said to myself—'I'll have her in my arms again! If she be cold, I'll think it is this north wind that chills *me*; and if she be motionless, it is sleep.' I got a spade from the tool-house, and began to delve with all my might—it scraped the coffin; I fell to work with my hands; the wood commenced cracking about the screws; I was on the point of attaining my object, when it seemed that I heard a sigh from some one above, close at the edge of the grave and bending down.

The reality of this is not the reality of Scott or of Poe, in, say, 'Ligeia' (published, incidentally, in 1838, nine years before *Wuthering Heights*); it has a reality which does not reappear in English until William Faulkner's tale of necrophilia in 'A Rose for Emily'.

Wuthering Heights is real because Emily Brontë was among the first novelists in English who, unconcerned with social realism, realized the importance of spareness in description, pace and distance in narration, and of probability in the midst of improbability. The famous and lovely speech of Cathy in which she describes her differences with Linton Heathcliff is an example of my meaning. Here we see the device of double narration: Ellen Dean is reporting the scene to Lockwood in Cathy's words, a device which lends both pace and distance, while the situation itself—Cathy's having been forbidden to visit the sickly Linton, together with her spirited transgression—is improbable but totally real within the narrative:

> 'One time, however, we were near quarrelling. He said the pleasantest manner of spending a hot July day was lying from morning to evening on a bank of heath in the middle of the moors, with the bees humming dreamily about among the bloom, and the larks singing high up overhead, and the blue sky and bright sun shining steadily and cloudlessly. That was his most perfect idea of heaven's happiness: mine was rocking in a rustling green tree, with a west wind blowing, and bright white clouds flitting rapidly above; and not only larks, but throstles, and blackbirds, and linnets, and cuckoos pouring out

music on every side, and the moors seen at a distance, broken into cool dusky dells; but close by great swells of long grass undulating in waves to the breeze; and woods and sounding water, and the whole world awake and wild with joy. He wanted all to lie in an ecstasy of peace; I wanted all to sparkle and dance in glorious jubilee. I said his heaven would be only half alive; and he said mine would be drunk; I said I should fall asleep in his; and he said he could not breathe in mine, and began to grow very snappish. At last, we agreed to try both, as soon as the right weather came; and then we kissed each other and were friends.'

The rhythm of the first half of the quotation is the prose of romanticism at its finest; but it is the conjunction of image, rhythm and antithesis in the second half that is startling and memorable. The use of antithesis is epigrammatic and controlled in a way that the English novel had not been controlled since Jane Austen. Yet Emily Brontë's emotional range shames Jane Austen, whose social comedies seem brittle and quaint in comparison.[1]

In terms of the present discussion, Emily Brontë's conception of reality was never to reappear in the English novel. It assuredly led, though in a tenuous manner, to D. H. Lawrence, but in Lawrence only the afflatus and none of the essence can be felt. The influence, if it is an influence, ran to ground in the dreary wastes of Charles Morgan's *Sparkenbroke*. For a convincing parallel to *Wuthering Heights*, we must look to Emily Brontë's American contemporaries, Melville and Hawthorne. Captain Ahab, Pierre Glendinning, Claggart, Chillingworth: these are the American Heathcliffs. But I anticipate my next chapter.

The degree of formal craftsmanship in *Wuthering Heights* was foreign to the serious English novel in 1847 and was to remain foreign to it until Conrad and James. The well-wrought novel had made an appearance in Jane Austen and a reappearance in Emily Brontë, when it passed not to the other masters of the nineteenth century, but to Wilkie Collins and the detective novel. Victorian taste, in the novel as in architecture and interior

---

[1] One must agree with Sir Herbert Read's comparison of the styles of Jane Austen and Emily Brontë, in which Emily Brontë comes off far better. *English Prose Style*, London, G. Bell, 1949, pp. 118–121.

decoration, ran to rococo fretwork and the elaboration of detail; writers like Trollope and Thackeray who obviously were capable of more workmanlike production chose to follow the taste of the day and at the same time to indulge in the English habit of the amateur, the off-the-cuff.[1] While today in the third phase brevity has supplanted prolixity and writers pay greater attention to actuality, the traditional attitude of the amateur still has great force. Careless writing is tolerated and even highly praised. The example of Lawrence comes to mind, or an even more egregious amateur of the novel, Wyndham Lewis. *Self Condemned* (1954), a novel which has received almost universal praise, reads like a first draft written by an unemployed newspaper reporter who has riffled through Arthur Machen, Sinclair Lewis, bad translations of Schnitzler, and the polemics of the elder Scaliger. 'Sudden death presents its card with a leer' is Lewis's way of disposing of the character, Mrs. McAffie, who is, incidentally, Dickensian in the worst sense. Both Wyndham Lewis and Lawrence were angry men who in any other country would have found a Bohemia in which to dissipate some of their anger and to place the rest in a more enriching context. But Lewis in particular resorts to tradition only to find a cliché to perform the work of imagination.

The journeymen of the contemporary English novel, like their fellows in America, France, Italy, or even Germany, go to school not only to a native tradition but to the international masters of the nineteenth century and of the great experimental period between 1910 and 1925; they nevertheless maintain a recognizable attitude towards reality in the novel. Whether we look to Ivy Compton-Burnett, Rex Warner, Elizabeth Bowen, Anthony West, P. H. Newby, Gerald Hanley, Henry Green, or Rosamund Lehmann we discover a common mastery of what were once experimental techniques, an admirable cultivation of the meanings and implications of those techniques, and a common degree of

[1] It invariably strikes the foreigner that in England, the most competitive society in the world, anyone with any claim to style affects not to work hard, not to struggle, not to admit that he is indeed competing with all his heart and soul. At the university, get a first by all means, but never admit that one worked for it.

stylization which relates their feeling for reality directly back to their eighteenth- and nineteenth-century forebears. Unlike many American writers, the contemporary English novelist need not relive the history of the novel within the limits of his own career. The English tradition serves him well and he begins work in full knowledge of what has been done in the novel form. At the same time, tradition not only can provide a standard for performance and a guide for craft, but it can also blight and diminish.

P. H. Newby's work characterizes the best that has occurred in post-World War II English fiction. *A Journey to the Interior* (1946), his first novel, is the work of a writer who knows his craft and has a view of human experience that is rich in present accomplishment and future possibility. Of the eight novels Newby has published since 1946, at least four are technical advances upon *A Journey to the Interior*. *A Step to Silence* (1952) and *The Retreat* (1953) are better novels than anything of Virginia Woolf or D. H. Lawrence, for example; they are the product of a writer of great literary energy whose sensibility is in the finest sense contemporary. Newby has learned creation of character from Dickens and perhaps from Dostoievski; he has learned pace, movement and a method of seeing from, I suspect, Conrad. His prose is clear with our twentieth-century kind of clarity, direct, straightforward, stronger in nouns and verbs than in the trappings of adjectives and adverbs. In these qualities he is traditional. His uniqueness rests in his conception of how human beings react upon one another; it is here that Newby's contemporary sensibility exercises its effect. *The Retreat* deals with Dunkirk and the period immediately following, yet it is only incidentally a war novel. Its real subject is that classical modern one, the difficulty of love and the terror of isolation. The confused relationship between Oliver Knight and Hesketh; Jane, Hesketh's wife, and Oliver's own wife—all of whom one had met in *A Step to Silence* —creates the subject and expresses it with intensity. Knight is wounded at Dunkirk and deserts the Air Force out of a compulsion to find Jane Hesketh in England. The substance of the novel, a frequent device for Newby, is pursuit, but he differs from the traditional novelist and from the quest-*Märchen* in never supplying a logical motive for the quest.[1] This amounts to the important insight that human beings frequently do act without logical motive, just as it conveys thematically and structurally the fact of fragmentation of experience under the impact of war. It is a welcome change from the traditional conception of the novel as a round and finished sphere of experience—that conception which dominated English fiction from its origins to the modern period. And yet, in spite of his ability to give his novels a structural reality that is unfacile and new, Newby's feeling for actuality remains literary; his novels have a 'written' quality which tends to negate his psychological insight and structural innovation. Regardless of literary energy and a fine sense of society, the traditional, stylized awareness of the real world in his work amounts either to blindness towards an important aspect of experience, or, more likely, to the fatal English impatience with the possibilities of language.

This same observation would apply to the rest of contemporary English novelists with few exceptions. Other writers stylize in other ways, but the net effect remains the same. Rex Warner writes a prose which demonstrates his knowledge of the classics, but it is a prose in which every character speaks like every other character: in the accents of a classical scholar. Ivy Compton-Burnett constructs novels entirely in dialogue, but the fluency of that dialogue does not compensate for a sameness of tone which causes the best-intentioned reader to confuse the characters from beginning to end and from novel to novel. Aldous Huxley's characters speak with crispness and wit, but they tend all to have the same crispness and the same wit; when in his later novels he attempts American speech, he sacrifices both wit and crispness and any vestige of the reality of American speech as well, as does Christopher Isherwood. Lawrence's characters, male and female, are indistinguishable from the Laurentian voice of the essays, and when he writes dialect in the mouth of Mellors, the game-

---

[1] In a monograph on Maria Edgeworth, Newby supplies a clue to his theory: 'The least we can ask of our serious writer, then (we exclude the comic writer, that most intellectual of beings, because we forgive anyone who amuses us), is that he should be occasionally puzzled.' *Maria Edgeworth*, London, Arthur Barker, 1950, p. 60.

keeper, or the elder Morel, he is unreadable. And when a writer like V. S. Pritchett presents a lower-class character like Mr. Beluncle he borrows shamelessly from Dickens.

The syntax of the English novel has changed very slightly in the last hundred years. A move towards simplicity can be seen, but for the most part English writers are all too content with a public-school standard of good taste. B.B.C.-English is a standard not only for the young man up from the provinces working at his first job in advertising, but it is a standard of that middle class who are so monotonously the subject of the English writer. This means that the English novelist can 'place' his characters out of his acquaintance with a literary tradition; he does not exercise himself to the observation of habits of speech which are essential to the creation of literary reality. The social fact that English writers either derive from or aspire to the middle class has produced a literature of *manners* at the expense of other genres. The English writer admittedly has a special problem; England has a vast variety of languages and the writer is forced either to the dialect of Mellors or to the middle-class tones of Mrs. Dalloway. James Joyce, as Cyril Connolly has pointed out,[1] was the first writer to realize —and it took an Anglo-Irishman to do so—that English syntax was in a state of decay. His answer was parody. Unfortunately Joyce's influence has been slight in England, the country to which his parody was directed.

I do not mean, in this discussion of the presence or absence of actuality in the English novel, to be making a plea for 'realism' or 'naturalism' or any other bare-boned theory of writing. What I do mean by the relationship between reality and tradition is contained in R. P. Blackmur's phrase, 'symbolic techniques'. Blackmur writes,

> By symbolic techniques I mean what happens in the arts—*what gets into the arts*—that makes them relatively inexhaustible so long as they are understood. I mean what happens in the arts by means of fresh annunciations of residual or traditional forces, whether in the language, culture, or institutions of the artist's society. I mean those forces that operate in the arts which are greater than ourselves and

[1] *The Condemned Playground*, p. 9.

come from beyond or under ourselves. .... I mean invokable forces, or raw forces, the force of reality, whatever reality may be, pressing into and transforming our actual experience. It is what bears us and what we cannot bear except through the intervention of one of the great modes of the mind, religion, philosophy, or art, which giving us the illusion of distance and control, makes *them*, too, seem forces greater than ourselves.[1]

In Blackmur's sense of the term 'reality', we can object that not enough gets into the English novel; a convention of realism has too often been substituted for reality itself. English poetry is rich in reality in a way that the English novel is poverty-stricken. Tradition and stylization, together with a suspicion of intellect and of high seriousness, have often been crippling. Evelyn Waugh and Graham Greene are as highly serious as the English novel has become, and it is all too relevant that one did his best work as the funny man of the 1930s and the other as a latter-day Wilkie Collins. The difference between the English and American awareness of reality in the novel is rather like Frank O'Connor's comment on the difference between the short story in England and the short story in Ireland and America. He said that the English short story is still in the stage where the last paragraph reads, 'As Col. Lascelles descended the staircase, his smile was the smile we had always known, but his whiskers were the whiskers of Tim the cat!' Somewhere between Blackmur and O'Connor lies the middle ground of accuracy. It remains for us to examine certain aspects of the American tradition in order to see more clearly the contours of that middle ground.

[1] R. P. Blackmur, *The Lion and the Honeycomb*, New York, Harcourt, Brace, 1955, pp. 210–211.

Chapter Six

TRADITION AND THE NOVEL: AMERICA

PERHAPS the leading difference between the English and the American tradition is not to be found in any single literary fact or group of literary facts, but in the attitude of writers to tradition. The English writer, like the continental, takes tradition for granted as something half-consciously absorbed in youth, like the principle of the family or the idea of monarchy. The American writer, on the other hand, must make his individual peace with tradition; he cannot put pen to paper without consciously accepting or rejecting a vast complex of literary, political, and sociological facts. Thus while tradition in England might seem devious, in contrast to America it is simplicity itself. Discontinuity takes the place of continuity and paradox the place of evolution in the American novel. The English novel has always had a close connection with English society, but from its origins the American novel has had the most ambiguous connection to society. To approach the American tradition, one must frequently leave literature for social and intellectual history and other non-literary considerations; not that the best American writing cannot stand alone, but that the American literary tradition is only partly literary.

The image of the American writer existing in scornful isolation from his society is familiar, valid in part, but finally facile and oversimplified. That view, stated frequently in the Marxist or proto-Marxist criticism of the 1930s,[1] has survived its political inspiration to become a cliché of the 1950s. It is hardly adequate for dealing with the thrust and counter-thrust of not one but

[1] For example, Newton Arvin, 'Individualism and the American Writer', in M. D. Zabel, ed., *Literary Opinion in America*, New York, Harper, 1951, pp. 544–549. This essay first appeared in *The Nation*, 1931.

several traditions in American writing; it has slight validity for
any real understanding of either Cooper or Henry James; it
helps to account for certain themes in the American novel, particularly the theme of dissolution that is strong in Cooper, Poe,
Dreiser, Faulkner, Fitzgerald, Wolfe and Nathaniel West, but it
hardly contributes to an understanding of the work of any one
of these writers, by relating it either piecemeal to one another's or
to the European traditions which they use in their various
ways.

It is certainly true, as William Phillips has said, that modern
European literature has been created and led by an intelligentsia
which has been able to discover, preserve, and simultaneously
recreate it within the framework of the great Western tradition
of beliefs and values. But when Phillips analyses the American
literary tradition and discovers not one tradition but a discon-
tinuous process in which each generation must recreate anew a
viable tradition, he is dealing in partial truth.[1] Within the discontinuity which Phillips emphasizes can be discerned the continuity
of the American writer's relationship to romanticism, while paradoxically we must be aware of the discontinuity within the work
of the single writer—Cooper, Steinbeck and Dos Passos are only
too flagrant examples. Again the American novelist's feeling for
reality offers a possible approach.

In this connection, I would vary Cyril Connolly's statement,
'. . . the vice of [English Literature is] Unreality',[2] to read, 'The
vice of American Literature is Reality.' Reality, or unreality,
has haunted the American novelist as memories of childhood
haunt old men. Where the English novelist's apprehension of
society has often hampered and diminished him, the American
writer has scorned conventional English social realism for ven-
tures into the interior of reality that have produced a few masterpieces and a large number of deplorable works which the average
European will not so much as admit to the discussion. V. S.
Pritchett remarks of James Jones's *From Here to Eternity*:

[1] William Phillips, 'The Intellectual's Tradition', *Partisan Review*, VIII,
November–December 1941, 481–490.
[2] *The Condemned Playground*, p. 80.

We are reaching the point where the European critic will have to admit that at least one school of American novelists is beyond his modest fishing tackle. One or two recent monsters roll about and sport like whales; if caught and disembowelled, they are remarkable for yielding tons of realism like so much undistinguishable blubber. The poet Clough, noting that the Colosseum in Rome was 'big' went on to ask 'if this is an idea?' Is it an idea to put down the literal life and obscene talk of an air force camp, to put the whole Pacific campaign into a novel, to describe word by unprintable word the hourly fatigues, promotion hunts, drunken blinds, crap games and fornications of a regular infantry company, stationed near Pearl Harbour?[1]

This is of interest not for its insensitivity to Jones's considerable abilities, but because the novel indicates how one American conception of reality differs intensely from the English conception— though not from one strain in continental writing. Pritchett's outrage is the emotion of a writer whose literature has seen little of naturalism and of the naturalist's primitive presentation of idea. This is another way of saying that American and English literary stylization differ in the degree that Savile Row tailoring differs from the cut of a cowboy's chaps. James Jones is an American phenomenon, inconceivable in England or even on the Continent. He is at once a product of romantic anti-intellectualism and of a social mobility which encourages a man to follow his inclination against logic, reason or common sense, and which may reward him handsomely into the bargain. Where English society has produced literature which is simply impatient of intellectual formulations, American society has produced an implicit anti-intellectualism which takes the form of a philistine demand for an easy optimism,[2] the raging denial of mind in

---

[1] V. S. Pritchett, 'Books in General', *New Statesman and Nation*, XLIV, 12 July 1952, 44.

[2] This view is usually seen on the periphery of literature itself. H. S. Commager, an historian, writes: 'We have little use, now, for the optimistic, the domestic, or even the democratic . . . fiction in our time is more concerned with aberrations of these qualities than with the qualities themselves, with repudiations of the optimistic, with violent departures from the domestic, with revelations of the insincerity and hollowness of our democracy. . . . It is easy to deride the doctrines that art must serve morality and that it must instruct rather than

From Here to Eternity, together with the highly intellectual novel of Henry James, or Norman Mailer in *Barbary Shore*.

This particular paradox is at once summarized and parodied in Nathaniel West's *Miss Lonelyhearts*, where Shrike, the newspaper editor, reviews in a scornful diatribe the possible modes of action for a citizen of the Waste Land world—and proves with drunken certainty the impossibility of escape either in the simple life, drink, art, women, drugs, or suicide: 'God alone is our escape', he concludes. 'The Church is our only hope, the First Church of Christ Dentist, where He is worshipped as Preventer of Decay. The Church whose symbol is the trinity: Father, Son and Wirehaired Fox Terrier. . . .' West's bitter and powerful satire has relevance to a traditional American feeling for reality while it demonstrates one place to which American, as opposed to European, experiment has moved.

Clearly neither Nathaniel West, James Jones nor virtually any other American writer of the third phase can actually be seen in depth without a fuller examination of the various American traditions. The figure of Henry James must loom large in any view of the American tradition, if only because he poses more urgently than anyone else the problem of the relationship between the English and the American novel. James has been victimized by two kinds of reader: the reader who sees James as a rootless and wistful European, denying his birthplace and satirizing his compatriots over his long career; and the reader who asserts James's Americanism as fervently as he sings 'The Star-Spangled Banner'. For him the fact of Americanism is sufficient and James is included with Sarah Orne Jewett and George Washington Cable as an American writer of fiction. One must agree with the second reader's conclusions while taking total exception to his

entertain, and it is almost irresistible to object to the principle that truth requires a sunny picture of American life. Clearly these are not the principles that have animated American fiction in the last half-century. From Crane, Norris and Garland through to Steinbeck, Faulkner and Dos Passos, and including even such traditionalist figures as Edith Wharton, Ellen Glasgow and Willa Cather, American novelists have concentrated on the misery, poverty, dullness and frustration of life in America.' H. S. Commager, ed., *Selected Writings of William Dean Howells*, New York, Random House, 1950, p. x.

reasons. 'To focus James's art against a background of Continental writers is not to focus it at all.' In an admirable examination of Hawthorne and Henry James, Marius Bewley performs an important service to criticism, while he poses questions whose implications lie outside his book, *The Complex Fate*. His quotation continues, 'and to eliminate Hawthorne from the history of his [James's] artistic development is simply to eliminate the best part of James—the part towards which his most serious moral interests gravitated'.[1] By placing Cooper, Hawthorne, Melville, and James within a single tradition, Bewley perceives a relationship which has escaped more pedestrian critics, while his legitimate impatience with the pedestrian critic's emphasis upon movements and influences—in this case romanticism in both its American and European manifestations—causes him to obscure the exact nature of the tradition he is describing. Again, the term 'moral' for Bewley, as for Yvor Winters and Dr. Leavis, is burdened with implications whose meaning is not explained. It has become a habit of our neo-neo-classicism to seek and find 'morality' up and down and back and forth across the entire landscape of Western literature. If a writer can be made moral he passes, otherwise he is discarded. 'Moral' in this connection seems to mean literature in which a series of significant choices is arranged by the author, and the more painful these choices, the more moral the author. This strikes me as a specious instrument in criticism, for it is quite arbitrary to divorce morality from ethics, and ethics, being patently non-literary, are never mentioned in the context of morality. To judge writing on moral grounds is to beg the question that all art is ultimately moral. Having said that, the critic must begin again with the process of criticism.

There is no question that moral choice, deriving from a theological framework, played an important part in the perception of their material by Hawthorne, Melville, James, Howells and Edith Wharton. In the third phase of the novel, moral choice based upon traditional Christianity hardly satisfies the demands of catastrophe. Yet the best of modern novelists in no sense eliminate morality from their view. I have emphasized the moral

[1] *The Complex Fate*, p. 6.

indignation in the naturalists, and it is hard to deny the presence of a moral basis in the work of Hemingway, Fitzgerald, Dos Passos or James Gould Cozzens. But again, having said this, we have said very little about peculiar and distinctive outlines of traditional American literature.

Hawthorne remains as fascinating a figure for us as for Henry James in that his prose caught and presented within a framework of various romantic clichés at least three themes which were to obsess American writers for a century: the theme of the place of the artist in society; the theme of disparity between traditional classicism and 'natural' man; and the international theme—the pressures and counter-pressures that are set up in the American mind as it conceives the idea of Europe. Hawthorne remains a minor writer in his inability to find a formal and stylistic vehicle adequate to his themes. James, in his way, remains compelling, because he was able to bring to Hawthorne's perceptions the formal equipment which their complexity and validity demand. Both James and Conrad occupy a unique position in the Anglo-American tradition. In our gratitude to James we have probably exaggerated his achievement; something of the same order applies to Conrad, whose work, however, lies outside this discussion. Hawthorne is minor because he allowed the traditional European machinery of romanticism to do too much of his work. Miles Coverdale in *The Blithedale Romance* wavers hazily before the eye, half author's disguise, half polite gentleman of a dozen conventional literary performances. Nevertheless he anticipates Strether of *The Ambassadors* as well as Nick Carraway of *The Great Gatsby* and even Jake Barnes of *The Sun Also Rises*. Coverdale is the prototype in American fiction of the perceptive centre, the moral mind which registers both the central action and its implicit resonances. Hawthorne's villains are Byronic in conception, pure products of a debased romanticism. Zenobia, Hawthorne's dark lady, like Hester Prynne, is a triumph within the stylized cliché of romanticism; almost in spite of the author, Zenobia and Hester are genuine women, sensual, rounded and full-blooded, the kind of women D. H. Lawrence attempted but failed to create. In his difficult affair with Europe, Hawthorne uncovered a rich literary subject, but again he lacked perhaps the mind, certainly the technique for presenting it in a literary context. *The Marble Faun* fails wretchedly, and we must go to the European and the American Notebooks to discover the degree of Hawthorne's preoccupation with the idea of Europe. As a Democrat and author of a campaign biography of Franklin Pierce, Hawthorne wanted to believe in the American national image, yet in his conscience he felt threatened and rejected by that national image. He looked to Europe as a man bred in a subpolar region looks to the Mediterranean—for warmth, light and spiritual nourishment.

Cooper had felt the same division in himself before Hawthorne, but Cooper had been able to confront, if not to resolve, the difficulty in social satire. Hawthorne was in no sense a satirist and it is depressingly typical of the nature of tradition in America that he learned nothing from Cooper. His English models, Mrs. Radcliffe and the Gothic strain in Horace Walpole, served him badly. The immediate influence of transcendentalism he perceived to be useless for his purposes. He went to seventeenth-century New England history partly out of taste, but more importantly out of a compulsion to fit his artist's instincts and perceptions into a usable pattern of human reality. A lesser artist would have stopped with Mrs. Radcliffe, as Charles Brockden Brown had done two generations before.

Dr. Leavis has indicated—and exaggerated—James's debt to George Eliot; he sees one of James's finest novels, *The Portrait of a Lady*, as a rewriting of the first section of *Daniel Deronda*.[1] Quite apart from the strange critical procedure of renaming George Eliot's novel *Gwendolen Harleth* and discussing it as an entity, Leavis chooses to ignore the fact that *The Portrait of a Lady* belongs to a long line of American novels which have as their theme the results upon the American consciousness of European experience. The bulk of James's work as well as his best work is devoted to that theme, hence the depth of James's American roots must be stressed.[2]

[1] *The Great Tradition*, p. 85.
[2] From its beginnings French criticism of James has emphasized his American

Quite apart from James's place as an artist it is worth noting that his main impact in England has been upon style—see Elizabeth Bowen, Anthony Powell or L. P. Hartley—while his influence in America has been first thematic and only secondly stylistic. James's following in his own lifetime was minor. Howells at best was a lesser James and Edith Wharton a still lesser female replica. As novelists of manners Howells and Edith Wharton have a certain interest, but Howells realized only crudely the importance of James's experiments; for example, he indicated his inability to maintain point of view with any consistency. Edith Wharton reproduced the trappings of James's social world, but with the exception of *The House of Mirth*, her least Jamesian novel, her writing has come to seem mildewed and dated.

James's technical contributions of course pervade the entire modern novel, but within the narrower limits of American writing we can see a specific tradition developing. Fitzgerald's two finest novels, *The Great Gatsby* and *Tender is the Night*, represent two poles of Jamesian influence within the work of a novelist whose considerable stature has not yet been fully granted. *Gatsby* is not just a novel of manners, but a Jamesian novel of manners. Fitzgerald's subject is money: money as it creates manners and money as a force in a society whose traditions are fading and being supplanted by codeless codes and by the raw cast of human character exposed to daily tests.

Tom and Daisy Buchanan have the attitudes and habits of a piratical aristocracy based on money and to a certain degree on birth, and Gatsby represents the anarchic force in American society that imitates the piracy of the aristocracy but lacks its codes and conventions. Gatsby is at once a comic figure in his aping the Buchanans, and he is genuinely tragic in his belief that the actual past does not matter, that only his invented version of the past has reality. Nick Carraway, the Jamesian narrator, centre of vision and judgment, establishes the link in tone between the two

quality and has even accused him of provincialism. Sartre has asked, 'Why read James when Flaubert is closer to hand?' implying that James has full meaning only in an American context. 'American Novelists through French Eyes', *Atlantic Monthly*, Vol. 178, No. 2, August 1946, 114–118.

N

extremities of action. He understands, likes and despises the Buchanans; he comes to understand Gatsby, and in a way to love him out of the completeness of his understanding. Carraway's understanding of the Buchanans and of Gatsby is of the same quality as Strether's understanding of Chad in *The Ambassadors*, or of Ralph Touchett's understanding of Isabel Archer in *The Portrait of a Lady*: it is a quality of love.

Fitzgerald's ability to convey undertones through style is also Jamesian. Writing of the Buchanans, Carraway says,

> Why they came East I don't know. They had spent a year in France for no particular reason, and then drifted here and there unrestfully wherever people played polo and were rich together. This was a permanent move, said Daisy over the telephone, but I didn't believe it—I had no sight into Daisy's heart, but I felt that Tom would drift on forever seeking, a little wistfully, for the dramatic turbulence of some irrecoverable football game.

> .   .   .   .   .

> [Tom Buchanan] had changed since his New Haven years. Now he was a sturdy straw-haired man of thirty with a rather hard mouth and a supercilious manner. Two shining arrogant eyes had established dominance over his face and gave him the appearance of always leaning aggressively forward. Not even the effeminate swank of his riding clothes could hide the enormous power of that body—he seemed to fill those glistening boots until he strained the top lacing, and you could see a great pack of muscle shifting when his shoulder moved under his thin coat. It was a body capable of enormous leverage—a cruel body.

> His speaking voice, a gruff husky tenor, added to the impression of fractiousness he conveyed. There was a touch of paternal contempt in it, even toward people he liked—and there were men at New Haven who had hated his guts.

Our last view of Buchanan takes the form of a judgment:

> I couldn't forgive him or like him, but I saw that what he had done was, to him, entirely justified. It was all very careless and confused. They were careless people, Tom and Daisy—they smashed up things and creatures and then retreated back into their money or their vast carelessness, or whatever it was that kept them together, and let other people clean up the mess they had made. . . .

I shook hands with him; it seemed silly not to, for I felt suddenly as though I were talking to a child. Then he went into the jewellery store to buy a pearl necklace—or perhaps only a pair of cuff buttons —rid of my provincial squeamishness for ever.

In *Tender is the Night*, a more ambitious novel than *Gatsby*, Fitzgerald eliminated the narrator and viewed his subject in the round. The tone and the quality of perception resemble that of *Gatsby*, but the subject, that other Jamesian theme of American experience in Europe, demands a broader technical range than the use of a narrator permits. Diver, the central figure, is a kind of twentieth-century Isabel Archer, a man of intellectual ability and basic decency who is almost corrupted by twentieth-century versions of Mme Merle, Osmond and Italy, the wealthy, cosmo-politan American family into which he has married and the enervation of life on the French Riviera. Diver's renunciation of his wife's money and of a potentially brilliant career as a psychia-trist is presented as failure; he is last heard from in a small-town general practice in upper New York State. But his failure re-sembles Henry Adams's failure and possesses the same irony. Set almost entirely in Europe, the novel can only be understood in terms of American society; thus James's great example is ex-tended.

Hawthorne remained suspended between history and litera-ture; James placed history within literature, and Fitzgerald and Hemingway followed him. Once we shear away the foliage of critical cliché, resentment, misunderstanding, and bloody-minded-ness about the nature and dimensions of Hemingway's achieve-ment, we can see how close he is to James's subject and to James's perception of social reality. Too much has been made of the slight connection between Gertrude Stein's experiments and Heming-way's prose, particularly in dialogue. Hemingway's best critic has pointed out that James's and Hemingway's dialogue is often virtually indistinguishable, especially in their common use of the 'hovering subject', that dialogue in which the actual subject is never mentioned but only implied.[1] I have already mentioned

[1] Carlos Baker, *Hemingway: The Writer as Artist*, Princeton, Princeton Univer-sity Press, 1952, pp. 182–186.

that Hemingway's manner of perception resembles James's;[1] their broader resemblance conforms to the logic of their parallel development as writers.

Both James and Hemingway were innocent of conventional education; in their different ways they educated themselves along the lines which were most profitable to them as writers. James read the English novelists and with unerring taste chose to work along the lines of one who had most relevance for him, George Eliot. He studied the Russians and the French, but always he built upon his model from the American tradition, Hawthorne. Hemingway discarded most of the English novelists as useless to him but centred upon one whom he could use, Ford Madox Ford. We have only to read the Tietjens series to discover how heavily Hemingway borrowed from Ford, and through Ford from Conrad. Hemingway, too, studied the Russians and the French, and he, too, always built upon his native tradition. But again the element of discontinuity appears, for Hemingway combined the anti-traditional tradition of Mark Twain by way of Sherwood Anderson, Stephen Crane, and of course James himself. Both James and Hemingway moved unhesitatingly to the international theme, the sounding of the depths of European experience upon the American mind. Both writers worked towards objectivity and both made heavy contributions to the art of the novel through their experiments in the techniques of objectivity: between them they created the modern American novel and a significant element of the modern English novel. Both writers took the fragmentation of society for their enveloping subject, but their great differences in tone and in impact help to explain the difference between the second and the third phase of the novel. That James anticipated with every nerve in his body the fact of social fragmentation as it has come to pass is apparent from his stylistic complexity, his humanity, and his moral preoccupation; it is also evidence of his greatness. His failures, and they are extensive, arose from his allegiance to a disintegrating society, a narrowness of vision, and a disposition to give the trivial the same attention as the significant. Born with the instincts of a rebel, he shrank from rebellion;

[1] See p. 95.

gifted with a unique literary sensibility, he expended it upon gossamer. Hemingway had luck; history, social fact and the accidents of his experience conspired to support his literary instinct; as devoted to the art of writing as James, Hemingway inevitably translates in his work a unique vision of our damned and fascinating recent history.

The cosmopolitanism of James and Hemingway not only establishes the paradox of continuity and discontinuity in the American tradition, it also emphasizes that the record of American writing in the nineteenth century was brief, thin, and in national terms, impure; whenever it attained purity, it was limited and provincial. Nothing distinctly American appeared until Cooper's Leather-Stocking series, begun in 1823. The so-called first American novel, William Hill Brown's *The Power of Sympathy*, dates conveniently from the year of the adoption of the Constitution, 1789. This novel was published anonymously to make it appear English, and English it was totally, in derivation and in feeling. Brown used Richardson's epistolary form, and like Richardson he said in his preface that he wished 'to expose the dangerous consequences of seduction' and to set forth 'the advantages of female education'. There any resemblance to Richardson ceases. The main plot involves a threatened incestuous marriage, the death by shock of the heroine, and the suicide of the hero, who dies with a copy of *Werther* on his table. The sub-plot deals coyly with seduction and further violent death. The sensational near-pornography of *The Power of Sympathy* set a low standard which was followed by Susannah Rowson in *Charlotte Temple* (London 1791, U.S. 1794), a novel whose popularity, 160 editions before 1860, was hardly justified by its quality; Susannah Rowson dealt in the English vogue for seduction and sentimentality in a style the elegance of which Mrs. Aphra Behn might have admired. Hannah Foster's *The Coquette* (1797) was more of the same, though its sensationalism was somewhat muted. The most interesting of these early derivative novels is Hugh Henry Brackenridge's *Modern Chivalry* (1792–1815). Brackenridge avoided Richardson and went for his model to Cervantes by way of Fielding. Capt. Farrago is his Quixote and an immigrant Irishman, Teague

O'Reagan, his Sancho Panza. Like Fielding, Brackenridge was a
Judge and a well-educated man. He wrote broad but witty satire
on a theme which would have interested Fielding: the nature of
liberty and the abuses of democracy. As a novel, however,
Modern Chivalry has even less form than Fielding's work, though
it remains an amusing and frequently well-written account of
American life at the end of the eighteenth century in backwoods
Pennsylvania, Washington and Philadelphia.

From William Hill Brown through Brackenridge, the novel
had been directed at the English eighteenth-century middle class;
as such it was without real significance to the American imagination. Charles Brockden Brown, however, went to English sources
which were to have large meaning in the American literary tradition. Brown clearly had read the English Gothic writers, Horace
Walpole, Mrs. Radcliffe, Monk Lewis, perhaps even Beckford.
He also read Godwin's *Political Justice*, Mary Wollstonecraft's *A
Vindication of the Rights of Woman*, and Godwin's novels, *Caleb
Williams* and *St. Leon*. The first professional writer in America,
Brown wrote with a peculiarly American seriousness. At least one
of his novels, *Wieland* (1798), is better than any of his Gothic
models, and *Edgar Huntly* (1799) has the dubious distinction of
being the first detective novel in English. Brown made good use
of the American scene in all his work, and he saw that to be
really effective, the 'Gothic' element needed to be more than atmosphere and machinery, had to be in fact psychological. Living in a
'Gothic' house near Philadelphia, Theodore Wieland is a psycho-
tic individual who hears on various occasions a strange voice
which he believes to be the voice of God. He becomes a victim of
religious delusions and slays his wife and children. We learn that
the voice was that of a wandering ventriloquist, Carwin. While
Brown used the conventional realistic explanation of his English
models, he created in Wieland the first fully realized character in
American fiction. *Ormond* (1799) is a chaotic failure which seems
to combine Goethe's Faust and Byron's Manfred with Richardson's Pamela and certain qualities of the elder Cenci. In spite of
his failures and in spite of much pedestrian writing in *Clara
Howard* and *Jane Talbot* (both 1801), Brown is still challenging in

himself, but more interesting to the tradition of the novel for his original use of the American scene. His American Gothic transformed the genre out of its English context, where it was a kind of *jeu*, a stylized mode, into a means of escape from a society which he saw with classic American eyes—a society to accept and to reject in the very act of acceptance, to portray for its own fascination and to leave for its impossible demands upon the individual who had no accepted place. These themes are shadowy in Brown's work, but, I think, indubitably there. Poe knew Brown and imitated his American adaptation of English Gothic. Poe in fact makes more sense when viewed in relation to Brown than to Germany, just as the macabre in Faulkner is more fully comprehensible in relation to both Poe and Brown. We know that Carwin's pained shock at the results of his experiments upon Wieland gave Mary Shelley the idea for *Frankenstein*; I wonder if *Arthur Mervyn* (1800) might not have given Melville the idea for *Pierre*. Whether Melville knew Brown or not, an affinity between the two novels surely exists.

With Brockden Brown German romanticism in English dress became established in the American novel with such solidity that it has never really been dislodged. In England, to the contrary, the novel has remained closer to its eighteenth-century models, and romanticism has touched it only fleetingly and intermittently. Emily Brontë's isolated romanticism was more a matter of geography or metaphor than of response to influence; the basic mode has been Jane Austen's anti-romanticism. Brockden Brown Americanized English Gothicism by eliminating its medieval character, a circumstance which testifies both to his sound instinct as an artist and to his undoubted provincialism. Cooper, a better artist and in no sense a provincial, discovered qualities in European romanticism which he could use in an American setting, while at the same time he travelled for material with Scott into the European past. Cooper's trilogy of Europe in late feudal times, *The Bravo*, *The Heidenmauer* and *The Headsman*, is too burdened with unassimilated idea to succeed, but it does not suffer from comparison with his master and rival, Scott. Cooper should still be read for his inspired adaptation of Scott's methods to native

American materials, but I would emphasize that Cooper is not merely an adapter but an original who made full use of an English tradition while he created an American one.

Cooper's masterpiece, the Leather-Stocking series, raises the problem of the place of the frontier in the American novel, both as a subject and as an intellectual force. For a generation in America Cooper and the literature of the frontier has been the property of the flag-waving school of academic apologists who rescued Cooper and Mark Twain from the children and placed them in the academic curriculum. The result has been profitable, but for the wrong reasons. To eliminate Cooper's debt to Europe is to slight his American accomplishment, and to centre attention on his use of the American setting forces one either into apology, or into satire like Mark Twain's upon Cooper's primitive sense of actuality.[1] The literature of the American frontier poses with urgency the question of the traditional and the anti-traditional. The existence of the series of geographical frontiers was a challenge to native writers who answered for non-literary reasons to the call for a national literature. At the same time, both as a physical obstacle and as an idea, the frontier concentrated the energy of American romanticism into a revolt against what was seen either as the restraints of cities or the excesses of urban corruption. Folk-lore and the all too self-conscious creation of folk myths took the place in America of the German *Märchen*; the literary rendering of frontier speech took the place of the intellectualized European research into remote languages and cultures; the European roman-tic distrust of reason and of urban life was fashioned into not only a glorification, but a full mystique, of the good primitive. Cooper realized the use to which the romantic formulas of Byron, Scott and Wordsworth could be put in the American setting. His apprehension was more imaginative than rational, a fact which explains both his successes and failures. In the Leather-Stocking series, Cooper manipulated the motifs of European romanticism

---

[1] Mark Twain writes a witty but irrelevant account of 'Fenimore Cooper's Literary Offenses', in Edmund Wilson, ed., *The Shock of Recognition*, New York, Doubleday, 1947, pp. 582–594; Twain's attack is rather like a criticism of Turner for not painting in the manner of Giotto.

in an interesting way. Natty Bumppo (also known as Leather-
Stocking, Deerslayer, Pathfinder, Hawkeye, and The Trapper)
personifies the superiority of the heart over the head, while he is
Byronic in his ability to perform superhuman feats. At various
times, Natty is the agent of proof of the superior wisdom of
savages, women, children, and idiots; he embodies the romantic
clichés, but Cooper recreates them not as clichés but as prototypes
of a reality which corresponded closely to frontier experience.
Natty Bumppo is neither a Lara nor even a Heathcliff; he is
superhuman not in lusts and rages but in his ability to drive a nail
in a plank with a bullet at 200 yards. He is an innocent, a naïf, a
child of nature born white but living by choice among the
Indians, possessing the 'natural' virtues of justice, honesty and
purity. If only for his Americanization of the European romantic
hero, Cooper's creation of Natty Bumppo would be of first
importance. But Cooper's image of the American primitive
scene has another importance for the American novel. His
biographer has remarked that Cooper's mind operated in reversed
chronological order;[1] we first meet Natty Bumppo in *The Pioneers*
(1823) when he is already advanced in age; *The Last of the Mohicans*
(1826) goes back in time to Natty's early middle age; *The Prairie*
(1827) presents Natty in 1804, almost ninety, and describes his
career on the western plains and his death; the remainder of the
series, *The Pathfinder* (1840) and *The Deerslayer* (1841), present
Natty as a young man in his full strength. Read in the order of
composition, the series becomes an elegiac idyll of the frontier, of
the disparity between the certain death of Natty and all he stands
for in the way of courage and integrity, and the equally certain
triumph of the white settlers whose rough-and-ready morals
allow for the breaking of treaties and the exploitation of the
natural resources of the country. As Cooper grew older his
imagination went even further back into the colonial period, and
the *Littlepage Manuscripts*, *Satanstoe*, *The Chainbearer* and *The
Redskins* deal with the fortunes of the Littlepage family through
three generations—a sequence in which the colonial past is

[1] James Grossman, *James Fenimore Cooper*, American Men of Letters Series,
London, Methuen, 1950, p. 32.

seen as a finer time than the mob-dominated present of the 1840s.

Commenting on Natty Bumppo's rejection of marriage as one of civilization's entanglements, Grossman presents an insight not only about Cooper's idyllic and elegiac imagination, but about a quality of imagination that appears many times in the American novel:

> With his refusal of Judith *The Leather-Stocking Tales* come to a close. It is a negative note, but Natty Bumppo is one of the great negative characters of literature, the man who will not be encumbered with the ordinary obligations of life and for whom freedom is the absence of permanent involvement. In *The Deerslayer*, the true end of the series, Natty, free of all of life's hampering restrictions, has the gift of youth not as the young live it but as old men dream of it. There is a recurrent American legend of the man who suddenly drops the burdens of civilization, usually a wife, and goes off by himself. Release may be sought by brutal direct action, as it is by Hawthorne's Wakefield, or may come gracefully of itself, as it does to Rip Van Winkle. In Natty Bumppo the grace is in never having become entangled. Cooper has invented, to use his own words in a context quite different from his own, 'a being removed from the every day inducements to err, which abound in civilized life'.[1]

I believe that this organizes with complete authority the American romantic attitude, and relates directly to the image of the good and innocent American who is misunderstood and victimized by wicked and corrupted Europeans: James's Christopher Newman in *The American*, Daisy Miller, Hemingway's Jake Barnes and Robert Cohn in *The Sun Also Rises*, and Fitzgerald's Dick Diver in *Tender is the Night*.

Faulkner's imagination, like Cooper's, gains depth from his feeling for the past. Gavin Stevens says to Temple in *Requiem for a Nun*, 'The past is never dead. It's not even past.' This could serve as an epigraph to virtually everything Faulkner has written. He constantly presents, in all its psychological complexity, the decadent present in contrast to the good, primitive past—Cooper's theme of the good Indians usurped by the civilized

---

[1] Grossman, pp. 148–149.

and therefore decadent whites. The theme appears in Faulkner's wonderful short stories about Ikkemotubbe and the Cherokees in Mississippi at the time of the arrival of the first white settlers, and it gives a powerful symbolic dimension to the novella, *The Bear*. Natty Bumppo's frontier virtues are the virtues of Faulkner's Indians too: in the story 'Red Leaves', an Indian who has been condemned to death by his tribe escapes and after several days is recaptured. His captors congratulate him and comfort him by saying, 'You ran well.'

Hemingway's ideals—it has been said many times—are the ideals of the American frontier, of Natty Bumppo and the Mohicans, and behind his vision of his native countryside lies another primitive idyll, directly described in the long story, 'Big Two-Hearted River' and indirectly stated in the episode in *The Sun Also Rises* in which Jake Barnes and his friend Bill go fishing in the mountains.[1] Jay Gatsby is still another kind of frontier figure in modern dress. By 1925 the wilderness was no more than a vivid folk-memory, and the romantic hero was threshing in the undertow of urban corruption; Gatsby emerges from one of the last remaining primitive areas of America, the north shore of Lake Superior. As a boy he made a living 'as a clam-digger and a salmon-fisher or in any other capacity that brought him food and bed. His brown, hardening body lived naturally through the half-fierce, half-lazy work of the bracing days.' But Gatsby, or James Gatz as he was born, is very much a latter-day primitive. He is corrupted young by a dizzying vision of wealth, but his corruption is his purification, salvation, and death, directed to a selfless and noble love for the unworthy Daisy. Gatsby masters one kind of American reality as a gangster, but he remains an innocent in his relation to Daisy. 'The truth', Carraway tells us, 'was that Jay Gatsby of West Egg, Long Island, sprang from his Platonic conception of himself.'

Gatsby is a realized symbol of the American past exerting its force upon the present; I can only interpret the novel as a classic and wonderfully brief account of how the romantic American

---

[1] Malcolm Cowley has discussed this aspect of Hemingway fully in his introduction to *Hemingway*, New York, Viking, Portable Library, 1944, pp. vii–xxiv.

image has been imprinted upon American society. The idyllic quality reappears in Nick Carraway's personal judgment of the superiority of the Middle West of his childhood to the urban East where the 'careless' Buchanans triumph over the innocence of a Gatsby:

> One of my most vivid memories is of coming back West from prep school and later from college at Christmas time. Those who went farther than Chicago would gather in the old dim Union Street Station at six o'clock of a December evening, with a few Chicago friends, already caught up into their own holiday gayeties, to bid them a hasty good-bye. I remember the fur coats of the girls returning from Miss This-or-That's and the chatter of frozen breath and the hands waving overhead as we caught sight of old acquaintances, and the matchings of invitations: 'Are you going to the Ordways'? the Herseys'? the Schultzes'?' and the long green tickets clasped tight in our gloved hands. And last the murky yellow cars of the Chicago, Milwaukee & St. Paul railroad looking cheerful as Christmas itself on the tracks beside the gate.
>
> When we pulled out into the winter night and the real snow, our snow, began to stretch out beside us and twinkle against the windows, and the dim lights of small Wisconsin stations moved by, a sharp wild brace came suddenly into the air. We drew in deep breaths of it as we walked back from dinner through the cold vestibules, unutterably aware of our identity with this country for one strange hour, before we melted indistinguishably into it again.
>
> That's my Middle West—not the wheat or the prairies or the lost Swede towns, but the thrilling returning trains of my youth, and the street lamps and sleigh bells in the frosty dark and the shadows of holly wreaths thrown by lighted windows on the snow. I am part of that, a little solemn with the feel of those long winters, a little complacent from growing up in the Carraway house in a city where dwellings are still called through decades by a family's name. I see now that this has been a story of the West, after all—Tom and Gatsby, Daisy and Jordan and I, were all Westerners, and perhaps we possessed some deficiency in common which made us subtly unadaptable to Eastern life.
>
> Even when the East excited me most, even when I was most keenly aware of its superiority to the bored, sprawling, swollen towns beyond the Ohio, with their interminable inquisitions which

spared only the children and the very old—even then it had always for me a quality of distortion. West Egg, especially, still figures in my more fantastic dreams. I see it as a night scene by El Greco: a hundred houses, at once conventional and grotesque, crouching under a sullen, overhanging sky and a lustreless moon. In the foreground four solemn men in dress suits are walking along the sidewalk with a stretcher on which lies a drunken woman in a white evening dress. Her hand, which dangles over the side, sparkles cold with jewels. Gravely the men turn in at a house—the wrong house. But no one knows the woman's name, and no one cares.

Despite a certain conscious naïveté in tone this passage is not sentimental in context and its very naïveté belongs to the emotional and intellectual complex that Fitzgerald was creating.

I have been dealing to this point with the adaptations by American writers of the basically European romantic strain. A parallel strain in the writing of the early American frontier from Cooper to Mark Twain needs to be mentioned, at least in passing. I refer to the vernacular literature of the frontier which is romantic for its concern with history, past and present, and for its emphasis upon adventure. It is anti-romantic for its tongue-in-cheek portrayal of the romantic hero and for its scornful treatment of themes which in pure romantic writing have dignity and grandeur. Novels composed in this vein were of minor importance except for their development of American diction and syntax. Bird's *Nick of the Woods* (1837) is interesting for its portrayal of the unnoble savage—Bird's Indians are brutal, nasty, bloodthirsty and sub-human—but as a novel it is sub-literary. The same can be said of most of the work of William Gilmore Simms, John Neal, and a long list of well and truly forgotten writers of the period between 1830 and 1860. Mark Twain was the only artist of the vernacular tradition, and even he belongs to the frontier only in a metaphorical sense. His great theme is that of Cooper and the European romantics, the conflict between wilderness and city, between the good natural man and the corrupted citizens of organized communities. *Huckleberry Finn* succeeds in part as a romantic document, in part as an American idyll, in part as a parody of romantic cliché (Huck's father is a

'natural' man), and most importantly in Twain's masterful use
of American idiom and syntax.

   Huckleberry Finn is the *Canterbury Tales* of the American novel,
for Twain put into successful practice the theory of diction which
Emerson had fashioned half a century before in *Nature*. Twain
established the literary use of American, as opposed to English,
and every subsequent American writer has had to choose whether
to write in literary English or unliterary American. This meant
a considerable shift away from the English tradition in the novel
which lasted until World War II, by which time a common
literary style in the novel had begun to reappear. But Twain and
the vernacular writers were not merely rebelling nationalistically
against English models. The peculiar turn of American romanticism and of the total American experience demanded a diction
which no traditional model had satisfied; at the same time, even
so anti-romantic a mind as Twain's was forced to certain modes
of romanticism.

   As one fierce apologist has written acutely (and with defiant
unclarity),

> Whoever speaks the American language is forced into romanticism.
> His strictest discipline is itself a spiritual oddity, and gives birth to an
> oddity—as witness *The Scarlet Letter*, Emily Dickinson, the early
> gas engine. The American landscape is not easily mistaken for an
> endless wallpaper of nymphs and fountains—in this language it takes
> hard application to achieve academic deadness. Precisely the fact
> that it gives them something to do and keeps them out of trouble is
> perhaps what makes the filing cabinets of tradition so desirable to
> the morally insecure.
>   . . . the American poetic impulse in this century has been given its
> most intimate hints toward self-knowledge by the French poetry of
> immediate presences, in which Poe's psychic experiments, Whit-
> man's vocabulary of objects, and the strange American fact have been
> steadily growing more intelligible.[1]

This statement simplifies and possibly vulgarizes conclusions of
sensitive observers of the American scene from Tocqueville and

---

[1] Marcel Raymond, *From Baudelaire to Surrealism*, New York, Wittenborn,
Schultz, 1950, Harold Rosenberg's Introduction, n.p.

Henry Adams to Perry Miller and F. O. Matthiessen. The very language forced American poets and writers of fiction to use the imagination in an unclassical manner; it forced writers to turn in upon themselves, sacrificing classical completion and form, dispensing with European and specifically English traditions which would have solved, though speciously and inadequately, the problem of form for the American artist. V. S. Pritchett's discomfort with the apparent primitiveness of many American novels, a common European complaint, is thus seen as a matter of language.[1] By definition, the romantic shuns the classical concern for order and pledges himself to the idea of incompletion and the unattainable. Even more than the European romantic, the American was pledged to incompleteness, for in each generation discontinuity still ruled; the challenge of experience was too great, and too much had to be surveyed.

Some successes and many failures in the American novel were successes or failures in diction. Melville went to the English seventeenth century for his basic diction, which he tempered with contemporary American idiom and occasional American rhythms. Hemingway's success derives from his full acceptance of American fact and his resolution to create his own, new mode of diction, which in fact is more his own than a product of tradition. Thomas Wolfe, like Melville, attempted to combine the language of the seventeenth with that of the twentieth century, but lacking Melville's intellectual power and taste, he failed. Wolfe can conveniently stand for the many American autobiographical writers who, egotistically submerged in their own experience, seem to manufacture a language, or various languages, from chapter to chapter. C. H. Rickword explains, I think, why this should be the case:

> . . . the main thing to be noted about the . . . 'subjective' novelists is their increasing tendency to rely for their effect not on set pieces of character-drawing, but directly on the poetic properties of words. The idea of a character's consciousness is created in the reader by the

[1] William Barrett, 'The End of Modern Literature', *Partisan Review*, XVI, September 1949, 942–950, writes a full and excellent discussion of American 'primitiveness'.

exploitation of the emotive powers of language used to evoke concrete imagery and sensation. The idea so created has unusual
reality. . . .

Following Whitehead, Rickword adds,

> Historically, character, as we now understand it, is an outcome of
> the Romantic Revival, a movement that has been discerned by some
> as one escape from the mechanistic and indifferent universe of science
> into the fastness of the individual soul and of an attempt to locate
> there the limitations that constitute value.[1]

Wolfe's characters conform precisely to this thesis; they depend
almost exclusively for their existence upon Wolfe's ability to
exploit 'the emotive powers of language'. The neo-romantic
writer cannot rely upon clichés or recognized social standards of
behaviour to communicate to his reader a particular character's
meaning; the writer himself does not recognize the cliché, and he
must recreate his character each time he returns to him within the
frame of the novel. Thus Wolfe's characters are constantly shifting before our eyes. O. W. Gant, for instance, is by turns a man
of great dignity and no dignity; he is comic, absurd, restrained,
licentious. These variations are due less to changes in the moods
of Gant, the character, than to changes in the mood of Wolfe,
the author. Gant becomes a vehicle rather than a character, but
a vehicle which belongs to the controlling idea of death. When
we first meet him, he is obsessed by thoughts of death. In the
first, expository pages of *Look Homeward, Angel*, he is at his most
'normal', and the novel at its least Wolfean stage. Very soon,
however, Wolfe's verbalizing dominates; by page twenty Gant
is '. . . like a senseless and infuriate beast' in his 'tragic consciousness of time'. When Gant returns from a trip to California, he
makes a 'Gulliverian entry' into Altamont; at once he is told by
a street-car motorman that a friend has died during his absence.
' "What!" howled Gant. "Merciful God!" he clucked mourn-
fully downward. "What did he die of?"' The word 'Gulliverian'
here is Wolfe's as he stands quite outside the character. The

[1] C. H. Rickword, 'A Note on Fiction', in William Van O'Connor, ed.,
Forms of Modern Fiction, Minneapolis, University of Minnesota Press, 1948,
pp. 269–301.

verbs 'howled' and 'clucked' belong to O. W. Gant, the violent and grotesque character. In his illness, Gant 'snivels' in self-pity, and when his son asks if he has eaten anything, Wolfe writes, ' "It stuck in my throat," said Gant, who had eaten heartily.' Of Mrs. Selborne, the 'grass-widow', '. . . forty-nine, with piled hair of dyed henna, corseted breasts and hips architecturally protuberant in a sharp diagonal, meaty mottled arms, and a gulched face of leaden flaccidity puttied up brightly with cosmetics. . . .' Gant says 'hopefully, "She looks like an adventuress, hey?" ' 'Adventuress' is Wolfe's word, not Gant's; it is just the proper word to give the episode its tone of hilarity, a tone by which author and reader can enjoy the lechery of a sixty-year-old sport who ogles a lady of forty-nine.

By the time Wolfe wrote the death of Gant in his second novel, *Of Time and the River*, the character had taken on tragic overtones and something like universality. The centre of meaning has shifted from Gant as merely the father of the autobiographical Eugene, a drunken, snivelling aged lecher, to Gant as a suffering human being, seeking in death his own father, and some private, elusive, world of childhood as distant as the Garden of Eden. In the actual death-scene, too long for quotation, Wolfe achieved a degree of control in diction rare in his novels; he combines with taste and propriety a tag from Keats, the father-son motif from Greek myth, and a suggestion of Christ crucified, concentrating in the episode his central themes of isolation, death, time, and suffering.

At other points in Wolfe's successful writing, the texture of the sentence is supported sheerly by felicity of phrase. Apart from dialogue, Wolfe's scenes are consciously 'written', a habit which he shares with Fitzgerald and one which derives from the nineteenth century, before Hemingway taught American writers the technique of producing immediacy without seeming to 'write'. The young virgins about the town of Altamont parade the streets, flaunting themselves before the local gallants, and entering shops 'to purchase small justifications'. Eugene Gant in the early morning hears 'the jinking bottles' of the milkman; at Harvard the 'intellectuals' have 'cold faces' and 'pale fox eyes'. Eugene

o

cannot talk to them, and feels that he is condemned '. . . to prowl the wintry, barren, and accursed streets of Friday night'. Alone in New York City and hating '. . . the sense of drowning daily in the man-swarm' (Whitman's word), Eugene remembers Spring in Old Catawba, remembers 'the facts' about the spring: '. . . these facts, as bright as herrings in a shining water, as literal as nails to fix the hides of falsehood to the wall, as real as April and all magic whatsoever, returned now under the furious light of his awakened and incontrovertible memory.' Without its concrete similes the sentence would be mawkish and inflated; Wolfe knew the necessity of the concrete image to pin down the abstractions that he tried so hard to capture.

No list of the beauties of Wolfean diction can obscure the fact that his writing is often no more than windy rhetoric. In his first two novels in particular, he is fond of archaic and bookish words: the 'ptotic' malevolence of Judge Tayloe's eye; throughout *Look Homeward, Angel*, all hands and feet are 'phthisic'; Eliza 'with desperate sadness . . . *encysted* herself within her house'; Helen 'fantasied' of France and Italy and a career in opera; in the early chapters of his second novel, when Wolfe was writing about the singularity of the Gants, words like 'tribal', 'earth', and 'animal' constantly obtrude. Some of this pretentiousness carried over into the later writing—Bear Joyner's 'coarse and swingeing' humour —although there was less of it after *Of Time and the River*. A careful combing of Wolfe's novels together with an examination of his personal library shows that Wolfe went to the Bible, to Shakespeare, Burton, Coleridge and Hardy for certain of his verbal habits, and to De Quincey for the authority and probably the model for his long, involved latinate sentences, rhetorical questions, addresses to the reader, his expansiveness, repetition and the needless explanations, elaborate humour, his sentence which seems always to be written in the second person plural even when it is not, his readiness to lapse into reverie.

De Quincey's periods were not the only source of Wolfe's rhetoric. I see in much of his writing, as in some of Faulkner's, a habit of the old-time Southern orator of the period when, as Tocqueville wrote, '. . . an American cannot converse, but he can discuss, and his talk falls into a dissertation. He speaks to you as if he was addressing a meeting; and if he should chance to become warm in the discussion, he will say "Gentlemen" to the person with whom he is conversing.'[1] Here is John C. Calhoun, in 1832, Senator from South Carolina and sometime Vice President of the U.S.:

> In a country having so great a diversity of geographical and political interest, with so vast a territory, to be filled, in a short time, with almost countless millions—a country of which the parts will equal empires, a union more intimate than that ordained in the Constitution, and so intimate, of course, that it might be permanently hostile to the feelings of more than a fourth of the states, instead of strengthening, would have exposed the system to certain destruction. There is a *deep* and *profound* philosophy, which he who best knows our nature will the most highly appreciate, that would make the intensity of the Union, if I may so express myself, inversely to the extent of territory and the population of a country, and the diversity of its interests, geographical and political; and which would hold in deeper dread the assumption of reserved rights by the agent appointed to execute the delegated, than the resumption of the delegated by the authority which granted the powers and ordained the agent to administer them. There appears, indeed, to be a *great and prevailing* principle that tends to place the delegated power in opposition to the delegating—the created to the creating power—reaching far beyond man and his works, up to the universal source of all power.[2]

And here is Wolfe, who in a single sentence out-Calhouns Calhoun:

> After the overwhelming impact of *impression and event* which a new world, a new life, had brought to him in so many varied, *chance, and unexpected* ways—after *the ship, the voyage,* the *enormous isolation,* the whole *earth-detachment* of the sea (itself a life, a world, a universe of new experience), after the weeks in England, the huge web of London, the brief but poignantly illuminating days in Bristol, Bath, and Devonshire, with fleeting glimpses of something so strange, yet

[1] Alexis de Tocqueville, *Democracy in America,* ed. Phillips Bradley, 2 vols., New York, 1945, I, 250. See also Vol. II, 77–78, 'Why American Writers and Orators Use an Inflated Style': 'Each citizen is habitually engaged in the contemplation of a very puny object: namely, himself.'

[2] *John C. Calhoun, His Life and Speeches,* New York, 1843, p. 60. My italics.

so familiar, so near, yet never to be touched, that it seemed to him he was looking in through a lighted window at a life which he had always known, but which he could never make his own; after the terrific impact of France and Paris—the month of bewildered, desperate and almost terror-stricken isolation in a new and hostile world—an atom, *wordless, tongueless*, almost drowned among the strange, dark faces of the Frenchmen; after all the confusion, grief, and error of that month—the night-time kaleidoscope of cafés, brothels, alcohol, and women, the frenzied day-time prowling through museums, bookstalls, thronging streets—the thousand monuments of an alien culture, the million faces of an alien race, until every atom of him was wrung, trembling, maddened and exhausted, sick with loss and hopelessness, weary with *despair*—after the huge first shock and flood-tide of immersion in an alien life— had come to his meeting with Starwick, Elinor, and Ann, the brief, fatal, furious weeks of their relation, the bitter loss and waste and rankling pain of parting; and finally the sweltering and incurable ache, the blind and driven aimlessness of wandering, the chance encounter with the Countess, and the brief interlude of *forgetfulness* and *oblivion* that had come to him while he was with her—and now, blank, silent loneliness again, the *blind fortuity* of *chance*, the arbitrary halt and desperate entrenchment of his spirit in this town of Tours.[1]

The two writers use embellishment for the sake of sound and rhythm. It is not necessary to Calhoun's meaning that philosophy be 'deep and profound', or that a principle be 'great and prevailing'. Neither is it necessary to the sense of Wolfe's sentence that ways be 'chance and unexpected', that Gant's interlude be one of 'forgetfulness and oblivion', or that the 'fortuity of chance' afflicts him. Calhoun's meaning is simple: as the union grows in size, states' rights become a more bitter issue. Yet he resorts to great periods in which dependent clause follows dependent clause and meaning is subordinated to mellifluousness. For the classical Southern orator as for Wolfe, the Southern novelist, mere meaning is not enough; meaning, in truth, is not meaning until the writer has proposed his idea, repeated it, fondled it, and put it tenderly down again. Wolfe includes more facts within his periods than Calhoun, but the rhetorical structure is clear.

[1] *Of Time and the River*, New York, 1944, pp. 856–857. My italics.

Wolfe's strange and wonderful ransacking of the English tradition in combination with his native American romantic impulses made for a style that was often empty and repellent. He criticized himself not at all and he wrote much that resembles a parody of his best work: at such times in utter failure of impulse and style he could write, 'It was as if God had lifted his baton sharply above the endless orchestration of the seas'; or preach in the pseudo-Old Testament style of

> O death in life that turns our men to stone! O change that levels down our gods! If only one lives yet, above the cinders of the consuming years, shall not this dust awaken, shall not dead faith revive, shall we not see God again, as once in the morning, on the mountain? Who walks with us on the hills?

At its worst, Wolfe's concentration upon himself resulted in self-pity; we should not accept most of the writing in 'The Return of the Prodigal' from a tabloid serial: 'His eyes, which were brown, had a curiously harsh and dark and hurt look in them, as though the man had been deeply wounded by life and was trying to hide the fact with a show of fierce and naked truculence as challenging as an angry word.' This same cleavage between the emotional flow of the episode and the embellishments led Wolfe into writing rhetorical essays, as when he stops the dramatic narrative of the Joyners, in *The Hills Beyond*, to deliver a long polemic on the history and sociology of the post-Civil War South.

In writers so various in quality as Thomas Wolfe, Sherwood Anderson, James Gould Cozzens and William Faulkner we can perceive still another quality of romanticism which American writers have made into a defining mode of the recent American novel. Marcel Raymond suggests the nature of that quality when he writes:

> While the classical writer, bent upon self-knowledge, relied on introspection and transposed the results of his observations to the plane of discursive intelligence, the romantic poet renounced all insights that did not convey a sense and an enjoyment of himself— and a sense of the universe experienced as a presence—and expected his imagination to compose a metaphorical, symbolic portrait of

himself in his metamorphoses. That is the core of the new mode of
expression inaugurated by Rousseau and Chateaubriand—a mode
of expression which is natural, and even direct, despite appearances
to the contrary, and which is superior to the analytical mode of
expression in that it restores some of the most ancient prerogatives
of language. . . .[1]

In terms of the novel this translates into the technique of point of
view. The romantic writer's 'sense of the universe experienced
as a presence' follows upon his identification of himself with the
cosmos, that state which Novalis and Rousseau had experienced
and wrote upon vividly: 'In this state of illusion', said Novalis,
'it is less the subject who perceives the object than conversely,
the objects which come to perceive themselves in the subject.'[2]
In the American nineteenth-century romantics and the twentieth-
century neo-romantics this experience is not wholly consum-
mated, in spite of the New England transcendentalists' effort to
systematize it, and the result for the modern novel was a kind of
double image or multiple point of view.

That double image or multiple point of view is first apparent
in Stephen Crane's *The Red Badge of Courage.* Crane wrote in the
traditional third person, but before the reader is very far into the
text, he is aware that Crane's use of the third person is different
indeed from traditional usage. The central character, Henry
Fleming, remains strangely anonymous; Crane refers to him as
the 'youth' and goes out of his way not to allow him to be central
in the usual sense. A brief work composed of a series of highly
wrought episodes on the theme of cowardice and courage, the
novel nevertheless has an underlying structure which results from
our awareness that for all its objectivity and surface brilliance, it
is a full though indirect image of Crane's own consciousness. It
is as though he were writing in the third and first persons simultaneously. A similar effect exists in reverse in E. E. Cummings's
The Enormous Room, which is so autobiographical that it is scarcely
a novel. Cummings describes his imprisonment in a French concentration camp for writing 'subversive' letters during the First

[1] *From Baudelaire to Surrealism*, pp. 8–9.
[2] *From Baudelaire to Surrealism*, p. 8.

World War. Outraged and indignant, he documents every aspect of his experience so fully that midway in the novel we can ignore the annoying first person in the discovery that the author has projected, almost in spite of himself, a second, objective point of view which enlarges the narrow and often naïve diatribe of the indignant narrator. Thomas Wolfe perceived the emotion if not the technique of the multiple point of view when he wrote in *Look Homeward, Angel*, of 'an eye within an eye, a brain above a brain, a Stranger that dwelt in him and regarded him and was him, and that he did not know'. In his autobiographical novels Wolfe frequently resorted to the double image in an attempt to achieve some kind of objectivity; his attempt usually took the form of pseudo-poetic incantation or interior monologue belonging not to his character but to Wolfe himself. Faulkner's success with stream-of-consciousness techniques can be charged to his modification of those techniques to allow for multiple point of view. When Faulkner places himself in the minds of the Bundrens in *As I Lay Dying* or in Quentin Compson's mind in *The Sound and the Fury*, whenever in fact he uses interior monologue with success, we hear the Faulknerian voice, the accent which can only be Faulkner's own. This is not a violation of point of view but a conscious, unifying technique that Faulkner uses to support the total architecture of his many novels. The emerging Faulknerian double image is Faulkner's answer to the fragmentation which, more than most contemporary writers, obsesses and challenges him.

The recent American novel has been interpreted in Europe almost entirely in terms of the theme of violence. Where the French, the Italians and even the Germans have been fascinated to the point of imitation, the English have been repelled—an emotion which aids in clarifying the nature of the relationship between American and English writing. Violence is basic to the romantic imagination; the romantic character, disdaining bourgeois compromise and petty restraint, can only resolve a dilemma by crashing violently through it. The English writer has never been able to accept the romantic solution as a solution; he has preferred to go to society and to his literary tradition for a rational reference, thus his greater attention to stylization and his continuing reliance upon experience conceived as a block. Both in substance and essence American experience has been violent; American individualism has never glossed over the resort to violence. At the same time the American writer's apprehension of European experience from 1914 to 1945 placed in stark outline the distinction between the American romantic idyll and memories of a pastoral boyhood, and the total, violent fragmentation of the wars and all that the wars implied in the destruction of individuality. If the cliché about American 'innocence' means anything, its meaning is here. Historical memory and social tradition educated the European from infancy to an awareness of wars and revolutions; in England it became bad taste to mention their possibility. When Basil Seal in Waugh's *Black Mischief* goes to the British Legation with the news that chaos has broken out in Azania and that the British will be murdered in their beds if they do not take measures, Lady Courteney says,

> 'Mr. Seal, . . . I think it's very mischievous of you saying all this. I'm sure that things are not nearly as bad as you make out. You're just talking. Now go and get yourself some whiskey and talk to Prudence and I think you might put that dirty gun outside in the lobby.'

English writers like Rex Warner and P. H. Newby, who have made the theme of violence basic in their work, are significantly without high critical honour in their own country; their reputations are wider in America than in England. American writers, prepared by their tradition, their history, and their special awareness of the place of violence in our world, have been forced by the climate of reality to that special theme.

Constance Rourke wrote that the genuinely native contribution to American literary culture was the 'quality of improvisation', which she saw in Emerson, Whitman, Hawthorne, James, and above all in Emily Dickinson.[1] This is, I suspect, another way of stating the American writer's paradox of traditionless tradition. In one sense the American writer has been more burdened with

[1] Constance Rourke, *American Humor*, New York, 1931, p. 270.

tradition than his English counterpart. His awareness of that burden has often driven him away from tradition to improvisation. Within the framework of romanticism the American emphasized reality, what Emerson called 'seeing'. Emerson wrote:

> We can never see Christianity from Christendom; but from the pastures, from a boat in the pond, from the song of a starling, we possibly may. . . . We must be great to see anything truly. Our weak eyes make goblins and monsters. But man thyself, and all things unfix, dispart, and flee. Nothing will stand the eye of a man, —neither lion, nor person, nor time, nor condition. Each bullies us for a season; but gaze, and it opens that most solid seeming wall, yields its secret, receives us into its depth and advances our front so much farther on into the recesses of being, to some new frontier as yet unvisited by the elder voyagers. And yet alas for this infirm faith, this will, not strenuous, this vast ebb of a vast flow! I am God in nature, I am a weed by the wall.[1]

And Thomas Wolfe wrote in *The Hills Beyond*, 'For it is not a question of having faith, or lack of it. It is a simple fact of seeing. Seeing, we are saved. Half seeing, we are worse than blind. And wrong.' Wolfe's threshing about in search of a form took him to major and minor English writers from Shakespeare to Hardy, but he responded most fully and wrote his best work under the impress of his native tradition, of Emerson, Melville and Whitman. He constantly emptied hardware-store windows and grocery stores of their physical facts, trying desperately, with meticulous care, to *see* them; even when he described the face of the madam in a French brothel he used the same care. I dwell on Wolfe's relation to tradition and underline his failure, because in his failure we can better understand the successes of greater artists. While his work emphasizes again the brevity and slightness of American tradition, it further emphasizes that the American novel is taking a new departure.

Since 1945 it has become apparent that the best American novelists have emerged from the period of experimentation of

---

[1] R. W. Emerson, *Journals*, edd. E. W. Emerson and W. E. Forbes, Cambridge, Mass., 1909–14, 10 vols., V, 407, 31 May 1840.

the 1920s and from the period of social and political formulas in
the 1930s, to create a novel with certainty of craft and an authority
of perception which were lacking in the best work of the past.
Norman Mailer, for example, served an apprenticeship to Joyce
and Dos Passos in *The Naked and the Dead* (1949), an interesting
but resounding failure, then went on to *Barbary Shore* (1951), an
unacknowledged success which combines the unpopular politics
of Trotsky from the period of the 1930s with the craft and the
communicated sensibility of the recent period. Unlike Wolfe,
Mailer does not blunder into the technique of the multiple image;
he uses it structurally to create his central character, Lovett, a
survivor of the war who has lost his memory and therefore his
past. Plastic surgery has transformed even his face so that he
becomes the complete symbol of isolated modern man, and
time his obsession. Mailer's diction is no longer self-consciously
native but a skilful blending of American and English speech:

> 'During one period I made prodigious efforts to recover the past.
> I conducted a massive correspondence with the secretaries of appro-
> priate officials; I followed people upon the street because they had
> looked at me with curiosity; I searched lists of names, studied photo-
> graphs, and lay on my bed bludgeoning my mind to confess a single
> material detail. Prodigious efforts, but I recovered nothing except
> to learn that I had no past and was therefore without a future. The
> blind grow ears, the deaf learn how to see, and I acquired both in
> compensation; it was natural, even obligatory, that the present should
> possess the stage.'

Both the private consciousness of the traditional romantic and
the public consciousness of the political writer meet in *Barbary
Shore*, as they do in Saul Bellow's fine novel, *The Adventures of
Augie March* (1953). Apparently abandoning technical experiment to return to the convention of the sprawling *Entwicklungs-
roman*, Bellow actually extends experiment in his depiction of a
variety of American experience which has been ignored in the
American novel. Augie March, born in a Chicago slum, reared
among juvenile delinquents, self-educated by stealing books and
reading them, is the unattached man, the observer who interprets
his experience with shrewd insight and a wild and wonderful

humour; he is not merely an observer, but a true hero of modern life, a knowing innocent, ironic, comic, sharp but never bitter. Although the notion is somehow ludicrous, an idea that Augie himself might propound, Bellow's technique in this novel resembles that of Emily Brontë in *Wuthering Heights*. He needs a narrator who can both act and interpret the action; like Ellen Dean who is a 'reader' and therefore acceptably literate, Augie the book-stealer is a kind of intellectual who bridges the greater gap which exists in America between the writer who would both entertain and remain an honest man, and a public which is even less interested than Emily Brontë's public in intellectual formulations. Bellow's success, in spite of lapses in taste and his inability to create credible women, is a success of diction, style and imaginative control. When Augie, both in love and in training for the Merchant Marine, writes,

> On Saturday, in a fever, I got off the base as soon as the usual parade shenanigans were over. What a state I was in! When I rode over the bridge from Brooklyn suspended on those heaven-hung struts over the brick valleys, then the fiery flux of harbor water, the speedy gulls, the battleships open like vast radio sets in the yards, beasthorns of Hengist and Horsa, and then the tunnel again, I felt that if I had to continue to ride and ride I would certainly not last but would give out.

he expresses one resolution of the various problems of tradition, both English and American, which have bedevilled American writers since Charles Brockden Brown. And when Ralph Ellison in *Invisible Man* creates a frame for negro experience in America which is indebted as much to German expressionism as to English social realism, in prose that is supple, clear and eloquent, he makes his peace with the savage naturalism of a novelist like Richard Wright, and demonstrates in still another way a maturity and a degree of achievement that have been rare at any point in the modern novel.

Chapter Seven

WAR AND POLITICS

THE terms 'war novel' and 'political novel' were coined to sell books, not to criticize them; nevertheless the themes of war and politics have created a literature which in variety, intensity and excellence claims a special place in the contemporary consciousness, one which is insufficiently identified by the category of ideas. The impact of war upon the novel has been so enormous that it is at once apparent that more than ideas is involved. Neither the English nor the American tradition gave the novelist a technique for dealing with the phenomenon of war. In England before 1914, war was a subject for the writer of adventure. In America Ambrose Bierce, DeForrest and Stephen Crane had written convincingly about the Civil War, but Bierce wrote only a few short stories, DeForrest went unread, and Crane, a novelist of the third phase living unhappily in the second, was without direct influence until Hemingway adapted some of the techniques of *The Red Badge of Courage* in *A Farewell to Arms*. The French tradition, on the other hand, offered fuller support to the war novelist, and it comes as no surprise to realize that André Malraux in *La Condition humaine* and *Les Noyers de l'Altenburg* has written the most impressive of war novels.

The physical fact of war is a severe test of the novelist's powers, and total war is total indeed in that it usurps the writer's attention and drains his energies in a particularly damaging fashion. War has often left in the vessel of literary energy a destructive, antiliterary residue which turns certain writers into mystical aesthetes or converts to exoticism and nihilism. But to the genuine novelist war and politics are facts of the real world to be faced, interpreted and imaginatively projected in his work.

With characteristic lucidity in paradox, Dylan Thomas in a

broadcast on Wilfred Owen went directly to the defining effect of war on literature when he referred to the 'position-in-calamity which, without intellectual choice, [Owen] chose to take'.[1] This same choice which is no choice, this relationship between calamity and intelligence, poses with urgency the problem of the novel of idea; I would propose to attack the problem from the rear, by first stating the case against the appearance of organized idea in literature—a case which would eliminate the possibility of the political novel. Both Julien Benda and Paul Valéry, for example, spoke for the extreme aesthetic position and for the people who basically hate literature when they said that literature is incapable of expressing thought, that the end of literature is the creation of style, a self-sufficient beauty; ideas, therefore, can have only a shadowy existence, and logic is obscured altogether. By its very nature, Valéry said, thought lacks style, and he accordingly denied style.[2] Valéry was of course justifying his own preoccupation with epistemology and perception, his private equation between the psychological processes of thought and literature. The difficulty in terms of the novel is that a theory which holds for poetry does not hold for prose; when put to work in the novel, Benda's and Valéry's ideas result in that monster, poetic-prose, at best in the unreadable poetic reverie of Gide's *Voyage d'Urien*. The modern political novel has demonstrated in rich variety how ideas receive statement, definition, and authority in an art-form which can and does deal with idea.

War and politics are not only inseparable in history, but in the third phase of the novel they have become inseparable in the literary sensibility. It is a fact that no major writer since 1914 has failed to deal with politics at some level in his work; often against his own inclinations, as with Gide; often in disgust, as with Wyndham Lewis; but no writer of any stature has been able to evade, or has really wanted to evade, the central and terrifying political circumstance. As George Orwell wrote, 'There is no such thing as genuinely non-political literature, and least of all

[1] Dylan Thomas, *Quite Early One Morning*, London, Dent, 1954, p. 103.
[2] Julien Benda, *Exercice d'un enterré vif*, III, Geneva and Paris, 1944; Robert L. Niess, 'Julien Benda: the Poet's Function', *Yale French Studies*, II, No. 2, 67–69.

in an age like our own, when fears, hatreds, and loyalties of a direct political kind are near to the surface of everyone's conscious-ness';[1] this was supported by Norman Pearson when he remarked with still wider reference of *Billy Budd*, 'No novel exists without history.'[2] Our increasing awareness of the contingency of history and imagination in England and America since 1914 again recalls that on the Continent catastrophe had impressed itself upon the literary imagination a century before. Stendhal, Büchner, Kleist and Flaubert prepared the way for a great and impressive modern series of continental novels on war and politics: Hermann Broch's *The Sleepwalkers*, Mann's *Dr. Faustus*, Hermann Hesse's *The Steppenwolf*, Malraux's *Man's Fate* and *Man's Hope*.[3] These novels underline the unintellectual aspects of the Anglo-American tradi-tion and the resulting emotional shock of the two World Wars upon the Anglo-American literary mind. We look to representa-tive novels of war and politics in English, then, for their special relevance to catastrophe and imagination.

Interesting and logical differences distinguish novels of the First World War from novels of the Second, English novels from American, and novels of immediate war experience from novels on the idea of war. The 1914–18 War clarified a long-standing ambiguity between American writers and society; they had long sensed their isolation from society and had made good literary capital of their intuition, but the war brought into the open, inescapably, the fact that writers stood on one side of an invisible, but real, line, and American society on the other. The majority of those who did good work in the twenties and thirties went to

[1] George Orwell, 'The Prevention of Literature', *Shooting an Elephant*, London, 1950, p. 123.

[2] In a lecture at Radcliffe College, February 1951. Wyndham Lewis adds further evidence: '"Is this a political book?" Not more, it can truthfully be answered, than some of Charles Dickens's books, and all by Mr. Shaw, to go no further afield. If my characters are obsessed by politics, it is because today our lives are saturated with them. It is impossible for a work of narrative fiction worth reading to contain less politics than *Rotting Hill*.' *Rotting Hill*, London, Methuen, 1951, pp. ix–x.

[3] *La Lutte avec l'ange*, a projected trilogy of which *Les Noyers de l'Altenburg* is the first instalment, promises to be Malraux's third masterpiece of war and politics.

the war physically, like Hemingway, Dos Passos, E. E. Cummings, Faulkner, Ernest Boyd, and Lawrence Stallings; or they identified themselves in spirit with the experience, like Fitzgerald, Katherine Anne Porter, and Thomas Wolfe. The war for this group was a rite of initiation in which the population at large could not possibly share, while the initiated could never regain even the illusions of social identity. They went to the wars out of boyish idealism in some cases, out of the American fondness for action, or to confront the enormous fact which war presented, but their enduring reaction was outrage. The Civil War was long past; the Spanish-American War had been no more than a patriotic orgy in which no one got hurt; nothing in recent American experience had prepared the literary volunteers, as they were to a man, for the overwhelming nature of their experience. Outrage was the dominant emotion of Cummings's *Enormous Room*, Dos Passos's *One Man's Initiation* and *Three Soldiers*, while Hemingway's farewell was a farewell to military arms and war's meaningless outrages to the individual. Faulkner's first novel, *Soldier's Pay*, was a denunciation of war and of the civilians' attitudes towards the demobilized forces.

The first crop of American World War I novels, Hemingway's excepted, was remarkably bad. Neither Dos Passos, Faulkner, nor Cummings more than dimly apprehended the idea of war behind the fact; they were busy with the fact itself and with the imperfectly realized emotion of outrage. When they returned to a prospering and uninitiated America, they felt totally cut off, contemptuous of the metatarsal arch cases and the businessmen who had stayed at home; they were repelled by a bourgeois civilization which seemed thin and unsatisfactory after their wartime whiffs of the delights of Europe. They became exiles and nomads, drawn back to Europe by movements which seemed to join the good fight against industrial standardization: the Dadaists, Futurists, Vorticists, the Surrealists. In the meantime, the experience of the war had to be purged through expression. The better writers realized that tradition no longer served, and they looked for new forms.

The Enormous Room (1922) is a total but symptomatic failure.

Writing in the first person and larding the narrative with heavy-handed satire, Cummings nevertheless groped towards a theory of time with reflections on how time differs for the prisoner from 'normal' sequence—an impulse to be central to the novel in the third phase; he also approximated a kind of bastard interior monologue, which is really exterior monologue, in his reporting of his fellow-prisoners' dialogues and monologues. Amateur and restless, varied in pace and attack, the novel suggests a mind in search of a more satisfactory form. Cummings tries every traditional device for size, approximating new ones on the way. But he was not a true novelist, and *The Enormous Room* is peripheral to his career as a poet.

John Dos Passos made better use of his war experience; from *One Man's Initiation* through the trilogy *USA* he met and with increasing mastery dominated the idea of war as a literary subject. The first volume of *USA*, *1919*, is a satirical commentary upon the peace of Versailles, but more interestingly, one of the earliest and best realized novels of the political perception which the war made possible. *1919* overshadows Dos Passos's first two war novels, written with narrow attention to immediate experience; they were primitive photography without being either actual or real, while in the later novels where Dos Passos went to the idea of war, both actuality and reality are enhanced. Faulkner's early short stories of war, like his war novels, *Soldier's Pay* and *Sartoris*, are wretched, but these failures, like Dos Passos's, are interesting in their anticipation of later methods. In spite of the embarrassing heroics of a story like 'Ad Astra', or the bungled construction of *Soldier's Pay*, we are again aware of a restless mind, of a writer trying out various techniques, using traditional methods and searching for new combinations and permutations. Without these early experiments, the finest of Faulkner's novels, *The Sound and the Fury* and *Light in August* would have been diminished and possibly non-existent.

Hemingway's first war novels were an exception to the American rule of ambitious, unrealized works not only because he was a finer artist, but also because he reversed the usual process. He began with the *idea* of war in his first novel, *The Sun Also Rises*

(*Fiesta* in England) of 1926, and went on to the *fact* of war three years later in *A Farewell to Arms*. Every 'war' writer who was a writer realized that the War of 1914–18 was the absolute end of a social order which had come into being with the French Revolution, which survived 1830 and 1848 and 1870, if only barely, and came crashing down in 1914. Traditional religion became a mockery for large masses of men; the various social élites lost status and social custom suffered fundamental changes; anarchy replaced manners; swinishness and barbarity replaced urbanity. European novelists were immediately aware of these changes in a way that American writers could not be. The differences between the first and last volumes of Proust's great novel are a measure of the European awareness: in the early volumes, the aristocracy is fast decaying, but it still represents meaningful, inherited forms; the Baron de Charlus, in the final volume, is fundamentally moribund. He has abandoned the society in which he formerly moved, and is no longer sure even of his own sex; he wanders the streets with painted cheeks picking up male lovers. In Hermann Hesse's *Steppenwolf*, Mann's *Magic Mountain*, and supremely in Hermann Broch's *The Sleepwalkers*, the same informing theme is rewritten again and again: the impact of war on society. The characters we remember are the embodiments of that theme—Charlus and Castorp, Harry Haller and Esch. Hemingway, too, in his first novel, treated this great theme, but in an American way. Like the other American novelists, he saw the war as a turning away from a virginal and innocent world to a world of evil and corruption. The two extremes, innocence and corruption, furnished the structure for his first, and in many ways greatest, novel.

The novel has structure, but a subtle one, and it has usually been read as 'picaresque'[1] and episodic; but once we perceive Hemingway's historical awareness of his theme, the structure becomes clear and beautiful in its appropriateness. *The Sun Also Rises* is

---

[1] As in M. F. Moloney, 'Ernest Hemingway: The Missing Third Dimension', in H. C. Gardiner, ed., *Fifty Years of the American Novel: A Christian Appraisal*, New York, Scribner, 1952, p. 187. The entire essay is typical of the wilful astigmatism of many of Hemingway's critics to his methods and purposes.

P

more than a parable about the 'lost' generation (that vapid cliché); it has endured until now, in spite of lapses in taste and tone, because Hemingway presented in the broadest sense of the term a political theme which defined a truth about the society in which he lived, and he wrote in a prose which used the past and answered to the present. When Bill Gorton says to Jake Barnes, 'You're an expatriate. You've lost touch with the soil. You get precious. Fake European standards have ruined you. You drink yourself to death. You become obsessed by sex. You spend all your time talking, not working. You are an expatriate, see? You hang around cafés', Hemingway sounds the tone which we have heard the American writer using before. Hemingway's scene is France and Spain, not because he avoids American society, but because he is seeing it in the relief one can only achieve abroad. He satirizes tourists—badly, and the satirical episodes lack fineness. At the same time, his satire shows the contempt of the initiates for the uninitiated, a theme which was to become mannerism in some of Hemingway's later, inferior work—*Across the River and into the Trees*, for example. Expatriation is more important in the character of Robert Cohn, and the narrator, Jake Barnes.

Cohn and Barnes are in every sense opposites, but each desires a quality basic to the other. Cohn is Jewish, wealthy, educated at Princeton where he was a good amateur boxer, and he fancies himself as a writer. He is a pseudo-intellectual, isolated from every individual in the novel; attached to a wretched woman, he lacks the resolution to leave her. He gravitates towards Jake, a man of good humour who relieves his loneliness; Jake in turn feels sorry for Cohn, is fond of him but despises him for weakness and envies his sexual competence, for Jake has been emasculated by a war wound. Cohn is a secondary, Jake a primary, by-product of the war. Cohn has particular reference to an American tradition in his isolation and his sense of time passing. He says to Jake, 'Don't you ever get the feeling that all your life is going by and you're not taking advantage of it? Do you realize you've lived nearly half the time you have to live already? . . . Do you know that in about thirty-five years more we'll be dead?' The idea is central in all literature, but it takes a particular American cadence in Henry James, Sherwood Anderson, John Dos Passos, Wolfe, and Paul Bowles. It is intimately connected with the American feeling for reality and for immediate experience. Cohn is driven from his mistress's arms to the delights of Brett Ashley, an unreal, tough, lovely, hard-drinking English nymphomaniac with whom Jake is in love and who loves Jake, to their mutual frustration. It is a tribute to Hemingway's craft that he can make this situation believable and moving. Cohn wants to seize experience, to take life by the throat and throttle some good out of it, hence his interest in Brett, who is exotic, intensely 'real', an illusion for ignoring time's passage.

Jake Barnes belongs with the character Krebs, in an early short story, 'Soldier's Home'. Krebs returns to Oklahoma after long and hard combat in France to find that he can talk to no one. The girls interest him, but he can no longer be bothered with the ritual of seduction. Jake is Krebs abroad, moving in a circle of American and English expatriates who are superficially happy as long as they can circulate freely about Paris, drinking hugely, talking their private Hemingway-language, cut off from the past and avoiding any impulse to cope with the future. With the exception of Jake, they are rotten and abandoned. Even in her own eyes, Brett's one gesture of nobility is to abandon Pedro Romero, the young Spanish bull-fighter whom she has seduced, because she knows she would corrupt him by remaining with him. The world of men contrasts with the corrupted world of Paris and women. Jake and Bill take a fishing trip which establishes the values that keep Jake uncorrupted; the fishing-idyll is also a metaphor for the cameraderie of armies, a symbol, along with bull-fighting, of fundamental qualities which Hemingway seeks in all social situations, qualities which lie outside post-war society. Fishing in the north of Spain is a return to boyhood purity and a release from the need to need women; the very concreteness of the prose contributes to the idyll.

> The path crossed a stream on a foot-log. The log was surfaced off, and there was a sapling bent across for a rail. In the flat pool beside the stream tadpoles spotted the sand. We went up a steep bank and across the rolling fields. Looking back we saw Burguete, white

houses and red roofs, and the white road with a truck going along it and the dust rising.

Beyond the fields we crossed another faster-flowing stream. A sandy road led down to the ford and beyond into the woods. The path crossed the stream on another foot-log below the ford, and joined the road, and we went into the woods.

It was a beech wood and the trees were very old. Their roots bulked above the ground and the branches were twisted. We walked on the road between the thick trunks of the old beeches and the sunlight came through the leaves in light patches on the grass. The trees were big, and the foliage was thick but it was not gloomy. There was no undergrowth, only the smooth grass, very green and fresh, and the big trees well spaced as though it were a park.

'This is country,' Bill said.

The relation of this episode to war is made clear when Jake remarks of a dinner during the festival at Pamplona, 'It was like certain dinners I remember from the war. There was much wine, an ignored tension, and a feeling of things coming that you could not prevent happening. Under the wine I lost the disgusted feeling and was happy. It seemed they were all such nice people.' War was not only violent and destructive, it gave men a possible and workable system of values—courage and loyalty and sometimes unselfishness. The bull-fight supplies Hemingway one metaphor for war.

He prepares us to accept Jake's emotions about bull-fighting by showing Jake at prayer in church. Jake has the capacity for religious wonder, but he can no longer respond to religion:

I knelt and started to pray and prayed for everybody I thought of, Brett and Mike and Bill and Robert Cohn and myself, and all the bull-fighters, separately for the ones I liked, and lumping all the rest, then I prayed for myself again, and while I was praying for myself I found I was getting sleepy, so I prayed that the bull-fights would be good, and that it would be a fine fiesta, ... and as all the time I was kneeling with my forehead on the wood in front of me, and was thinking of myself as praying, I was a little ashamed, and regretted that I was such a rotten Catholic, but realized there was nothing I could do about it, at least for a while, and maybe never, but that anyway it was a grand religion, and I only wished I felt religious and maybe I would be next time; . . . .

We accept the bull-fight motif because Hemingway presents the incidentals of the sport as ritual, from the unloading of the bulls and their awesome run through the streets to the pens in the arena, to his description of Romero dressing for the fight, as formal as Greek and Latin epic in fullness of detail, as are the descriptions of the bull-fights proper. Hemingway is thus able to deal with primitive and basic themes: religion, initiation, war, death, and their attendant ritual. Jake Barnes, a fisher-king figure from the wasteland, moves in a context of metaphor which allows Hemingway to draw upon sources of emotion that civilization has coated over with convention. The treatment of war at one remove in *The Sun Also Rises* is thus superior to *A Farewell to Arms*, good as that novel is, for its transcending metaphor.

A Farewell is a fine demonstration of what an artist can do with naturalism in the third phase of the novel, but it seems meagre and local in contrast to *The Sun Also Rises*. Hemingway perceived in war his particular theme, and his novels of war have sanity, a human and moral base, a technical competence, and a degree of awareness which no other writer in English has achieved. Only Malraux and Broch have approximated his achievement, but neither has surpassed him. The First World War did not shock English novelists as it did the Americans, though it did outrage them even more fundamentally, and again in English war novels the sense of outrage, though not the same kind of outrage, dominates. History prepared the English for the Great War as it had not prepared the Americans; English schoolboys were brought up on legends of the thin red line marking a desperate and successful stand against hordes of murderous tribesmen absurdly resisting the extension of Empire, while angel choruses hummed 'God Save the King' above the din of battle. Where the Americans were stunned and unhappy at the thought of having to raise an army in 1917, the English, a militaristic race in comparison, responded in 1914 with comparative enthusiasm and a doughy idealism. The shock and the outrage came later, after the bloody defeats of 1915 and 1916, when the troops and finally the population at large realized the enormity of the adventure in which they were engaged.

These differences and gradations in social response were rendered competently in English war novels, but without the innocence and bravura of the young Americans. Most English novels of World War I were not written by professional novelists, but by poets like Siegfried Sassoon and Richard Aldington, who used the novel form as catharsis for ideas and emotions which the stricter discipline of verse does not immediately accommodate. H. M. Tomlinson and Ford Madox Ford were professionals, but Tomlinson's *All Our Yesterdays* has survived, I suspect, for its sentimental picture of the British soldiery carrying on. Ford's Tietjens series, happily, is another matter.

Although Ford challenges criticism in a manner of which Richard Aldington is incapable, the latter's *Death of a Hero* portrays more nakedly the complex relationship between English literary tradition and the political occurrence of the war, between English society and one reasonably competent artist's perception of society. *Death of a Hero* was published in 1929, the same year as *A Farewell to Arms*, but it reads as though it had been written from the trenches in the full heat of indignation. It is a sprawling, ambitious book which sets out to recreate the Victorian background not only of George Winterbourne, the 'hero' in question, but of his parents and grandparents. At the same time, Aldington attempts a satire upon London literary and artistic society of 1912–14, a political account of the background of the war, and a full portrait of the war itself in France, of the men who fought it and the civilians in England who cheered them on. Composed in three parts complete with prologue, verse-epilogue, a prefatory note about censorship of obscenities and a personal letter to a friend of the author, *Death of a Hero* departs conscientiously from the Edwardian well-made novel of E. M. Forster and returns to the late Victorian example of Samuel Butler. The first two sections of *Death of a Hero*, in truth, read like an uneasy mixture of Butler seasoned with early, uninspired Aldous Huxley. That Aldington was sensitive to criticism is clear in the public-private letter he carefully reproduced: 'I am all for disregarding artistic rules of thumb. I dislike standardised art as much as standardised life. Whether I have been guilty of Expressionism or Super-realism or not, I don't know and don't care. I knew what I wanted to say, and said it. And I know I have not tried to be "original".' This bombast typifies Aldington's approach to his material, and one goes on reading the first two parts of the novel only for their revelation of how bad writing can be and still survive. Tenacity is rewarded by the third part, which suddenly takes on life and power; when Aldington turns to the fact of the war itself, he ceases to be an absurd, angry amateur and becomes a writer.

The story-line of the novel—Aldington carefully avoids plot— is simple, and is related in entirety by the author in the prologue: Winterbourne is born to Victorian parents who are ignorant, self-deceiving, floridly pious, snobbish, materialistic, and incompetent; he attends a bad public school and after the failure of his father's business, goes to London to paint and earn a meagre living as an art-critic. He rebels sexually and socially against his parents' 'values', takes both wife and mistress, becomes trapped between the two women's personalities, enlists when war breaks out and serves until 1918 when he commits suicide by exposing himself to German machine-gun fire. The tone of the prologue, that of a D. H. Lawrence or Thomas Wolfe essay, is the tone of the first two sections of the novel; indignation substitutes for the rudiments of craft, and unrealized idea gets in the way of imagination. The end of the prologue reads,

The death of a hero! What mockery, what bloody cant! What sickening putrid cant! George's death is a symbol to me of the whole sickening bloody waste of it, the damnable stupid waste and torture of it. You've seen how George's own people—the makers of his body, the women who held his body to theirs—were affected by his death. The Army did its bit, but how could the Army individually mourn a million 'heroes'? How could the little bit of Army which knew George mourn him?

.   .   .   .

That is why I am writing the life of George Winterbourne, a unit, one human body murdered, but to me a symbol. It is an atonement, a desperate effort to wipe off the blood guiltiness. Perhaps it is the wrong way. Perhaps the poison will still be in me. If so, I shall search for some other way. But I shall search. I know what is poisoning me. I do not know what is poisoning you, but you are poisoned. Perhaps you too must atone.

This raving continues in Aldington's attempts to reproduce dramatically the situations he had already outlined editorially. It alternates with a heavy brand of satire, as when Winterbourne is in London just before the war meeting the literary set:

As for Mr. Waldo Tubbe, who hailed (why 'hailed'?) from the Middle Western districts of the United States, he was an exceedingly ardent and patriotic British Tory, standing for Royalism in Art, Authority in Politics, and Classicism in Religion. Unfortunately, there was no dormant peerage in the family; otherwise he would certainly have spent all his modest patrimony in endeavouring to become Lord Tubbe. Since he was an unshakeable Anglo-Catholic, there were no hopes of a Papal Countship; and Tory Governments are proverbially shabby in their treatment of even the most distinguished among their intellectual supporters. Consequently, all Mr. Waldo Tubbe could do in that line was to hint at his aristocratic English ancestry, to use his (possibly authentic) coat-of-arms on his cutlery, stationery, toilet articles, and book-plates, and know only the 'best' people.

Aldington's pettiness is exceeded only by his nastiness in the sexual episodes.

It is relevant that when Aldington finally turns to combat in France, his mind and his style become purified and the novel takes on meaning for the first time; a curious illustration of what happens to the English novelist when he attempts notebook-naturalism. Scenes of great documentary force mingle with further editorial raving, but despite the mixture of styles the war episodes have an honesty and directness which the rest of the novel lacks. When Aldington does not try to 'write' he demonstrates a good command over dialogue and individual accent together with a feeling for pace and the placing of scenes. Winterbourne's death has dignity and taste, but the moments of dignity and taste are too few and the novel as a whole is embarrassing in its obvious autobiographical basis and annoying in its wealth of cliché and innocence of craft.

Death of a Hero took English war fiction a step beyond Sassoon's barely disguised diary notations, but as a novel it demonstrates how inadequate the tradition was and how urgently a new form was needed for the various themes that Aldington had botched. More unoriginal than he knew, Aldington was firmly rooted in the Victorian era he so violently disliked. When he tried to cope with ideas, for example, he used the methods of Disraeli or H. G. Wells; like these novelists of the first two phases, his ideas are deductive, based on untested vision and presented in superficial reportage. Only his anger was new.

Ford Madox Ford's Tietjens novels, *Some Do Not*, *No More Parades*, *A Man Could Stand Up*, and *Last Post* (1924–28) proved Ford to be the only war novelist to advance the form of the novel in the decade after the war was fought. And yet even the Tietjens series contains grave lapses and remains a minor effort. It was Ford's bad luck that in his war novels he worked out a series of experiments, making the errors that an experimenter usually makes, and moving towards a technique which other writers, notably Ernest Hemingway, were to perfect in later work. Ford is a fascinating historical figure, for he was completely and intensely aware of the English tradition in the novel, devoted to the novel as a great literary form in a degree which is startling in England, fully conscious of the contributions of James and Conrad, and equally conscious that the war as a political event and as a subject demands from the novelist an approach which nothing in the tradition provided. Ford is the Ezra Pound of the novel: like Pound he encouraged numbers of young writers; by insisting on the importance of their art as an art and emphasizing in his own novels, criticism and conversation the achievements of the French nineteenth century, he provided a good influence which is as ubiquitous as it is difficult to define.

Unlike Pound, Ford's own powers were unequal to his demands, and the Tietjens novels, his best work, are an unfinished monument to his place in literary history. Ford perceived with characteristic sensitivity that the theme of war involved the destruction of a social order, but gave the novelist an opportunity to treat the individual consciousness with a depth that the usual invented situations made difficult. He further perceived that this opportunity was in the nature of necessity for the art of the novel, rather like the opportunity of a man driving fast with faulty brakes through a railroad-crossing just ahead of an express train. Sincerely devoted to his notion of traditional English society, Roman Catholic and conservative in a way that shames the easy conservatism of the 1950s, Ford established in Tietjens a very knight of a Christian English gentleman of landed Yorkshire stock. Tietjens is a man of greatness whose goodness is his undoing. His very nobility is his tragic flaw; he will lift not a finger in his own behalf. Trapped into marriage, he will not divorce Sylvia, a wife who persecutes him for his very superiority virtually to his death. From the beginning to the end of the series Tietjens is the moral point of reference for an entire society—the Edwardian cabinet ministers and civil servants in *Some Do Not*, the various army cliques in *No More Parades* and *A Man Could Stand Up*, and the *nouveau riche*, American and English, who take over county-society in *Last Post*. His purpose, Ford wrote, was to explain to the public,

> 'This is what the late war was like: this is how modern fighting of the organized, scientific type affects the mind. If, for reason of gain or, as is still more likely, out of dislike for collective types other than your own, you choose to permit your rulers to embark on another war, this—or something very accentuated along similar lines—is what you will have to put up with!'

Like Aldington, Ford accuses the Victorians, but unlike Aldington his accusation is dramatic and structural. Tietjens is in love with Valentine Wannop, whose Victorian father, a classical scholar, taught her Latin and Greek, and died, leaving her impoverished and without any capacity to make a living. She says of her father, 'Look here: I disapprove of this whole thing: of what my father has brought me to! Those people . . . the brilliant Victorians talked all the time through their hats. They evolved a theory from anywhere and then went brilliantly mad over it. Perfectly recklessly. . . .' Situations, of which this is representative, are developed entirely through the dialogue, a technique which Ford adapted from Henry James with fine effect and one which

Hemingway in turn seems to have taken from Ford. Ford also makes extensive use of interior monologue, but his success with the device is mixed; he goes from character to character distractingly, though for the most part he uses Tietjens's mind as a centre of consciousness. Ford seems to ignore Dorothy Richardson's and Virginia Woolf's errors, and to go directly back to the experiments of James. He failed notably with Sylvia Tietjens, a monster of wantonness and perversity, an *Ur*-bitch whose unreality and unpleasantness Hemingway appears to borrow directly in such characters as Brett Ashley, or in American guise, Mrs. Macomber. Hard, brittle and snobbish, she never loses a theatricality which cheapens the series.

Ford succeeds in conveying by indirection, understatement and irony the pain and the outrage of combat, where Aldington and Sassoon had resorted to overstatement. He communicates a notion of the vastness of the war which no other novelist but Hemingway approached. His knowledge of Conrad's technique of presenting ideas through visual imagery is put to good use when Tietjens says to a fellow-officer,

'If you got a still more extended view over this whole front you'd have still more enormous bodies of men. . . . Seven to ten million. . . . All moving towards places to which they desperately don't want to go. Desperately! Every one of them is desperately afraid. But they go on. An immense blind will forces them in the effort to consummate the one decent action that humanity has to its credit in the whole of recorded history. The one we are engaged in . . . .'

But in *Last Post* the series degenerates. Understatement has become a habit, and more serious, the symbolism obvious and tasteless. The war is over, and Mark, Tietjens's brother, who had been a powerful administrative officer in the war government, lies totally paralysed, while Tietjens himself is reduced to dealing in antique furniture, the only living for which his experience has prepared him. Neither is able to save the ancestral manor, Groby, from the American tenant who cuts down the ancient Groby yew—Old England has gone under, and we can no longer take seriously Tietjens's Christian, Tory nobility.

Ford seemed unable to sustain his own imaginative vision, and his final text is no more compelling than Galsworthy's. If for no other reason, however, we would still read the Tietjens series as a focal point in the development of fiction of the third phase. Ford's perceptions were important ones, as the political novel of between the wars and the novels of World War II have demonstrated. He was one of the first novelists to realize the possibilities of the cognitive novel, of the inseparable interaction between the purely technical devices at the writer's command and that external history which makes up an important part of his materials. In this sense only he helped to advance the novel. Both as fact and as idea, the First World War set a crucial test for the English tradition in the novel, a tradition which was admirably suited to an ironic handling of idea in social comedy, and suited not at all to dealing with fact. Where the Americans could draw with profit on both doctrinaire and native naturalism, English writers for the first time turned to naturalism as a necessary instrument for dealing with the fact of war. The result was a curious split between idea and fact, between the presentation of the idea of war in social terms through traditional devices, and the presentation of fact through the devices of naturalism. This very split was necessary and ultimately healthy for the English novel, but it meant that with the exception of Ford's, English war novels lacked the excitement, the restlessness in formal and technical terms, of the Americans.

A Farewell to Arms is deservedly well known and I shall not linger over textual details; it is instructive, however, to compare it with the Tietjens series, where Ford was defeated by his attempt to marry social conservatism to technical experiment. His social perceptions tend to negate his artist's conscience, and vice versa; his defence of a social system which produced people like Sylvia Tietjens and General Campion led him into anomalies which no amount of artistry could resolve. He demonstrated brilliantly Tietjens's ambiguous feeling about the war, but his honesty in perceiving the corruption of Tory values after the war axiomatically made the post-war Tietjens into a quaint 'character' of slight literary reality. Hemingway, on the other hand, aware of the value of Ford's technical experiment, realized with a surer instinct

the split in society which the war had made and the futility of
defending an indefensible position. Society is present only at
second remove in Hemingway's work; there are no factories or
politicians, not because he could not create them but because he
chose to go to the direct issue, the disparity between the good
individual and a meaningless society. *A Farewell to Arms* survives
as the only excellent novel of the first war in English because,
unlike other novelists, Hemingway made the connection between
the fact of the war and an intellectually defensible idea of the war.

The First World War was comparatively easy to write about
in universal terms; France provided a frame and the very nature
of the fighting made possible a helpful economy. The Second
World War, which was fought all over the world, has defied
universal treatment, and novels have been little more than vig-
nettes. Novels of the First World War established a series of
clichés which large numbers of young writers have followed,
but we may leave that fact to the sociologists. While it is still
too early to look for the great novels of the Second World War
it is possible to assess the problem it poses and to see how the war
has affected the imaginations of a few good writers.

'All the novels about the Second World War could never
convince an intelligent observer from Betelgeuse that such an
event did ever occur. . . .'[1] So reads a comment by a usually
perceptive American writer, who goes on to argue that recent
war novels are no more than geographically far-flung imitations
of novels of the First World War. This view is widely held both
in England and in America, and while it describes with accuracy
the bulk of recent war fiction, it reveals a blindness to a few works
which deny the generalization so fully as to make it absurd. The
comment interests me for its revelation of a conflict in the writer
concerning World War II itself, a conflict which is also present in
virtually all recent novels about the war. It relates to what I have
described as the White Russian attitude toward literature and
society; it sees the pacifism of the first war generation as naïve,
and the passiveness of the second war generation toward war as

[1] Leslie Fiedler, 'The Ant on the Grasshopper', *Partisan Review*, XXII, No. 3,
414.

irresponsible and guilt-laden. The White Russian attitude masks a new *Hurra-Patriotismus* which justifies any mode of warfare since 1939 by the unanswerable argument that Hitler was evil and evil must be fought with evil.[1] Much writing of excellence about World War II has been passed over for failing to observe the White Russian attitude, while a novel like John Hersey's *The Wall* is praised for its unassailable orthodoxy in spite of a technical slickness which parades as serious art.

The great debasement of naturalism that took place between the wars prepared the way for the large number of novels about the Second World War, in which the rich possibilities for vulgarity and dishonesty of the Book-of-the-Month club were fully realized: Irwin Shaw's *The Young Lions*, Steinbeck's *The Moon Is Down*, Herman Wouk's *The Caine Mutiny*, and in England, Nicholas Monsarrat's *The Cruel Sea*. A comparison between *The Caine Mutiny* and Warren Eyster's *Far from the Customary Skies*, a relatively unknown novel on the same subject, Naval war in the Pacific, establishes the difference between the popular writer who polishes clichés like jewels and places them in glossy new settings, and the writer of integrity who uses war for its test of mind and character in extreme situations. *The Caine Mutiny* is a uniquely contemporary product that summons to mind the underworld of Hollywood and television where men of great ability create parodies of their own ambitions in return for swimming-pools. The novel is a trivial projection of a Technicolor war upon a Technicolor sea to be ignored as literature, but it represents a point at which literature and sociology unfortunately coincide. It has been read by at least six million people, and in the form of play and film seen by further millions: in short, it has become a cultural artifact. Because Wouk's version of the Second World War has been accepted by vast millions, it becomes a

---

[1] Mr. Arthur Koestler is the High Priest of this cult which spreads west from Berlin to San Francisco; while Koestler's own writings are condescended to by the more sophisticated members of his cult, his ruthless political view is followed to the letter. Koestler, himself uprooted, spiritually and politically, one-time religious Communist become religious anti-Communist, political activist and intellectual analyst, is the embodiment for literature and for politics of all that is intended in the term 'catastrophe'.

literary duty to discover why; within the reasons lies the challenge
of communication which the serious novelist increasingly feels.

Wouk has the sharp American reportorial eye, his dialogue is
skilful, and he knows all the tricks about scene-setting, pace and
compression. The surface of his long novel is consistent and possesses texture. His style is simple without being simple-minded,
and he has wit and a literary kind of intelligence. By placing the
action on a mine-sweeper he does not attempt to represent a
cross-section of America, nor does he indulge in false heroics;
that is to say he avoids the obvious clichés of the war writer. The
novel has a convincing plot which is well served by Wouk's
undoubted narrative ability. The situation is fresh and potentially
important: the conflict between the sense of military duty as
conceived by the regular Navy, and the rebellion which civilians
in uniform feel at having to obey without question apparently
stupid orders. The first third of the novel develops with subtlety
and wit the fact that the regular Navy commander of the *Caine*,
Queeg, is at best an ignorant martinet, and at worst a psychopath
who is unfit for responsible duty. Queeg harasses his junior officers
and crew to the point where his second officer relieves him of
command at the height of a typhoon in accordance with naval
regulations and in full knowledge that he may be committing
mutiny. These episodes are presented through the consciousness
of Ensign Willy Keith, the central figure of the novel, a comic
anti-hero for half of the book and a true hero for the remainder.
Keith is supposed to be an attractive, thoughtless young man just
out of Princeton, who volunteers for the Navy only to escape
conscription into the Army. His parents are wealthy and disapprove of his affair with an Italian night-club singer. In Keith we
have the first inkling that Wouk may be writing with one hand
on his wallet and one eye on Hollywood, but there is the possibility that he may purposely be manipulating his all-American
cliché in order to create an ironic centre for his true theme. Once
Keith is aboard the *Caine*, the theme of responsibility develops
with a certain power. We meet Maryk, an ex-fisherman, who
hopes to enter the regular Navy after the war, a plodding, good
man who will relieve Queeg of command. We also meet

Lieutenant Thomas Keefer, purported to be writer and intellectual, the man who first diagnoses Queeg's condition as paranoia
and urges Maryk to his act of mutiny. Although Wouk creates
suspicion about Keefer's integrity, we are convinced up to the
point of Maryk's court martial that Queeg is indeed a sorry
specimen and that Maryk was correct in his action. But in the
clever, meretricious court-martial episode, Queeg is presented as
a wronged man and Maryk as the dupe of the false Keefer. Maryk
is saved from disgrace by a *deux ex machina* in the person of Barney
Greenwald, a Jewish lawyer turned fighter-pilot, grounded for
wounds, who gets Maryk off by legal trickery, assuring him he
is 'guilty as hell', and describing Keefer as a kind of wolf in
intellectual's clothing who represents all the rottenness in American life.

The crux of the novel is Greenwald's appearance at a party to
celebrate the publication of Keefer's novel and Maryk's verdict.
Greenwald arrives late, drunk, and eloquent, saying that if he
wrote a war-novel he would make Queeg the hero:

> His speech was halting and blurry. He was gripping the spilling
> glass tightly. The scars on his hand made red rims around the bluish
> grafted skin.
>
>   'Well, sure, you guys all have mothers, but they wouldn't be in
> the same bad shape mine would if we'd lost this war, which of course
> we aren't, we've won the damn thing by now. See, the Germans
> aren't kidding about the Jews. They're cooking us down to soap
> over there. They think we're vermin and should be 'sterminated
> and our corpses turned into something useful. . . . But I just can't
> cotton to the idea of my mom melted down into a bar of soap. I
> had an uncle and an aunt in Cracow, who are soap now, but that's
> different, I never saw my uncle and aunt, just saw letters in Jewish
> from them, ever since I was a kid, but never could read them. Jew,
> but I can't read Jewish. . . .
>
>   'I'm coming to Old Yellowstain [Queeg]. Coming to him. See,
> while I was studying law 'n' old Keefer here was writing his play
> for the Theatre Guild, and Willie here was on the playing fields of
> Prinshton, all that time these birds we call regulars—these stuffy,
> stupid Prussians, in the Navy and the Army—were manning guns.
> Course they weren't doing it to save my mom from Hitler, they

were doing it for dough, like everybody else does what they do. Question is, in the last analysis—*what* do you do for dough? Old Yellowstain, for dough, was standing guard on this fat dumb happy country of ours. Meantime me, I was advancing my little free non-Prussian life for dough. Of course, we figured in those days, only fools go into armed service. Bad pay, no millionaire future, and you can't call your mind or body your own. Not for sensitive intellectuals. So when all hell broke loose and the Germans started running out of soap and figured, well it's time to come over and melt down old Mrs. Greenwald—who's gonna stop them? Not her boy Barney. Can't stop a Nazi with a lawbook. So I dropped the lawbooks and ran to learn how to fly. Stout fellow. Meantime . . . who was keeping Mama out of the soap dish? Captain Queeg.

'Yes, even Queeg, poor sad guy, yes, and most of them not sad at all, fellows, a lot of them sharper boys than any of us, don't kid yourself, best men I've ever seen, you can't be good in the Army or Navy unless you're goddamn good. Though maybe not up on Proust 'n' *Finnegans Wake* and all.'

By this point the opaque image of the serious novel Wouk might have written vanishes completely, never to reappear in the long coda, in which Willy Keith turns into Naval hero and mature man who gets the chaste girl. The issues in Greenwald's speech display a remarkable depth of literary cynicism. Wouk consciously manipulates the public urge to congratulate itself upon fighting the war in a good cause and for its liberalism regarding anti-semitism, rather like royalty congratulating itself for being well-born. The anti-semitic theme, totally extraneous to this novel, is commercially rewarding in America, and the 'bestseller' war novel is rarely without it: Shaw's *The Young Lions*; John Horne Burns's *The Gallery*, even *The Naked and the Dead* (in which the theme is structural). Wouk, in brief, avoids the old clichés but manipulates new ones. Keefer, the 'intellectual', is so by virtue of taking to sea with him a volume of Kant, *Finnegans Wake*, by writing a sonnet and a sexy war novel; a large public accepts this parody as the real thing, and answers with indignation to Wouk's smearing of the intellectual when he makes Keefer into a parlour pink of the thirties. But the most remarkable example of cynicism is the glorification of the military

Q

by creating a wry hero out of Queeg; Wouk plays upon the post-war disposition, forced by history, to rely upon the military, to elect General Officers as Presidents. As Faulkner has somewhere suggested, perhaps we do not deserve to survive. *The Caine Mutiny* places Wouk at the head of the other plutocrats of the American novel, John Marquand, John O'Hara, John Cheever, Edward Newhouse, Irwin Shaw; writers who do not actually pimp and prostitute, but who adjust their vision and contort their imaginations ever so slightly in the direction of a popular taste that corrupts, emasculates, and finally kills.

The majority of novels about the Second World War have been written by men old enough to have experienced the anti-war sentiment of the thirties and the political furor of the Spanish Civil War; behind their work lie an idea of war and an idea of Europe in relation to America which colour their treatment. Burns's narrator in *The Gallery* says, for instance,

> A Liberty ship in convoy brought me to Casa [blanca] from Camp Patrick Henry, Virginia. In the nineteen days of crossing the Atlantic, I remember that something happened to me inside. I didn't know what adjustment to make for where I was going, but I think I died as an American. I'd climbed the gangplank with some of that feeling of adventure with which all soldiers go overseas. All the pacifist propaganda of the twenties and thirties couldn't quite smother that dramatic mood of well-here-we-go-again-off-to-the-wars.

Eyster's *Far from the Customary Skies* displays none of that mood, and none of the preconceptions about war of the older novelists; yet in a literary sense, Eyster, too, in crossing the Pacific, may have 'died as an American'. Even more than *The Naked and the Dead*, an intellectually stronger book, Eyster's novel treats the idea of war as a literary idea in a manner that few Americans have been able to master. *Far from the Customary Skies* (the difficult title is from a couplet of Yeats: Many a son and daughter lies . . .) has none of Wouk's professional patina, but its weaknesses are not those of false intellectual clarity, reaction disguised as liberalism, or film-script disguised as novel. It lacks plot, but it has that rarer quality, inevitability.

Eyster describes life on a destroyer in the South Pacific from the battle for Guadalcanal to the invasion of the Philippines from the enlisted man's point of view, avoiding the implicit sentimentality of the common sailor as sub-human beast, or in the manner of Thomas Heggen's *Mr. Roberts*, as rich humorous Character. He conveys with fidelity the routine of shipboard life with techniques of naturalism which are relieved of deadness and reportage by an unintrusive symbolic framework. The novel is without a hero, though it has a central point in vision in the Fire-controlman Ham, a slight, ill, childlike man whose sensitivity to the difficulties of human relationships and whose reactions to natural beauty are communicated with unhackneyed insight. His fellow Fire-controlman, Ross, is tougher and more sophisticated, but Ross shares something of Ham's sensibility.

Neither character is the cliché of the aesthetic young man gone to war; they have nothing of the Dos Passos young man's whine, like Andrews in *Three Soldiers*. Ham's innocence and sense of wonder are more comparable to Sherwood Anderson's George Willard of *Winesburg, Ohio*, though I do not mean to suggest an influence. The humanity of Ham and Ross contrasts with the brutishness of Malone, the Boatswain's Mate, a giant of a man who instinctively hates the Fire-controlmen for their physical weakness and their intelligence, himself craftily intelligent and domineering, a born sailor who works with epic endurance and leads his deckhands to emulate him. Malone is not the traditional naturalist's human animal, neither a McTeague nor a Byronic superman, but a finely observed human being of a type which occurs with some frequency in the American Navy, men who exemplify in a corrupt degree traditional American qualities and perform with tragic heroism in extreme situations.

Early in the novel when the newly commissioned *Dreher* is on its training cruise, Eyster prepares for the final scenes and Malone's death in a shark-hunting episode which Malone takes on as a bet against Ham. He angles for a shark, brings the thing aboard almost unaided and kills it with a boat-hook. When Ham tries to pay the five dollars he has lost, a 'fin' in sailor's slang, Malone refuses the money and says that the fin that he wants is the shark's dorsal fin, and that Ham must cut the fin from the body and give it to him. In the final episode, after three years of combat, the *Dreher* goes into action off the Philippines and is badly hit by Japanese gunfire. Malone, in charge of a gun-crew, refuses to abandon ship and with a broken arm forces his crew to continue at their doomed post. Ham tries to argue Malone away from his gun, and Malone stabs him to death. Only Polock, a small-time criminal, survives the *Dreher's* end. Thus outlined the novel would appear to be one more example of lurid naturalistic violence; it is in fact neither lurid nor violent. Eyster's sailors are realistically convincing without being forced to symbolize social or political facts. The absence of the overt political theme gives the novel a curious, cool detachment; it is not so much a war novel as a novel of the sea on which a war is taking place. Eyster brings to writing that literary vision which sees the familiar un-familiarly; this gives him a style which only occasionally lapses into purple patches and the insight to dispense with either the understatement of Hemingway's imitators or the stereotyped cast of characters of Monsarrat, Shaw, or Mailer. The novel has been neglected since publication in 1953, but I would predict that it will be read long after the vulgarities of *The Caine Mutiny* are forgotten.

Recent English fiction of the *fact* of war has been thin and disap-pointing. Novels like *The Cage* of Dan Billany and David Dowie, and *The Trap* of Billany were no advance upon the faintly dis-guised memoir of Sassoon, while a novel like Alexander Baron's *From the City, from the Plough* is a kind of Second War *All Our Yesterdays*, a celebration of the stout British heart (' "Another thing," said the Brigadier. He blew harshly through his empty pipe. "The Hun mustn't know that the main assault isn't coming from this side any more. You'll have to keep your crowd active" '). Indignation was no longer possible to the English writer of the Second War, and his honeyed naturalism in no manner challenges the ambitiousness of Mailer or the originality of Eyster. English war novelists as a group have written with a superficial command which stops at competence and evades the challenge of the theme. Only Gerald Hanley's *The Consul At*

Sunset has the scope and the finish to do justice to his material but Hanley, like the American Alfred Hayes, has borrowed too generously from Hemingway, and his novel of the British Army in North Africa has too many echoes to survive as an original work. In the war theme the defining differences between English and American writers tend to disappear. The English adopt the devices of naturalism rather gingerly but without the taste for violence and the controlling philosophy which naturalism demands in order to be successful. The result is something like *The Cruel Sea*, in which episodes from corvette life in the Atlantic are written brilliantly and honestly but which as a novel becomes trivial in Monsarrat's unnecessary insertion and handling of the love scenes, his cliché of a heroic ship commander, and his flagrantly tasteful celebration of the Royal Navy and the British cause.

English novelists have done their best work not with the military fact but with the idea of war in the civilian consciousness; only here can the unique English reaction to our most recent of catastrophes be discovered. Elizabeth Bowen in *The Heat of the Day*, Rosamund Lehmann in *The Echoing Grove*, P. H. Newby in *The Retreat* and, above all, Rex Warner in *The Aerodrome* leave the unruly immediacies of warfare in the background and go directly to social disruption and the aspect of war that can create and harden, or shatter and corrupt the individual consciousness. Miss Bowen's novel is the least satisfactory in that she seems unable to strike a balance between intensity and the implied scope of her ambitious theme; her description of London during the air attacks is too carefully wrought. It is as though someone had moved a Jamesian interior into a windswept field. Miss Lehmann has a tougher mind, if a less careful technique, and she captures something of the largeness of the war theme that Miss Bowen misses. P. H. Newby does not actually broach the subject of war and is content to treat it at second remove; within the confines of his own purpose he succeeds, but *The Retreat* remains peripheral to this discussion.

The Aerodrome, one of the finest English novels for decades, confronts the issue which English novelists have always preferred, the effect of the seemingly exterior event upon society. Warner is one of the few modern novelists in English—Ralph Ellison is another—who has been able to escape the vice of social realism *cum* naturalism and yet create the essence of social reality. The material of the novel is simply the effect upon the townspeople of the location of an aerodrome near an English country village. The ruthlessness of the military under the command of the Air Vice-Marshal and the inexorable corruption of the villagers by his lieutenants creates an anti-war novel the subtlety of which makes the shot-and-shell realism of Alexander Baron seem like crude preaching. Liberated from social realism but exposed to the literary dangers of allegory and the temptations of a Kafkaesque surrealism, Warner dominates his difficult medium through a series of carefully controlled incidents within a plot deriving from Greek myth and drama. As in his other novels, Warner's narrative economy and Greek directness permit him to write of things which have come to seem tawdry and platitudinous: love, hope, faith, suffering, and endurance. Few other writers could adopt without absurdity the tone and diction of the narrator's final speech: ' "That the world may be clean," I remembered my father's words. Clean indeed it was and most intricate, fiercer than tigers, wonderful and infinitely forgiving.' Warner presents ideas, and *The Aerodrome* is a novel of ideas, directly and dramatically, while with his conviction of the pathos in the discrepancy between goodness and simplicity and the necessary corruption of war, he writes tragedy, an achievement of enduring authority and stature.

The Aerodrome, together with the best American novels of the Second World War, *The Naked and the Dead*, *Far from the Customary Skies*, and *From Here to Eternity*, have not been celebrations of the sacred cause, but anti-war and anti-military. Mailer's treatment of war—the corruption of armies, the barren wastes in the professional soldier's being, his black view of society—is essentially supported by Jones, Eyster, and Warner. It is an unpopular view, but one whose validity has certainly not been challenged by the confections of Herman Wouk or Nicholas Monsarrat.

Shallow American parallels to the English treatment of the *idea* of war occur in Albert Guerard's *Night Journey*, John Hawkes's *The Cannibal*, and in Faulkner's *A Fable*. Guerard and Hawkes struggle earnestly to escape from realism and naturalism by apprenticing themselves to Gide and Kafka. Their novels are earnestly tortured, surrealistic products of an imagination flogged beyond its capabilities; in comparison to Rex Warner's their work seems lifeless. *A Fable* proves finally the dangers of the war theme even to a writer of greatness. Faulkner follows his own example in *Light in August* of adapting the biblical story of Christ's passion and death into a modern setting; where he succeeded triumphantly in *Light in August*, he fails abominably in *A Fable*. Faulkner returns to his basic idea of contemporary man's relation to history, not only Southern United States history but all of human history; he would assert the precedence of man over the final corruption of war. To this epic theme he brings a Christ-figure in the person of a Central European Corporal and twelve followers who wander back and forth between the lines of the allies and the central powers, trying to stop the war. They almost succeed, but the consternation of the Generals quells the rebellion they have incited and leads to their execution. It has been pointed out that Faulkner is not making a traditional interpretation of the Bible, but a heretical one, that he is merely demonstrating the futility of the Christian legend to redeem a civilization which has lost and damned itself.[1] Faulkner's bitter heresy places him among the greatest writers on the subject of war, but his ambitious theme betrays him into new turgidities of style, and his sometimes sound narrative instinct deserts him. The net effect is that of a film-scenario of Passion Week collaborated upon by Matthew, Mark, Luke, and Dostoievski.

The best writing inspired by the wars emphasizes the connection in the novel of the last thirty-five years between society and politics. We have been told many times that 'life' and art cannot mix, that the degree of involvement in immediate experience which war and politics imply is too raw a diet for literature. The

[1] Ursula Brumm, 'Wilderness and Civilization: A Note on William Faulkner', *Partisan Review*, XXII, No. 3, 340–351.

unruly nature of modern politics has indeed defeated many
novelists, just as war has defeated many more. The unpleasant
facts of existence in the last generation have sent writers scurrying
to the Church or to the *Bhagavad-Gita*, just as it has sent others to
homosexuality and an arid aestheticism. The novel like life
itself has required toughness and integrity; it has set tests for the
English and American writer which they had not to face in
earlier generations. Thus we are forced to distinguish between
early and late Aldous Huxley or John Dos Passos, and we cannot
evade the fact that the memorable novels of the past generation
have been, directly or by implication, political. In the case of
George Orwell and Wyndham Lewis, politics have prevented
their full development as novelists. Idea dominates imagination
in most of Orwell's work and in all of Lewis's. In America,
Robert Penn Warren in *All the King's Men* and Norman Mailer
in *Barbary Shore* show a similar, though not so crippling, limitation. Both use the novel as a means for clarifying their own personal political perceptions; they do not quite succeed in projecting
their perceptions into the finality of great art. Americans and
Englishmen alike lack the continental tradition of the political
novel, but their awareness of the need has created a crisis, not a
desperate but a fruitful crisis, in the novel of ideas. It may be
useful to conclude this discussion with a glance at the work of
André Malraux, a continental who does not belong to this study,
but whose novels provide an illuminating contrast to novels of
war and politics in English, while they may indicate one direction
in which our novelists are moving.

In his life and in his art Malraux anticipated with the vision of
literary genius a political formulation and a pattern in the novel
which would do justice to his knowledge and feeling. Never a
Communist but allied with the Communists in China in the
1920s, in France in the 1930s and in the *maquis* during the war,
he knew from inside the nature of collective politics and knew
with the isolation of the modern artist the effect of ideology upon
human beings. *Les Conquérants* (1928), *La Condition humaine*
(1933) and *L'Éspoir* (1937) are all major novels of revolution and
of the human condition. The first novel describes the successful

phase of the Kuomintang uprising in South China; *Man's Fate*
reverses the situation and deals with the disintegration after the
collapse of the Wuang government and the liquidation of the
Left by the Right-wing Kuomintang generals. *Man's Fate* is not
only a perfect piece of craftsmanship but an accurate prediction of
recent Chinese history in the portrayal of Chiang Kai-Shek. It is
a study in contemporary politics and more. Observing the human
condition in the midst of cataclysm, Malraux creates the atmosphere of revolutionaries at work and simultaneously explores the
idea of the contemplative life as against the active life through
Gisors-père ('ideas were not to be thought, but lived'). In
Gisors, a saintly man, the Christian ethic is contrasted with the
Buddhist's, the Marxian ethic with the individualist's. He says,
'. . . it is less hard to serve man than to serve the state. Do we live
for ourselves? We are nothing. We live for the state in the present, for the order of the dead through centuries. . . .' The other
characters too are saintly in their own manner, even the corrupted
Clappique, even Katow and Hemelrich, the hardened revolutionaries. Ch'en, the terrorist, Kyo, the central character: in their
deaths Malraux constructs a martyrology in which the only sur-
viving value is each man's conception of his own dignity, which
each reaches in isolated and devious ways. 'Gisors [thought] of
one of Kyo's [his son's] ideas: all that men are willing to die for,
beyond self-interest, tends more or less obscurely to justify that
fate by giving it a foundation in dignity: Christianity for the
slave, the nation for the citizen, Communism for the worker.'
And Katow says that he would go to prison for someone else,
even though he did not love that person deeply, '. . . for the idea
he has of life, of himself. . . . It's not for someone else that one
goes to prison.'

Man's Hope develops Malraux's ideas more fully. It is Malraux's
longest and most 'intellectual' novel; within the narrative he sets
forth through dramatic action and in the explicit words of the
characters his complicated but always wonderfully clear exposition of what those characters are about and why. Malraux's
clarity is never the simple-minded clarity of Steinbeck or, say,
C. P. Snow; he is always aware of the shifting focus of his various

projections of reality. Characters in the political novel are always
in danger of becoming walking ideas; Malraux's never do. Puig,
the Anarchist and student of Bakunin, '. . . saw no hope for the
world, exemplary revolts were the utmost he could hope from
anarchism. And so for him every political crisis resolved itself
into a test of character and courage.' These are the eternal values
for Malraux, courage in the midst of hopeless chaos, and Puig is
perhaps his most extreme exemplar. Puig is killed as he drives an
unarmoured car upon a Fascist field-piece in the streets of Madrid.
Magnin, the unmistakable portrait of Malraux himself, the Negus,
Jaime, Manuel, Puig—all the best of these characters are willing
to give up their lives. But not for a warm, sentimental dream of
liberty; each in his way knows precisely what he is doing; each
in his way creates one aspect of the irony in the title of the novel.
    Malraux scrutinizes the official Communist Party carefully: a
nameless old man tells Lopez, a Communist sculptor,

> 'I'll paint a picture of an old man toddling off and a young fellow
> having a bath. The nincompoop who bathes, and goes in for sports,
> who can't keep quiet for a moment—that's a Fascist.'
>   Lopez looked up; the man who spoke was an excellent Spanish
> painter. Obviously he had half a mind to add: 'Or else, a com-
> munist.'

Ximenes, the former regular army officer, a Catholic who has
remained with the Loyalists, presents fully the liberal Catholic
position with regard to the Communist Party; he virtually wins
over Manuel, his protégé, to his position. Yet Manuel remains
within the Party. 'The age of parties is beginning', Garcia says,
and man can act only within the limits laid down by that age.
    But above all, the world of *Man's Hope* is the apocalyptic
world, and Malraux even obliges us with the history of that
apocalypse. Garcia and a group of Russian Communists have
been arguing, and Garcia reflects,

> For him the term anarcho-syndicalism consisted of two opposed
> elements. The positive element was the syndicalist activity of the
> anarchists; the negative element, their ideology. Once the glamour
> was ruled out, anarchist theory fell absolutely into line with

syndicalism; the more enlightened anarchists took their stand on Sorel's teachings, not on theosophy.

Still later, Garcia thinks back to one of the Russian's views, that men must 'change—or die'. Garcia says, 'Many men . . . hope to find in the apocalypse a solution of their own problems.' And he adds to Hernandez,

> 'It's quite likely, Hernandez, that you're on the way to meet your . . . destiny. It's never easy to give up what one has loved, all the things one's lived for. I'd like to help you; but the cause you're staking on is doomed from the outset. Because you have to live politically, you have to act in terms of politics; and your duties as an officer bring you every moment in touch with politics. Whereas the cause you have in mind is not political. It is based on the contrast between the world in which you live and the world of your dreams. But action can only be envisaged in terms of action. The business of a political thinker is to compare one set of hard facts with another, one practical proposition with another; our side or Franco's; one system or another system. He is not fighting against a dream, a theory, or another apocalyptic vision.'

Throughout these three major novels as in *Days of Wrath* (*Temps du mépris*, 1934) and in *Les Noyers de l'Altenburg* (1943) Malraux continues to develop the distinction between action and contemplation within the framework of the political system which resembles Leninist and Stalinist Communism but which, as Trotsky pointed out, is not even Marxist. For Trotsky *Les Conquérants* contained too much individualism, too much of aesthetic caprice.[1] Answering Trotsky's attack, Malraux replied that *Les Conquérants* was first of all an 'accusation' against the human condition; 'accusation' is the strategic word. We then read *Man's Fate* as an ironic commentary. Man's dignity and heroism are embodied in apocalyptic, isolated, and long before Sartre, existentialist acts. Secondly Malraux makes the obvious point that political critics always ignore, '*L'optique du roman domine le roman*'—the perspective of the novel dominates the novel. And finally Malraux says, 'as to Hong [the terrorist prototype of

[1] Léon Trotsky, 'La Révolution étranglée', *La Nouvelle Revue Française*, No. 211, 1 April 1931, 489.

Ch'en in *Man's Fate*], he represents not the proletariat but *anarchy*; . . . his end is ethical, not political—and without hope'.[1]

Malraux's force derives in part from his choice of a philosophy upon which to construct an imaginative vision: it is the philosophy of Georges Sorel in *Reflections on Violence*. Malraux takes from Sorel what T. E. Hulme described as the dissociation between the working-class movement and the working-class ideology in Sorel's work.[2] Sorel was a political anti-intellectualist of Mephistophelian cast who set forth a rationale of violence in his chapters on the proletarian strike and the political general strike. He constructed in intellectual terms an anti-intellectual mystique according to which the proletariat must seize upon a myth, specifically the myth of the general strike, in order to achieve 'dignity'. Their violence is not directed to any immediate end; social benefits, if they result at all, are reserved for the remote future. War, similarly, is a benefit, for it prepares the apocalyptic climate in which heroism is possible.[3] 'Heroism and a sense of the sublime are the highest virtues—they are military virtues and whether practised inside the society in case of civil war or outside the society in case of national wars, they raise the dignity of the individual and endow him with the pride which dignity requires.'[4]

Sorel's syndicalism, then, provided the genesis of Malraux's

[1] André Malraux, 'Réponse à Léon Trotsky', *La Nouvelle Revue Française*, No. 211, 1 April 1931, 502–505.

[2] T. E. Hulme, *Speculations*, ed. Herbert Read, London, 1936, Appendix A, 'Reflections on Violence', pp. 249–260. Hulme translated *Reflections*.

[3] Georges Sorel, *Reflections on Violence*, trans. T. E. Hulme and J. Roth, Glencoe, Ill., 1950, pp. 136–201 and ff.

[4] Edward A. Shils, introduction to *Reflections on Violence*, p. 17. The difference between the Marxist myth and the Sorelian myth is implicit in Sorel's letter to Daniel Halévy, in which he argues the case for *Reflections on Violence*. He writes (in 1907) of Utopianism,

> The revolutionary myths which exist at the present time are almost free from any such [Utopian] mixture; by means of them it is possible to understand the activity, the feelings and the ideas of the masses preparing themselves to enter on a decisive struggle; the myths are not descriptions of things, but expressions of a determination to act. A Utopia is, on the contrary, an intellectual product; it is the work of theorists who, after observing and discussing known facts, seek to establish a model to which they can compare existing society in order to estimate the amount of good and evil it contains. (*Reflections on Violence*, p. 57.)

apocalyptic hero, his vision of a decaying society formed by this century and supported by the prophetic intuition of a philosopher whose main work appeared in 1906–7.

I am not suggesting that English and American novelists should turn to Sorel or even to Malraux; I am only emphasizing that Malraux's great novels have profited from having an intellectual base which neither Indian mysticism nor even heretical visions of Christianity like Faulkner's have been able to supply. The dangers of mystique are apparent in both Malraux's life and art; he has controlled them in his art by a firm intellectual discipline which has been lacking in traditional English and American writing. The need felt in England and in America for a controlling discipline has led many writers to a reliance upon mystique, to a concept of the novel as obsession.

Chapter Eight

THE NOVEL AS OBSESSION

L'Art sans poitrine m'a trop longtemps bercé dupe. La Forgue.

D. H. LAWRENCE wrote in a letter to Aldous Huxley, 'I am doing a novel, a novel which I have never grasped. Damn its eyes, there I am at p. 145 and I've no notion what it's about. I hate it. F. says it is good. But it's like a novel in a foreign language I don't know very well—I can only just make out what it's about.' And in another context Lawrence wrote, 'My great religion is the belief in the blood, the flesh, as being wiser than the intellect. We can go wrong in our minds. But what the blood feels, and believes, and says, is always true.'[1] Jean Paul Sartre has said, 'I am condemned to freedom', to which statement he added a footnote in *Huis Clos*, 'Hell is other people.' In Virginia Woolf's *To the Lighthouse* we read of Mrs. McNab:

As she lurched (for she rolled like a ship at sea) and leered (for her eyes fell on nothing directly, but with a sidelong glance that deprecated the scorn and anger of the world—she was witless, she knew it), as she clutched the banisters and hauled herself upstairs and rolled from room to room, she sang. Rubbing the glass of the long looking-glass and leering sideways at her swinging figure a sound issued from her lips—something that had been gay twenty years before on the stage perhaps, had been hummed and danced to, but now, coming from the toothless, bonneted, care-taking woman, was robbed of meaning, was like the voice of witlessness, humour, persistency itself, trodden down but springing up again, so that as she lurched, dusting, wiping, she seemed to say how it was one long sorrow and trouble, how it was getting up and going to bed again, and bringing things out and putting them away again. It was not easy or snug this world she had known for close on seventy years. Bowed down

[1] Aldous Huxley, *The Olive Tree and other Essays*, p. 129; p. 136.

she was with weariness. How long, she asked, creaking and groaning on her knees under the bed, dusting the boards, how long shall it endure?

In *Light in August*, Faulkner writes of the Reverend Gail Hightower, who often cannot distinguish the present from the past and confuses his own tortured career with that of his grandfather, a cavalryman killed in the Civil War,

> It is as though they had merely waited until he could find something to pant with, to be reaffirmed in triumph and desire with, with this last left of honor and pride and life. He hears above his heart the thunder increase, myriad and drumming. Like a long sighing of wind in trees it begins, then they sweep into sight, borne now upon a cloud of phantom dust. They rush past, forward-leaning in the saddles, with brandished arms, beneath whipping ribbons from slanted and eager lances; with tumult and soundless yelling they sweep past like a tide whose crest is jagged with the wild heads of horses and the brandished arms of men like the crater of the world in explosion. They rush past, are gone; the dust swirls skyward sucking, fades away into the night which has fully come. Yet, leaning forward in the window, his bandaged head huge and without depth upon the twin blobs of his hands upon the ledge, it seems to him that he still hears them: the wild bugles and the clashing sabres and the dying thunder of hooves.

And in *Miss Lonelyhearts*, a savage story of a male 'sob-sister' who becomes so oppressed by the suffering of his semi-literate correspondents that he comes to identify himself with the figure of Christ, Nathaniel West writes,

> After a long night and morning, towards noon, Miss Lonelyhearts welcomed the arrival of fever. It promised heat and mentally unmotivated violence. The promise was soon fulfilled; the rock became a furnace.
>
> He fastened his eyes on the Christ that hung on the wall opposite his bed. As he stared at it, it became a bright fly, spinning with quick grace on a background of blood velvet sprinkled with tiny nerve stars.
>
> Everything else in the room was dead—chairs, table, pencils, clothes, books. He thought of this black world of things as a fish.

And he was right, for it suddenly rose to the bright bait on the wall.
It rose with a splash of music and he saw its shining silver belly.

Christ is life and light.

'Christ! Christ!' This shout echoed through the innermost cells
of his body.

He moved his head to a cooler spot on the pillow and the vein in
his forehead became less swollen. He felt clean and fresh. His heart
was a rose and in his skull another rose bloomed.

The room was full of grace. A sweet, clean grace, not washed
clean, but clean as the innersides of the inner petals of a newly
forced rosebud.

Delight was also in the room. It was like a gentle wind, and his
nerves rippled under it like small blue flowers in a pasture.

He was conscious of two rhythms that were slowly becoming one.
When they became one, his identification with God was complete.
His heart was the one heart, the heart of God. And his brain was
likewise God's.

God said, 'Will you accept it, now?'

And he replied, 'I accept, I accept.'

He immediately began to plan a new life and his future conduct as
Miss Lonelyhearts. He submitted drafts of his column to God and
God approved them. God approved his every thought.

In their various ways, Lawrence, Sartre, Virginia Woolf,
Faulkner and West display one quality of the recent novel which
can only be described as obsession. These writers and many like
them seem to be chained to their typewriters like the German
soldiers of the atrocity story chained to their machine-guns.
Their writing has an immediately recognizable feverishness which,
upon analysis, reveals a particular and defining aspect of the novel
in its third phase. In the obsessed novel we discover a total atomization of human experience which can only be charged to our
wars, revolutions and social upheavals. The majority of these
writers seem to have nothing in common with frankly political
writers like Orwell and Dos Passos, who set out to analyse lucidly,
in social terms, the effects of catastrophe upon imagination. But
a connection does exist, one which has a good deal to do with the
writer's trust or mistrust of intellect, and even more to do with his
control as an artist over his themes and his material. At first

glance it would seem that the obsessed writer is anti-intellectual, badly disciplined as a craftsman and often floundering in the web of a mystique. It might also seem that the obsessed writer, in terms of traditional literary categories, is a survival of romanticism, a post-war Poe or a machine-age Scott. None of these apparent explanations, however, really satisfies.

That the obsessed writer is in part anti-intellectual is as clear as sunlight after fog. His first allegiance is to intuition, to the blinding flash that substitutes for logic and for the rational processes of the writer who believes in the adequacy of mind. This process is not confined to writing: we know that one of the most frightening effects of total war is its corrosion of public faith in reason and polity. War and industrialism together have turned entire populations in upon themselves—a truism. Indirectly, but no less witheringly, the corrosion of public faith has penetrated beneath the immediately political to all art, all manner of intellectual formulation, and of course to writers everywhere. Europe has been affected differently from America, and the European public is just beginning to turn into the basically anti-intellectual mass audience that America has been for two generations. Just as American faith in the ideals of the Enlightenment had been more intense than the Europeans', so American disillusion was swifter and more profound. The efficiency of American industrialism, in turn, consolidated the mass audience with a speed that Europe is only beginning to attain.

We have already seen anti-intellectualism as a romantic survival, particularly in America with its special connections to and modifications of European romanticism. I would emphasize here that the struggle between the contemplative and the creative ideal is as old as American history, and that by the nineteenth century the activist had supplanted in the popular mind any momentary eighteenth-century ascendance of the contemplative. Thus Malraux could write, '. . . the essential characteristic of contemporary American writing is that it is the only literature whose creators are not intellectuals . . . they are obsessed with fundamental man'[1]

[1] Henri Peyre, 'American Literature through French Eyes', *Virginia Quarterly Review*, XXIII, Summer 1947, 434.

—a partial truth, but a truth for all that. I have noted previously the absence in American fiction of the intellectual as a subject. Hemingway's Robert Jordan in *For Whom the Bell Tolls* is an intellectual of sorts, but his intellectuality is subordinate to his deeds. Dos Passos's intellectuals are not the real thing; they are frauds and fools when they are activists and ineffectual when they are contemplatives. Faulkner does a good deal of intellectualized preaching in the person of Gavin Stevens, but Stevens is made to appear as a folk-character, the village lawyer, who although he has been to Harvard, pronounces with the folk-voice the collective wisdom of the South. In Burns's *The Gallery*, a collective portrait of the stupidity and rapaciousness of American troops in Italy, the wry protests of a bespectacled little Private are always followed by the author's comment, 'But he was only a Jewish Communist and nobody ever listened to anything he said.' Robbins, the President of a women's college in Randall Jarrell's *Pictures from an Institution*, is an ex-Olympic diver who solicits funds from his Hollywood alumnae, sitting on the edge of a swimming-pool in Hawaiian bathing-costume, looking like 'some boy star who, playing Tom Sawyer, fancies for the moment that he is Narcissus'. 'On the table in the President's waiting-room', Jarrell writes, 'there are copies of *Town and Country*, the *Journal of History of Ideas*, and a small magazine—a little magazine—that had no name.' Until very recently, that is, American writers have preferred to satirize the intellectual rather than to analyse him—a variety of self-hatred, for the satirists have usually been intellectuals themselves, striking out at their kind. In place of the intellectual American writers have often preferred the sensitive young man, isolated, suffering, and not a little sentimentalized. This figure recurs in Dreiser, Dos Passos, Wolfe, Farrell, and Glenway Wescott. In England the intellectual is not so much satirized as ignored, but the sensitive young man appears in D. H. Lawrence, Aldington, Sassoon, Isherwood, and Olivia Manning; for each country the list could be extended.

English and American anti-intellectualism present an identical silhouette when contrasted with the continental variety. Again Malraux is the tantalizing and paradoxical exemplar, one of the most intellectual of writers who turns anti-intellectual out of reasoned conviction. Unlike a frantically obsessed anti-intellectual such as Céline, Malraux makes clear the connection between politics and anti-intellectualism: in *Espoir*, Garcia portrays Malraux's mystique of action when he says,

> 'The great intellectual is a man of subtleties, of fine shades, of evaluations; he's interested in absolute truth and in the complexity of things. He is—how shall I put it?—"antimanichean" by definition, by nature. But all forms of action are manichean, because all action pays a tribute to the devil; that manichean element is most intense when the masses are involved. Every true revolutionary is a born manichean. The same is true for politics, all politics.'

The most vivid episode in the novel is 'manichean', the scene at Toledo in which 10,000 Loyalist troops throw down their arms and desert—a powerful incident out of Malraux's apocalypse. One of the Communists says that the '. . . cynical outlook *plus* a taste for action makes a man a fascist, or a potential fascist— unless there's a loyalty behind him'. Malraux's central characters always possess two of these elements: the cynical outlook and a taste for action. Most of them, however, have a loyalty behind them, or realize the need for loyalty. Malraux's career has been devoted to a search for the necessary loyalty and a way to avoid the apocalypse of Shanghai, Toledo, or the Russian front in *Les Noyers de l'Altenburg*. Malraux's implied anti-intellectualism was even more explicit in *The Psychology of Art*, where he wrote,

> Threatened in its prime, the European spirit is undergoing a metamorphosis; as did the spirit of the Middle Ages when, in the stress of never-ending war, it built that fifteenth-century hell with the ruined hope of the cathedrals. Whether dying or not, menaced assuredly, and fraught with rehabilitations of the past she will not yet let go, Europe seems now to contemplate her future less in terms of freedom than in terms of destiny.

And again, 'What our tragic modern art is sweeping away, by dint of barbaric styles, is primarily that monstrous clot of lies with which civilization stifles the voice of destiny.'[1] The mystique of

[1] André Malraux, *The Psychology of Art: Museum Without Walls*, trans. Stuart Gilbert, New York, 1949, p. 83; p. 127.

action and the reliance upon 'destiny' are neither rational nor ordered, but obsessed and anti-intellectual. In his novels, Malraux is in control as an artist; the mystique of action is made to fit into a pattern. But in his essays and public pronouncements, Malraux suffers from the difficulty of D. H. Lawrence or Wolfe; idea, at once philosophical, political, even religious, imperfectly formulated and zealously fostered, seems to block off the critical faculties in the mind, bringing Lawrence to 'blood' and Malraux to 'destiny'.[1] The great difference between Malraux and the English and American obsessed novelist, is that the latter are controlled by idea in their novels, where Malraux maintains a distinction between his novels and his other writing.

Lawrence, I believe, was incapable of any such distinction; it is difficult to understand why he chose to write novels, a form which he never mastered and upon which he tried to impose mystique in the place of craft. His admirers discover strength in his artlessness. It is perhaps a tribute to the intensity of his obsession that it won him the many followers who forgive lapses which would condemn another writer to oblivion. From his first novel to his last, Lawrence's habit was to write and rewrite his autobiography, rejecting along the way a civilization he had never penetrated, preaching his obsessed sermon of man's depravity, and urging the necessity for a vaguely fascist system based on his version of 'love', the recognition of 'the joy of obedience', and the 'dark flow of blood'.

Kangaroo, one of Lawrence's calmer novels, can be taken as representative of his entire technique. Richard Lovat Somers arrives in Australia with his wife Harriet after the First War, strikes up an acquaintance with Callcott, an Australian working man, becomes involved in an Australian nationalist movement and finally leaves the country out of fear of committing himself to the Australians, whom he in turn admires and hates. Within this simple narrative we discover all the Laurentian gestures and

---

[1] A similar struggle can be seen in the career and work of Hermann Hesse and Thomas Mann, particularly in *Dr. Faustus*. Malraux's struggle appears in his two prose styles. The style of the novels is lucid and straightforward; the style of the essays is turgid, cramped, overladen with meaning and most difficult to read.

posturings. Somers is a small man with a beard, a writer whose personality is described but never explained. Somers is of course Lawrence himself, the figure with or without beard who appears in most of the novels, whether as Paul Morel in *Sons and Lovers*, the groom in *St. Mawr*, Birkin in *Women in Love*, or, ludicrously, *both* as Kate, the heroine, and Don Cipriano in *The Plumed Serpent*. Harriet is the familiar wife, a German woman whose status as an aristocrat is carefully emphasized and who leads a difficult married life with her difficult husband—Lawrence did not bother to disguise his own wife. Every detail in the domestic routine of the Somers—the kind of jam they ate for tea and the price of a pound of tomatoes—is endowed with transcendent meaning, not because Lawrence was concerned with the texture of actuality, but out of his arrogant conviction that any autobiographical trivia somehow fitted his mystique. His consciousness of actuality was slight, as the first paragraph of the novel makes clear:

> A bunch of workmen were lying on the grass of the park beside Macquarie Street, in the dinner hour. . . . Some were eating food from paper packages. They were a mixed lot—taxi drivers, a group of builders who were putting a new inside into one of the big houses opposite, and then two men in blue overalls, some sort of mechanics.

The vagueness of 'a bunch' of workmen and 'some sort of mechanics' is typical of Lawrence's carelessness in details which do not interest him.

Lawrence intends the novel to stand or fall on his ideas, which upon examination prove not to be ideas, but mystique. Early in the narrative Lawrence hammers home his notions of class distinction: 'Only nihilists aim at the removal of all class distinction, in Europe.' The Australians displease Somers for their lack of class distinction; they are irresponsible: '. . . it was a granted condition of Australia, that Demos was his own master.

'And this was what Richard Lovat Somers could not stand. You may be the most liberal Liberal Englishman, and yet you cannot fail to see the categorical difference between the responsible and the irresponsible classes.'

These strictures relate to the central theme, which again typically involves half-realized homosexual relationships between Somers and Callcott, and between Somers and Benjamin Cooley, the 'Kangaroo' of the title. Cooley is one of the leaders of the group of fascist nationalists who attempts to bring Lovat into the fold. Lovat almost succumbs but is repulsed in the end not by the politics of the group but by a fastidious distaste for Cooley's body, which resembles that of a kangaroo. Cooley, like Ramón in *The Plumed Serpent*, embodies Lawrence's obsession and makes the fullest enunciation of his mystique:

> 'Man that is born of woman is sick of himself. Man that is born of woman is tired of his day after day. And woman is like a mother with a tiresome child: what is she to do with him? What is she to do with him?—man, that is born of woman.
>
> 'But the men that are born like ants, out of the cold interval, and are womanless, they are not sick of themselves. They are full of cold energy, and they seethe with cold fire in the ant-hill, making new corridors, new chambers—they alone know what for. And they have cold, formic-acid females, as restless as themselves, and as active about the ant-hill, and as identical with the dried clay of the building. And the active, important, so-called females, and the active, cold-blooded, energetic males, they shift twig after twig, and lay crumb of earth upon crumb of earth, and the females deposit cold white eggs of young. This is the world, and the people of the world. And with their cold, active bodies the ant-men and the ant-women swarm over the face of the earth.
>
> .   .   .   .   .
>
> 'But I am a son of man. I was once a man born of woman. And by the warm heart of the mother that bore me, even if fifty wives denied me, I would still go on fighting with a warm heart to break down the ant-hill. I can fight them with their own weapons: the hard mandibles and the acid sting of the cold ant. But that is not how I fight them. I fight them with the warm heart. Deep calls to deep, and fire calls out fire. And for warmth, for the fire of sympathy, to burn out the ant heap with the heat of fiery, living hearts: that is what I stand for.'

Lawrence drops his normal awkward style and lapses into pseudo-poetic incantation to achieve his effect—a common evasion of the obsessed writer. Readers who admire Lawrence presumably admire this sort of thing. Obsession becomes ridiculous, though, when Lawrence tries to dramatize the conflict between Somers and Cooley:

'Generous, generous men!' Kangaroo muttered to himself. 'At least you can get a blaze out of them. Not like European wet matches, that will never again strike alight—as you've said yourself.'

'But a blaze for what? What's your blaze for?'

'I don't care,' yelled Kangaroo, springing with sudden magnificent swiftness to his feet, and facing Somers, and seizing him by the shoulders and shaking him till his head nearly fell off, yelling all the time: 'I don't care, I tell you, I don't care. Where there's fire there's change. And where the fire is love, there's creation. Seeds of fire. That's enough for me! Fire, and seeds of fire, and love. That's all I care about. Don't carp at me, I tell you. Don't carp at me with your old, European, damp spirit. If you can't take fire, *we can*. That's all. Generous, passionate men—and you dare to carp at them. You— What have you to show?' And he went back to his chair like a great, sulky bear-god.

By means of an awkward flashback Lawrence used *Kangaroo* as the record of his experience during the war when because of his German wife and his conscientious objection to war he was made to feel his isolation from other Englishmen with particular vividness. In the chapter, 'The Nightmare', he drops any pretence of fiction and places in Somers's mind the memory of being forced to leave various provincial residences, and of having to subject himself to the indignity of medical examinations to determine his fitness for military service. Here again Lawrence's self-pity and egotism fail to convince anyone who is not already convinced:

It was Christmas—winter—very cold. He and Harriet were very poor. Then he became ill. He lay in the tiny bedroom looking at the wintry sky and the deep, thatched roof of the cottage beyond. Sick. But then his soul revived. 'No,' he said to himself. 'No. Whatever I do or have done, I am not wrong. Even if I commit what they call a crime, why should I accept their condemnation or verdict. Whatever I do, I do of my own responsible self. I refuse their imputations. I despise them. They are canaille, carrion-eating, filthy-mouthed canaille, like dead-men-devouring jackals. I wish to God I could kill them.'

This frenzy seems to have impressed Lawrence's contemporaries; Aldington, who admires Lawrence, adopted the same tone in *Death of a Hero*.

As the years pass, Lawrence's widely touted 'genius' appears increasingly to be a product of the literary quarrels of the twenties. His undoubted service to Anglo-American literature in helping to free it from a constricting sexual puritanism is offset by his arrogance, ignorance, anti-semitism, political fascism, and most seriously, by his wilful disregard of the form in which he wrote: he egregiously lacked the 'courteousness in regard to matter' that Genet defined as talent. Lawrence's novels are not novels, but tracts, editorials, and the ravings of an unpleasant mind. Once separate from his image all the biographical nonsense and little more than sociological curiosities remain.

Like an illiterate midwife who sometimes can diagnose symptoms before the trained physician, Lawrence went unerringly to a fact rich in literary possibility for the modern novelist, the fact of human isolation; to pursue the simile, he then brewed up a potion of political mystique to counter the fact of isolation, and the strength of his brew was the degree of his obsession. Isolation, indeed, has frequently been the central theme of the obsessed writer. Virginia Woolf dealt with the theme almost exclusively in her rather arty novels, while in America, obsessed novelists like Sherwood Anderson and Thomas Wolfe discovered in the theme of isolation broad possibilities for the organization of American experience. In contrast to the English and consistent with American tradition, their perception of isolation can be described as sociological; they are more concerned with reasons and effects.[1]

[1] The testimony of Röpke, a Swiss sociologist, about urban life is to the point: The more tightly individuals are packed together and the greater their dependence on each other, the greater is their inner isolation and loneliness, and there is a direct connection between the grinding down of society into the sand-heap of myriads of individuals and its conglobation into unorganized, structureless and amorphous mass formations, which provide a luxuriant breeding ground for the mass instincts and mass emotions which are responsible for the befuddled and hysterical instability of present-day society.
Wilhelm Röpke, *The Social Crisis of Our Time*, trans. Annette and Peter Schiffer Jacobson, London, Hodge, 1950, pp. 10–11.

Anderson and Wolfe between them formed an American composite of D. H. Lawrence. Wolfe shared Lawrence's political mystique in his attraction to German Nazism, while his obsession with isolation, and the related themes of love and death, was expressed in a style very like Lawrence's in which poetic incantation alternated with rhetorical bombast. Isolation, Anderson's only effectual theme, provided him with two excellent books, *Winesburg, Ohio* (1919) and *Poor White* (1920); it also led him to direct and barren imitation of Lawrence to the end of his days. *Winesburg* is neither a novel nor a collection of short stories, but a series of delicate sketches unified by the recurrent, central character, George Willard, a newspaper reporter whose sympathy for various of his townsmen is such that he is the agent of their infrequent, mystical moments of communication. Anderson's style, too, is very like Lawrence's, though it is somewhat less gnarled. His version of the 'poetic' in Lawrence is what a sympathetic critic has called the 'hushed bardic chant, low-toned and elegiacally awkward, deeply related to votive speech rhythms yet very much the result of literary cultivation'.[1]

Anderson's later, Laurentian career was depressing; *Dark Laughter* (1925) is proof of the dangers of one kind of obsession. Bruce Dudley, the central character, is an American Birkin or Somers who resolves the familiar struggle with his wife by leaving her and his newspaper job in Chicago to wander to New Orleans, where he becomes a gardener for Aline Grey, who plays a sort of Lady Chatterley to his Mellors. The novel turns into a debased romantic celebration of the primitive, the erotic, and in a naïve schoolboy's idea of Europe, the exotic. The dark laughter of the title is the laughter of Aline Grey's negro servants at the antics of the neurotic whites. But Anderson's negroes are clichés: 'Negro women have no moral sense. They will do anything. They like it . . .'; and his heavy-handed contrasts between the evil of industrialism and the good of the old craftsmen is a weary repetition

[1] Irving Howe, *Sherwood Anderson*, American Men of Letters Series, London, Methuen, 1951, p. 108. Howe analyses with authority the influence of Lawrence on Anderson, as well as that of George Borrow, Mark Twain, and Turgeniev, pp. 91–97; 181–196.

of the theme which had given genuine strength to *Poor White*.
The longer he wrote, the more closely his novels approximated
Laurentian essays; the bitterness of his later, sterile career until his
death in 1941 resembled Lawrence's final bitterness—for both,
life and art uncomfortably merged.

Wolfe resembled Lawrence not only in style and political
mystique, but also in his fierce preoccupation with autobiography,
his formlessness, his eroticism, and his eagerness to defy society.
Wolfe's only character is himself, a self that is even less disguised
than Lawrence's. In the case of both men, formlessness resulted
from their inability to escape self, for as long as the self goes on,
the novel, too, must go on. Both are novelists of the moment,
miniaturists who attempt to enlarge their momentary intuitions
into vast prototypes of all human history. The obsession with
self, understandably, produced nausea. Lawrence described men
as canaille, and Wolfe in *Look Homeward, Angel*, wrote about

> . . . the vicious doll-faces of the movie women, the brutal regularity
> of the faces in the advertisements, and the faces of most of the young
> college-men and women, were stamped in a mould of enamelled
> vacancy, and became unclean to him.
>
> The national demand for white shiny plumbing, toothpaste, tiled
> lunch-rooms, hair-cuts, manicured dentistry, horn spectacles, baths,
> and the insane fear of disease that sent the voters whispering to the
> druggist after their brutal fumbling lecheries—all of this seemed
> nasty. Their outer cleanliness became the token of an inner corrup-
> tion: it was something that glittered and was dry, foul, and rotten
> at the core.

This fails as an intellectual analysis of social habit because the
intensity of the author's emotion is insufficiently projected into
Gant, the character.

For Lawrence, human isolation was a secondary product of his
sexual-social mystique. For Wolfe, isolation was a primary subject, to the degree that his heroes are set apart from average
humanity not only temperamentally but physically, like Wolfe
himself. Although it is a much-flawed novel, *Of Time and the
River* is Wolfe's most successful struggle with the theme of isolation; as one of the most ambitious statements of obsession in recent

American fiction, it may be rewarding to trace Wolfe's technique in some detail. Significantly, the form is that of the *Bildungsroman*, the effort of the hero to attain maturity—the least formal design that tradition supplies. Wolfe writes a series of loosely connected episodes establishing Eugene Gant's inability to reach other human beings, and he inserts in each episode a lyrical set-piece in which obsession appears nakedly: an anonymous traveller leaves a train at a nameless stop '. . . and looks into the faces of all the people passing with the same sense of instant familiarity, greeting, and farewell—that lonely, strange and poignantly wordless feeling that Americans know so well'. Gant's first journey from his native South into the 'secret North' recalls '. . . the huge mystery of the night and darkness, and the image of ten thousand lonely little towns . . . across the continent'. A small town seen in the night is a '. . . haunting and lonely memory'; there is a '. . . ghastly imitation of swarming life . . . and the almost total absence of life itself'.

Wolfe wrestles with language to state what he believes to be a fundamental emotion to the American, that lonely man, whose fondness for

> brilliant, blazing incandescence. . . . is as if he feels again the ancient fear of—what? Of the wilderness, the wet and lidless eye of shame and desolation feeding always on unhoused and naked sides. It is as if he fears the brutal revelation of his loss and loneliness, the furious, irremediable confusion of his huge unrest, his desperate and unceasing flight from the immense and timeless skies that bend above him, the huge, doorless and unmeasured vacancies of distance, on which he lives, on which, helpless as a leaf upon a hurricane, he is driven on forever, and on which he cannot pause, which he cannot fence, wall, conquer, make his own.

A hundred pages later Wolfe in effect repeats this passage at greater length, in the same vocabulary: 'Immense and cruel skies bend over us.' In spite of the repetition, the reader feels that Wolfe experienced the emotion again, that he was still striving to delineate the nebulous aura of an emotion that resisted delineation. When Wolfe fixes upon such vague emotion, even the players in a baseball game become '. . . bright, desperate solitary

atoms encircled by that huge wall of nameless faces. . . .' At the
end of a drunken evening in Boston, Eugene Gant's story is
interrupted by a paragraph composed of a single sentence: 'We
are so lost, so lonely, so forsaken in America: immense and savage
skies bend over us, and we have no door.' By this point the repetition has become thematic and is united with the symbols of
isolation which Wolfe carries over from *Look Homeward, Angel*:
the stone, the leaf, the door—Eugene's tags of memory, calling
forth a sweet, sad, sentimental despair.

In *Of Time and the River* Wolfe takes up again a thread which
began in the first novel, the alienation of the Gant family from the
city of Altamont and from one another. Even the warm, crass,
and explosive sister, Helen, vividly experiences the sensation of
isolation. She reflects in the course of a sleepless night that while
she has been acquainted with various people all her life, she really
knows nothing about any one of them. '. . . and suddenly, this
fact seemed terrible and grotesque to her, and she thought desperately: "What is wrong with people? . . . Why do we never get
to know one another? . . . Why is it that we get born and live
and die here in this world without ever finding out what any one
else is like?"' The passage begins rather like an episode in
Winesburg, Ohio, but soon the adjectives begin to flow, the tem-
perature to rise, and the section is indubitably Wolfe's again.

In non-lyrical sections of the novel the theme of isolation is
further developed in three important episodes: Eugene's relationship with the wealthy Joel Pierce; with the homosexual, Frank
Starwick; and with the Bostonian girl, Ann. Eugene is attracted
to Joel Pierce by the glamour of his wealth, by the ease of his
manner, and the flattery implied in his invitation to visit the family
mansion up the Hudson River. In the course of his visit Eugene
discovers that the disparity in their social and financial position is
unacceptable. Pierce offers him a loan to aid him to take a trip
to Europe, but Gant refuses.

> And he never knew exactly the reason why: there was, perhaps, the
> growing sense of something alien and irreconcilable in the design
> and purpose of their separate lives . . . [there was] a feeling of loneli-
> ness and finality and farewell—as if a great door had swung forever

closed between them, as if there was something secret, buried, and essential, in the soul of each, which now could never be revealed.

Eugene is unable to accept the proffered hand and unable to accept the truly pure affection that Joel embodies. With Starwick, something of the same obtains, though Starwick is an intellectual fraud, a despised aesthete and a homosexual, which Eugene is not. Early in their relationship at Harvard, Eugene believed that Starwick '. . . was the greatest young man of his time and generation'. Yet he cannot accept the man's friendship, and after realizing in Europe Starwick's true character (he is sexually ambidextrous, and wins away Eugene's Ann), in spite of pity and full understanding of the reasons for Starwick's failings, in a fit of disgust and jealousy Eugene almost kills him by driving his head against the corner of a building. By this action, Eugene cuts himself off from the one person with whom he has kept up a relationship from university days, the one person with whom his acquaintance has been more than casual.

Eugene's relationship with Ann, whom he admires for being big, blonde and stupid, indicates, I suspect, the depth of Wolfe's hatred for women. Gant's ideal lady is one who will cook for him, sleep with him, be on hand when he wants to talk, and vanish into the air when he wants to be alone, or as his mistress says, be present and absent simultaneously. There is no place in the Gantian universe for a woman's ego; when Ann asserts that she is in love with Starwick, Eugene's love turns to disgust and hatred. Throughout all his work, Wolfe's characters are closer to hatred than love for women; their isolation from the demands of other people for understanding and love is self-imposed. In fact, Wolfe's only successful writing about women occurs in a slight incident near the end of *Of Time and the River*. Gant has broken finally with Starwick, Ann, and their cicerone, Eleanor, and in revulsion from his entire experience he sets out from Paris for the South of France. When the train stops near Orléans, a handsome peasant girl enters the carriage, but leaves again at Orléans; Eugene helps her with her basket, unable in his indecision and desire to speak. 'And he told himself, as he had told himself so many times before, that he would certainly find her again, knowing in his heart he never would.' However slight, read in context the incident is poignant and true; yet even in his successful writing, Wolfe never can detach his own emotion from his character's—a fatal lapse in literary intelligence.

At this point one might object that the obsessed novelists with their themes of isolation, love and death are simply carrying on against a contemporary background the romanticism of the nineteenth century. After all Tennyson, Arnold and Hardy in poetry; Hawthorne, Melville, Gissing, Conrad and again Hardy in the novel fully apprehended the fact of isolation and treated it convincingly in their best work. The differences, I believe, are considerable. Nineteenth-century romantic writers went to the theme of isolation out of their prescience of things to come, and because it suited the prevailing mood of melancholy. After 1914, however, isolation was no longer a mood but an enveloping fact unavoidably to be recorded in any literature that was not escapist. The romantic agony ceases to be romantic, and agony becomes obsession; love becomes eroticism, and eroticism leads to death— almost to necrophilia. The difference between Hardy's literary realization of the death-wish of Jude Fawley and Faulkner's realization of the suicide of Quentin Compson, differences in technique and in the climate of actuality,[1] are a measure of the distance between the nineteenth-century late romantic writer and the twentieth-century obsessed novelist.

Again comparison with the continental novel lends perspective, and again I find in Malraux's *Man's Fate* the archetypal delineation of modern obsession. That novel is finally a concentrated study of solitude and alienation; of the irony implicit in men's seeking dignity and communion in desperate acts prompted by the most idealistic interpretation of the Marxist-Sorelian vision which can lead only to their deaths. The motif of isolation is sounded in the very first scene of the novel, when Ch'en, the terrorist, stabs to death an anonymous victim who is compared to a sleeping animal; Ch'en thus becomes a living symbol of isolation throughout the narrative. Ch'en's particular problem is to find acceptance within

[1] I do not mean to imply that Faulkner's treatment is superior to Hardy's, merely different.

a system which will be politically tolerable and intellectually acceptable. Smithson, the American clergyman, holds out to him Christianity and peace. Ch'en replies that he does not want peace, unless through political faith—in two hours he will kill a man. 'He was alone. Still alone.' In battle his difficulty is the same: 'In spite of the intimacy of death, in spite of that fraternal weight which was pulling him apart, he was not one of them. "Is even blood futile?"' he thinks. Once he enters upon the ultimate act of terror that will mean his certain death, Ch'en seeks brotherhood with his fellow-terrorists, Pei and Suan; before they set out to kill Chiang Kai-shek, Ch'en tries with ritualistic fervour to bind Pei to him in the solidarity of their act. Pei fails to respond, making only a conventional promise, 'I shall go with you.' Malraux closes the scene with Ch'en turning away: 'Never had Ch'en thought one could be so alone.' In the moments before he throws his bomb at Chiang Kai-shek's car, Ch'en reflects:

> The oldest Chinese legend came to his mind: men are the vermin of the earth. It was necessary that terrorism become a mystic cult. Solitude, first of all: let the terrorist decide alone, execute alone; the police derive their whole strength from informers; the murderer who operates alone does not risk giving himself away. The ultimate solitude, for it is difficult for one who lives isolated from the everyday world not to seek others like himself.

And as the car approaches, he thinks, 'Was not Destiny itself the force that was pushing them towards the end of the avenue where the archway on the edge of the shadowy river, illuminated by indistinguishable signs, was like the very gates of death?'

Ch'en is the starkest example of isolation in the novel, but Kyo, Gisors and his wife, Katow and old Gisors, are alienated from one another and from the political movement in which they believe with only a part of their minds. The action of the novel pivots on Kyo's activity as a Party organizer. In his agonizing isolation he is unable, in the course of a trip to Party headquarters at Hankow, to make the Central Committee understand the desperate position of the group under him at Shanghai. He knows that the suppression and death of his comrades is implicit in his failure; he discovers that '. . . to be obliged to seek refuge entirely in oneself is almost unbearable'. Kyo's situation contrasts with Katow's, the revolutionary who survived the fighting in Russia ten years before and went voluntarily to the lead-mines with his companions. As a result of his experience he is able to articulate the situation of all desperate men. 'The main thing is not to be alone', he says to Hemelrich, whose child has a mastoid, whose wife enchains him with her selfless understanding of the insurrection, who feels '... like a lamp-post that everything in the world comes and pisses on'. Inevitably these men are condemned to death by fire. As they wait for execution, Katow gives Kyo one of his last two cyanide capsules, and while he waits for his own death with the frightened Suan, tasting his own fright, he thinks of 'human dignity'. In the darkness the guards tell stories, and the condemned men wait.

> In spite of the hum, in spite of all these men who had fought as he had, Katow was alone, alone between the body of his dead friend and his two terror-stricken companions, alone between his will and that whistle [of the steam-engine in whose fire-box the condemned are executed] far off in the night. But a man could be stronger than his solitude and even, perhaps, than that atrocious whistle.

Katow gives his remaining capsule to Suan, and the central movement of the novel ends with Katow's isolated, heroic, very possibly meaningless act.

Kassner in Malraux's *Days of Wrath* says at one point, 'For love is choice, and one has nothing to choose when one has nothing to give'; a text which comments upon Katow's act and provides one connection between love and death. Hemingway's heroes go to their deaths in much the same spirit: Robert Jordan in *For Whom the Bell Tolls* and Harry Morgan in *To Have and Have Not*. In *A Farewell to Arms* Frederick Henry and Catherine Barkley are permitted to love each other only in a total isolation created by Henry's desertion from the Army, and the end of their idyllic affair in Catherine's death is a necessary, not a contrived, conclusion to the novel. Wolfe's characters can communicate only in the presence of death, and some of his best writing was on the subject of death.

No writer has been so obsessed with death as Faulkner, nor used it to better literary effect. As a pervading theme in his work, death has evoked writing of extraordinary power, and it has also accounted for tasteless, *Galgenhumor* jokes in *Intruder in the Dust*, or a story like 'A Rose for Emily'—lapses that mark veritable obsession. But in his finest work, *As I Lay Dying* and *Light in August*, the joke surmounts mere humour and devices of plot to become shattering irony, or in the case of Joe Christmas's death, the starkest tragedy of Southern society.

As I Lay Dying begins with Addie, the mother of the poor-white, back-country Bundren family, listening on her death-bed to the sounds of an adze, wielded by Cash, her eldest son, as he constructs her coffin. The narrative proper is presented through the minds of the family, Cash, Darl, Jewel, Vardaman, Addie's daughter Dewey Dell, and her husband Anse, as they make an epic ten-day journey to fulfil Addie's wish to be buried in Jefferson, her birthplace. Impeded by rains, mud and accidents they succeed in transporting the stinking flesh to its burial ground to discover that Anse has taken a second wife in Jefferson, whom he presents to his family in the final scene. With such macabre and unlikely material, Faulkner constructs a remarkable image of the illiterate mind holding to concepts of duty and dignity, in narrative presented entirely in interior monologue and dialogue, a model of directness and economy. The contrast between the single-minded efforts of the Bundren family to carry out Addie Bundren's request and the bad joke of Anse Bundren's marriage to a 'kind of duck-shaped woman all dressed up, with them kind of hard looking pop eyes like she was daring ere a man to say nothing' produces an effect of anti-tragedy, a cruel, harsh, yet humane irony unique in fiction.

The method of *Light in August* displays Faulkner's obsession at an opposite pole of technique and emotional range. The bleak, tough-minded narrative of the life of Joe Christmas resembles only Céline's *Voyage au bout de la nuit* in tone and quality of hatred, but Faulkner's novel is superior to Céline's in that Faulkner is able to contrast with hatred the human decency and endurance of Lena, Byron Bunch, and of the countrymen, Armstid and Ratliff.

S

Christmas, who dominates the novel, is identified with the figure of Jesus Christ, but he is a heretical Christ, a bastard who grows up believing he is a mulatto, conceiving a desiccating hatred for both whites and blacks and particularly for women. The parallel to the New Testament is carried out with subtlety but without a limiting consistency. The simple, ignorant Lena is a kind of Virgin Mary and Byron a Joseph; Christmas's mad grandfather believes that he is God the Father, and Lucas Burch, who betrays Christmas to a lynch-mob after Christmas has beheaded Joanna Burden, is a kind of Judas. Christmas embodies the theme of isolation even more totally than Malraux's Ch'en. He is constantly described as a man moving fast, running, seeking to establish a recognition of his own being. Faulkner's style conveys obsession, but with a control of which Lawrence and other obsessed writers are incapable:

His way was sure, despite the trees, the darkness. He never once lost the path which he could not even see. The woods continued for a mile. He emerged into a road, with dust under his feet. He could see now, the vague spreading world, the horizon. Here and there faint windows glowed. But most of the cabins were dark. Nevertheless his blood began again, talking and talking. He walked fast, in time to it; he seemed to be aware that the group were Negroes before he could have seen or heard them at all, before they even came in sight vaguely against the defunctive dust. There were five or six of them, in a straggling body yet vaguely paired; again there reached him, above the noise of his own blood, the rich murmur of womenvoices. He was walking directly toward them, walking fast. They had seen him and they gave to one side of the road, the voices ceasing. He too changed direction, crossing toward them as if he intended to walk them down. In a single movement and as though at a spoken command the women faded back and were going around him, giving him a wide berth. One of the men followed them as if he were driving them before him, looking over his shoulder as he passed. The other two men had halted in the road, facing Christmas. Christmas had stopped also. Neither seemed to be moving, yet they approached, looming, like two shadows drifting up. He could smell Negro; he could smell cheap cloth and sweat. The head of the Negro, higher than his own, seemed to stoop, out of the sky, against the sky. 'It's a white man,' he said, without turning his head, quietly. 'What you want, whitefolks? You looking for somebody?' The voice was not threatful. Neither was it servile.

'Come on away from there, Jupe,' the one who had followed the women said.

'Who you looking for, cap'm?' the Negro said.

'Jupe,' one of the women said, her voice a little high. 'You come on, now.'

For a moment longer the two heads, the light and the dark, seemed to hang suspended in the darkness, breathing upon one another. Then the Negro's head seemed to float away; a cool wind blew from somewhere. Christmas, turning slowly, watching them dissolve and fade again into the pale road, found that he had the razor in his hand. It was not open. It was not from fear. 'Bitches!' he said, quite loud. 'Sons of bitches!'

After Christmas murders Joanna Burden, the parallel with Christ's death becomes precise and moving. Christmas escapes from the scene of the murder and wanders for three days, from Gethsemane to Calvary. On the third day, a Friday, he is taken by the mob. We know that he is thirty-three years old, and Faulkner writes that the mob is looking for someone 'to crucify'. The actual death in Hightower's house at the hands of Percy Grimm, a small-town fascist and a sadist, in its luridness and violence represents the farthest point to which obsession can go; in context we accept it for the intention which Faulkner expresses in the final quoted sentences. Hightower tries to prevent Grimm from his act:

'Jesus Christ!' Grimm cried, his young voice clear and outraged like that of a young priest. 'Has every preacher and old maid in Jefferson taken their pants down to the yellowbellied son of a bitch?' He flung the old man aside and ran on.

It was as though he had been merely waiting for the Player to move him again, because with that unfailing certitude he ran straight to the kitchen and into the doorway, already firing, almost before he could have seen the table overturned and standing on its edge across the corner of the room and the bright and glittering hands of the man who crouched behind it, resting upon the upper edge. Grimm emptied the automatic's magazine into the table; later someone covered all five shots with a folded handkerchief.

But the Player was not done yet. When the others reached the kitchen they saw the table flung aside now and Grimm stooping over the body. When they approached to see what he was about, they saw that the man was not dead yet, and when they saw what Grimm was doing one of the men gave a choked cry and stumbled back into the wall and began to vomit. Then Grimm too sprang back, flinging behind him the bloody butcher knife. 'Now you'll let white women alone, even in hell,' he said. But the man on the floor had not moved. He just lay there, with his eyes open and empty of everything save consciousness, and with something, a shadow, about his mouth. For a long moment he looked up at them with peaceful and unfathomable and unbearable eyes. Then his face, body, all, seemed to collapse, to fall in upon itself, and from out the slashed garments about his hips and loins the pent black flood seemed to rush like a released breath. It seemed to rush out of his pale body like the rush of sparks from a rising rocket; upon that black blast the man seemed to rise soaring into their memories forever and ever. They are not to lose it, in whatever peaceful valleys, beside whatever placid and reassuring streams of old age, in the mirroring faces of whatever children they will contemplate old disasters and newer hopes. It will be there, musing, quiet, steadfast, not fading and not particularly threatful, but of itself alone serene, of itself alone triumphant. Again from the town, deadened a little by the walls, the scream of the siren mounted towards its unbelievable crescendo, passing out of the realm of hearing.

We accept Faulkner's instinct for violence and his bleak view of a lost society because his own communicated conviction argues the accuracy of his view, but more particularly because Faulkner as a literary artist presents his conclusions in convincing literary form. I have already mentioned the chronology of *Light in August*; by means of beginning at the end and carrying us both backward and forward in time Faulkner achieves a simultaneity of effect and a validity to experience which saves him from the Gothic luridness of Poe. His method enables us to hold in mind a double vision of humanity and depravity, religious in intensity, combined with a frightening analysis of the human capacity for outrage. Sartre comments on *The Sound and the Fury*, a masterpiece similar to *Light in August*, and provides by the way the distinction between the obsessed writer, Faulkner, and the non-obsessed writer, Proust.

Proust really *should have* employed a technique like Faulkner's; that was the logical outcome of his metaphysic. Faulkner, however, is a lost man, and because he knows that he is lost he risks pushing his thought to its conclusion. Proust is a classicist and a Frenchman; and the French lose themselves with caution and always end by finding themselves. Eloquence, a love of clarity and a rational mind led Proust to preserve at least the appearance of chronology.[1]

Faulkner is an exception among obsessed writers. His command of technique exempts him from the excesses of the Laurentian school of obsession. Faulkner's obsession is not so much mystique as it is a personal interpretation of history and a personal vision embracing a largely heretical Christian element. Wolfe is more typical of lesser American writers who contrive a national mystique. Wolfe and a large number of historical novelists feel compelled to catalogue the various physical countenances of the country in order to understand their society. Whitman had begun the device of the catalogue in his verse, and Wolfe was at least partially imitating Whitman. The device of the catalogue was virtually the only formal element in Gertrude Stein's experiments in prose. One of her critics has said in explanation of the catalogue:

Gertrude Stein as usual began at the beginning, with the question of how anything is put together, of how anyone puts something together. . . . And how does one really put the data of experience together to make a sense? Things are together well enough by being next to each other and very well if inside something, whether a moment of consciousness, a space, or an action. But how does one get together with anything? The simplest way is by counting it. . . . But almost as simple a way is to name it—love, apple, mantelpiece, or whatever—and so relate it to vocabulary, or to a category like passion, fruit, or furniture, or to its habitual situation in a story if there is one, all of this belonging not to the original perceived thing but to us, to the human interior. Thus the perceived thing is accounted

[1] Frederick J. Hoffman and Olga W. Vickery, edd., *William Faulkner: Two Decades of Criticism*, E. Lansing, Michigan State College Press, 1951, p. 185.

for, organized, possessed. It is converted into a substantive, a settled thing, quite as if it had been counted.[1]

While this explanation is principally psychological, by inference it contends that the catalogue solves one problem in technique. For both Gertrude Stein and Wolfe, mystique and technique meet in the device of the catalogue. To maintain that either writer reached a satisfactory form through the catalogue, which in turn is imaginatively related to the very essence of that which they were trying to convey, does not absolve them from the sin of formlessness, but it suggests that conventional notions of form may be insufficient to the task of assessing exactly what these writers were about.

Wolfe's notebooks abounded in lists of physical facts, and these lists frequently appear in his novels: '. . . the rank slow river, and . . . tomatoes rotten on the vine; the smell of rain-wet plums and boiling quinces; of rotten lily-pads; and of foul weeds rotting in green marsh scum; and the exquisite smell of the South, clean but funky, like a big woman; of soaking trees and the earth after heavy rain'. The listing of physical facts in nature goes on to fantastic length. A second sort of catalogue is that in which Wolfe is attempting to elicit an emotional apprehension of the component items of his list, thus, from *Of Time and the River*:

> And finally the whole design of that earth, with the casual and powerful surveys of its great fields, its dense still woods of moveless silence ringing with the music of the birds, its far-off hills receding into time as haunting as a dream, and the central sorcery of its shining river—that enchanted thread which ran through all, from which all swept away, and towards which all inclined—was unutterably the language of all he had ever thought or felt or known of America: . . . . an America that was so casual and rich and limitless and free, and so haunted by dark time and magic, so aching in its joy with all the bitter briefness of our days, so young, so old, so everlasting, and so triumphantly the place of man's good earth. . . .

Regarded as an extension of the catalogue, this kind of writing takes on fuller meaning; Wolfe strains language much as a poet

[1] Donald Sutherland, *Gertrude Stein, A Biography of Her Work*, New Haven, 1951, pp. 74–75.

strains language (which is not to say that this is 'poetic prose') to express an inner state and to weave it into his fiction. Wolfe was trying, he wrote to a friend, to move away from rigidity in the processes of thoughts, speech, art, and life. He maintained that America had never been fundamentally explored but merely surveyed.[1] Unfortunately his catalogues were little more than further exploration, testimony to a failure in technique. Wolfe's obsession with the size of America conforms to his attempts to catalogue it. A favourite device was to place his central character aboard a train and in a modified interior monologue to reflect upon the extent of the country being traversed, while always a concept of size and extent dominated. Wolfe's writing about the size and extent of America was evocative and lyrical. The danger of such writing to Wolfe and a multitude of minor novelists is that it becomes a habit and finally a cliché. In *The Hills Beyond*, for example, Wolfe's last fragment, instead of an evocation of mood, place and personality, we frequently find only a vapid trance: Wolfe writes in fairly objective fashion about a murder trial, but then we read abruptly that the trial, 'a scene which, with all its strange and terrible contradictions, is somehow memorable and as moving as it is thrilling; for in it, somehow, is the whole enigma of our violent and tormented life—this huge complex of America, with all its innocence and guilt, its justice and its cruelty, its lawlessness and its law'. It is not merely complexity, but 'huge complexity', and we know that Wolfe is once more writing an essay; obsession with size forces itself into an inappropriate context, making his point meaningless. Similarly, the catalogue loses thematic purpose, and therefore meaning, in most of Wolfe's later writing. In an experiment with point of view, the short story 'The Return of the Prodigal', the following occurs:

> Each of us has his own America, his own stretch, from which, here outward, the patterns are familiar as his mother's face and the prospect is all his. Eugene's began at Gettysburg, his father's earth; then southward through Hagerstown, and down the Valley of Virginia.

[1] Wolfe to Hamilton Basso (probably July 1937). Unpublished manuscript in Harvard College Library, accession No. *46AM-15.

First, the great barns, the wide sweep and noble roll of Pennsylvania fields, the neat-kept houses. Lower down, still wide fields, still neat-kept houses, white fences and painted barns, a grace and sweetness that still lingers in the Valley of Virginia. . . .

Wolfe thus repeats in two paragraphs a motif which formed entire chapters of *Look Homeward, Angel*, but here the motif has become weak and empty.

Another component of Wolfe's mystique was his feeling for night-scenes, his conviction that a study of the night-happenings of America would clarify something about Americans themselves. Like Sherwood Anderson,[1] Wolfe seemed instinctively to feel that human beings are closer to knowledge of one another at night, further from their daytime isolation. The Gant family finds its only moments of communication in the depths of the night—after the death of Ben, in *Look Homeward, Angel*, and of old Gant, in *Of Time and the River*. 'Gentlemen of the Press' is a part of the night pattern, as are the effective scenes in the all-night lunch-room in *Look Homeward, Angel*. There is in fact more literary reality in the night-scenes than in the scenes of day, in all Wolfe's work. With Whitman's assertion of identification, Wolfe gave his apprehension of night its most emotional expression in the story, 'Death the Proud Brother'. The narrator has not found 'the grandeur, and the immortal beauty of America' by day:

I had found the dark land at the heart of night, of dark, proud, secret night: the immense and lonely land lived for me in the brain of night. I saw its plains, its rivers, and its mountains spread out before me in all their dark immortal beauty, in all the space and joy of their huge sweep. . . . And my heart was one with the hearts of all men who had heard the strange wild music that they made, filled with unknown harmonies and a thousand wild and secret tongues crying to

[1] Irving Howe writes, '*Winesburg* is a book largely set in twilight and darkness, its backgrounds heavily shaded with gloomy blacks and marshy grays—as is proper for a world of withered men who, sheltered by night, reach out for that sentient life they dimly recall as the racial inheritance that has been squandered away. Like most fiction, *Winesburg* is a variation on the theme of reality and appearance, in which the deformations caused by day (public life) are intensified at night and, in their very extremity, become an entry into reality.' *Sherwood Anderson*, p. 98.

men the exultant and terrible music of wild earth, triumph and discovery, singing a strange and bitter prophecy of love and death.

'Love and death': the accent is Whitman's, and the diction might be that of Hesse, Malraux, or Mann, while the total expression is very close to Wolfe's meaning in his futile attempts to discover 'America'. He can find love only by night, and then only in conjunction with death.

Wolfe's mystique was based on his awareness of the combination of social faith, naïve optimism, and progressive activism to which social historians have given the useful name, 'The American Dream'. By the twenties the American Dream had become troubled, and Wolfe's reproduction of it, like Anderson's, Dos Passos's and Faulkner's, contained much darkness. Unlike Faulkner Wolfe wavered between an emotional and an intellectual apprehension of that darkness, but toward the end of his life he moved closer to an intellectual apprehension. In *The Hills Beyond* we learn that the two generations before the Civil War were 'good' men; ignorant and uncultivated pioneers who lived, uncorrupted, close to nature. Bear Joyner is the noble primitive, American style; he belongs in the select company of Deerslayer and the Daniel Boone of myth. But unlike Chateaubriand's or Cooper's primitives, Bear Joyner and his kind possess humour and the knowledge of humanity necessary for humour.

The Civil War marks the end of the older, good, frontier community. When the Joyners move to town, they become avaricious, educated, and they share all the evils of the educated. Bear Joyner's virtues live on only in Zachariah Joyner, in whom they are corrupted; he is a politician, with all the politician's craft and guile. The American earth itself suffers from these post-War Americans who strip the forests and mines, spending their profits on the construction of an inferior society dominated by money. Virtue is still possible; Eugene Gant's father, in *Look Homeward, Angel*, is still a pre-War man; his failings are 'good' failings because they are 'natural'—drink and whoring—though toward the end of his life he is tainted by his wife's 'bad' failings—cupidity for land and cash profit. So, too, George Webber's father in *The Web and the Rock*, though he remains uncorrupted.

Wolfe did not really believe his own chronological formulation of American decay, for the body of his writing was dominated by rural visions of the 'good' America beyond the cities where the earth smells sweet and life is free, where a poor man can get an honest trial, no matter what the indictment, in contrast to Europe, where 'the laws are all made for the rich, a poor man never can get justice *there*'—in the words of Nebraska Crane in *The Web and the Rock*. And as George Webber rides through Manhattan on his way to a party, he reflects upon the American small town and the city too: 'Here was the American hope, the wild, nocturnal hope, the hope that has given life to all our poetry, all our prose, all our thoughts, and all our culture—the darkness where our hope grows, out of which the whole of what we are will be conceived.'

And yet, despite these utterances, the ultimate impression of Wolfe's mystique, as of Hawthorne's, Melville's and Whitman's, is pessimistic. In *The Hills Beyond* the county courthouse is his symbol for the American betrayal:

> The county courthouse was, in short, America—the wilderness America, the sprawling, huge, chaotic, criminal America. It was murderous America soaked with murdered blood, tortured and purposeless America, savage, blind, and mad America, exploding through its puny laws, its pitiful pretense. It was America with all its almost hopeless hopes, its almost faithless faiths—America with the huge blight on her of her own error, the broken promise of her lost dream and her unachieved desire; and it was America as well with her unspoken prophecies, her unfound language, her unuttered song. . . .

In his mind's eye, Wolfe conceived of himself as the prophet-novelist who would speak the 'unspoken prophecies', the *Dichter* who would uncover America's 'unfound language'.

Wolfe's bardic conviction helps to explain, though it does not forgive, much that seems belatedly romantic and provincial in the American novel. Obsession in the form of a mystique of history accounts for at least two household goddesses of American Literature, Willa Cather and Ellen Glasgow, and for the many fumbling attempts to shape a national myth, a simplified legend defying the fact of catastrophe and its attendant complexities for the literary mind. That fumbling, Laurentian period has come to an end, I think, in America as well as in England. Inevitably many writers continue to be obsessed, but since World War II their obsession has turned them back to stricter forms, within the confines of which absorbing experiments continue to take place: I refer to the related forms of allegory and satire.

Chapter Nine

ALLEGORY AND SATIRE

THE greatest novelists have always used their material in such a way that symbol and allegory have emerged seemingly without the conscious manipulation of the writer. English and American novelists, with their special affinity for actuality, their allegiance to the medium of prose and its implicit logic, have traditionally been equivocal about the conscious use of symbols and frankly suspicious of the organization of symbols into allegory. Recently, however, a group of novelists has adopted symbol and allegory as conscious devices. Not only are many of these writers interesting in themselves for their firm talents, but their literary tactics pose problems for any interpretation of the tradition and for any understanding of the contemporary situation.

Paul Bowles, for example, begins *The Sheltering Sky* (1949) with Port Moresby and his wife, Kit, in North Africa, picking their joyless way through the wreckage of their marriage, and travelling deep into the savage interior, where Port dies—a meaningless end to a meaningless man—and Kit survives only to become a half-crazed, sub-human nymphomaniac, whose only explained action is her rejection of rescue by the French authorities and her return at the end of the novel to her horrifying life among the Arabs. *The Sheltering Sky* is fastidious and restrained in comparison with *Let It Come Down* (1952), the story of a wretched American bank clerk who flees his own nonentity from New York to Tangier, where he becomes involved in petty smuggling, takes to drugs, and in the lurid conclusion drives a spike into the skull of his Moorish accomplice, a hashish parody of *l'acte gratuit*. These truly shocking novels differ qualitatively from earlier American novels of violence; they make the violence of Hemingway, or even the absurdities of Faulkner in *Sanctuary*, seem like the products of a sweet, calm and rational mind. Bowles's apprehension of catastrophe in his obsessed writing can only be described by that dubious term, neurotic. It demonstrates the dangers inherent in obsession, as does the work of the group of recent American novelists which he dominates by his greater ability.

This group—the American Ronald Firbanks—composed of Carson McCullers, Truman Capote, Tennessee Williams, Gore Vidal, Frederick Buechner, and numbers of writers too minor to list, shares the Firbank turkish-bath kind of imagination which rejects, or is incapable of holding, what we fondly call 'normal' experience. The belated decadents gravitate to extreme situations and inflate extremity with giggling gusto to the point where it becomes ridiculous and nauseating. Unlike Firbank, they write well, commanding every trick and device of the craft, but the extremity of their sensibility leads them inevitably to allegory, and often with Firbank, to the periphery of satire, burlesque. In the extremity of their work, the question arises of the relationship between obsession and form, between the disparateness and atomization of experience, and the need to order and communicate it. The allegorists of extremity also return us to a consideration of the place of ideas and of manners in the novel, and provide, incidentally, a most useful method for clarifying similarities and differences between English and American practice, past and present.

'For even satire is a form of sympathy.' Lawrence's passing intuition in *Lady Chatterley's Lover* accurately defines satire in the first and second phases of the Anglo-American novel, but it lacks validity in the third phase. It satisfies with reference to George Eliot and Mark Twain, but the fact that it seems off the point with reference to Aldous Huxley, Evelyn Waugh, Ring Lardner or Mary McCarthy suggests the need for a look at the tradition of satire on both sides of the Atlantic. The basic device of eighteenth- and nineteenth-century satirists in England and America was that of the 'Anatomy', to use Frye's term, in which men were described as types, social and political customs were analysed with varying degrees of subtlety, and both men and society derided from a discernible moral point of view. In its origins, American satire was modelled upon English. I have already noted the strong resemblance between Hugh Henry Brackenridge's *Modern Chivalry* and Fielding's satires;[1] the best satire in early nineteenth-century America, Cooper's *The Monikins* (1835), was modelled upon Swift's *Gulliver*. Like Swift, Cooper perceived and directly used the connection between allegory and satire. The Yankee sea-captain, Noah Poke, meets in Paris four monkeys who have been touring Europe: Dr. Reasono, Lord Chatterino, Lady Chatterissa and Mistress Vigilance Lynx. With his friend, Sir John Golden-calf, Poke travels with the 'Monikins' to their native Polar regions, where in Leaphigh (England), excellence is determined by the length of one's tail; they visit Leapthrough (France), a region of scoundrels; and Leaplow (America), where democracy levels all men under the National Allegory (or the Constitution) and low motives are disguised by high-sounding principles.

The Monikins demonstrated again Cooper's strong sense of society and combined through allegory a tone of bitterness with good humour. While Cooper was placing Swift in an American setting, his contemporaries, mainly in the theatre, were composing broad burlesques on local politics, women's rights, free love, and false romantic attitudes towards the American Indian, thus creating a native tradition that Poe and Hawthorne, in fiction, extended in a significant manner. Neither writer's satire was at all important; Poe's was childish and verbal in stories like 'Loss of Breath', 'X-ing a Paragrab', and 'The Devil in the Belfry'. Hawthorne's satire on the transcendentalists, 'The Celestial Railroad', derives weakly from Bunyan. What is of very great importance, though, was their perception of the formal cleavage between satire and allegory as modes of the imagination. Both writers omitted satire from their best prose fiction, and with a characteristically American attempt to cope with experience by removing it from actuality, concentrated on allegory. Poe's novella, *The Narrative of Arthur Gordon Pym*, remains a literary curiosity, a prose version of *The Ancient Mariner*. Hawthorne exhausted himself as an artist by trying to reconcile actuality with

[1] See pp. 181–182.

allegory. *The Scarlet Letter*, *The House of the Seven Gables*, and *The Blithedale Romance* are uneasy masterpieces, imperfect, agonizing, honest attempts to make congruent formal tradition and American history. As Hawthorne's later career demonstrated, his method was inadequate to his ambitions, and he was unable even to complete the manuscripts of *Septimius Felton*, *The Dolliver Romance*, *Dr. Grimshawe's Secret* and *The Ancestral Footstep*—all variations on a single allegorical theme. The humourless and stark allegorical imagination of Poe and Hawthorne has often recurred in American fiction: in Mark Twain's final work, in Ambrose Bierce's Civil War stories and later sardonic extravagances, in a social utopian novel like Howells's *Traveller from Altruria*, and most recently in Faulkner's *A Fable* and in the work of Paul Bowles and his unmerry crew.

Melville belongs to this tradition, but his work presents a special problem. As with Hawthorne, the split between satire and allegory occurs in the same mind, but more dramatically, providing a source of literary energy, and accounting for resounding failures. Allegory dominates in *Moby Dick* and *Billy Budd*, and these novels have a consistency of tone that is lacking in *Mardi*, *Pierre*, *Israel Potter*, and *The Confidence Man*, novels in which allegory and satire are neither balanced nor reconciled. In *Mardi* Melville attempted the philosophical epic with which he later succeeded so well in *Moby Dick*, but he failed to invent a formal structure which would allow him to allegorize through the romantic motif of the quest, and to satirize in the manner of *Gulliver* or *The Monikins*. The result is an unreadable book. *Israel Potter*, the record of the Job-like sufferings during forty-five years of exile of an American revolutionary war soldier, is a failure in tone similar to *Mardi*, and hardly more readable. Where *Mardi* is the failure of an apprentice and *Israel Potter* the failure of an experimenter, *Pierre* and *The Confidence Man* are the brilliant failures of a great writer, straining to display in the novel 'more reality than life itself can show'. In *Pierre*, the tragic theme of incest and the hero's obsession with purity and justice is presented as a parody upon the sentimental fiction of the day, a parody which fails when the tragedy gets out of hand and scenes of

emotional torture and suffering tower over the burlesque style,
destroying tone and structure. The sub-title, *The Ambiguities*, is
Melville's rationalization, but an inadequate one. *The Confidence
Man* is not so much a sustained novel as a savage and bitter
excoriation of American society. The scene is a Mississippi River
steamboat and the basic device, a brilliant use of allegory, describes
the Confidence Man in a series of disguises, now pitiful, now
malevolent, requesting the world of the passengers to trust him.
Early in the novel he appears as a negro who has lost both legs
and must beg charity. His face is compared to a Newfound-
land dog's, and when the passengers throw him coins, he catches
them in his teeth. As a herb-doctor, and later as a barber, the
Confidence Man becomes an evil figure who solicits and fails to
find any of the basic human virtues in his fellow-man. Although
the novel is again marred by Melville's superfluous freight of
unassimilated philosophy, the power of allegory and satire places
it deeply in the mind, and episodes from it rise to one's consciousness at unexpected times. In its extremity and bitterness, Melville's
satire expressed his uneasiness in American society, a condition
which made him incapable of the politer and more stylized satire
of his English contemporaries. His frequent failures in structure
must be attributed to the split between allegory and satire. Like
Hawthorne's, his greatest work was allegorical, and again like
Hawthorne he was uneasily aware of the limitations for a novelist
in the method of allegory.

English satire in the nineteenth century was both purer and
more refined than the American variety. With the exception of
Dickens and Peacock, English writers on the whole addressed
themselves directly to society without the American compulsion
to turn from satire to allegory. Peacock was of course a satirist
first and foremost and when he approached the methods of
allegory, he did so with sanity and good humour, remaining in
complete control of his method. There is nothing in Peacock of
Melville's compulsive, driven emotion, nor of Dickens's feverish,
sometimes splendid, effects. When Dickens abandoned burlesque
for satire, he invariably wrote allegory. In *Martin Chuzzlewit*,
Dickens's inspired attack on American manners of the 1840s,

Colonel Diver, Jefferson Brick, and 'The Watertoast Association of United Sympathizers' are all cartoons and burlesques which reappear in Mark Twain and Sinclair Lewis. When Dickens writes of American businessmen, 'Whatever the chance contributions that fell into the slow cauldron of their talk, they made the gruel thick and slab with dollars. Men were weighed by their dollars, measures gauged by their dollars; life was auctioneered, appraised, put up, and knocked down for its dollars', he conveys an emotion that is at once personal and social, but the basic dimension is still social. But when in *Bleak House* the fantastic Chancery suit of Jarndyce and Jarndyce provides the basic structure of the entire novel, Dickens treats society at the remove of allegory. The mad Miss Flite has not the fictional dimensions of Mr. Jefferson Brick's; she has at once less reality in social terms, but greater reality as a figure of allegory. Dickens probably anticipated one mode of modern obsession in his allegories, but his cavil on the social subject shaped the emotion underlying his obsession in a traditional manner.

Virginia Woolf's comment on the nature of satire is valid for the English nineteenth century and to a lesser degree for America in the same period: '. . . the more complex a vision the less it lends itself to satire: the more it understands the less it is able to sum up and make linear. For example: Shakespeare and Dostoievsky, neither of them satirise [*sic*]. The age of understanding: the age of destroying—and so on.'[1] That is to say, the satire of writers so different as Jane Austen, Disraeli, George Eliot, Henry Adams, Howells, and James is an important though incidental technique; it supports their criticism of society in novels whose first purpose is to reveal and support society. Among these writers only Henry James approaches the allegorical; he is significantly American and in his use both of satire and allegory we meet again the split in consciousness which we have seen in Melville and Hawthorne. James's earlier satire in *The Bostonians* (1886) is employed with humour and a light heart; Miss Birdseye is closer to one of Dickens's burlesques than to Melville's Confidence Man:

[1] *A Writer's Diary*, entry for 6 May 1935, p. 274.

T

She always dressed in the same way: she wore a loose black jacket, with deep pockets, which were stuffed with papers, memoranda of a voluminous correspondence. . . . She belonged to the Short-Skirts League, as a matter of course; for she belonged to any and every league that had been founded for almost any purpose whatever. This did not prevent her being a confused, entangled, inconsequent, discursive old woman, whose charity began at home and ended nowhere, whose credulity kept pace with it, and who knew less about her fellow-creatures, if possible, after fifty years of humanitary zeal, than on the day she had gone into the field to testify against the iniquity of most arrangements. . . . She looked as if she had spent her life on platforms, in audiences, in conventions, in phalan-steries, in séances; . . . . when Miss Chancellor explained that she had brought Mr. Ransom because he was so anxious to meet Mrs. Farrinder, she gave the young man a delicate, dirty, democratic little hand, looking at him kindly, as she could not help doing, but without the smallest discrimination as against others who might not have the good fortune (which involved, possibly, an injustice) to be present on such an interesting occasion. . . . No one had an idea how she lived; whenever money was given her she gave it away to a negro or a refugee. No woman could be less invidious, but on the whole she preferred these two classes of the human race. Since the Civil War much of her occupation was gone; for before that her best hours had been spent in fancying that she was helping some Southern slaves to escape. It would have been a nice question whether, in her heart of hearts, for the sake of this excitement, she did not sometimes wish the blacks back in bondage. She had suffered in the same way by the relaxation of many European despotisms, for in former years much of the romance of her life had been in smooth-ing the pillow of exile for banished conspirators. Her refugees had been very precious to her; she was always trying to raise money for some cadaverous Pole, to obtain lessons for some shirtless Italian. . . .

Miss Birdseye is The Feminist, a type whom James describes from the outside in the tradition of the Anatomy. But when in the late novels, *The Golden Bowl* or *The Sacred Fount*, James wrote his elaborate allegories, he wrote without humour, in the dedicated, compulsive tone that obsessed novelists of the third phase may well have taken from him. In the portrait of Miss Birdseye James did rather crudely what George Eliot had done superbly with her portrait of Rosamond Vincy in *Middlemarch*, but the method was the same, the method of the novelist of manners from Jane Austen to Edith Wharton in America and C. H. B. Kitchin or Anthony Powell in England.

Native American satire in the nineteenth century typically faltered at the social theme and turned to burlesque; Henry Adams's *Democracy* (1880), however, represents the closest treatment of manners outside of James that was produced. His description of his heroine has a bitter American sweep which differentiates it from the satire of, say, Thackeray:

> Was it ambition—real ambition—or was it mere restlessness that made Mrs. Lightfoot Lee so bitter against New York and Philadelphia, Baltimore and Boston, American life in general and all life in particular? What did she want? Not social position [Adams describes her birth, her fortune, her cleverness]. . . . She had travelled in Europe, and after several visits, covering some years of time, had returned home, carrying in one hand, as it were, a green-gray landscape, a remarkably pleasing specimen of Corot, and in the other some bales of Persian and Syrian rugs and embroideries, Japanese bronzes and porcelain. With this she declared Europe to be exhausted, and she frankly avowed that she was American to the tips of her fingers; she neither knew nor greatly cared whether Amercia or Europe were best to live in; she had no violent love for either, and she had no objection to abusing both; but she meant to get all that American life had to offer, good or bad, and to drink it down to the dregs, fully determined that whatever there was in it she would have, and that whatever could be made out of it she would manufacture. 'I know', said she, 'that America produces petroleum and pigs; I have seen both on the steamers; and I am told it produces silver and gold. There is choice enough for any woman.'

Adams was an obsessed man, but his two excellent though minor novels are conceived without the eccentricity or the compulsion of modern obsession. *Democracy*, a skilful satire upon Washington society, develops fully Whitman's description in *Democratic Vistas* of social life in the capital as '. . . a sort of high-life-below-stairs business'; Whitman objected to labourers' and mechanics' sons imitating the pomps of foreign courts, 'As if any farce could be funnier . . . than the scenes of the crowds, winter nights, meandering around our Presidents and their wives. . . .'[1] In theme and treatment, *Democracy* (as well as *Esther* of 1884) urges comparison with Howells's work, but Adams's fiction is never merely 'calisthenic', as so much of Howells's was. *Democracy* is the point in American writing outside James's work where social criticism and individual psychology are conceived as one and the same. Adams brought to social and political satire an intellectual integrity that Howells, a more conscious and dedicated artist, often lacked.

The native cast of Mark Twain's satire, together with his late conversion to allegory, ought not to obscure his English debt. Like Adams's *Democracy*, Twain's first novel, *The Gilded Age*, is a kind of cross-road between English and American tradition, with its curious blending of manners, satire and burlesque. If Colonel Sellers is modelled directly on Micawber, Senator Dillworthy is a native product, and Twain's presentation of him establishes a line of tradition in American satire which runs through the work of George Ade, Ring Lardner, Sinclair Lewis, and Thomas Wolfe, to John O'Hara and Randall Jarrell. The Senator's speech to the citizens of Hawkeye is discreetly stylized and not quite broad enough to lapse into burlesque:

'Fellow-citizens: It gives me great pleasure to thus meet and mingle with you, to lay aside for a moment the heavy duties of an official and burdensome station, and confer in familiar converse with my friends in your great state. The good opinion of my fellow-citizens

[1] Walt Whitman, *Democratic Vistas and Other Papers*, London and New York, n.d., p. 166. Whitman's essay, 'Society', is further to the point:

I have myself little or no hope from what is technically called 'Society' in our American cities. New York, of which place I have spoken so sharply, still promises something, in time, out of its tremendous and varied materials, with a certain superiority of intuitions, and the advantage of constant agitation, and ever new and rapid dealings of the cards. Of Boston, which its circles of social mummies, swathed in cerements harder than brass—its bloodless religion, (Unitarianism,) its complacent vanity of scientism and literature, lots of grammatical correctness, mere knowledge, (always wearisome, in itself)—its zealous abstractions, ghosts of reforms—I should say, . . . there is, at present, little of cheering, satisfying sign. In the West, California, etc., 'society' is yet unform'd, puerile, seemingly unconscious of anything above a driving business, or to liberally spend the money made by it, in the usual rounds and shows.

of all sections is the sweetest solace in all my anxieties. I look forward with longing to the time when I can lay aside the cares of office——'
['Dam sight,' shouted a tipsy fellow near the door. Cries of 'Put him out.']
'My friends, do not remove him. Let the misguided man stay. I see that he is a victim of that evil which is swallowing up public virtue and sapping the foundation of society. As I was saying, when I can lay down the cares of office and retire to the sweets of private life in some such sweet, peaceful, intelligent, wide-awake, and patriotic place as Hawkeye [applause]. I have traveled much, I have seen all parts of our glorious Union, but I have never seen a lovelier village than yours, or one that has more signs of commercial and industrial and religious prosperity——'.

Twain, a master of the methods of satire, used exaggeration, invective, burlesque, irony, parody, and understatement with a nice sense of balance that his immediate followers, Ade, Lardner, and Sinclair Lewis, quite lacked.

Twain managed to entertain a wide popular audience and still to achieve, intermittently, high literary quality. His followers added to American satire the notebook-habits but not the power of naturalism; Ade and Lardner, pretending to be no more than entertainers, worked out a cutting and deadly method of reproducing the speech of illiterates or semi-literates which was often no more than buffoonery, though occasionally in Lardner's case literary in spite of the author. Ade's *Fables in Slang* (1899), Aesopian, brutal sketches aimed at the easy target of provincial pettiness, were themselves provincial and petty and are no longer readable. But they gave a method to Ring Lardner, an artist-*manqué* who began his literary life as a sports-writer and who maintained the sentimental anti-intellectual attitude of many American newspapermen throughout his career. Like Ade, he expressed a loathing for American life and American popular ideals that was and remains frightening in its breadth and thoroughness. Fundamentally a mordant satirist, again like Ade he assumed the pose of a humorist, with perplexing results. His novel, *The Big Town*, and the best of his short stories, 'Champion', 'The Golden Honeymoon', 'Gullible's Travels', are far more sweeping indictments of America in the 1920s than anything in Sinclair Lewis, Faulkner or Erskine Caldwell. They approach allegory in their bitterness; his stupid baseball players, small-town capitalists on their travels, the harridans and their ignorant husbands carry far beyond naturalism or social realism; they stop on the near side of allegory for lack of resonance and for a fatal American lack of mind. Lardner never realized his own talents because the beginnings of vision broke down into grotesque buffoonery and cruel literary practical joking.

Sinclair Lewis's failure as a novelist provides a curious contrast to Lardner's. Both men satirized the same aspects of American life from roughly the same level of observation; Lardner failed because of his unwillingness to give up his pose as newspaperman and honestly to face the problems of an artist, while he possessed the mind to evaluate both his material, and his relationship to his material, with precision and without illusion. Lewis was fundamentally less talented than Lardner, but he worked harder at his craft. His failure was an intellectual failure to establish a satisfactory relationship to the society he castigated; his castigation turned into defence; his sensibility, never supple nor subtle, hardened, and his final novels became parodies of his earlier work. Lardner began on firmer ground than Lewis; his observation was always immediate and clear. Lewis began with satirical novels embracing a cliché about American society, the cliché fostered by pseudo-intellectuals like H. L. Mencken and George Jean Nathan when Mencken edited the appropriately named *Smart Set* (1918–24), and later the fatuous but potent *American Mercury*. According to this cliché, America was a barren place, inhabited by the 'boo-boisie' in the cities and by semi-literate Bible-readers in the country, a nation incapable of fostering the arts, and incapable of appreciating the chance work of art that might appear. Americans were all one variety or another of swine whose collective spirit transformed wine, women, and song into near-beer, your own wife, and community singing. Lewis developed the cliché in *Main Street* (1920), *Babbitt* (1922), *Elmer Gantry* (1927), and *Dodsworth* (1929), although it was obvious that he knew it to be a cliché from his attempts to modify it; George Babbitt is at once

a triumphant apostle of a civilization run by dentists and real-
estate men, and a troubled man of conscience who sides momen-
tarily with the local Bolshevist.

They met at the Union Station for the midnight train to Monarch.
All of them, save Cecil Rountree, who was such a snob that he
never wore badges, displayed celluloid buttons the size of dollars and
lettered 'We zoom for Zenith.' The official delegates were magnificent with silver and magenta ribbons. Martin Lumsen's little boy
Willy carried a tasseled banner inscribed 'Zenith the Zip City—Zeal,
Zest and Zowie—1,000,000 in 1935.' As the delegates arrived, not
in taxi-cabs but in the family automobile driven by the oldest son or
by Cousin Fred, they formed impromptu processions through the
station waiting-room.

It was a new and enormous waiting-room, with marble pilasters,
and frescoes depicting the exploration of the Chaloosa River Valley
by Père Emile Fauthoux in 1740. The benches were shelves of
ponderous mahogany; the news-stand a marble kiosk with a brass
grill. Down the echoing spaces of the hall the delegates paraded
after Willy Lumsen's banner, the men waving their cigars, the
women conscious of their new frocks and strings of beads, all singing
to the tune of Auld Lang Syne the official City Song, written by
Chum Frink:

> Good old Zenith,
> Our kin and kith,
> Wherever we may be,
> Hats in the ring,
> We blithely sing
> Of thy Prosperity.

. . . Babbitt was stirred to hysteric patriotism. He leaped on a
bench, shouting to the crowd:

'What's the matter with Zenith?'
'She's all right!'
'What's best ole town in the U.S.A.?'
'Zeeeeeen-ith!'

Two things are immediately apparent in this account of Babbitt
and his fellow realtors on their way to a convention: a purposeful
avoidance of subtlety and the familiar notebook-naturalism of
the American writer. The scene has actuality, as almost any

American would admit, but it lacks literary reality, and it therefore dates, along with all of Lewis's work. Lewis's method was not adequate to sympathy, yet he tried to evoke sympathy and he constantly reached for effects that were beyond him., When Paul Riesling shoots his wife in *Babbitt*, for instance, Lewis departs even from actuality. He remained a Daumier with the ambitions of a Goya.

Lewis's curiously inflated reputation as a serious novelist is already declining, but he retains a secondary literary importance for his large influence on other writers. Thomas Wolfe, whose reputation was similarly inflated, largely through Lewis's efforts,[1] imitated him both in material and in technique, though Wolfe added a crazy humour of his own. Eugene Gant, in *Look Homeward, Angel*, believing he has caught what is colloquially known as a dose, declaims to McGuire, the doctor,

'Why should I bear the stigma for what others get away with? Hypocrites—a crowd of damned, dirty, whining hypocrites, that's what they are. The Double-Standard! Hah! . . . Why should I be blamed for what people in High Society——' . . . 'Who's blaming you? You don't think you're the first one who ever had this sort of trouble, do you? There's nothing wrong with you, anyway.' . . . McGuire . . . scrawled a few hieroglyphics on a prescription pad. 'Give this to the druggist,' he said, 'and be a little more careful hereafter of the company you keep. People in High Society, eh?' he grinned. 'So that's where you've been?'

This sort of satire, like much of Lewis's, relies for success on verbal effects, in contrast to intellectual satire of situation. English satire in Waugh and Huxley is much more likely to be satire of situation; verbal effects are careless and limited. Lewis, Wolfe, Steinbeck, and one could add, Faulkner and Hemingway in their inferior work, are indebted for verbal effects to Mark Twain and the tall-tale, a debt which is at once an advantage and a disadvantage.

Lewis and Wolfe appear in skilful combination in Burns's *The Gallery*, but with a difference. Burns, an obsessed writer of the

[1] In his Nobel Prize acceptance speech in 1930, Lewis singled out Wolfe as one of the most important writers at work in America.

third phase, brings to his portrait of Captain Motes, the ignorant Southerner turned military man, a coward, a homosexual and a nasty martinet, a degree of loathing which makes Lardner's wrath look like tea-party politeness and wide-eyed naïveté. The portrait of Motes is exceeded only by the portrait of Motes's wife, a frigid poetess who publishes her own books. Before Motes entered the Army, he was a petroleum engineer:

> Yet they saw little of each other in their Roanoke apartment. She wrote her poems and read them at women's clubs, where she was applauded by wrenlike elderly ladies who then drank iced tea and champed on shortcake. He in his laboratory brooded on the possibilities of gasoline. Sometimes he forgot to take any food for a whole day, and she was too preoccupied with what she called her muse to bring him anything.
>
> —Ours is the ideal love, she'd say with a towel round her head in the steaming Virginia summers. Few men or women have had a relationship as spiritual as ours.
>
> Or sometimes when a visiting business associate was about to slide under the table from bourbon, he'd read him excerpts from his wife's poetry.
>
> —Has she any children? the business associate would say.

This has the subtlety that both Lewis and Wolfe lacked, but the link to their work appears in the verb 'champed', and in the exaggerated drunkenness of the business associate. Wolfe's verbal invention also appears in one of Burns's soldier narrators, who says,

> I know my army officers pretty well, having observed them for years from the perspective of a pebble looking up and squinting at the white bellies of the fish nosing above it. Americans usually go mad when by direction of the president of the United States they put a piece of metal on their collars. They don't know whether they're the Lone Ranger, Jesus Christ, or Ivanhoe. Few Americans I ever knew could sustain the masquerade of an officer. Their grease paint kept peeling in unexpected places. I heard that in combat the good officers simply knew their men well and did them one better in daring. But to be a good officer out of combat demands a sort of shadowboxing between truth and posing. Europeans know the

secret. But few Americans can play the nobleman without con-descension or chicken.

Burns's satire exists within a muddied intellectual context. A high degree of unassimilated emotion still dilutes the acid effect with the sugar of sentimentality, as it had done in the satire of Lewis and Wolfe. John O'Hara's work resembles that of Burns in being half-intellectualized, but the more important half is made up of a series of classic American poses: toughness, understated emotion, together with a basic sentimentality, an absolute mastery of craft. *An Appointment in Samarra* is almost *The Great Gatsby* of the 1930s. It is a fine satirical rendering of an American small city country-club society set against the background of the depression, in which O'Hara demonstrated an un-Jamesian but keen awareness of manners. The novel's weakness is in the slight but discernible reliance upon easy, fashionable effects, a tendency which has become a habit in his later work. *An Appointment in Samarra* and O'Hara's occasional brilliant short stories, like 'Graven Image' in *Pipe Night*, suggest how the novel of manners has been approached in the third phase—almost invariably through satire. According to one critic who questions by implication the possibility of a novel of manners in America,

> There are rigidities in the Jamesian 'given' in both of the worlds the novelist must unite which probably can never be wholly reduced. But a reasonable solution of these difficulties is nonetheless the task the 20th Century novelist has to face. . . . The possibility for such a solution is always present in writers like Fitzgerald and Faulkner and Hemingway. Still none of these writers has as yet produced a novel in which the eccentrically conceived and obsessive personal moral problem has not to some extent seriously distorted or even excluded a satisfactory account of the conditions which were its occasion . . . .[1]

This, of course, is the White Russian mind again, which reveres James as the eldest Cardinal if not the Pope of the modern novel, and seems incapable of assessing what has been done since. If

[1] Arthur Mizener, 'The Novel of Manners in America', *Kenyon Review*, XII, 1950, 19.

Fitzgerald in *Gatsby*, Hemingway in *The Sun Also Rises*, or Faulkner in *The Sound and the Fury* did not write novels of manners, then neither did James. I suspect that the American critics who discuss manners without mentioning satire—generally the same critics who read Faulkner and the rest without any apparent consciousness of their humour—regard satire later than Pope's as too frivolous for Literature. 'Literature is real, Literature is earnest,' these people seem to say, 'Literature is also our bread and butter, and we must not jeopardize our positions by mixing business with pleasure.' The horrible party given by Tom Buchanan's mistress, Myrtle Wilson, in *Gatsby* remains a full realization of Fitzgerald's 'given'; that his problem differed from James's is not particularly important. Nick Carraway's report of the party is as subtle a comment on class behaviour as anything in James. It is also comic.

> Mrs. Wilson had changed her costume some time before, and was now attired in an elaborate afternoon dress of cream-coloured chiffon, which gave out a continual rustle as she swept about the room. With the influence of the dress her personality had also undergone a change. The intense vitality that had been so remarkable in the garage was converted into impressive hauteur. Her laughter, her gestures, her assertions became more violently affected moment by moment, and as she expanded the room grew smaller around her, until she seemed to be revolving on a noisy, creaking pivot through the smoky air.
>
> 'My dear,' she told her sister in a high, mincing shout, 'most of these fellas will cheat you every time. All they think of is money. I had a woman up here last week to look at my feet, and when she gave me the bill you'd of thought she had my appendicitus out.'
>
> 'What was the name of the woman?' asked Mrs McKee.
>
> 'Mrs Eberhardt. She goes around looking at people's feet in their own homes.'
>
> 'I like your dress,' remarked Mrs McKee, 'I think it's adorable.'
>
> Mrs Wilson rejected the compliment by raising her eyebrow in disdain.
>
> 'It's just a crazy old thing,' she said. 'I just slip it on sometimes when I don't care what I look like.'

The party comes to a catastrophic, drunken end when Buchanan breaks Myrtle's nose with a single blow. Mr. McKee, the man from downstairs, and Carraway leave together.

> 'Come to lunch some day,' he suggested, as we groaned down in the elevator.
>   'Where?'
>   'Anywhere.'
>   'Keep your hands off the lever,' snapped the elevator boy.
>   'I beg your pardon,' said Mr McKee with dignity, 'I didn't know I was touching it.'
>   'All right,' I agreed, 'I'll be glad to.'

This needs only to be compared with Cyril Connolly's attempt at the same effect, the difference between the *haute* and the *petite* bourgeoisie in *The Rock Pool*, to establish the difference between the expert novelist and the knowing dilettante. The scene is the French Riviera, and Naylor, the despicable English hero, has just met a countrywoman who runs a pub:

> 'Of course, it's much worse for Duff, she's the real thing,' went on Varna, lowering her voice as the English do at mention of these sacred subjects. 'The way that child was brought up—yachts, motor cars, her own aeroplane—everything regardless! Why, my own people were very wealthy, you know, but, well, well—I mean!' She broke off into a breathless little giggle and fixed her wide-set green eyes upon him. Naylor suddenly realized that she was middle-class and, worse, was assuming that he was. So she expected him to gape with her at Duff's superior breeding! He decided that she was profoundly antipathetic—that voice like a medium's, those clair-voyant eyes, and that sturdy little body in inappropriate sailor trousers!

The Rock Pool is hardly representative of the best in recent English satire, for it is little more than Evelyn Waugh's devices in Norman Douglas's setting. Neither Waugh, Connolly, nor Aldous Huxley, the obvious candidates, has approached Fitzgerald's treatment of manners through satire; their satire comes directly from the English tradition through a sensibility that apprehends the modern setting with a bilious English loathing, unalloyed by Fitzgerald's sense of history, or his larger and more serious ambitions.

Yet the comparison is hardly fair, for in their best work Huxley and Waugh are 'pure' satirists, while Fitzgerald used satire as an incidental method. Pure satire, in turn, defies foreign appreciation. It tends to be national and local, and finally private. Germans and Frenchmen do not read Waugh with any pleasure; to many Americans who like their own local satire in Jarrell or Mary McCarthy, Waugh is a bore, and Huxley an increasingly pretentious bore. *Crome Yellow* or *Vile Bodies* takes the American into the private, public-school world of the English upper middle classes, where a dithering word like 'elevenses' is standard diction, where grown men, even in self-parody, express approval with the phrase, 'Rather heavenly'—a world more exotic than the expected exoticism of the Orient, stranger to the American than Mau-Mau or Moroccan atrocities.

Time has been unkind to Huxley, though just. Between *Crome Yellow* (1921) and *Point Counter Point* (1928) Huxley caught and expressed a tone and a mood in English society which has departed for ever, rather as Dorothy Parker caught a similar tone and mood in America. That tone—bright, *chic*, cynical, anarchic—presented crisply and entertainingly, had about it a frantic gaiety that was not gay, a quality of hatred which was not merely cynical; somewhat as though St. Paul had turned to the description of Roman society instead of missionary work among the Ephesians. In retrospect, we can now see that in Huxley's beginning was his end. The early Huxley who entertainingly satirized Wordsworthian pantheism, sexual love and materialism foreshadowed the Huxley of *Eyeless in Gaza*, *After Many a Summer*, and all the later work which has become monstrous and horrible. Until *Point Counter Point*, there was still a quality of *odi et amo* in Huxley's attitude; since then, it is simply *odi*. Theodore Gumbril and Coleman, in *Antic Hay*, were frightening enough upon analysis, but they were also entertaining. We could read them as stylized representations of valid human types. By the end of the 1920s, however, Huxley's nerve began to fail, and just as he turned to Gerald Heard's brand of mysticism, so Coleman turned into the Anthony Beavis of *Eyeless in Gaza* who makes sterile, loveless love on a rooftop, and on whom a dead dog drops from an aeroplane to spatter him and his victim with its guts. Beavis, in turn, foreshadowed the eighteenth-century nobleman in *After Many a Summer* who has found the secret of eternal life, but who lives his eternity in a cave eating guts and beating his mate.

Huxley's method, this is to say, was from the beginning that of the obsessed satirist who turns to allegory, but to an allegory that ceased to have anything to do with the human condition. The reader becomes an embarrassed psychiatrist, witnessing the decline of a mind. The fantasy-parody of the night-club play in *Antic Hay* tipped off the secret; Huxley's own inability to love turned into hatred of women and of humanity. What had been merely a scene in *Antic Hay* became a basic method in *After Many a Summer* and *Time Must Have a Stop*. In re-reading Huxley the conclusion is inescapable that his vaunted brilliance is the pseudo-brilliance of the precocious schoolboy, the clever undergraduate, written for schoolboys and undergraduates. His erudition is little more than information smacking of the encyclopaedia and smatterings of esoterica. His models were Peacock, though he hates women, and Firbank, but Firbank outweighed Peacock to make Huxley a writer not for the male world or the world of mature humanity but for a smutty, sniggering schoolboy world. He uses the typical English minor writer's escape through madmen and fantasy, rather than true allegory. The mad Miss Elvira of *Those Barren Leaves* and the dwarf Sir Hercules in *Crome Yellow* belong to the same family as the obscene horrors of the later novels. And Huxley is the writer who published, in 1930, a pamphlet entitled 'Vulgarity in Literature'. Mysticism led inevitably to Mescalin, to California and the atmosphere which produced that other vulgar libel on humanity, Isherwood's *The World in the Evening*, a novel directed to and written about the same sexually-neuter audience as Huxley's.

The decline and imminent fall of Evelyn Waugh provides a certain parallel to that of Huxley; it is even more depressing, for Waugh once possessed the real toughness of the pure satirist, as opposed to the mere feline stringiness of Huxley. Waugh obviously borrowed from Huxley, as did numerous other young men in the thirties and even into the forties—I think of Angus

Wilson.[1] Where his minor imitators took over Huxley's entire attitude and embellished it with their own kind of obsession (Wilson borrowed the madmen in numerous short stories and added the homosexuals in *Hemlock and After*), Waugh simply took over Huxley's tone, particularly the tone and atmosphere of *Antic Hay*; it is that tone which created Gumbril and Coleman, and Waugh's Peter Pastmaster and Basil Seal. There resemblance ceases. Huxley always toyed with ideas, usually borrowed— from Lawrence and Gide, for example, in *Point Counter Point*— while Waugh, a better craftsman and a better artist, had the taste to allow idea to remain implicit in his work. Beneath the truly comic nonsense of *Vile Bodies*, *Decline and Fall*, or his best book, *Black Mischief*, lies a system of total condemnation; entirely logical, flawless, true to itself and its author's vision. The antics of the Welsh brass band in *Decline and Fall*, the diary entries in Azania of Dame Mildred Porch of the League of Dumb Chums in *Black Mischief* ('Road to station blocked with motor lorry. Natives living in it. Also two goats. Seemed well but cannot be healthy for them so near natives') are conceived with wild comic abandon, but they both conceal and express a metaphysic of loathing for society that is never equalled and rarely approached in modern writing. From Waugh's first novel *Decline and Fall* (1928), through *Black Mischief* (1932), there is a crescendo of comic invention and of the logic of rejection. Where the first novel only dipped into society by way of university and school-teaching, with excursions into white-slavery and the corruption of the wealthy, *Black Mischief* presents an entire society dominated by scoundrels who in turn are dominated by Basil Seal, a lewd fornicator who steals his own mother's jewels and literally eats at a cannibal feast the girl he has sworn he loved. These novels are perfect minor work; every element is assimilated, nothing is attempted that is not brought off.

The difficulty, even in Waugh's early, successful work, lay in

[1] Since writing this, I note with the pleasure of vindication that Mr. Wilson has acknowledged a debt to Huxley in a contribution to a 'critical' symposium on Aldous Huxley, 'The House Party Novels', *The London Magazine*, II, No. 8, August 1955, 53–56.

his models. He shared Firbank's girlish urge to outrage; with Firbank, he would *épater* not only the bourgeois, but everyone in the social scale. Unlike either Firbank or Huxley, the one sustained in his isolation by a mauve-coloured, post-Oscar Wilde aestheticism, the other by an easy surrender to exotic mysticism, Waugh honestly believed in society—not the post-war society of industrial wealth, but in a snobbish society of birth, land, unostentatious plenty—his private vision of aristocracy. Cyril Connolly's remark in 1936 that *A Handful of Dust* showed Waugh to be a Tory satirist, and that Tory satire, 'directed at people on a moving staircase from a stationary one, is doomed to ultimate peevishness',[1] takes on the cast of prophecy which the novels since *Put Out More Flags* (1942) have more than vindicated. When Basil Seal is resurrected in war-time, apparently unchanged, but then announces, 'There's only one serious occupation for a chap now, that's killing Germans. I have an idea I shall rather enjoy it', we know that Waugh has given up. The old Basil would have joined the Nazis and ended up at Potsdam running the General Staff. *Brideshead Revisited* became as inevitable after Basil Seal's conversion to God and Country as *Eyeless in Gaza* was after Huxley's conversion to Gerald Heard. Waugh's literary surrender to Roman Catholicism and County snobbery is perhaps more palatable than California mysticism, but as far as his work goes, he now writes with a sentimentality approximating Huxley's. And he lacks Huxley's intellectual façade. Basically an anti-intellectual, he is now in a position where he must propose intellectual positions. The result is a strange and sad confusion. Waugh still lashes out with the old fury, at the same time attempting to defend a position, but the lash is not a weapon of defence.

To this point I am conscious of having disparaged allegory in the novel without, perhaps, having supplied sufficient direct reasons. The careers of Huxley and Waugh in England, of Wolfe in America, and of various continental writers, notably Franz Kafka, considered together, may clear the critical air. Medieval and renaissance allegory subsisted upon and succeeded through the existence of spiritual and social systems with which the limited

[1] Reprinted in *The Condemned Playground*, p. 116.

reading public was familiar: Christianity, and the conventions of courtly love. These were exterior modes, readily available to the writer. The modern obsessed writer who turns to allegory in reaction to catastrophe, lacks that useful, exterior machinery; and because of the nature of allegory as a literary device, he also lacks a subject. This lack sends him into himself, both for subject and for the symbols with which to make objective his obsession. Unless he is a great writer indeed, he tends to become subverted stylistically in the direction of 'poetic' prose, as in the case of Wolfe; or in the direction of abstractions of a personal, often neurotic vision, as in the extreme case of Kafka. Huxley and Waugh both react to the world about them in horror, and they proceed to develop attitudes which will allow them to cope with the world; their early work remained fairly objective, but their later work was a retreat into the private allegory of mysticism, or what Waugh asserts still to be public property, Catholicism and the codes of the aristocracy. Still other and less gifted writers follow Kafka in technique, but attempt to allegorize the abstraction which can only be called the theme of appearance and reality: I think of Paul Bowles, Albert Guerard Jr., John Hawkes, and William Sansom. Kafka and the 'Kafkaesque' thus become crucial.

Even if we knew nothing about Kafka's biography—and we know too much—it would be clear from his work that he was born without any nerve whatsoever, incapable of erecting the inadequate defences of Huxley. The resulting degree of obsession accounted for novels and short stories that speak directly to a body of modern intellectuals with a voice of authentic prophecy. They speak to the real victims of catastrophe, the men of thin blood for whom art is a justification, a retreat, a mystique, and an obsession. Kafka's work is slight and unfinished; he habitually responded to catastrophe with a mild, weak variety of satire that readily turned into allegory. *The Trial* and *The Castle*, his two novels, were pieced together by Max Brod. They satirize the German *Beamter*, though only incidentally. The real burden of both novels is their presentation of the ways of an Old Testament, orthodox Jewish God of wrath to uncomprehending, suffering, stumbling man, in the person of Joseph K, that very unconvincing

U

symbol of mankind. A Poesque nightmare atmosphere and an occasional gift for comedy, together with an unusually uncomplicated, direct German style, are Kafka's total stock-in-trade, yet he enjoys the idolatry of a large cult, and has been compared favourably with Joyce, Proust, and Dante.[1]

I am not here concerned with Kafka as Kafka, but with the fact that the atmosphere we have come to call 'Kafkaesque' has become common property—a mixture of satire and nightmare— and that writers in England and America have used his method and example in varying ways. Apart from Kafka's minor imitators, there exists a group of other writers who have apprehended Kafka's feeling for catastrophe but responded in a different manner; to this group belong some of the finest among contemporary novelists.

Rex Warner's *The Wild Goose Chase, The Aerodrome, The Professor,* and *Men of Stone*; Anthony West's *On a Dark Night*; Norman Mailer's *Barbary Shore*; Ralph Ellison's *Invisible Man*; these novels are Kafkaesque in a general sense, but they uncover an entirely new and different aspect of the modern use of allegory. Kafka and his direct imitators write with the hysterical tones of obsession; their characters are willingly crucified in one manner or another. The tension in a novel like Graham Greene's *The End of the Affair,* one of the better examples of remote derivation from Kafka, is created in the efforts of the heroine to find a manner of surrender, and of the hero to grasp that her surrender is a turning from his stale and unpleasant world to God.[2] In the second group of allegorists, allegory is justified not for its easy solution to the problem of motivation, but it is a method of asserting bravery; McLeod in *Barbary Shore,* the anonymous narrator of *Invisible Man*, John Wallis in *On a Dark Night*, the Professor in Warner's novel are all brave men who suffer catastrophe heroically, conquering it even when crushed by it, unlike the characters of the *echt*-Kafka school who whine, cringe and lie down.

[1] See Angel Flores, ed., *The Kafka Problem*, New York, New Directions, 1947.

[2] An anonymous essayist wrote that novelists like Graham Greene and François Mauriac say in effect, 'Let us go sin and not enjoy it; then God will punish us and we shall be happy.' 'London Diary', *New Statesman and Nation*, XLIX, 14 May 1955, 674.

In method, the English and the American allegorists differ considerably. As might be expected, the English novelist is more tempted to fantasy than the American. I have mentioned how fantasy negates the potentialities of Warner's *The Wild Goose Chase*, his first attempt at allegory;[1] *The Aerodrome* succeeds where the first novel failed, for the setting in an English village contains the necessary modicum of actuality to allow us to accept the implicit allegory. The same is true of *The Professor*, a political novel set in a middle-European country which undergoes the experience of Czechoslovakia at the time of the Communist coup. Warner does not imitate Kafka; rather, he creates an atmosphere which resembles Kafka's. He frees his method of the conventions and limitations of realism and writes a convincing novel of ideas of strength, and in contrast to Kafka or the Kafka-like, of bravery.

Anthony West's problem in *On a Dark Night* is even more formidable, for he invites the complete unreality of fantasy in his narrative of existence after death. As the novel opens, John Wallis, an English lawyer in Germany, shoots himself out of disgust with a misspent life and hatred for the war-crimes trial in which he has been responsible for the execution of General Von Kenelm. Wallis discovers that he is condemned to eternal companionship with Kenelm. They begin eternity in a kind of concentration camp, which they eventually leave for pleasanter surroundings where the possibilities of duplicating their mortal failings, sins and corruption are always present; hell, in brief, is in themselves. By remembering and facing his past with responsibility, Wallis discovers that heaven, like hell, is within himself, to be uncovered by the act of the responsible will. After an uncertain beginning marred by an attempt at American soldiers' diction, West proceeds with style and taste to solve the problem that has defeated Graham Greene in his sombre gospels, and Charles Williams in his fantasies: the presentation of a religious theme without the trappings of sectarian theology; an impressive accomplishment. The novel is limited by the amount of cleverness West must exert to create literary actuality—the undue

[1] See p. 63.

demand upon the imagination that fantasy always makes. But like Rex Warner's novels, *On a Dark Night* is important as a rare example in the contemporary English novel of the serious confrontation of a serious theme. It is free of Huxley's façade of intellectualism and of Waugh's flippancy, and it departs from the tradition of manners and social realism that limits the writing of L. P. Hartley and much of Elizabeth Bowen.

Invisible Man is as unmistakably American in method as *On a Dark Night* is English. Where West projects allegory through the basic convention of fantasy, either inviting or forcing us, according to his skill, to suspend disbelief, Ellison varies from the direct presentation of actuality through brutal naturalism, to the fantasy and surrealism of writers so disparate as Kafka and the Melville of *The Confidence Man*. At the same time, Ellison is serious in a different manner from West or Warner. He displays the recent tendency of English and American writers to combine the methods of the nineteenth century with the devices of the twentieth: he does not hesitate to state ideas directly through the narrator, while Warner and West allow idea to remain implicit. Ellison avoids the disaster of Wolfe's or Lawrence's editorializing, however, because his narrator is not merely a disguise for the author's obsession; he is a created being, having his own voice and development. The narrator opens the novel with a prologue in which he states the basic theme:

> I am an invisible man. No, I am not a spook like those who haunted Edgar Allan Poe; nor am I one of your Hollywood-movie ectoplasms. I am a man of flesh and bone, fiber and liquids—and I might even be said to possess a mind. I am invisible, understand, simply because people refuse to see me. Like the bodiless heads you see sometimes in circus sideshows, it is as though I have been surrounded by mirrors of hard, distorting glass. When they approach me they see only my surroundings, themselves, or figments of their imagination—indeed, everything and anything except me.

In a series of artful, sometimes too artful, episodes, the theme of 'invisibility' is restated and dramatically developed: in a southern negro college, in Harlem, in a paint factory and in a hospital—episodes directly out of Kafka in their unreality and undisguised

symbolism, but tempered with naturalism when Ellison describes
the powerful attraction of Communism for Harlem negroes, or
when he presents the climactic Harlem riot, based on the actual
ugly riot of 1936, in a masterly counterpoint of comedy and
Walpurgisnacht horror. The heavy demands upon style are fully
satisfied in the basic diction, which is American and West Indian
negro, in all its suppleness. Ellison's touch fails at times and he
becomes pretentious, as in his simile of music 'as full of Welt-
schmerz as flamenco'; or vulgar, 'I felt a swift uneasiness'. These
lapses are trivial, however, in comparison with Ellison's many
successes: the invention of 'Ras the Exhorter', who leads a negro
fascist movement; or the episode of Clifton's death, with its
muted Christian symbolism; or again, the brilliant device of the
'invisible' man wearing dark glasses to escape from Ras and his
gang, being mistaken for a gambler, a numbers man, a minister
of the church, and a pimp—recalling *The Confidence Man*.
Although no other novelist has conveyed the bitterness of relations between whites and negroes so successfully, we do not read
Invisible Man as a documentary study in race-relations; its allegory
is broadly political, not narrowly racial. The novel is a work of
high art, a full and brave statement of the need for men to be
individuals and to be human. In spite of its occasional debt to
Kafka, it contains not the slightest suggestion of the Kafka-cult
lament.

That lament has been particularly loud in England because it
blended readily with the English disposition to prefer fantasy to
actuality. I do not refer to the totally fantastic conception such as
Charles Williams's in *The Place of the Lion*; I question that 'pure'
fantasy has anything to do with the art of the novel. I refer to
novels like Francis King's *The Dark Glasses*, Brigid Brophy's
Hackenfeller's Ape, and specifically to the work of Wyndham
Lewis: novels in which fantasy is a device rather than a total
mechanism. Fantasy guides these novelists to the symbols which
are intended to communicate the basic meaning of narratives
otherwise conventional in construction. Recognizable human
emotions are twisted into unreal and, finally, incommunicable
and absurd expressions of disturbance, in sharp contrast to the

fantasy of Warner, Ellison, or West, in which imaginative control never falters.

The Dark Glasses broaches an habitual theme of Somerset Maugham and Norman Douglas, the tendency of Englishmen to go to pieces when they settle at any point south of Milan. Patrick Orde, a dilettante botanist and photographer, tries to fit into the atmosphere of Corfu, the home of his wealthy but not entirely sympathetic wife. The dark glasses of the title symbolize Patrick's infirm grasp upon his 'real' English self which he readily loses in his new and exotic surroundings. When he puts on the glasses, '. . . the whole landscape of jagged rocks, laboriously terraced vineyards and dazzling sky relaxed; expanded; lost its flatness, hardness and clarity. A mysterious veil descended. . . . All at once he had experienced a sensation of almost melancholy calm, combined with a vague premonition, he could not have said of what.' This passage, early in the novel, alerts us like the blow of a club for the sequel: Patrick's sexually ambivalent affair with Soula, a native girl, and Stavro her scornful brother (who *finds* the glasses when lost), his flight on Easter Sunday from the intolerable reality of Corfu amidst lambs being sacrificed on street-corners, and his belated discovery that Stavro murdered Soula upon learning that she was pregnant by Patrick. The reasonably competent, modified Jamesian style breaks down with Patrick's knowledge of the tragedy: '. . . and then there was a baffled agony in which he asked himself over and over again— Why? Why? Why?' The mild fantasy of the dark glasses, in short, is all too central and obvious for the heavy freight of emotion which the author validly creates in the first two-thirds of the novel, and we turn back, disconsolately, to Somerset Maugham. *Hackenfeller's Ape*, Miss Brophy's parable on the wickedness of amoral scientific research, tries to combine the actuality of the London Zoo with fairy-tale whimsy about a particularly human ape needed for rocket-experiments; both the reader and Miss Brophy conclude the novel within the ape's consciousness.

With a consistency in eccentricity which over the years we have come to expect whenever he has uttered a reluctant, hieratic word about the novel, T. S. Eliot writes that he '. . . can only *suspect* that Mr. [Wyndham] Lewis is the most distinguished living English novelist'. This remarkable statement is not made out of loyalty to an old comrade, for Mr. Eliot goes beyond the most generous limits of loyalty by adding, 'The opinion to which I do not hesitate to commit myself, is that Mr. Lewis is the greatest prose master of style of my generation—perhaps the only one to have invented a new style.'[1] For a parallel, we would have to imagine William Faulkner announcing that John Betjeman was the most distinguished English poet alive and the only master of the art to have invented a new poetic style; it is only necessary to read the published fragments of Lewis's novel, *Monstre Gai*, the object of Eliot's generosity, *The Childermass*, to which *Monstre Gai* is a sequel, or, for that matter, any other example of Lewis's fiction to realize that my parallel is no conceit. Lewis provides the supreme object-lesson on the dangers of allegory for the obsessed writer, while the crashing irony of his satire makes his American contemporary, Sinclair Lewis, seem like Voltaire. Wyndham Lewis is hardly a novelist, in fact, but an amateur Kafka, English-bred, whose stock-in-trade is limited to fantasy, allegory, and Laurentian essays expressing the village-thinker's conviction that the world is out of step with him.

Lewis's novels apparently divide themselves into two groups, those like *Tarr*, *The Revenge for Love*, and *Self Condemned*, which are set in the actual world and pretend to some sort of social reality; and *The Childermass* and *Monstre Gai*, set in limbo, possibly heaven—no one yet knows. The division is more apparent than real, for the energy in all his fiction seems to be adapted from Lewis's theory of painting, 'Vorticism'. Vorticism, in brief, asserts the metaphor of experience as a vortex, the only important aspect of which is the still centre, as opposed to the violent but unimportant flux of the mass in motion around the centre. Whatever its possible virtues for painting, translated into the novel,

---

[1] Mr. Eliot covers his tracks by adding, 'And by "style" I do not mean "craftsmanship" nor do I impute impeccability.' His qualification, however, only creates a mystery about his definition of style. T. S. Eliot, 'A Note on *Monstre Gai*', *Hudson Review*, VII, No. 4, Winter 1955, 525–526. The entire work excluding *The Childermass*, has since appeared as *The Human Age*, Methuen, 1955.

the still centre is a cataclysm, an inhuman, exterior catastrophe that negates characterization, narration, tone, the use of motif, all the devices of the novelist. In his best novel, *The Revenge for Love* (1937), where in spite of an ignorant reading of Spanish politics and a series of wooden satirical portraits of London 'bohemians', he creates two nearly believable people in Victor Stamp and Margot, the quality of Lewis's obsession—hatred—causes him to plunge these characters over a cliff in a motor-car. In *Self Condemned* (1954), a turgid satire on academic orthodoxy, a rich subject of which Lewis obviously knows little, the narrative does not progress but it jerks from cataclysm to cataclysm: René Harding's self-exile in a vile Canadian hotel during the war, the destruction of the hotel by fire, his wife's suicide, his death-in-life as a professor at an American university. These novels, like *Tarr* (1918), recall D. H. Lawrence in their repetition, shoddiness, and above all in the quality of obsessed hatred, but they have nothing of Lawrence's virtues—his communicated feeling for inanimate nature and his indubitable sincerity.

The Childermass was obviously an incompleted experiment, too confused and confusing to require judgment; the appearance of *Monstre Gai*, however, clarifies some of the confusion and makes possible certain preliminary conclusions. The setting invites comparison with West's *On a Dark Night*, in that Lewis is dealing with experience after death, but there all resemblance ceases. Eliot praises Lewis for taking his characters not, like Swift, to a landscape in which comparisons with human experience are a mere matter of scale, or like Dante, as human excursionists beyond the grave, but as denizens of the other world, so that he sacrifices 'normal standards of consistency'. The difficulty is that 'normal' or human standards of consistency are the only standards human readers know, so that Lewis and every other allegorist inevitably draws a parallel with those standards.[1] *The Childermass* is con-

[1] Samuel Johnson's comment on *Paradise Lost* is pertinent: 'The plan of *Paradise Lost* has this inconvenience, that it comprises neither human actions nor human manners. The man and woman who act and suffer are in a state which no other man or woman can ever know. The reader finds no transaction in which he can by any effort of imagination place himself; he has therefore little natural curiosity or sympathy.' *Lives of the English Poets*, London, Everyman, 2 vols., n.d., I, 107.

cerned entirely with presenting the central characters, two of the more unpleasant creatures of modern fiction, Pullman and Satterthwaite, who have hardly met since public-school days, and who maintain their former relationship of prefect and fag. The two find themselves in The Camp, a redistribution centre where they are unhappily kept waiting before they may go on to other destinations across a Styx-like river. They have been aware of a figure known as the Bailiff, upon whom they are somehow dependent. *Monstre Gai* picks up the action with Pullman and Satterthwaite (Pulley and Satters, for heaven's sake) safely over the river, inserting themselves into the Magnetic City, where they meet various inhabitants, graded socially according to their earthly positions, and where the forces of heaven are threatened by the hosts of hell. The proletariat of the Magnetic City speak cockney, the ambiguous figures around the Bailiff speak B.B.C. English, and the action involves an encounter between the heavenly forces and a deputation from Old Nick. After drawing heavily on medieval painting for descriptions of the diabolical band, Lewis presents the struggle between a 'blond giant' and Satan's deputy. A roar is heard:

> 'Demon!' it began, and had a terrible echo. 'Demon, I will crush you like a fly! I will annihilate you on the spot. Hell-bird, you will regret the day you brought your filthy troop to this city.'
> Hell's envoy struck the other on the face, and the blow was a climax of alarm. . . .
> The blond giant returned the blow, and both the escort of demons, and the blond followers of the Padishah's sprouting envoy, scuttled to the rear to avoid being trodden on. But the giants were now firmly fastened together, rocking about from side to side. Such panted remarks as 'T-t-take your claws away from my throat,' or 'Blast you, I will tear your eyes out,' could be heard, in the midst of enormous breathing and threatening grunts.

The struggling bodies burst out of their clothes, 'suddenly levitated' and 'made their exit buttocks uppermost'. In this manner the most distinguished living English novelist plunges into still greater absurdities, seeming to write a Miltonic parody, but maintaining a basic seriousness of tone, hard in the grip of obsession and allegory, quite out of control of his own materials. Fundamentally a satirist, Lewis depends upon ideas for the final validity of his work, but he lacks the integrity to deal honestly with them. Idea in his novels is like a tennis ball in the twilight, elusive and impossible to control.

If Wyndham Lewis is like a man playing bad tennis in the twilight, still another group of satirists I wish to consider are like men playing tennis in total darkness. These, to change the figure, are the knight companions of the turkish bath first frequented by Ronald Firbank, writers who prefer to giggle at civilization rather than to reject it, projecting fantastic parodies of man's weakness, compressing all human emotion into a jelly of *chic*. Osbert Sitwell unconsciously speaks to the point in his introduction to a post-war reprinting of five of Firbank's dated and enervated productions:

> With a few chosen belongings, he standardised each temporary home, whether it was a tent in the desert, a palace in Portugal, a furnished flat in London, an old house in Constantinople or rooms at Oxford. In every country, they provided a sufficiently personal setting for him and spread over his dwelling-place an indefinable but luxurious atmosphere. Chief among these objects, were two drawings by Downman, a bronze bull (would it be Greek or Renaissance?), a Felicien Rops drawing, a pencil portrait of Firbank by Albert Rutherston, a little green-bronze Egyptian figure of some bearded god or pharaoh, standing rigidly above a miniature marble pedestal, all the latest novels, a number of the silliest illustrated weekly papers (which provided him with a constant source of amusement), several of his own published books and manuscripts bound in white vellum, a photograph of his mother wearing Court Dress, mounted in a large silver frame, elaborate inkpots, coloured quill-pens, a vast tortoiseshell crucifix, and cubes of those large, blue, rectangular postcards upon which it was his habit to write. To this collection he subsequently added a fine drawing by Augustus John. There was always, too, a palm-tree near him, and in some way the author's personality was able to translate it back into a tropical and interesting plant, so that here it lacked that withered, 1880-boarding-house air which it usually assumes in England.[1]

[1] Ronald Firbank, *Five Novels*, London, Duckworth, 1949, pp. xiii–xiv.

This precious catalogue of Firbank's precious baggage by a fond admirer and imitator defines very well the quality of imagination in Firbank's own work, as well as that of his immediate and distant imitators: all the Sitwells, Cyril Connolly, William Sansom, and Angus Wilson; and in America, Truman Capote, Tennessee Williams, Paul Bowles, and Frederick Buechner. The majority of these writers share with Firbank a taste for excessive stylization, an adolescent desire to shock, a fondness for exotic paraphernalia, and an inadequately reasoned and therefore irresponsible attack on social shibboleth. Firbank's neuter giggle echoes through his tasteless burlesques, as in this from *The Flower beneath the Foot*:

> The Countess became reminiscent.
> 'In Venice,' she said, 'the indecent movements of the gondolieri quite affected my health, and, in consequence, I fell prey to a sharp nervous fever. My temperature rose and it rose, ah, yes . . . until I became quite ill. At last I said to my maid (she was an English girl from Wales, and almost equally as sensitive as me): "Pack . . . Away!" And we left in haste for Florence. Ah, and Florence, too, I regret to say I found very far from what it ought to have been!!! I had a window giving on the Arno, and so I could *observe*. . . . I used to see some curious sights! I would not care to scathe your ears, my Innocent, by an inventory of one half of the wantonness that went on; enough to say the tone of the place forced me to fly to Rome, where beneath the shadow of dear St. Peter's I grew gradually less distressed.'[1]

The giggle turns into a snigger in *The Rock Pool* of Connolly, *Hemlock and After* of Angus Wilson, and *The Grass Harp* of Truman Capote. Firbank's mental contortions to invent unusual situations —two women struggle to reach their confessor, and push over the confessional—are duplicated at the beginning of William Sansom's *A Bed of Roses*, which opens with the heroine locked in an armoire by her lover. Firbank's possible derivation from Henry James is suggested by still another of Firbank's more remote imitators, L. P. Hartley, who also imitates James. Firbank actually takes the Jamesian formula and turns it inside out; his characters (*Prancing Nigger* excepted) are Jamesian, and his situations are grotesque

---

[1] Firbank's ellipses.

burlesques of James's; it is as though some blasphemer had written a musical comedy on the story of the Crucifixion. Hartley uses the Jamesian style, but the aimless symbolism that litters Firbank's page reappears in essence, though with more order, in his novels. In *The Boat*, for example, the hero attempts to assert himself in a village to which he has removed by getting the local authorities to permit him to operate his boat; this slight symbol becomes the inadequate machinery of the entire, very long novel. Again, in *The Shrimp and the Anemone*, as in *The Sixth Heaven* and *Eustace and Hilda*, a trilogy, the sea beasts of the first novel represent the weak Eustace at the mercy of the female, Hilda, a symbolically savage relationship enacted with something approaching obscenity, though with considerable power, in the experience of children. Hartley is not a satirist, nor is he necessarily influenced directly by Firbank; his almost excellent novels indicate how the climate of writing can be adversely affected by sub-literary but fashionable work.

The primary objection to the Firbank-Connolly sort of writing is that it carries the cachet of intellectualism without being intellectual; it is made up of attitudes that answer to our apparent need for snobbery of some description. Firbank's attitude was the last gasp of the decadence; Connolly's a quasi-leftist political stance; Bowles's a parody of existentialism. As satirists, this group attempted to eliminate the traditional strength that satire derived from the assertion of morality; without morality, their work became expressions of disgust or unconvincing buffoonery. A hope for satire has recently arisen both in England and in America in the work of writers who have seen through the attitudinizing of the Firbank cohort, who maintain a genuine intellectual position, a moral base, and generally a more competent technique. In America, Randall Jarrell and Mary McCarthy are nothing if not clear in their approach to satire. They are intellectuals writing for intellectuals with cleverness and taste, in the case of Jarrell, often only with cleverness in the case of Miss McCarthy. However minor and local their satire, it is adult and professional in calibre; its appearance suggests that the long process of maturation in the American novel is now complete.

At least three writers promise better things for English satire. Iris Murdoch's *Under the Net* (1954) was a welcome departure from the elaborate arcana of the upper-middle-class atmosphere, but the suggestion of Firbank fantasy is still present. The haphazard symbolism of the down-at-heel hero backstage in a pantomime theatre making love to an elusive mistress amidst masks, a bear-skin and other theatrical props is unfortunate, but Miss Murdoch's intellectual spiv calls to mind Augie March and the previously ignored areas of fiction that Bellow so successfully invaded. John Wain's *Hurry on Down* (1953) and Kingsley Amis's *Lucky Jim* (1954) are negligible as novels, but they are satires from the point of view of not the under- so much as the middle-dog in English society, and the enthusiastic response indicates a public appetite for a liberalizing of the ground-rules of English satire. Both novels seem hastily written, but their errors are professional, not amateur errors, and they display an intellectual honesty of which smoother writers like, say, Angus Wilson appear incapable. Above all, they are free from the emasculating fantasy and the escape into allegory that has encrusted large areas of English and American fiction for too long.

Chapter Ten

THE UNWITHERED BRANCH

A FEW years ago, an English critic published a book on the modern English novel with the bleak title of *The Withered Branch*, the conclusions of which were the exact opposite of my own. As a novice of the new piety according to Tolstoy, Kierkegaard and Berdyaev, this critic discovered in Hemingway 'a clear form of the slavery to war and to violence'; in Forster 'a marked slavery to the bourgeois spirit and to society'; in Margiad Evans 'a pronounced slavery to passion and to nature'; in Aldous Huxley 'the erotic lure is prominent'; in Joyce 'the aesthetic lure dominates everything'; and in Virginia Woolf 'we see the elementary bewilderment of a mind incapable of formulating a clear view of her world of experience consequent upon inability to establish foundations in belief of whatever order'. 'The lesson of the modern novel', he concludes,

> as displayed in these figures, is that of the disintegration of the consciousness of modern man, resulting from his divided and de-polarized being, sundered from its absolute centre. But while as a thinker I am interested in the organic manner in which, in these examples, one form of disorientation is connected with another, as a critic I note above all that each path here traced leads to a condition which may fitly be described as *the impossibility of speech*.[1]

This is interesting peripherally for its tentative arrogance and its hint of critical mystique (what exactly is the 'absolute centre' of man's consciousness?), but centrally for the writer's conviction that 'disorientation', or what I have called 'catastrophe', is responsible for the end of communication in the novel ('*the impossibility of speech*') rather than for the important technical and imaginative

[1] D. S. Savage, *The Withered Branch: Six Studies in the Modern Novel*, New York, Pellegrini & Cudahy, n.d. [written 1944–48], p. 19. Savage's italics.

triumphs of the modern novel that I have tried to describe. *The Withered Branch* is interesting as a whole in that it makes no distinction between English and American tradition, and displays in the author's choice of writers a survival of the once dominant provincial English hostility to American literary secession, the attitude implied in Virginia Woolf's comment on James's *The Wings of the Dove*: 'Very highly American, I conjecture, in the determination to be highly bred, and the light obtuseness as to what high breeding is.'[1] Fully aware of the dangers of chauvinism, I have tried to demonstrate that the American novel historically has not been simply the English novel *manqué*, but a legitimate heir of the early common form, with a development now parallel, now deviating, but always maintaining a curious and complex relationship with the English novel.

Looking back, we do not distinguish between the English and the American novel until the early nineteenth century, when American writers began to draw their material from their own history and their own people, and drifted into the close association with the Continent which led to a technical and philosophical treatment of their problems that departed from English practice, but which at base was a response to a common need: for synthesis, and a reconciliation in art of the contradictory demands of individualism and an increasingly industrialized and mechanized society. At the end of the century, this development culminated in the American allegiance to naturalism, the products of which brought into the open different, but again parallel, modes of seeing and communicating experience. While individual writers differed in their attitudes toward themselves and their art, English and American writers remained fundamentally anti-intellectual, empirical, and suspicious of continental formulations. Living close to a comparatively homogeneous society, believing for the most part in the society he occasionally scorned, the English writer favoured the novel of manners and practised a degree of stylization that was foreign to the American, who by contrast lived apart from a heterogeneous society, unable and indeed unwilling to stylize his perceptions.

[1] *A Writer's Diary*, p. 40.

The lines of development in the two countries ceased to run parallel in the second phase of the novel, the period of doctrinaire naturalism, but they curved back toward the parallel in the third phase, with the common response to the catastrophe of the First World War and the fragmentation of the traditional social and intellectual structure. In this period, Englishmen and Americans alike rediscovered the uniqueness of the novel as a form peculiarly suited to the problems of fragmentation, and they came in that first period of experimentation to grapple with the old romantic paradox in new and unromantic context: the division in the mind and in life between action and contemplation, between the humane tradition of what society ought to be, and the political facts of society as they found it. They came to say with Malraux, 'I don't doubt that it is hard to be at the same time both artist and man of action, because art, in any field, involves a kind of obsession, in order to distil the whole world into the work of art, while action implies the distillation of the world into the action itself. The two forms of distillation are different, but they can be successive.'[1] They turned, that is, to the concept of art as obsession, a concept that took them far from the 'normal' pursuits of society, even while it was emphatically linked to their sense of society's direction and to their duty to interpret society to itself.

Even more than the poet or the dramatist, the novelist turned away from the classic ideal of literature which Gide defined when he wrote, 'Le classicisme tend tout entière vers la litote. C'est un art de pudeur et de modestie.'[2] The obsessed writer, with his conception of experience as a process of unfolding, a process which never hesitates long enough to allow for litotes, rules out the classic restraint of Gide's ideal, and allies himself more closely to the spirit of Dostoievski. Like Dostoievski, the novelists who answer most fully to our demands regard human life as a trial to be endured: a manner for discovering action, a recognition of evil, an achievement of balance between the contrary tides of action and contemplation, mind and instinct. The obsessed writer

[1] André Malraux and James Burnham, 'The Double Crisis', *Partisan Review*, XV, April 1948, 438.
[2] André Gide, *Incidences*, Paris, 1924, p. 40.

conveys to us what the late F. O. Matthiessen once described as 'the sensation of experience breaking through the pattern of form'. This in turn often means uncertainty of control, emotion become destructive, direction lost in a Sargasso Sea of nervous negation. That unclassic form, the confession, or thinly disguised autobiography, has emerged as a legitimate genre of the novel. For, as an English writer has said of verse, with equal relevance to the novel,

> Such is the paradox of our time that the more a poet draws on an objective tradition, the less on subjective experiences, the more obscure he will seem. It is important to realise that neither *The Waste Land, The Cantos*, nor even *Finnegans Wake* is obscure to us chiefly because the author refers to some subjective and private world, but for the opposite reason. All these works assume a knowledge of a common fund of traditional culture, that few any longer in fact do possess. . . . Anybody's dreams today are more likely to be understood than an allusion to Bede's or Caesar's histories . . . or to the gods of the Druids, or to the Christian liturgy. . . .[1]

The burgeoning ego of the subjective novelist has produced Lawrence and Wolfe with their near-successes and frequent failures, but the confession has also developed into the modern novel of ideas, which in England and America is just coming into its own.

The novel of ideas, in turn, has demonstrated anew the uniqueness of the novel form, and the pointlessness of the 'classical' criticism whose terms of reference are so frequently borrowed from the other arts. Gertrude Stein's mannered explanation of the presence of objects in painting provides both a parallel and a metaphor of the purely aesthetic notion of the relationship between ideas and the novel:

> I think the annoyance comes from the fact that the oil painting exists by reason of these things the oil painting represents in the oil painting, and profoundly it should not do so, so thinks the oil painting, so sometimes thinks the painter of the oil painting, so instinctively feels the person looking at the oil painting. Really in everybody's

---

[1] Kathleen Raine, 'Books in General', *New Statesman and Nation*, XLIV, 22 November 1952, 607.

heart there is a feeling of annoyance at the inevitable existence of an oil painting in relation to what it has painted people [*sic*], objects and landscapes. And indeed and of course as I have already made you realize that is not what an oil painting is. An oil painting is an oil painting, and these things are only the way the only way an oil painter makes an oil painting.[1]

One of the most prominent ideas embedded in the novel throughout its history has been the idea of society, which the English novelist often continues to treat in the realistic novel of symbolic incident, and the American with a desiccated, debased naturalism. The low point in the recent English novel of society has been reached by writers aware of the social challenge but truculently resistant to experiment: C. P. Snow's attempt to revive the *roman-fleuve*; William Cooper's relentlessly minor *Scenes from Provincial Life* which by title promises the social subject, but which in content is no more than a pastel study in sexual inversion, set for a change in the provinces rather than in London. The essence of these novels is baldly stated by Olivia Manning in *A Different Face*:

> In Coldmouth there was a point at which certain people—those of exceptional social position or attainments—were above criticism. 'Oh, well, people like that, of course! What do you expect.' His desire was not to change himself but to change his status, but he knew that nothing he did here would reassess him. He would have to go away.

In America the social challenge is often answered in two opposing ways: by the pretentiousness of a novel like John Steinbeck's *East of Eden*, with its historical backgrounds and Biblical parallels; or by watered-down versions of the Jamesian sensibility in a novel like Jean Stafford's *The Catherine Wheel*, and the allied work of the *New Yorker* ladies with elaborate memories of childhood, quaintly furnished houses, and delicately conveyed emotions—writing which merits the slander on James contained in the quip that he chewed more than he bit off.

[1] Quoted in Sutherland, *Gertrude Stein*, pp. 97–98. Sutherland refers this statement to Gertrude Stein's own writing and to the problem of idea in her writing: 'This literary bother about ideas in the work is something like the painter's bother about the subject-matter in the painting.'

All, in short, is not necessarily well with the modern novel, even though it is far from moribund. The situation of both American and English writers is determined of course by aesthetic motives, but powerfully determined by economic and social considerations as well. The enduring aesthetic considerations are more interesting than the economic, but the two are inextricably confused, today perhaps more than ever before. The contemporary English novel arises out of the genuine homogeneity of the English, and out of the more apparent than real homogeneity resulting from the fact that all literary production is dominated by the upper-middle-class intelligence. To the foreigner, the English novel seems tame and cursed by gentility. The English novel has always lacked intransigence, I think, but it has compensated in the past by setting a high standard of technical expertness, and by producing in writers and readers alike a unique sensitivity to the possibilities of language and a remarkable intensity of emotion.

Edmund Wilson has overstated his case against the place of the eternal schoolboy in English culture,[1] but again the foreigner cannot fail to be impressed by the importance of the public school —either its presence or absence—in the experience of English writers. Cyril Connolly wrote with boasting regret and greater irony than he knew of his 'corruption' by the Classics at Eton;[2] Anthony Powell's characters live in an enduring haze of school impressions, and the foreigner thinks, ah, satire—but always the gnawing doubt arises as to how far the satire is intended; Christopher Isherwood's school experience pervades his work in content and manner, a cruel limitation; the autobiographies of middle-aged English literary figures that regularly appear evoke most vividly not the university, not marriage, war, politics, the experiences of mature people in other parts of the world, but memories of school. This ironically adolescent atmosphere creates an attitude which I think of as Cyrillism—a mixture of scornful sentimentality, repressed intellectual cleverness, flippancy, and subtle, complicated snobberies. Cyrillism is not of the slightest

[1] In *Europe without Baedeker*, London, Secker & Warburg, 1948, pp. 9–11.
[2] See *Enemies of Promise*, and Connolly's introduction to *The Rock Pool*, English edition.

importance to the art of the novel, though in pervading minor
novelists it must affect the potentialities of the art; it is of great
importance in the economics of English publishing, reviewing,
and in the doling out of official largesse.

The Cyrillist is the writer of high potential ability but limited
energy, fatally lacking in devotion to the demands of art. He
turns out one novel, one volume of verse, one biography, then
makes his living by literary journalism, talks on the B.B.C.,
eventually moving into an editorship or a permanent post on one
of the almost superb literary weeklies. Or the Cyrillist may turn
to the B.B.C., where he helps to exert the velvet stranglehold
which that organization, together with the British Council, has
on English cultural life. It is all too easy to believe that if Sainte-
Beuve were to go to the B.B.C. with a series to be called *Causeries
de lundi*, he would be turned away politely but firmly with the
judgment that they were not dramatic enough, not suited to the
medium of broadcasting.[1] But that elegant amateur, the Cyrillist,
does infinitely more harm through his place in the mechanics of
book-reviewing than in the B.B.C. Unlike America, England
has had for a century and a half a remarkable literary press which
has occasionally attracted critics of highest calibre. Today, however, the literary and politico-literary weeklies, two new monthlies
and even the literary columns of a daily as intelligent as the
Manchester Guardian are dominated by the Old-School Book,
while the work of genuine artists—novelists and poets—is
ignored, or denigrated by compression into omnibus reviews:
five novels in 200 words. Typographically dominating the omnibus review is the double-column examination of the Old-School

---

[1] Even the staid and starchy *Times Literary Supplement* concurs: 'The typical
English poet, of some reputation, in his thirties or forties, has today probably been
absorbed either into the cultural side of administration or the administrative side
of culture; he plans lecture courses on folk-dancing in Timbuctoo or produces
dramatized features on the rise of the wool trade for the B.B.C.' Editorial,
'Hopes for Poetry', *T.L.S.*, No. 2612, 22 February 1952, p. 141.

It would be churlish and unjust to deny that the B.B.C. does a good job at
what it is supposed to do—broadcasting; but a by-product of its efficiency is the
consumption and waste of many men's talents. If writers could live by writing,
they would not need to go into the B.B.C., but they cannot, partially because the
B.B.C., with television and films, has taken over their audience.

Book, which may be, in the season, a sensitive young man's contribution to the travel literature of Sicily or the Greek isles; a description of English caves and grottoes; archaeology in Northumberland; the latest biography of Christina Rossetti; a thriller from the pen of a Roman Catholic don; or imaginary conversations with Attila the Hun. Meanwhile, the prestige of the reviews is maintained by a score of brilliant historians and political scientists, and by the one or two indubitable literary critics who carry the entire burden of serious examination of the novel on their backs. Novel reviewing is the province of academic charlatans, of young men trying to gain a foothold in literary journalism, and of the middle-aged gamin who already has his place and will yield it to no one. Since the death of George Orwell there seems to be no one in England to say nay; only the dissembling Wyndham Lewis survives, and he no longer bothers with other writers.

In America, the situation is different but not necessarily better. A novel is often not only reviewed, but criticized as a novel, though few readers are aware of the fact. A healthy intransigence still exists, but the work of the intransigent is read only by other intransigents. The country manages to support, barely, a few excellent literary periodicals, and many second-rate ones, but it lacks a British Council, a B.B.C., and a literary press of the quality of *The Observer* or *The Times Literary Supplement*. In the place of the British Council, America has an official Information Agency loosely attached to the State Department, concerned only with the propaganda value of American writing, and staffed by a corps in which the American novelist, poet, musician, painter, or even professor is notable for his absence. In the place of a B.B.C. or Arts Council, America has philanthropic foundations whose high intentions are belied by their support, in literature, of a vaguely official version of American achievement. The effect of these agencies upon specific writers is occasionally fortunate, but their effect upon American writing at large is minor or non-existent. In the place of the English literary press, America has a disgrace to literature, *The Saturday Review of Literature*, the weekly book-review supplements of the New York *Times* and *Herald Tribune*,

and the literary departments of periodicals like *The Nation* and
The New Republic. *The Saturday Review* is edited by businessmen
who hate literature and are interested only in the Book Club
mind; the New York review supplements are incompetently
edited, and seem designed to sell, not to criticize books. When
they occasionally print articles by writers of authority, those
articles often disgrace the writer's talent, written off the top of the
mind in dreary journalese, expressing commonplaces and intellectual clichés. The political weeklies are so tendentious that they
are read only by the few converted; they cannot compare in
literary quality with the *New Statesman*, or even the feeble
Spectator, in England.

While Cyrillism has made an appearance in America, having
been introduced by English expatriates, it is not the problem that
it is in England. America has its native kind of literary deceit,
exercised by Henry Miller, the American Wyndham Lewis,
and by an allied group of charlatans too tedious to list. It suffers
from the dissipation of literary and economic energy in the
printing, distribution and sale of the works of the businessmen of
the novel: Wouk, Marquand, the 'historical' novelists—the vast
number of talented, cynical writers who litter the landscape with
their trumpery. It suffers from an excess of arrogant, bad literary
criticism, and from the inability of its few good critics to get a
hearing from any but the already convinced. This in turn leads
to the inflation of reputations of writers of small merit and to the
public enthusiasm for bad work. Eudora Welty, who mixes one
part inferior Faulkner with two parts L. P. Hartley, is proposed
as a major writer; Robert Penn Warren, who writes florid, forced
studies of southern history, is touted as a philosopher; an entire
crew of sickly, second-rate southern writers poses as a 'renaissance'.

What I am saying in this melancholy catalogue of circumstances
surrounding the novel is that as an art-form the novel is neither
dying, dead, nor even in crisis, but that literary society, and society
at large, is in serious crisis. We are still fond of crying Crisis!
Crisis! even though we are all bored by the notion of crisis.
Nevertheless, our crisis is genuine and urgent, in England as in

America. It is as much political as literary, for it grows out of the increasing coincidence of literary, social and political facts over the past twenty years. It is a crisis of the manner in which catastrophe impinges not upon imagination, but upon the writer's rational processes, limiting, in turn, the range of his imagination.

Since the fading of Communist ideology as a possible faith for intelligent men at some point in the late thirties, writers in particular have been placed in a new relationship to society. This has nothing to do with membership in, sympathy for, or tolerance of Communism as a political system, but rather with the fact that the possibilities of Communism or some other radical political solution had allowed writers a scope for idealism, irresponsible perhaps, but emphatically broad in imaginative scope as they then stood in relation to society. The American writer more than the English writer had traditionally been alien to society, standing apart from it, but deriving from alienation a rich source of literary energy. Traditionally, the American has been able to go to the roots of society *because* of his alienation, not for any fleeting identity with it. When, like Howells, he tried to identify himself with society, he became 'calisthenic' and superficial, or like Steinbeck, mystical and vapid.

With the recent closing in of the political horizon, and particularly since 1945, the intellectual in America, as Irving Howe has written in an important article, has been granted, grudgingly, an honoured place in the new capitalism. 'It is a society', Howe says, 'in which ideology plays an unprecedented part: as social relations become more abstract and elusive, the human object is bound to the state with ideological slogans and abstractions—and for this chore intellectuals are indispensable, no one else can do the job as well.'[1] The 'prosperous ruins' of Greenwich Village attest to their defection, and in place of an earlier, and for literature necessary, stance of opposition, we now hear 'a whining genteel chauvinism'. Writers are lured into institutions, academic, governmental, even industrial, and *'cease to function as intellectuals'*. (But they are not lured into agencies in which they could be

[1] Irving Howe, 'This Age of Conformity', *Partisan Review*, XXI, January–February 1954, 9.

expected to function as intellectuals.) Machiavelli supersedes Marx.[1] The English writer is similarly afflicted, but he has been afflicted for a longer time and has learned, if not to bite, then to snap at the hand that feeds him. P. H. Newby, after all, is a talks-producer for the B.B.C. But the American is hardly comfortable in his new prosperity; he becomes defensive and writes ambiguous pieces for magazines that at one time he would not even have read.

When an English reviewer says that 'The novel only breathes when it has its roots in society',[2] he repeats a truism and evades the meaning of 'society' at this particular point in contemporary history. The parallel lines of English and American writing again converge; Peter Taylor, Truman Capote and Eudora Welty take over the traditional English mannerism, writing with taste and sensibility of children, madmen and homosexuals; Americans produce their own Francis Kings and C. H. B. Kitchins, and call their work important literature. Politics and society conspire anew to make valid André Gide's complaint that generally speaking one meets among men of intelligence only the impotent (*des perclus*), and among men of action only fools.[3] This libels the best work in the English and American novel, but it underlines the seriousness of the crisis.

Fools and *hommes perclus* we have in abundance, but also *honnêtes hommes*. Great novels have never been abundant, and they have always been produced in unlikely circumstances. The modern period has already produced its fair share of work that promises to last, and in spite of our wish to see a masterpiece every week-end, it will probably continue to produce its fair share, though no more. The change in the novel-form which I have tried to describe is not a change for the worse, nor necessarily for the better, but the continuing vitality of the novel made it inevitable. The strength of the novel as an art-form still lies in its resilience and in its resistance to definition. It remains one art-

---

[1] 'This Age of Conformity,' pp. 9–19. Howe's italics.
[2] C. P. Snow, 'Storytellers for the Atomic Age', pp. 1 ff.
[3] André Gide, *Journal*, Paris, Gallimard, 1948, p. 785 (3 June 1924). My translation.

form that is closely linked to the abstraction we term 'reality'; it is still a full and satisfying means by which the artist can simultaneously delight us and order the political and social chaos of contemporary existence. The novel retains, in spite of experiment —indeed, because of it—an immediacy to common experience, together with the separateness and the wonder that give art its power in any time or place.

The final image of the novel in England and America is not clear; it cannot be, for its components are too complex; it is like the shadow created by a swaying lamp on an irregular wall, by turns sharp and dim, sometimes seeming to have three dimensions, at other times shadowy and insubstantial. In America there is no one to write, as Whitman wrote not very long ago, '. . . while England is among the greatest lands of political freedom, or the idea of it, and in stalwart personal character, etc.—the spirit of English literature is not great, at least is not greatest—and its products are no models for us'.[1] England has so often been a model, and more important, has so often set a standard, without which the American novel would have been impoverished. Since Cooper, it has not been a question of leader and follower, as far as the novel is concerned, as much as the development of a corporate sense of the fitness of certain modes for the expression of common experience. The national question, after all, however useful as a method, is minor; it is accidental that attitudes toward the art of the novel do differ in the two countries. There appears to be no one in England to demand the high seriousness in the art of the novel that Eliot and Pound demanded in verse, a generation ago, and succeeded in getting. Whether the Ezra Pound of the novel will be English, or as I suspect, American, is also unimportant. The important element is the art itself; that writers and their critics know the challenge of the past, that they remain humane as well as human in perceiving the present, so that in their work this indispensable, still-developing form be increased, not as fat increases on a glutton's belly, but as muscle and sinew are renewed in the ever-young flesh of art.

[1] *Democratic Vistas and other Papers*, p. 162.

INDEX

B4P18268